# Brazil Built

**Brazil Built** is an examination of the architecture of the Modern Movement in Brazil. In the 1940s and 1950s, Brazil acquired unprecedented prestige in the world of Modern Architecture. Brazil was regarded as the country which had inherited the progressive Modernism of the pre-war period in Europe, and which, furthermore, had initiated a new phase of the assimilation of cultural and environmental considerations. The major buildings – the Ministry of Education, the Brazilian Pavilion at the New York World's Fair 1939, the Brazilian Press Association, Santos Dumont Airport, the Pampulha complex – became widely known and highly influential, launched by the exhibition 'Brazil Builds' at the Museum of Modern Art, New York in 1943 and the publication of *Brazil Builds*.

This book constitutes a unique presentation of the major Modern buildings in Brazil in their historical context. Prompted by the contemporary revaluation of Modernism and the renewed interest in Brazil, this book examines how the buildings came into being, how they came to be so highly regarded, and the changing reactions to them in Brazil and abroad.

**Zilah Quezado Deckker** is an architect with an MSc and PhD in architectural history.

# Brazil Built

## The Architecture of the Modern Movement in Brazil

## Zilah Quezado Deckker

SPON PRESS
Taylor & Francis Group

London and New York

First published 2001
by Spon Press
11 New Fetter Lane, London EC4P 4EE

Simultaneously published in the USA and Canada
by Spon Press
29 West 35th Street, New York, NY 10001

*Spon Press is an imprint of the Taylor & Francis Group*

Typeset in Frutiger Light by Wearset, Boldon, Tyne and Wear
Printed and bound in Great Britain by TJ International, Padstow,
Cornwall

*British Library Cataloguing in Publication Data*
A catalogue record for this book is available from the British Library

*Library of Congress Cataloging in Publication Data*

Quezado Deckker, Zilah.
   Brazil built: the architecture of the modern movement in
   Brazil/Zilah Quezado Deckker.
      p. cm.
   Includes bibliographical references and index.
   1. Modern movement (Architecture)–Brazil. 2. Architecture,
Modern–20th century–Brazil. I. Title.

NA855.5.M63 Q47 2000
720'.981'0904–dc21
                                        00–030082

ISBN 0-415-23407-7 (Hbk)
ISBN 0-415-23178-7 (Pbk)

To Dr. Maria Quezado Soares

# Contents

*Colour illustrations appear between pages 18–19 and 146–147*
*Acknowledgements*                                                    ix
*Foreword*                                                            xi
*Introduction*                                                         1


PART I
Revolutions                                                            5

  1  Vargas, Le Corbusier, and reinforced concrete                7


PART II
The Heroic Period                                                     23

  2  The Ministry of Education and Health Building              25
  3  The Brazilian Pavilion at the New York World's Fair 1939   54
  4  'A whole new school'                                       64


PART III
The Museum and the war                                                87

  5  The Museum of Modern Art, New York, and architecture       89
  6  'America for the Americans'                                95
  7  'the MUSEUM and the WAR'                                  103


PART IV
The exhibition and the book                                          109

  8  The planning of the exhibition 'Brazil Builds'            111
  9  The 'Brazil Builds' exhibition                            127
10  *Brazil Builds: architecture new and old 1652–1942*                 135

PART V
The 'Brazilian Style'                                              145

11   *Brazil Builds* and the press                                147
12   The 'Brazilian Style' observed                             164
13   Le Corbusier and the 'Brazilian Style'                      172
14   *Construção Brasileira*: the 'Brazilian Style' in Brazil    188

*Conclusion*                                                      207
*Appendices*                                                      209
*Bibliography*                                                    227
*Index*                                                           247

# Acknowledgements

This book was developed from my PhD thesis submitted to the University of East Anglia in 1992. For this research I must thank the Coordenação Aperfeiçoamento Pessoal Nível Superior (CAPES) of the Ministry of Education in Brazil for the grant which made the project possible, Dr. Stefan Muthesius for the supervision of the thesis, and Dr. Nicholas Bullock and Professor Tim Benton for their positive appreciations in their capacities as external examiners.

The nature of this work made research, both in Brazil and abroad, of equal importance. The sources were to be found in three countries in addition to Britain, i.e. Brazil, France and the United States. Several institutions in each country generously made their archives available for my research: in Brazil, the Serviço do Patrimônio Histórico e Artístico Nacional (SPHAN) in Rio de Janeiro, in particular Augusto Guimarães Filho and the group responsible for the conservation of the Palácio Capanema (the former Ministry of Education); in Paris, the Fondation Le Corbusier, and in New York, The Museum of Modern Art, New York both had fascinating archives of their Brazilian connections. I am especially grateful to the warm reception of Lucio Costa and Oscar Niemeyer in Rio de Janeiro, and to Roberto Cerqueira Cesar of Rino Levi Associados and Pietro Maria Bardi, then Director of the Museu de Arte de São Paulo, São Paulo.

For the book itself, thanks are due to Allen Cunningham who supported the project in his capacities as Chairman of docomomo-UK and consultant to Spon Press, and Caroline Mallinder, Commissioning Editor at Spon Press. I must thank the friends who assisted me with my last minute enquiries: Marina Quezado and Juan Zapatel for Brazilian sources and Laurence Taillandier for the French ones.

Finally, and most importantly, the person to whom most thanks are due is Thomas Deckker for his unfailing support and intellectual contributions throughout both the PhD thesis and this book.

# Foreword

The processes whereby ideas and enthusiasms move around the world cannot be adequately described by any simple model of transmission and reception. In no case is this more true than in that of Le Corbusier's international influence in the 1930s. He invariably had the greatest influence in precisely those countries and among those people from which the master himself had most to learn. This was particularly true during the phases of transition in his work, such as that which followed his first Modernist period in the 1920s. Contact with the vernacular architecture of Spain and North Africa in 1928–30, his first South American trip in October 1929, and his flirtation with the USSR from October 1928, all conspired to change his ideas about machine-made architecture. Furthermore, from the winter of 1926 (during the heavy drafting work on the League of Nations competition), the studio at the rue de Sèvres was filled with young architects from Europe, South America and Japan. These young people also influenced Le Corbusier, just as he mesmerised them. From this there arose a number of awkward cases where his young disciples could argue, with some reason, that their master had taken credit for their own originality.

The story of Le Corbusier's 'discovery' of Argentina and Brazil in 1929, his subsequent invitation to Rio de Janeiro in 1936, and involvement with the Ministry of Education and University projects and his later involvement with Oscar Niemeyer in the United Nations project in New York (1946–7), is well told in this book. It emerges clearly that the young Brazilian architects who took Le Corbusier's work as their starting point in the 1930s went on to develop buildings and a tradition which went further than Le Corbusier's own work in many ways, at a time when the work of the atelier in the rue de Sèvres in Paris was signally short of built output. Much of what Le Corbusier learned from the Brazilian architects found its way back into the *Œuvre Complète* at the end of the 1930s, much of it lifted directly from the pages of *Brazil Builds*, the book accompanying an important exhibition at the Museum of Modern Art, New York in 1943. This story, of the origins and successful launching of the exhibition and book, is well told here, and intersects nicely with the narrative of the Corbusian *diaspora*.

The links between Le Corbusier's interaction with Brazil and that of the Museum of Modern Art in New York help to explain the flowering of

Brazilian modern architecture in the 1930s and its unexpected *succès d'estime* in North America and across the world. The 1930s witnessed the collapse of confidence in the International Style at precisely the moment when Henry-Russell Hitchcock and Philip Johnson codified it as a style in the Museum of Modern Art exhibition and book of the same name in 1932. The period 1928–32 also witnessed the first major internal schism within Modernism. Architects like Mies van der Rohe and Le Corbusier were attacked both by the traditionalists (often from a far right, nationalist perspective) and by the radical avant-garde (often Communist or far left). The very status of architecture as an art was called into question in these debates, under the hard functionalist critiques of Karel Teige, Hannes Meyer and Mart Stam. Although Fascism, National Socialism and Stalinism accelerated the backlash against Modernist Architecture in the 1930s, modern architects had mixed fortunes in countries like the USA, Britain, France and Holland where a mixture of academic orthodoxy, the interests of government and big business, and the resentment of 'foreign' innovations effectively restricted modern architects to a handful of commissions. Paradoxically, therefore, the *diaspora* of influences from the pioneers of modern architecture took on new qualities and enterprise as it distanced itself from the countries of origin of the Modern Movement.

It is curious, but instructive, to compare the cases of England and Brazil. Like Brazil, England came late to Modernism in architecture, largely missing out on developments in the 1920s. Modernist architecture in England was influenced by two factors: the immigration of key protagonists such as Berthold Lubetkin, Walter Gropius, Marcel Breuer and Eric Mendelsohn and the predominant influence of Le Corbusier's books (and especially their illustrations). Although English Modernists rejected prestigious public commissions as irredeemably in the hands of traditionalist academicians, they were occasionally able to develop further some of the European prototypes. Thus, the Zoo buildings by Lubetkin and Tecton (1932–5), the Boots factory by Owen Williams (1935–6) and the De La Warr Pavilion by Eric Mendelsohn and Serge Chermayeff (1933–5) can be compared favourably with anything in the rest of Europe at the time. Le Corbusier was gracious enough to say as much, celebrating the opening of Lubetkin and Tecton's High Point I in London as the first of the vertical garden cites. Le Corbusier had not yet had the opportunity to build housing as ambitious and well-finished as this in 1936. Similarly, it is utterly inconceivable that he or anyone else could have received a commission to build a prestigious Ministry building in the centre of London or Paris. The challenge of Modernist monumentality, laid down by Le Corbusier and Pierre Jeanneret in the League of Nations building competitions (1926–8) was partially picked up in the Centrosoyuz building in Moscow (1928–33) (but with disappointingly slow and obstructive progress), but it was to Algiers and Rio that Le Corbusier looked to execute his grander visions. That his dream of replanning Rio and Algiers remained unfulfilled was not as important as his influence on those local architects who did transform their cities into two of the most vibrant architectural communities of the 1930s.

Another interesting comparison emerges by contrasting two single-party states in the 1930s, Italy and Brazil, connected by their history and a number of specific interventions. The Brazilian President Getúlio Vargas admired Benito Mussolini and introduced a number of Italian Fascist features into Brazil long before his regime tightened into a truly authoritarian one. Le Corbusier, too, followed events in Italy very carefully, cultivating a number of correspondents and awaiting the call that never came to build something spectacular in Milan or Rome. The Triennale exhibition in Milan, 1933, was arguably the most enterprising and advanced display in Europe in the 1930s. Architects like BBPR (Banfi, Belgioso, Perressuti and Rogers), Terragni, Moretti, Libera and Sartoris competed for all the monumental public commissions in the Fascist era and endeavoured to win over Mussolini, who visited the opening of the second modern architecture exhibition in Rome. The new towns in the Pontine marshes (Sabaudia, Littoria, etc.) and the unfinished apotheosis of Fascism, the new exhibition town of EUR, caught Le Corbusier's attention and helped to develop his theories of a new Mediterranean direction to European Modernism, between the poles of Barcelona, Marseilles, Rome and Algiers. It would only have taken a slight adjustment to the pattern of events for Le Corbusier to have built on the scale of the Brazilian Ministry of Education in Fascist Italy. Dr. Deckker explains with precision the circumstances which led to Le Corbusier's involvement in Brazil, and many of these circumstances (the invitations to lecture, the attempts to muscle in on existing commissions, the visits of admiring young men in Paris) were duplicated in both cases. In those cases, too, Le Corbusier found himself jousting with the intelligent, politically astute official architect of the Fascist regime, Marcello Piacentini.

That Brazilian modern architecture turned into a Brazilian style was partly due to the unifying dominance of Le Corbusier over the imagination of the new generation of Brazilian architects and partly to the importance of local traditions and conditions. As in Fascist Italy, the Brazilian authorities wanted both to connect with their heritage and distance themselves from it. The authentically 'Brazilian', as opposed to Portuguese, influences from the past came from the district of Minas Gerais and, in particular, the work of the liberated slave O Aleijadinho (c. 1738–1814). Modern architects like Lucio Costa and Oscar Niemeyer paid particular tribute to Aleijadinho's work, writing articles and introductions to exhibitions and resisting the nationalist view that this black sculptor could not have been an informed and able architect. The powerfully expressive quality of Aleijadinho's work, its relative absence of superfluous decoration, and the intricacies of the plans, made him eminently suitable as a father figure of modern Brazilian architecture. The fact that American and European scholars were just beginning to discover the Baroque architecture of Minas Gerais in the late 1930s was, as Dr. Deckker says, a significant factor in the interest of the Museum of Modern Art to promote the work of the Brazilian modern architects. Of course, there were political factors too, which gained urgency during the Second World War. But even if the Museum of Modern Art tried to present *Brazil Builds* as some kind of token representation of democratic individuality particularly congenial to the free spirits of America, the individuality of the work and its distinctive originality resisted this pigeonholing.

Tim Benton

# Introduction

In the 1940s and 1950s, Brazil gained unprecedented prestige in the world of Modern Architecture. This new architecture was praised by architects all over the world and placed among the international avant-garde of the post-war years. Britain and the United States, and later France, looked to Brazil as the country which had inherited the progressive Modernism of the pre-war period in Europe, and which, furthermore, had initiated a new phase of the assimilation of cultural and environmental considerations.

The main contribution to publicising the new Brazilian architecture came from the timely exhibition 'Brazil Builds' held at the Museum of Modern Art, New York in 1943 and the publishing of its catalogue as the book *Brazil Builds*.[1] The international press received the exhibition and the book with great enthusiasm. *Brazil Builds*, beautifully produced and lavishly illustrated, was the pioneering study of the new Brazilian architecture. It immediately became the major source of information on Brazilian Modern Architecture abroad.

While *Brazil Builds* represented the discovery of Brazilian architecture by foreigners, it also came to be the discovery of its architecture by Brazilians themselves. Within Brazil, the acclaim that these innovative buildings received gave public credibility to progressive architects emerging from the shadow of a colonial heritage, both cultural and economic. While *Brazil Builds* showed the old and new architecture in Brazil to the world, at home it helped to dismiss the 'colonial complex': contemporary critics described with great irony that Brazilians were surprised, even astonished, by the book which proved to them that they had a modern architecture of international status. That Brazil had Modern Architecture exciting enough to be promoted as a model for the future obviously depended on circumstances which preceded the planning of the exhibition; however, the new architecture displayed there gained public acceptance in Brazil which encouraged the demand for modern buildings. The original buildings consisted of a group of isolated examples mainly financed by government bodies, but after 1943 Modern Architecture became a widespread phenomenon.

The optimism of the Modern Movement, with its ideals of rationality and technology, and its conscious separation from the preceding era, embodied the Brazilian political climate, stimulated by President Getúlio Vargas. His 'Revolução de 1930' was a kind of 'New Deal' to promote modernisation together with economic and social progress. The 'Brazilianisation' of all things European was actively and officially encouraged in all branches of the Arts. The ideal ambience thus existed for the creation of an architectural form which incorporated nationalistic features within a more rational framework. The definition of a Brazilian cultural identity was seen as a central problem among intellectuals in many different fields. In painting, Tarsila do Amaral mixed tropical colour and life within a cubist framework. In music, Heitor Villa-Lobos incorporated the sounds of Brazilian fauna and used indigenous and traditional musical themes within a classical form. In architecture, a group of architects absorbed the principles of Modern Architecture, as exemplified by Le Corbusier, and almost immediately created a 'national' style which assimilated their own cultural and environmental requirements. By the end of World War II a number of highly-regarded buildings had been produced.

The initiative behind the exhibition 'Brazil Builds', on the other hand, having come from the United States, was seen as part of its foreign policy of 'America for the Americans' which President Roosevelt developed towards Latin America during World War II, when he sought to replace European political and economic interests in Latin America with those of the United States. The Museum of Modern Art, New York became intimately linked to the 'New Deal' and Pan-Americanism through its policies in the Arts.

The Museum of Modern Art had been a major propagandist of Modernism in architecture since its exhibition 'Modern Architecture: International Exhibition' of 1932. During the war, it turned its attention away from Europe towards America, North and South. It found in Brazil exactly the material it needed to display that Modern Architecture had found international acceptance. The well-chosen title 'Brazil Builds' conveyed the impression that the whole country had become one vast building site while construction abroad was at a virtual standstill.

Fortunately, 'Brazil Builds' came at a time of transition between the International ideals of the pre-war era and the consciously regional post-war attitude. By the 1950s, reaction to the new work was mixed; after Brasília was built, 'Brazilian-style' architecture was virtually abandoned in Brazil, and Brazilian architecture in general was forgotten by those countries which had previously praised it so highly.

It was a rare situation, then, which allowed Brazil in the post-war years, with its economy stimulated by war and spared from destruction, to emerge into the world of Modern Architecture. To understand the importance and ultimate influence of the 'Brazil Builds' exhibition, the context of the period and the content of the show and the book need to be examined: how the buildings came into being and around what concepts, how they came to be so highly regarded, and the changing reactions to them in Brazil and abroad.

The most important buildings are studied in great detail, to establish the interests and objectives of the main architects and patrons. *Brazil Builds* is used as the source of contemporary views, both pictorial and written. Where appropriate and possible, up-to-date photographs are used to juxtapose the present condition or alternative aspects of the buildings. All quotes and titles of books and periodicals retain the original language and orthography. Portuguese orthography in particular was undergoing revision at this time in Brazil and varied considerably.

**Note**

1    Philip Goodwin: *Brazil Builds: architecture new and old, 1652–1942*. Photographs by G.E. Kidder Smith (New York: Museum of Modern Art 1943; 2nd edn September 1943; 3rd edn November 1944; 4th edn May 1946).

# PART I
## REVOLUTIONS

*Quand tout est une fête,*
*quand, après deux mois et demi de contrainte et de repliement, tout éclate en fête;*
*quand l'été tropical fait jaillir des verdures au bord des eaux bleues, tout autour des rocs roses;*
*quand on est à Rio-de-Janeiro,*
*– des baies d'azur, ciel et eau, se succèdent au loin en forme d'arc, bordées de quais blancs ou de plages roses; ou l'océan bat directement, les vagues se roulent en lames blanches; où le golfe s'enfonce dans les terres, l'eau clapote. Des allées de palmiers droits, aux troncs lisses, galbés par de la mathématique, courent en rues droites; l'un veut qu'ils aient quatre-vingt mètres du haut, je me contente de trente-cinq. Les autos américaines, luxueuses, brillantes, roulent d'une baie à l'autre, d'un grand hôtel à un autre et contournent les promontoires successifs qui tombent dans la mer.*

Le Corbusier: *Précisions* 1930

# 1 Vargas, Le Corbusier, and reinforced concrete

When *The Times* undertook a survey on Brazil, published on 21 June 1927 as '*The Times* Brazil Number', the outstanding works of architecture that it illustrated – the Escola Nacional de Belas Artes [National School of Fine Art] (Adolfo Morales de los Rios 1908), the Teatro Municipal [Municipal Theatre] (Francisco de Oliveira Passos 1909), and the Biblioteca Nacional [National Library] (Francisco Marcelino de Souza Aguiar 1910) – were all in the Second Empire style (Figure 1.1). These all lay on the Avenida Rio Branco, the main artery of the city, which had been cut through the colonial centre of Rio de Janeiro from 1904 by the Mayor, Pereira Passos (1836–1913), in emulation of the Parisian Boulevards. The architectural section, however, presented Neo-Colonial as the true and only style of the country.[1] The author, José Mariano (1881–1946), was Director of the Escola Nacional de Belas Artes, and had been a leading figure in promoting the style.

In 1935, the Minister of Education, Gustavo Capanema (1901–85) invited Marcello Piacentini (1881–1960) to Rio de Janeiro to submit a design for the Cidade Universitária, the campus for the new Universidade do Brasil. Piacentini was Mussolini's chief architect and had previously planned Rome's University City. By 1936, the same Minister had invited Le Corbusier (1887–1965) to Rio de Janeiro to be a consultant on the design of both the Cidade Universitária and the new headquarters of the Ministry of Education and Health.

When Philip Goodwin (1885–1958) arrived in Rio de Janeiro in 1942, he found a group of Modern buildings, almost all within sight of one another, which convinced him that a Modern movement, and one, moreover, with a unique and identifiable national character, had taken root in Brazil. Philip Goodwin's discoveries were displayed to an international audience and to universal admiration in the exhibition 'Brazil Builds' at the Museum of Modern Art, New York in January 1943 and the publication *Brazil Builds*.

In 1927, however, when José Mariano was writing in *The Times*, the problem of identifying an authentic Brazilian architecture was central in discussions among architects. These discussions sprang from the wider search for a national identity in Brazil. *Os Sertões* (1902) by Euclides da Cunha (1866–1909), a mythological account of the first urban settlements in the *sertão*, the north-east of Brazil, closely matched the contemporary

1.1 'The TImes Brazil Number'.

*The Beauties of Brazil.*

Top left: *THE MAIN AVENUE of Rio de Janeiro, the magnificent Avenida Rio Branco. It was cut through the older part of the capital about 20 years ago.*

Top right: *VIEW OF THE AVENIDA RIO BRANCO showing the Municipal Theatre on the left and the National Library on the right.* (The Escola Nacional de Belas Artes is in the background).

Middle left: *THE CITY HALL of Rio de Janeiro, an example of the handsome architectural style which distinguishes public buildings in Brazil.*

Bottom right: *RIO DE JANEIRO BY NIGHT – A panoramic view of Rio de Janeiro showing the Brazilian capital lighted up by night. The long curve of the beach of Copacabana is seen stretching along the open Atlantic Ocean.*

Decorations of cotton bolls, pineapples, palm leaves and caravels.

*The Times* (21 June 1927).

search for national cultures in Europe. The tendency towards nationalism during the first century after Independence in 1822 had initially led Brazil to distance herself from Portugal. In architecture this meant an affiliation to the architecture of the École des Beaux-Arts; the Academia Imperial de Belas Artes was created in 1826 (renamed the Escola Nacional de Belas Artes in 1889), with an architectural course organised by the French architect Grandjean de Montigny (1776–1850). The Second Empire naturally became the accepted style for official buildings.

The Neo-Colonial movement gained impetus from 1914, encouraged by the Portuguese architect Ricardo Severo (1869–1940) with a conference in São Paulo entitled 'A Arte Tradicional no Brasil' and subsequent publications in the press of Rio de Janeiro campaigning for the 'renaissance of the traditional spirit of Brazilian architecture'.[2] José Mariano, a doctor by training who had become an art critic, advocated a return to the architecture of the Colonial past which he claimed 'had developed in accord with Brazilian necessities, and specially adapted to the exigencies of the Brazilian climate'. He built his own house, the Solar do Monjobe (demolished, 1974) in Rio de Janeiro, as an example of the style, and coined the term 'Neo-Colonial'.[3]

The Neo-Colonial rapidly became a fashionable style for domestic architecture and official buildings, but its Brazilian character was in doubt. José Wasth Rodrigues (1891–1957), an artist and critic, thought that, because of the lack of any serious survey of Colonial architecture, the practitioners of Neo-Colonial had no claim to authenticity and were borrowing more from the contemporary 'Mexican' and 'Mission' styles popular at the time in the United States. Rodrigues could speak with authority because he was undertaking a survey, later published as *Documentário Arquitetônico*, of the then still little-known eighteenth-century architecture in Minas Gerais and the north-east.[4] With hindsight, it is apparent that Neo-Colonial architects were using elements of Colonial architecture freely for decorative effect, rather than replicating the sober townscape facades of eighteenth-century domestic architecture. At that time, however, Neo-Colonial was considered radical for trying to assert a national identity in opposition to the international character of the École des Beaux-Arts.

The Neo-Colonial style achieved its zenith in two events in 1922: the exposition of the Centenary of Brazil's Independence from Portugal in Rio de Janeiro, and the Semana de Arte Moderna 1922 [The Week of Modern Art 1922] in São Paulo. While the exposition of the Centenary of Independence was an official enterprise which exemplified how patronage in Rio de Janeiro was the prerogative of the State, the Semana de 22 in São Paulo was undertaken by leading members of the emerging class of industrial entrepreneurs who were leading Brazil's economic development, such as the 'coffee baron' Paulo Prado (1869–1943).

The Semana de 22 is generally considered a break with Academism and the first expression of a 'Modern' attitude in Literature and the Arts in Brazil (Figure 1.2). The event, which ran from 13 to 17 February, consisted of seminars and poetry readings by leading writers such as Oswaldo de Andrade (1890–1954), Mario de Andrade (1893–1945) and Paulo Menotti Del Picchia (1892–1988), music performances by the composer Heitor Villa-Lobos (1887–1959) and exhibitions of paintings and sculptures by artists

1.2 Catalogue of the Exhibition 'Semana de Arte Moderna', São Paulo (1922). Cover by Emiliano Di Cavalcanti. Amaral: *Artes Plásticas na Semana de 22*.

including Emiliano Di Cavalcanti (1897–1976), Anita Mafaldi (1896–1964) and Victor Brecheret (1894–1955). They advocated reconciling the values of Brazilian culture and its primitive forms with those of the French avant-garde. The two small exhibitions of architecture did not share this progressive attitude, however: they showed designs in the Neo-Colonial style.[5]

By 1930, a younger group was also present; they took their lead from the more radical European architects. The spokesman for this group was Lucio Costa (1902–98), born in Toulon, France of Brazilian parents; he grew up in France and England before returning to Brazil in 1917.[6] Costa studied at the Escola Nacional de Belas Artes in Rio de Janeiro. Following

his graduation in 1924, he travelled for a year in Europe in 1926–7; on his return he travelled through the interior of Brazil to the Colonial towns in Minas Gerais. He abandoned his established practice as a Neo-Colonial architect, in which he had already built a series of houses and won two competitions – the Brazilian Pavilion at the Philadelphia Exposition in 1926 and the Argentine Embassy in Rio de Janeiro in 1928 (both unbuilt) – in 1930 when he believed he saw a parallel between the functionalist principles of Le Corbusier (1887–1965) and the constructional honesty of Colonial architecture (Figure 1.3).

The image, at least, of the new architecture had already arrived in Brazil with the Russian émigré Gregori Warchavchik (1896–1972) and Rino Levi (1901–65), a Brazilian of Italian origin, who had both studied in Italy. Warchavchik had been born in Odessa, where he had trained as an architect; in 1918, he attended the Instituto Superiore di Belle Arti in Rome and worked with Marcello Piacentini, before settling in São Paulo in 1923. In 1925 he published a provocative article, 'Acerca da Arquitetura Moderna', in a daily newspaper in Rio de Janeiro in which he quoted Le Corbusier's concepts of the *machine à habiter* and the inherent aesthetic beauty of the automobile.[7] It is certain that this article, published as it was – four small columns among a miscellany of advertisements – had no impact at all. Warchavchik, however, became associated with the patrons and artists who were responsible for the Semana de 22 through his marriage to Mina Kablin, who came from a wealthy family of industrialists. He achieved notoriety through an exhibition 'The Modernist House' (Figure 1.4). 'The Modernist House' was built in the Rua Itápolis in São Paulo, and opened to the public between March and April 1930, with furniture and fixtures designed by the architect himself, pictures and sculptures by various Modernist leading artists, and a Bauhaus tapestry (Figure 1.5).

While Warchavchik talked about Functionalist ideals, his houses remained more 'Moderne' than Modern; Le Corbusier, who saw the house

1.3 Lucio Costa: Fontes House, Rio de Janeiro (1930).
The last neo-Colonial house designed by Lucio Costa.
Costa: *Lucio Costa: registro de uma vivência*.

1.4 Catalogue of the Exhibition 'Exposição de Uma Casa Modernista', São Paulo 1930. Ferraz: *Warchavchik*.

1.5 Gregori Warchavchik: 'Casa Modernista', Rua Itápolis, São Paulo (1930). Ferraz: *Warchavchik*.

in the Rua Itápolis under construction in 1929, compared it to works by Rob Mallet-Stevens; nevertheless, Le Corbusier elected Warchavchik to be a member of the Congrès Internationaux d'Architecture Moderne (CIAM).[8] The plan of 'The Modernist House' was not a *plan libre*, but resembled contemporary American suburban houses in its accommodation and distribution; the detailing was closer to an Art Deco with the lavish use of colour and different materials. Several compromises had had to be made: the parapets concealed not the desired flat roofs, but pitched tiled ones. Warchavchik described, in his report to the 1930 CIAM, the difficulty of producing Modern designs in Brazil: iron, glass and cement were imported, which considerably increased the building cost, as opposed to brick, tiles and wood which were of good quality and abundant.[9] Nevertheless, Warchavchik was important as a catalyst in the debate; he was taken up by the group of the Semana de 22 to represent the Modernist trend in architecture which they had already exhibited in literature and painting. The garden, filled with cactus by Mina Kablin, was highly praised for its national character.

The technology already existed in Brazil, however, for the development of the new architecture: reinforced concrete frames had been used since the 1910s for large-scale constructions. The first tall buildings in Rio de Janeiro and São Paulo, at the turn of the century, had been built with steel frames, along with bridges and similar structures. Steel proved to be an expensive system in Brazil, however. There were no rolling facilities for structural steel members in Brazil; these, and the technical supervision of the construction, had to be imported from the United States. Although Brazil did not initially produce either cement or reinforcing rods, reinforced concrete had the advantages of being prepared on site and of not requiring specialised labour, which greatly reduced the cost.

The new technology was adopted by engineers and used in the early skyscrapers in Brazil. The Martinelli Building in São Paulo (1929) was an ornate tower in the eclectic taste; the A Noite Building in Rio de Janeiro (1928) (Figure 1.6) was a simple tower in a Moderne style. These buildings were closely based on contemporary skyscrapers in the United States. Emilio Henrique Baumgart (1889–1943), a Brazilian engineer who developed the use of reinforced concrete structures in Brazil, set a world record for the height of reinforced concrete structures at 102.5 m with the design for the A Noite Building.

So successful was the use of reinforced concrete that it came to supplant steel even in situations where steel would have normally been used, such as the roofs of aircraft hangars and long-span bridges.[10] The unusual application of concrete structures in Brazil merited the attention of contemporary technical periodicals in France and Germany.[11] The affinity of Brazilian engineers to concrete construction led to the creation of a technical periodical, *Concreto*, in 1932, in which research into, and achievements in, the application of the material were discussed.

It was not until the 'Crash' of 1929, which shattered the economy, that the necessity or possibility of an official policy of industrialisation arose. Brazil had been an independent nation since 1822, but a century later it was still suffering from a colonial economy, exporting raw materials and agricultural products – sugar, rubber, and most recently coffee, while

1.6  A Noite Building, Rio de Janeiro (1928).
The tallest concrete frame building in the
world when completed in 1928. Emilio
Baumgart, engineer.
Postcard, 1948. Collection: Zilah Quezado
Deckker.

importing manufactured goods. During the 1920s, the rapidly increasing
industrialisation in São Paulo and, to a lesser extent, Rio de Janeiro, had
provoked – unsuccessfully – a series of political crises against the ruling oligarchy. During the Crash, the price of coffee fell to the point at which
Brazil could no longer import essential materials; the economy – and political structure – collapsed.

The resulting power vacuum was filled in 1930 by Getúlio Vargas
(1883–1954) in the 'Revolução de 30' [Revolution of 1930]. The success of
Vargas' tenure, from 1930 to 1945, lay in his effort to experiment with
new forms of national organisation. Profound changes took place in the
economic, political and institutional fabric of the nation: industry expanded
to fill the gap left by the decline of imported goods; locally-produced
goods replaced those which Brazil no longer had the foreign exchange to
import. The State was centralised and the power of the regional

oligarchies neutralised by the use of centrally-appointed Mayors. Vargas chose Ministers whom he trusted would be sympathetic to his policies of industrialisation and nationalism. Although not democratically elected, the early years of his 'Revolução de 30' had liberal overtones; intellectual endeavour was encouraged. Young progressives, including Lucio Costa and Heitor Villa-Lobos, were appointed to key positions in education.[12]

Many of the commissions for Modern buildings stemmed directly from the policies of the modernisation of the economic and social structures of Brazil promoted by the Vargas government and its newly-created Ministries. From the Ministry of Education and Health came the Ministry of Education and Health Building and the Cidade Universitária; from the Ministry of Labour, Industry and Commerce, the Brazilian Pavilion at the 1939 New York World's Fair; from the Civil Aviation Department, Santos Dumont Airport; and from the appointed Mayor of Belo Horizonte, the Pampulha complex.

The first Minister of Education, Francisco Campos, appointed Lucio Costa Director of the Escola Nacional de Belas Artes in October 1930, on the advice of his *chefe de gabinete* [Secretary], Rodrigo Mello Franco de Andrade (1898–1968), with the intention of reforming it. With diplomatic consideration, Costa added a 'Functional' course, parallel to the existing 'Beaux-Arts' course. It is certain that Costa knew little about the actual nature of Modern architectural education, but, as he knew of Warchavchik's works in São Paulo, he appointed him as Professor, with Affonso Eduardo Reidy (1909–64), a recent graduate, as his assistant. Atilio Corrêa Lima (1901–43), who had studied urbanism at the Sorbonne, established and held the chair of Urban Planning.

The overwhelming success of the 'Functional' course led to a violent reaction from the other professors in the School; José Mariano, whom Costa had supplanted as Professor, was still a powerful political figure and attacked him openly in the press. In his defence against these vitriolic attacks, Costa wrote of his profound admiration for the Colonial architecture of Brazil, and exposed contemporary Neo-Colonial practice as a sham; he derided the practice of finishing machine-sawn timber by hand to give it an authentic appearance. He claimed that he was maintaining a continuity in principle with the Colonial past, by responding to contemporary social and technical forces; he stressed that only the straightforward use of the new technology – reinforced concrete – could bring about a contemporary architecture of equal quality.[13] Costa did not believe that he could maintain a credible position in the face of such determined and underhand opposition and resigned in September 1931. His resignation sparked a student revolt in October 1931, which found support from Frank Lloyd Wright, then visiting Brazil.[14] Before he left, Costa held an exhibition, known as the 'Salão de 31', where he introduced several artists from the Semana de 22 in São Paulo to Rio de Janeiro.[15]

Costa was unable to complete his reforms, but his success may be judged by the fact that most of the Modern architects, such as Luiz Nunes (1908–37), Milton Roberto (1914–53), Álvaro Vital Brazil (1909–97), Jorge Machado Moreira (1904–92), Carlos Leão (1906–83), Oscar Niemeyer (b. 1907) and Ernani Vasconcellos (1909–88), as well as Roberto Burle Marx (1909–94), were students during his brief reign. They were, in his words, 'a

1.7 The Modernists, 1931.
Including: Lucio Costa (4th, front row),
Gregori Warchavchik (3rd, front row),
Carlos Leão (7th, back row) and Cândido
Portinari (5th, front row).
Costa: *Lucio Costa registro de uma vivência.*

1.8 Gregori Warchavchik and Lucio Costa:
Schwartz House, Rio de Janeiro (1932).
The gardens were by Roberto Burle Marx.
Costa: *Lucio Costa registro de uma vivência.*

purist battalion dedicated to the impassioned study of Walter Gropius, Ludwig Mies van der Rohe and especially Le Corbusier' (Figure 1.7).[16]

After Costa left the Escola Nacional de Belas Artes, he entered into partnership with Warchavchik, with Carlos Leão as their associate, opening an office in the A Noite Building; they built a few private houses and a group of low-cost houses in Gamboa, a working-class district of Rio de Janeiro. The Schwartz House (1932) was a much more relaxed version of the Modern style than Warchavchik's own houses (Figure 1.8); Roberto Burle Marx was in charge of the garden design, his first commission. The partnership ended in 1933 because their ideas were very different; Warchavchik eventually retreated from his Modernist position. Costa built little until 1935; he described those intervening years as '*chômage*' [unemployed].[17]

During these years, Costa continued in practice with Carlos Leão, but carried out almost no commissions, as they were sought out by clients who wanted Neo-Colonial houses. Instead, he studied the work of Walter Gropius (1883–1969), Ludwig Mies van der Rohe (1886–1969) and above all Le Corbusier (1887–1965), and designed what he called '*casas sem donos*' – houses without owners.[18] Costa consolidated his ideas in 1935 in an article 'Razões da Nova Arquitetura', in which he stated his beliefs on the relationship between the newly-emerging industrial society and Modern architecture. His principles found a parallel with Le Corbusier's doctrines, which Costa came to consider 'almost the Holy Scripture of our architecture'.[19]

'Razões da Nova Arquitetura' was published in the *Revista da Directoria de Engenharia da Prefeitura do Distrito Federal* (*PDF*) in January 1936. *PDF*, an official magazine of the Prefeitura do Distrito Federal [Prefecture of Rio de Janeiro] was founded in July 1932; it was edited by the engineer Carmen Portinho (b.1906), the wife of Affonso Eduardo Reidy. It became the mouthpiece of the Modern architects with the publication of innumerable unbuilt projects.

In 'Razões da Nova Arquitetura', Costa elaborated his two main points: first, that the new architecture must be responsive to the society in which it was based, and, second, that it must be responsive to climate and construction methods. Without the former, it would not be accepted; without the latter, it would not function in the rigorous climate of Brazil. He did not address the issue of 'style': he believed that this would follow naturally from the first two conditions. Costa viewed history as a cyclical process, and the Modern period as one such transformation. Therefore, for Costa, traditional architecture was out of place in a Modern society; only when the Arts had achieved a synthesis with society could they be considered authentic. Costa believed that the methods of machine production would define the new aesthetic:

> it is vital that industry supports construction, producing, conveniently, all those elements that it requires, with the same degree of perfection that the coachwork of automobiles shows.

He did not believe, however, that the new architecture was international, but emphasised its Latin roots, which would make it more acceptable for Brazil:

> the new architecture, which is linked, in its most characteristic examples [...] to the most pure Mediterranean tradition, that same Reason of the Greeks and Romans, which was reborn in the Renaissance, and which afterwards was wrecked by the artifices of academic decoration – is today resurgent, with impressive and renewed vigour.

Lastly, he emphasised Le Corbusier's position of authority among contemporary architects:

In this great work of opening up the path to industry, innumerable architects, world-wide, are dedicating themselves, some with faith, some with talent, and one – with genius.[20]

Le Corbusier was initially important to Brazilian architects, Lucio Costa in particular, because he seemed to be the only Modern architect to present a complete social and technical basis for Modern architecture. It would be easy to assume that Le Corbusier was the only influence on Brazilian architecture in this period, and that he uniquely represented Modernity in Brazil. He was taken up by the more progressive Modern intellectuals mainly because his rhetorical approach was in accord with the way they saw that Modernism could be propagated in Brazil. Furthermore, his use of reinforced concrete was within the practical grasp of architects in Brazil; on the other hand, some of his technical features were certainly greeted with scepticism: the *mur neutralisant* was quickly answered with *brise-soleils*. Because Costa was appointed architect of two important buildings, and because he saw Le Corbusier's work as uniquely expressive, Le Corbusier assumed a pivotal role in the development of Brazilian architecture. Although he was to become the single most important influence, his first visit in 1929 had had remarkably little impact. There was no evidence of the importance he was to play in Brazilian architecture nor of the impact Brazil was to play in his life.

Le Corbusier had been planning to go to South America since 1926, when Fernand Léger (1881–1955) and Blaise Cendrars (1887–1961) had introduced him to the idea that the Brazilian government was considering building a new capital on the central plateau of Brazil.[21] Through them, Le Corbusier had met the cultural elite of South America: Vitoria Ocampo, who invited him to Argentina, and Paulo Prado, sponsor of the Semana de 22, who invited him to Brazil.[22] He did not make the journey until 1929, however. He was well received in both Rio de Janeiro and São Paulo, and met many political figures.

Le Corbusier had been invited to give a lecture tour of four cities in South America – Buenos Aires, Montevideo, São Paulo, and Rio de Janeiro. His lectures were based on his plans for the Ville Contemporaine (1922), the Centrosoyuz Building, Moscow (1929–33) and the Villa Savoye, Poissy (1929–33), these last two still under construction. The Centrosoyuz Building was a prominent part of these lectures, in particular its supposedly rational climatic features. He promoted the use of the *mur neutralisant* as suitable for any climatic region from the tropics to the poles, although this was to prove one of the most problematic features of his buildings.[23]

While Le Corbusier was proselytising the mechanistic world of 'L'Esprit Nouveau' in Rio de Janeiro, his own work underwent a transformation. It was his first contact with the extraordinary landscape of Rio de Janeiro and the extraordinary warmth of the *carioca* people, in contrast to the provincial and restrained cultures of the other cities (Figure 1.9). It had been presaged by his flights in an open aeroplane over the Argentine *pampas* with the pioneer aviator Antoine de Saint-Exupéry (1900–44) and his meeting with the American singer Josephine Baker (1906–75) on board the SS *Giulio Cesare* from Buenos Aires to Rio de Janeiro.[24] In Rio de

1 Alfred Agache: Plan for Rio de Janeiro (1926–30).
Agache: *Cidade do Rio de Janeiro.*

2 Le Corbusier: Plan for Rio de Janeiro (1929).
FLC 32091: *Précisions* p.243.
© FLC/ADAG, Paris and DACS, London 2000.

3 Le Corbusier: Plan for Rio de Janeiro (1929).
FLC 33425: *Précisions* p.243.
© FLC/ADAG, Paris and DACS, London 2000.

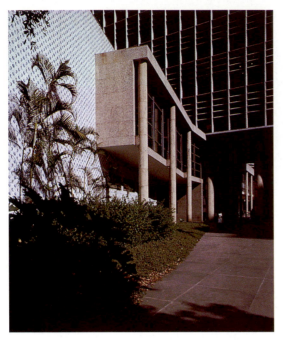

4 Lucio Costa and Team: Ministry of Education and Health, Rio de Janeiro (1936–45).
Auditorium and Minister's private entrance.
© Zilah Quezado Deckker.

5 Lucio Costa and Team: Ministry of Education and Health, Rio de Janeiro (1936–45).
Public Entrance underneath the colonnade.
© Zilah Quezado Deckker.

6 Lucio Costa and Team: Ministry of Education and Health, Rio de Janeiro (1936–45).
Reception hall of the Minister's quarters.
Murals by Portinari. Carpet by Niemeyer.
© Zilah Quezado Deckker.

7 Marcelo and Milton Roberto: Central Terminal, Santos Dumont Airport, Rio de Janeriro (1937–44).
Exterior: view from the land side.
© Zilah Quezado Deckker.

8 Atilio Corrêa Lima: Seaplane Terminal, Santos Dumont Airport, Rio de Janeiro (1937–8).
South façade to the land side.
Originally the vehicle approach to the terminal.
© Zilah Quezado Deckker.

9 Rino Levi: 'Sedes Sapientiæ', São Paulo (1942).
Exterior.
© Zilah Quezado Deckker.

10 Oscar Niemeyer: Casino, Pampulha, Belo Horizonte (1940–2).
Entrance façade.
© Zilah Quezado Deckker.

11 Oscar Niemeyer: Casa de Baile, Pampulha, Belo Horizonte (1940–2).
View across the lake from the Casino.
© Zilah Quezado Deckker.

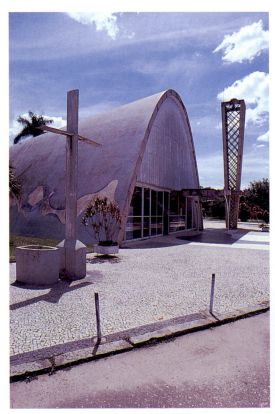

12 Oscar Niemeyer: Church of São Francisco, Pampulha, Belo Horizonte (completed 1946).
Entrance façade, towards the street. Azulejos by Portinari.
© Zilah Quezado Deckker.

13 Oscar Niemeyer: Church of São Francisco, Pampulha, Belo Horizonte (completed 1946).
Interior. Painted panels by Portinari.
© Zilah Quezado Deckker.

1.9  Le Corbusier and Monteiro de Carvalho, Rio de Janeiro, 1929.
FLC LI (2) 9–1.
© FLC/ADAGP, Paris and DACS, London 2000.

Janeiro, he stayed at the newly-built and considerably luxurious Hotel Gloria in Flamengo, and swam in the bay.[25] Le Corbusier filled sketch-book after sketch-book with drawings of the tropical landscape and mulatto women.[26] This new-found sensuality marked the appearance of *objets à réaction poétique* in his work.

There was a further reason which attracted Le Corbusier to Rio de Janeiro: the presence there of the French urbanist Alfred Agache (1875–1959), who was working on the master plan for the city (Plate 1). In *Précisions*, Le Corbusier claimed that he had not originally intended to go to Rio de Janeiro because of Agache, but this must be seen as ironic.[27] Firstly, his ship had already stopped in Rio de Janeiro on the way to Buenos Aires (and would stop there on the way back) and Le Corbusier had already noted in his sketchbooks the extraordinary landscape, and secondly, he may have seen an opportunity to challenge Agache's Beaux-Arts proposals for the city, at least on a theoretical level.[28]

For all the four cities he visited in South America – Buenos Aires, Montevideo, São Paulo, and Rio de Janeiro – Le Corbusier proposed urban plans based on the Ville Contemporaine.[29] The plan for Rio de Janeiro, however, showed a significant departure from the plan for the other cities: Le Corbusier abandoned the orthogonal rigidity of the other schemes for fluid curves (Plates 2 and 3).[30] He proposed a single long motor-viaduct, 100 metres high, looping around the various bays and promontories from the Centre to Gávea, a distance of six kilometres. This may have been due to the complex geography of the area, the 'violent and sublime landscape', which demanded, and gave an opportunity for, a more subtle response.[31]

Le Corbusier's work made little impact in Brazil at the time, however. Of what was to become the 'purist battalion', only Carlos Leão had attended his lecture at the Escola Nacional de Belas Artes; Lucio Costa had passed by but left without much thought about it.[32] Brazilian architects only embraced Le Corbusier's doctrines after the publication of *Précisions*, with the plans for Rio de Janeiro and São Paulo, because Le Corbusier had written enthusiastically about Brazil's problems and possibilities and showed how his work might be applicable to Brazil.[33] The subsequent publication of *La Ville Radieuse* and the *Œuvre Complète 1929–34* in 1935 had an immediate impact; the Centrosoyuz Building, the League of Nations project, the Maison Locative in Algiers, the Lotissement in Barcelona, and the Errazuris House, were all to become influential in Brazil. It led directly to his official invitation to Brazil in 1936.

Le Corbusier's second visit to Brazil was due to an extraordinary patron within the Vargas government. The new Minister of Education and Health, Gustavo Capanema, was an extraordinary cultural figure and patron of the arts: he created the Universidade do Brasil and the Serviço do Patrimônio Histórico e Artístico Nacional (SPHAN), as well as programmes of national health and public education. Two important commissions of the Vargas regime stemmed directly from Capanema: the Ministry of Education and Health Building and the Cidade Universitária. Costa, established as the major theoretician of Modernism in Brazil, was appointed architect to both these projects. His Cidade Universitária was never built, but the Ministry of Education and Health received immediate international recognition and launched what became known as the 'Brazilian Style'.

Unusually among Modern architects at that time, Costa was not concerned exclusively with new buildings. SPHAN was established in 1937, under the direction of Rodrigo Mello Franco de Andrade; in the pilot plan of 1936, Mario de Andrade, who had been instrumental in the discovery of the Colonial towns of Minas Gerais in 1924, described the purpose as 'to identify, organise, conserve, defend, and publicise the national heritage'.[34] The definition of national heritage encompassed archaeological, Amerindian, popular, historic, fine and applied art, Brazilian and foreign. It was more than a Commission for Ancient Monuments; it included a number of young progressives:

> In the first years of SPHAN, its director counted on the collaboration of Mario de Andrade [writer], [. . .] José de Sousa Reis [architect b. 1909], Lucio Costa [architect], [. . .] Carlos Drummond de Andrade [writer 1902–87], Gilberto Freire [sociologist 1900–87], [. . .] Joaquim Cardoso [engineer 1897–1978], Vinícius de Morais [poet 1913–80], [. . .] Sérgio Buarque de Holanda [historian 1902–82]. They formed themselves into a team of researchers, historians, lawyers, architects, engineers, conservationists, restorers, foremen.[35]

At SPHAN, Costa became the architect of the Museum of the Church of São Miguel (1937), Brazil's finest Jesuit mission church in Rio Grande do Sul, as well as taking charge of the restoration of Colonial towns such as Ouro Preto in Minas Gerais.

The strong national character of the 'Brazilian Style' and the exploration of the historical roots of Brazilian architecture were part of a wider political picture. The Vargas regime, as it strove to develop industries and implement social and political reforms, was necessarily highly nationalistic; the cornerstone of its policies was the concept of *brasilidade*, which implied cultural as well as economic self-sufficiency, with the state giving direction and organisation to political, social, and cultural institutions. Some degree of paranoia within the Vargas regime is understandable. During the 1930s, Brazil was a strategic battleground between Nazi German, Imperial Japanese, and Soviet Russian interest groups. Vargas crushed the Soviet-backed communist revolution of 1935 as well as the right-wing Integralist uprising in 1937.

The 'Revolução de 30', liberal and democratic, was formalised into the Estado Novo in 1937. The Estado Novo was not really a Fascist state, although Italian fascism was a desirable model for many in the Vargas government. While the state did not tolerate opposition, it was relatively open in its treatment of opinion; while it was nationalistic, it was not racial or reactionary.[36] In as far as Modernism was a consciously abstract style, the Estado Novo did not seek to impose an aesthetic of ideological representation; for Vargas, 'modernisation' was the key issue. Furthermore, it was a time of enormous popular hope in the future in Brazil. Vargas and his ministers were:

> prepared to fight for ambitious plans of economic and social change, full-scale national re-organisation [. . .] [with] a willingness to experiment with new political forms in a desperate attempt to discard the old.[37]

However certain they were about discarding the old, they were less certain about the direction of the new.

## Notes

1 José Mariano: 'Palm Thatch and Patio Gardens' *The Times* (21 June 1927) p.xviii. Review in *The Builder* (8 July 1927) p.43.

2 *The Times* (21 June 1927) p.xviii.

3 José Mariano: 'Os Dez Mandamentos do Estilo Neo-Colonial aos Jovens Architectos' *Architectura no Brasil* (September 1924) p.161.

4 José Wasth Rodrigues: *Documentário Arquitetônico* (São Paulo: Martins 1944; 4th edn. Belo Horizonte: Itatiaia/São Paulo: Editora Universidade de São Paulo 1979).

5 Aracy Amaral: *Artes Plásticas na Semana de 22* (São Paulo: Perspectiva 1976) p.50. Georg Przyrembel (1885–1956) was a Polish architect and Antonio Garcia Moya (1891–1956) an architect of Spanish origin.

6 His father was a naval engineer. In 1910 they moved to Newcastle upon Tyne. Lucio Costa spoke fluent French and English. Conversation with Lucio Costa, December 1988.

7 *Correio da Manhã* (1 November 1925). Geraldo Ferraz: *Warchavchik e a Introdução da Nova Arquitetura no Brasil 1925 a 1940* (São Paulo: Museu de Arte de São Paulo 1965) p.25.

8 Ferraz: *Warchavchik* p.260.

9 Gregori Warchavchik: 'L'architecture d'aujourd'hui dans L'Amerique du Sud' *Cahiers d'Art* no.2 (1931) p.107.

10 The Herval Bridge in Santa Catarina was the longest span reinforced concrete bridge in the world and was built entirely with cantilevered shutters. 'Long Rigid-Frame Bridge Erected by Cantilever Method' *Engineering News-Record* (6 August 1931) pp.208–9.

11 'Le Théâtre João Caetano' *La Technique des Travaux* (February 1931); 'Le Pont Rio de Peixe au Brésil' *Le Constructeur de Béton Armé* (February 1932); 'Einige Eisenbetonbauten in Brasilien' *Der Bauingenieur* no.9/10 (1938).

12 Thomas E. Skidmore: *Politics in Brazil 1930–1964: An Experiment in Democracy* (New York: Oxford University Press 1967).

13 Lucio Costa: 'Uma Escola Viva de Belas-Artes' *O Jornal* (31 July 1931). *Arquitetura Moderna Brasileira: depoimento de uma geração* (São Paulo: Pini/Associação Brasileira de Ensino de Arquitetura/Fundação Vilanova Artigas 1987) pp.47–50.

14   Frank Lloyd Wright: *An Autobiography* (New York: Longmans Green; London: Faber & Faber 1932; repr. London: Quartet Books 1977) pp.541–6. Wright gives the date of this visit incorrectly as 1930.

15   Lucio Costa: 'Salão de 31' in *Lucio Costa: registro de uma vivência* (São Paulo: Empresa das Artes 1995) pp.70–1.

16   Lucio Costa: 'Testimony of a Carioca Architect' *Atlantic Monthly* (February 1956) p.44.

17   Conversation with Lucio Costa, December 1988.

18   *Lúcio Costa: registro de uma vivência* pp.83–9.

19   Lucio Costa: 'Testimony of a Carioca Architect' *Atlantic Monthly* p.44.

20   Lucio Costa: 'Razões da Nova Arquitetura' *Revista da Diretoria de Engenharia da Prefeitura do Distrito Federal (PDF)* (January 1936) pp.3–9.

   *é imprescindível que a indústria se apodere da construção, produzindo, convenientemente apurados, todos os elementos de que ela carece, para podermos chegar àquele grau de perfeição de que as carrocerias de automóvel são amostra animadora.*

   *Filia-se a nova arquitetura, isto sim, nos seus exemplos mais característicos [. . .] às mais puras tradições mediterrâneas, àquela mesma razão dos gregos e latinos que procurou renascer nos Quatrocentos, para logo depois afundar sob os artifícios da maquilagem acadêmica – só agora ressurgindo, com imprevisto e renovado vigor.*

   *é nessa obra grandiosa de abrir caminho à indústria que, em todo o mundo, inúmeros arquitetos se empenham com fé, alguns com talento e um – com gênio.*

21   Blaise Cendrars (Frederic Sausur) had been born in La Chaux-de-Fonds within a month of Le Corbusier (Charles-Edouard Jeanneret), and they remained friends. Blaise Cendrars to Le Corbusier 13 July 1926. FLC E1–13.8; Fernand Léger to Le Corbusier 1926. FLC U2–9.1–2.

22   Le Corbusier: *Précisions sur un état présent de l'architecture et de l'urbanisme* (Paris: Editions Crè 1930; repr. Paris: Vincent Fréal 1960) p.19.

23   For the problems of the *mur neutralisant* in Moscow see Jean-Louis Cohen: 'Le Corbusier and the Mystique of the USSR' in *Oppositions* 23 (1981) pp.85–121. None were actually built.

24   Antoine de Saint-Exupéry was the Director of the Argentine Air Mail Service between 1929 and 1931.

25   Letter addressed to Le Corbusier in Rio de Janeiro, 2 September 1936. FLC I3–3.52.

26   Le Corbusier: *Sketchbooks* I (London: Thames and Hudson/Paris: Fondation Le Corbusier 1981) pp.227–90. His earlier experiments in life drawing appear to have been made from pornographic postcards. Stanislaus von Moos: 'Le Corbusier as Painter' and Christopher Green: 'The Architect as Artist' in *Le Corbusier: Architect of the Century* (London: Arts Council of Great Britain 1987) pp.90–1, p.126.

27   Le Corbusier: *Précisions* p.241, 245.

28   He illustrated Agache's proposals alongside his own in *La Ville Radieuse* (Boulogne-sur-Seine: Editions de L'Architecture d'Aujourd'hui 1935; repr. Paris: Vincent Fréal 1964; English edn *The Radiant City* London: Faber & Faber 1957) pp.222–3.

29   Le Corbusier: *Précisions* p.240, 243. *Œuvre Complète 1929–34* p.138.

30   For Le Corbusier's urban plans for Rio de Janeiro see Yannis Tsiomis (ed.): *Le Corbusier Rio de Janeiro 1929–1936* (Centro de Arquitetura e Urbanismo do Rio de Janeiro: Prefeitura da Cidade do Rio de Janeiro 1998).

31   *Précisions* p.244. 'paysage violent et sublime'.

32   Conversation with Lucio Costa, December 1988.

33   Conversation with Lucio Costa, December 1988.

34   Mario de Andrade: 'Anteprojeto de Criação do Serviço do Patrimônio Nacional'. *Mario de Andrade: Cartas de Trabalho* (Brasília: SPHAN Pró-Memória 1981) p.39.

   'determinar, organizar, conservar, defender, e propagar o patrimônio artístico nacional.'

35   *Rodrigo e seus Tempos* (Rio de Janeiro: SPHAN Pró-Memória 1986) pp.20–1.

   'Nos primeiros anos do SPHAN, seu diretor contou com a colaboração de Mario de Ae, [. . .] José de Sousa Reis, Lucio Costa, [. . .] Carlos Drummond de Andrade, Gilberto Freire, [. . .] Joaquim Cardoso, Vinícius de Morais, [. . .]. Formou-se uma equipe com pesquisadores, historiadores, juristas, arquitetos, engenheiros, conservadores, restauradores, mestres-de-obras.'

36   Eric Hobsbawm: *The Age of Extremes: The Short Twentieth Century* (London: Abacus 1995; 1st publ. 1994) p.135.

37   Skidmore: *Politics in Brazil 1930–1964* p.7.

# PART II
## THE HEROIC PERIOD

In thinking about Europe as it then was and as it is today, and in watching these young Brazilians, in the space of a few years, bridge an intellectual gap that one might have expected to hold up development for decades, I have come to understand how societies decline or come into being, and to realise that those great historical upheavals, which, when one reads about them in the textbooks, appear to be the outcome of anonymous forces working in profound obscurity, can also, in a moment of lucidity, be brought about by the vigorous determination of a handful of talented young people.

Claude Lévi-Strauss: *Tristes Tropiques* 1955

# 2  The Ministry of Education and Health Building

Historians of that period of Brazilian history known as the Estado Novo claim that the common citizen retained certain impressions of it:

> The social memory, represented by the common man, keeps some traces, however contradictory, of the period: censorship; the police of Filinto Müller (1900–73) [responsible for the crushing of the communist uprising]; the construction of Volta Redonda [the first steel mill, set up in 1943]; labour legislation and workers' demonstrations in the Vasco da Gama stadium; the building of the Ministry of Education in Rio de Janeiro; the figure of Villa-Lobos; the National Radio; Carmen Miranda (1909–55) [a singer and dancer mythicised by Hollywood as the personification of Brazilian popular culture]; Zé Carioca [a Walt Disney cartoon parrot who personified a citizen of Rio de Janeiro, see plate 15]; and, obviously, Vargas.[1]

The Ministry of Education and Health Building, however, should not be linked to the Estado Novo, but to the 'Revolução de 30' which preceded it. During the stricter *brasilidade* campaign of the Estado Novo, Le Corbusier's participation would neither have been feasible, nor the involvement of a foreign architect possible under Brazilian law. As it was, between 1930 and 1937 there was a period of liberalism during which most of the social and cultural changes in Brazil took place, of which the project for the building of the Ministry of Education was part.

The Ministry of Education and Health was created in the first year of the Vargas government. The building of new headquarters for Ministries was part of the general Government campaign of Modernisation, although the kinds of Modernity embodied in these buildings were strikingly different. The Ministry of Finance, built at the same time as, and adjacent to, the Ministry of Education, was a stripped classicist building typical of contemporary American practice, while the Ministry of Education was to become one of the most highly-regarded and influential Modern buildings of the period.[2]

The site for the new Ministries lay on the Esplanada do Castelo adjacent to the Avenida Rio Branco, along which lay cultural institutions such as the Escola Nacional de Belas Artes, the Teatro Municipal and the Biblioteca

2.1  The Esplanada do Castelo in 1930.
Street lay-out in progress according to the
Agache Plan.
Agache: *Cidade do Rio de Janeiro*.

2.2  The Esplanada do Castelo in 1930.
The dotted line indicates the position of the
razed Morro do Castelo.
Agache: *Cidade do Rio de Janeiro*.

Nacional. The Esplanada do Castelo was part of a monumental commercial complex and Federal District surrounding a plaza proposed by Alfred Agache on the site of the Morro do Castelo, the sixteenth-century Colonial centre, which had been razed to create more space in the centre (Figures 2.1 and 2.2).[3] The Esplanada do Castelo was to be the show-piece of the modernisation of Rio, and included many of the new Ministry buildings and impressive boulevards. The site reserved for the Ministry of Education – Quadra F – was a long narrow site surrounded by other large Ministry buildings and with a main road, the Rua Araújo Porto Alegre, on one narrow side.[4] Quadra F and its surroundings were initially developed as the Agache Plan, but this Plan was later abandoned (see Plate 1).

The Ministry of Education Building was very much the inspiration of the Minister, Gustavo Capanema, himself. Capanema had no conception of what a Modern Brazilian architecture might be; he undertook, therefore, a long and involved process to arrive at a design which fulfilled his dream. However incidentally he arrived at the result, it became intimately linked with the character of the man and his Ministry:

The Ministry of Education in Rio de Janeiro, built in his tenure, according to the modernist lines of Le Corbusier, symbolises until today the image that stayed for many of an open-minded Minister, ahead of his own time, defender of culture and the arts, and promoter of education.[5]

When he took office in July 1934, at the age of 33, Gustavo Capanema was virtually unknown in the circles of Federal Government. Capanema had graduated in Law in his native State of Minas Gerais; he was a great supporter of Vargas and had participated actively in the 'Revolução de 30'. He entered government as assistant to the Secretary of the Interior, and later became Minister of Education and Health, where he remained until the downfall of Vargas in 1945. He surrounded himself with Modernist intellectuals from his native state such as the poet and writer Carlos Drummond de Andrade and Rodrigo Mello Franco de Andrade, who greatly assisted him in promoting cultural enterprises and commissioning modern artists. Capanema became known for his capacity to balance the dual aims of being an intellectual and a politician:

Capanema [...] never renounced his intellectual pretensions, which he maintained through his concern with questions related to education and culture; he cultivated personal friendships with writers, painters, and artists in general, and the habit of study and reading. He tried to be, always, an intellectual in power.[6]

Despite the enormous public acclaim which the Ministry of Education and Health Building was to receive, for the architects, however, it was not, as it seems today, the most important commission to come from Capanema's office. The most important undertaking by the Ministry was not its own building, but the Cidade Universitária. Like the Ministry, the Cidade Universitária project involved not only the buildings but also the programme of the Universidade do Brasil itself. The Italian architect Marcello Piacentini had originally been appointed to design the campus in August 1935;[7] at the same time, Capanema established a commission of professors to work on the programme. The academic committee supported Piacentini on ideological grounds: Italy was a desirable model in the fascist quarters of Vargas's government. However, before Capanema could advance his plans for the campus, which was a much more complex undertaking, the Ministry Building took priority.

A competition for the Ministry was announced in the *Diário Oficial* of 23 April 1935 and was further publicised through the Instituto de Arquitetos do Brasil [Institute of Brazilian Architects] and major newspapers in Rio de Janeiro, São Paulo and surrounding states. It established a two-stage competition and a maximum budget, and, fortuitously, included a clause which freed the government from contracting the winning project.[8]

There was a high degree of expectation surrounding this competition. It attracted a good response with 35 entries, a large number for Brazil in 1935; all from Rio de Janeiro and São Paulo.[9] The periodical *PDF* announced the competition as being the great opportunity to do '*realmente arquitetura*' [real architecture], meaning 'Modern': first of all, because its function was to house the Ministry which was to deal with the '*questões de arte*' [questions of art], and secondly, because the brief seemed to have been organised to give architects a considerable degree of freedom.[10]

The result of the competition did not fulfil their expectations, however. The judges, in addition to Capanema himself and his assistant, had been designated by the various architectural institutions in Rio de Janeiro and were mainly conservative.[11] Only three finalists had been chosen, instead of the five stipulated in the brief (Figures 2.3–2.5).[12] In the final results,

2.3 Archimedes Memória: Competition entry for the Ministry of Education and Health (1935). First prize.
Front elevation.
PCMESP I.100 Courtesy of SPHAN.

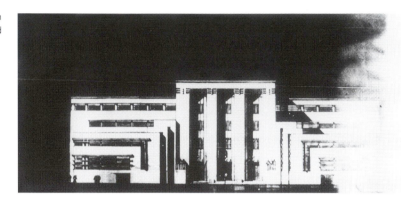

2.4 Mario Fertin and Raphael Galvão: Competition entry for the Ministry of Education and Health (1935). Second prize.
Front elevation.
PCMESP I.111 Courtesy of SPHAN.

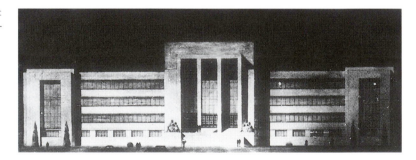

2.5 Gerson Pinheiro: Competition entry for the Ministry of Education and Health (1935). Third prize.
Front elevation.
PCMESP I.122 Courtesy of SPHAN.

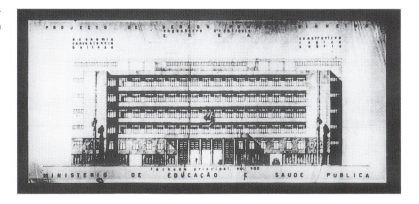

announced on 1 October 1935, it was apparent that the jury had chosen the most conservative of the three: a Beaux-Arts plan within a stripped classicist envelope, by Archimedes Memória (1893–1960).

From the beginning of the competition, however, Capanema had pursued his own investigations of recent office buildings abroad.[13] His abstention from voting in the second phase and avoidance of the debate over the winning design indicated that he had been dissatisfied with all three finalists. He moved instead behind the scenes to free himself of the winning project: he persuaded Vargas to revoke the law he had just passed requiring public buildings to be chosen in competition.[14]

At that time, rejecting the competition winner had many implications and would not have been an easy alternative to take. The press was aggressively attacking the expenditure of public funds on the new Ministry buildings; worse still, in the case of the Ministry of Education and Health, the cost of the competition and the prizes had not been a cheap exercise and the press would not spare a word of criticism; above all, the Minister was accused of an undemocratic attitude by contemplating the possibility of contracting another architect without competition.[15] The prize winner, Archimedes Memória, a very influential figure who had replaced Costa at the Escola Nacional de Belas Artes, protested directly to Vargas.[16] To justify his decision publicly, Capanema sent the schemes for specialist appreciation. As perhaps he had expected, these reports condemned the project as being out of step with contemporary practice: the plan was not functional and stylistically it would not provide a notable work of art.[17]

To choose an architect for the Ministry Building, Capanema then turned to the group of Brazilian architects nominated for the Cidade Universitária. Although Piacentini had originally been appointed architect in August 1935, protests from local professionals against the employment of a foreign architect for such an important project had led Capanema to establish simultaneously a group of Brazilian architects to carry out his design. This group of architects and engineers, nominated by three architectural institutions,[18] was mainly Modernist, and had their own ideas – a political as well as an architectural antipathy.[19] Lucio Costa had established himself as their spokesman; because of this, Capanema appointed him architect for the Ministry, on 30 March 1936. He justified the choice officially by saying that Costa had been nominated by two institutions.[20]

Costa immediately formed a team of Modern architects to undertake the Ministry Building. Initially, he had intended to collaborate only with Carlos Leão, with whom he had shared an office since 1933, Jorge Moreira and Affonso Eduardo Reidy. The inclusion of Oscar Niemeyer had been a gesture of compassion towards his young employee after his earnest appeal; this was also the case with Ernani Vasconcellos who had been co-author with Moreira in their competition entry.[21] Every member of the team had entered, and been rejected, in the initial competition.[22]

Of the Modern competition schemes, the drawings of only two – Moreira and Vasconcellos, and Reidy – have survived due to their publication in *PDF* (Figures 2.6 and 2.7).[23] Both were based on Le Corbusier's Centrosoyuz Building: specifically the *projet d'execution* illustrated in the

2.6 Affonso Reidy: Competition entry for the Ministry of Education and Health, Rio de Janeiro (1935).
Perspective.
*PDF* (September 1935).

2.7 Moreira and Vasconcellos: Competition entry for the Ministry of Education and Health, Rio de Janeiro (1935).
Perspective.
*PDF* (September 1935).

*Œuvre Complète 1910–29*. Not only had Le Corbusier proselytised this building extensively during his lecture tour of 1929 as an ideal office type, but the *projet d'execution* had also been illustrated in the local *Revista de Arquitetura* in 1935 following its publication in the *Œuvre Complète 1929–34*.[24] Centrosoyuz was a broadly symmetrical seven-storey 'H'-shaped building containing an auditorium between one set of wings. Significantly, the *projet d'execution* was rectilinear rather than angled to follow the site boundaries as built.[25]

Both these schemes followed the *projet d'execution* almost exactly. Moreira and Vasconcellos proposed the central block running along the site; Reidy proposed the central block running across the site. Costa's new plan also followed the *projet d'execution*; he kept Reidy's orientation on site, but extended both arms towards the Rua Araújo Porto Alegre. Unlike the 'H' shape of the original, his plan was 'U' shaped: the wings did not extend around the auditorium (Figures 2.8 and 2.9).[26] It was obviously an extremely awkward form, made worse by the use of open *pilotis* (as in Centrosoyuz) under the lower side wings; the architects quickly nicknamed it the '*múmia*' [mummy].[27]

The new scheme was distinguished by the treatment of the elevations. In his competition entry, Reidy had drawn a parallel between his principles of '*orientação*' [orientation] and '*ventilação*' [ventilation] and Le Corbusiers's principles of '*chauffage*' [heating] and '*ventilation*' [ventilation], and the Costa plan retained them. The offices were placed facing east and

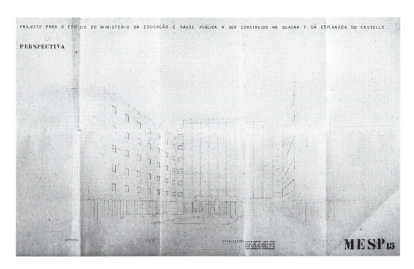

2.8 Lucio Costa and Team: First project for the Ministry of Education and Health, Rio de Janeiro (1936).
MESP 15, Perspective.
PCMESP III.219 Courtesy of SPHAN.

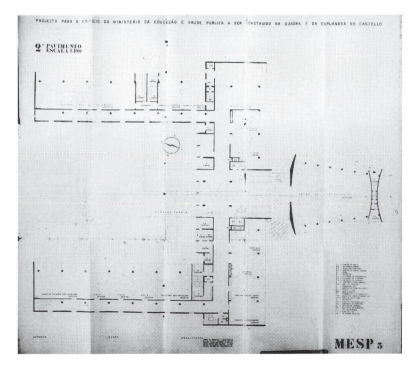

2.9 Lucio Costa and Team: First project for the Ministry of Education and Health, Rio de Janeiro (1936).
MESP 3, Second floor plan.
Le Corbusier's comments scribbled in pencil: *Dommage, rentrez l'escalier, trouvez une autre forme d'escalier pas symétrique pour pouvoir le rentrer/Grouppez les 4 acenseurs/Dommage, que pas un fait niveau.*
PCMESP II.207 Courtesy of SPHAN.

south which were the shady sides, while the halls and corridors faced north and west. The corridors located between the offices and the north façade were also intended to protect the working areas from intense heat. With this internal arrangement, they could use *fenêtres en longeur*, with venetian blinds for extra protection, for the offices on the east sides of the arms; *pan-de-verre* was applied to the south side of the main block. On the sunny sides of the building, the corridors were protected by *mur mixte*, solid walls with square windows at equal intervals, and the halls of the main block, which faced north, were protected with *brise-soleil*. In their optimistic words, they claimed, 'It will be the first time, in the whole of the city, that an important building managed to satisfy entirely the impositions of orientation.' The architects credited Le Corbusier and Pierre Jeanneret with having proposed the 'ingenious' use of *brise-soleil* for a project in Algiers. In fact, much more should have been credited to Le Corbusier: the 'Memorial Descritivo' which accompanied the drawings can be read as an eulogy to his principles.[28]

It was exactly this clear affiliation with Le Corbusier's principles which was the contentious point of the design. Capanema decided to seek criticism of the design from various technical experts. One 38 page report, by the engineer Saturnino de Brito Filho, sought to prove that Le Corbusier was representative of a minor European style with a dubious future. Instead, it suggested better examples in the Los Angeles County General Hospital, the Maison de l'Agriculture and the new Hôtel de Ville in Algiers, and concluded by aggressively stating that if Capanema really wanted to be Modern he could have a building with no windows as the apotheosis of artificial light and ventilation. Le Corbusier's books circulated even among his detractors: Saturnino de Brito Filho quoted extensively, in French, from *Une Maison Un Palais*, *La Ville Radieuse*, and *Urbanisme*.[29]

Capanema, however, was soon going to be able to receive Le Corbusier's ideas first-hand: he had already planned his visit. His invitation was twofold: since August 1935, Costa had been pressing Capanema to invite Le Corbusier as a way of counterbalancing the involvement of Piacentini on the project for the Cidade Universitária, and to seek his advice on the forthcoming commission for the Ministry of Education and Health Building. On 29 January 1936, Capanema had made a request to Vargas that both Le Corbusier and Piacentini be invited to Brazil to give advice on the Cidade Universitária.[30]

Costa's invitation to Le Corbusier should be placed within the context of the relative isolation of Brazil in the 1930s and Costa's relative youth. Although the major theoretician of Modernism in Brazil, Costa was uncertain what Modernism actually entailed in practice. He had not seen any Modern architecture during his sojourn in Europe in 1926–7, and Brazil was far from the rich cultural interchange possible there. Furthermore, he had never built any large buildings, let alone Modern ones; he built nothing between 1932–5 because of the middle-class preference for the so-called 'Colonial' style. While Le Corbusier consciously cast himself in the role of prophet, the much younger Costa could think of no better artist to demonstrate what Modernism actually was.

Costa sought Le Corbusier through Alberto Monteiro de Carvalho, a wealthy engineer who had met Le Corbusier during his first visit to Brazil (see Figure 1.9). Monteiro de Carvalho explained that he had been approached by Carlos Leão and Lucio Costa who had 'just been put in charge of the project for the new Ministry of Education', and had thus been able to convince Capanema to invite him to Brazil. He proposed that Le Corbusier, in addition to lecturing, give advice on the project for the Cidade Universitária:

The two [Lucio Costa and Carlos Leão] as well as a group of modern comrades faithful to Le Corbusier, like Affonso REIDY, Jorge MOREIRA, Oscar NIEMEYER, Ernani VASCONCELLOS, etc. think that the Minister might ask you to come here to give a course at the Escola de Belas Artes and when you are here the Minister would certainly ask your advice on the University campus as well and it will be easy to arrange things so that you can at least manage to direct the project to the benefit of the young Brazilians.[31]

Although Monteiro de Carvalho specifically mentioned only the Cidade Universitária project, his letter, written on 21 March, listed the Ministry team even before their official appointment on 30 March 1936.

Le Corbusier, ever the opportunist, immediately proffered his collaboration on both projects: while he was happy to accept Monteiro de Carvalho's terms that he should only give advice on the Cidade Universitária, he considered his participation in the Ministry '*essentiel*'. He assured Monteiro de Carvalho of his discretion and mentioned his experiences with the Centrosoyuz Building, and how his research in the United States had armed him with 'very modern ideas on the conception of a university campus'.[32]

The prospect of an opportunity to design the Ministry of Education and Health Building and the Cidade Universitária must have been particularly attractive to Le Corbusier in 1936. Firstly, it was a Government enterprise and Le Corbusier believed in the power of authority to accomplish new ideas; in his first lecture in Rio de Janeiro in 1929, Le Corbusier had praised the work of Mayor Pereira Passos, who had undertaken the renewal of Rio de Janeiro in a Haussmannian fashion at the turn of the century.[33] Doubtless Le Corbusier believed that Capanema had that combination of authority and vision which he so much admired. He even invited himself to meet Vargas: 'I would like to have some contact with the President if possible to put to him my famous plan of 1929', although there is no record that they met.[34] Secondly, the possibility of getting a major commission in Brazil came at the time of his return from a lecture tour in the United States where he had received a cold reception; not only had he not found any commissions but he had been criticised severely by the press.[35] He concluded that 'I had the unfortunate surprise of not being able to declare myself happy with what I found in the U.S.A.'.[36] In contrast, he felt sure of a warm welcome in Brazil, not only because Rio de Janeiro was a 'a city which is Latin and as a consequence, is part of the zone which I like to work: Athens, Algiers, Barcelona, Paris',[37] but because his previous trip to Rio de Janeiro in 1929 had left him with the best of memories:

What a pleasure it will be for me to return to Rio, the most beautiful city in the world, and to find that warm atmosphere of friendship which I could never forget.[38]

During the negotiations, however, he pressed for a commission: 'it is essential that I get some serious work out of such a trip, because the profession of being a prophet has started to weigh heavily on my shoulders'.[39] Monteiro de Carvalho, however, continued to stress that Le Corbusier would only be able to be involved on the Cidade Universitária project; he assured Le Corbusier that 'The project for the Ministry of Education – they [Costa and Leão] have already done it.'[40] A building was still very much on Le Corbusier's mind; he appealed directly to Capanema that a trip to Brazil would only be worthwhile if he received a commission, whether large or small:

I am at an age in which I can not move myself to purely and simply give lectures to students. It is essential that I find the opportunity to create works of architecture small or large, but significant.[41]

Capanema certainly had no intention of offering Le Corbusier a commission; his invitation was a concession to Lucio Costa. Le Corbusier's consultancy had to remain an informal agreement between Capanema and Le Corbusier. This was within the Government policy at the time of inviting intellectuals from abroad to lecture in Brazil.[42] A contract was neither possible under Brazilian law, nor convenient under the nationalistic mood of Vargas' regime. It was necessary to cover Le Corbusier's consultancy fee within the fee for his lectures. He was offered 30,000FF, based on 500FF a day absence from the office in Paris, plus travel expenses, but he insisted that he would not accept less than the 6,000FF per lecture, plus travel expenses, that he had received on his 1929 trip. The final payment was apparently 86,000FF plus travel expenses, accommodation, and an official automobile at his disposal.[43]

The invitation coming from official quarters, however, seemed to have caused some confusion. Le Corbusier apparently believed – possibly even wished – that the invitation had come directly from a client seeking his services as an architect, rather than from the architects themselves looking for support from a much-admired fellow professional. It may explain his cavalier treatment of the Brazilian architects and his later claims towards the design of their building.[44]

By 19 June 1936, a formal invitation, properly authorised by Vargas, had been sent to Le Corbusier and a passage arranged on the Zeppelin flight on 8 July.[45] Le Corbusier arrived on 13 July, and stayed again at the Hotel Gloria and swam every day in the Bay before work.[46] In the following six weeks, Le Corbusier gave six lectures at the Escola Nacional da Música, developed plans for the Cidade Universitária, and developed two schemes for the Ministry of Education and Health Building.[47]

On the first day of his stay in Brazil, Le Corbusier received a formal request from Capanema to comment on the Ministry of Education and Health project.[48] He made an initial set of comments scribbled in pencil on the drawings which criticised the symmetrical arrangement and elaborate form [see Figure 2.9].[49] His official comments started by praising the project of the Brazilian architects: 'This project can be classified for its architectural value among the best which have been built in any country.'[50] A diplomatic approach can be felt throughout the report; perhaps he was following the advice he had received from Lucio Costa prior to his departure:

One more word. One of your tasks to the Minister will be to make him aware of your opinion on the project of which I am sending you photos. If it displeases you, say it straightforwardly to us, but, I beg you, do not say brusquely to Mr. Capanema: 'That's ugly . . . they haven't understood me' – because then we will be lost, because the 'others' have already condemned it, and we have asked you to vouch for us.[51]

Le Corbusier quickly moved to display his own ideas, however: 'I propose not to change the project which is excellent but to change the site which is bad.'[52] He found the site at Castelo within Agache's urban grid to be inappropriate for such a significant building and searched for another location; he found what he believed to be the ideal site on the Praia de Santa Luzia – a beach directly opposite the Hotel Gloria, formed, ironically, from the spoil from the Morro do Castelo – which could take advantage of a panoramic view of the Bay and Pão de Açúcar, and made contact with the Municipality, who owned the site, to transfer the ownership to the Federal Government.[53]

Continuing his report in the same tactful tone, Le Corbusier stated that his project for the Praia de Santa Luzia was but an adaptation of the existing project to a new site: 'I insist on the fact that it is not a new Palace *but the same* in which the wings are simply opened out.'[54] This new design was presented in nine sheets of drawings (Figures 2.10 and 2.11).[55] The project continued the type evolved through his League of Nations,

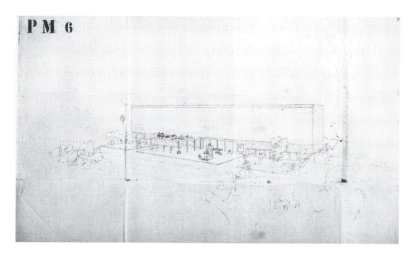

2.10 Le Corbusier: Project for Ministry of Education and Health, Rio de Janeiro at the Praia de Santa Luzia (1936).
PM 6, Perspective view from Avenida Beira Mar.
PCMESP V.343 Courtesy of SPHAN.

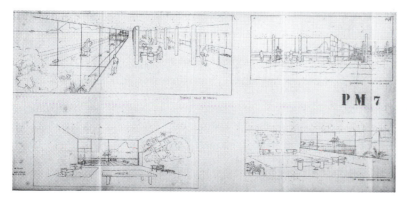

2.11 Le Corbusier: Project for Ministry of Education and Health, Rio de Janeiro at the Praia de Santa Luzia (1936).
PM 7, internal perspectives. *(Etages) Salle de travail/(Entre-sol) Foyer de la Salle 1er Etage Audience du Ministre/1er Etage Gabinet du Ministre.*
PCMESP V.344 Courtesy of SPHAN.

Centrosoyuz, and Palace of the Soviets projects. It consisted of a single horizontal block eight storeys high, on *pilotis*, with *pan-de-verre* on the south side, which allowed a full view of the Bay, and *brise-soleil* on the glazed parts of the rear façade – one fifth of the block on each edge – which faced north. The building occupied only part of the site, leaving the rest landscaped with open parking areas. A sculpture, planned to be 'O Homen Brasileiro' by Celso Antonio (1896–1984), was positioned in front. Most striking about Le Corbusier's design was the systematic asymmetry; symmetry had been, in fact, the major drawback that he had seen in Costa's project.

For inspiration for this proposal, Le Corbusier returned to the sketches he had made in 1929 of a serpentine motor-viaduct, to which he added a proposal to replace the entire remaining urban fabric of Rio de Janeiro with the 'Y'-shaped Cartesian skyscrapers he had developed in reaction to New York in 1935.[56] It was, however, the contrast of the horizontal architecture with the landscape which remained his obsession: the markedly horizontal proportions of his Ministry of Education proposal and its prominent site on the Praia de Santa Luzia relate it to the sketches of the proposed viaduct he had made from a boat in Guanabara Bay [see plates 2 and 3].

Le Corbusier's drawings displayed the building in three dimensions, in contrast to the two-dimensional drawings by the Brazilian architects. The exterior perspectives were complete with landscape, including a row of *palmeiras imperiais*, the palm trees which were such a notable feature of neo-classical urban lay-out in Brazil. His interior perspectives revealed the beautiful landscape views through the windows, suggested furniture – all Corbusian – and displayed murals showing other Corbusian schemes, including his Cité Universitaire.

After receiving Le Corbusier's report and the new set of drawings for the Praia de Santa Luzia, Capanema asked him to propose modifications to the design 'in case' it should need to be built on the site at Castelo.[57] Le Corbusier tried to persuade Capanema of the importance of the other site by affirming that:

> If the Palace is built at Castelo, public opinion could one day reproach such a choice. If it is built at Praia de Santa Luzia, public opinion, not only that of Rio, but also that of all the foreigners and tourists, will be unanimous in praising a solution which makes the most of the natural splendours of Rio, splendours which are precisely the object of world-wide admiration, and which so far have been scorned in the construction of the majority of the city, except for the great Mayor Passos who attached his name to the glories of Rio.[58]

However, Capanema was not convinced that a change of site was either necessary or possible and, in fact, no attempt was considered for exchanging the sites.

Only a few days before his departure on 15 August 1936, Le Corbusier sketched a new proposal which adapted the Praia de Santa Luzia project for the site at Castelo. This consisted of four sheets containing free-hand drawings and a few written notes: one sheet with three façades and an external perspective, and three sheets with plans of the ground floor,

2.12 Le Corbusier: Project for the Ministry of Education and Health, Rio de Janeiro at Castelo (1936).
Side façade/South façade
North façade/Perspective.
*Projet du Palais Ministère Education et Santé Publique du Castello, Rio 13 août 1936.*
PCMESP V.348 Courtesy of SPHAN.

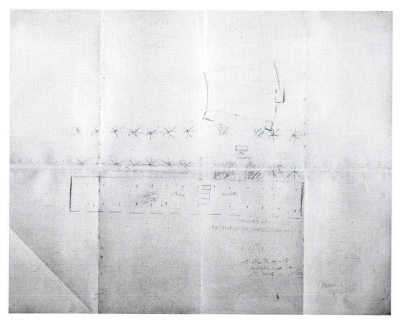

2.13 Le Corbusier: Project for the Ministry of Education and Health, Rio de Janeiro at Castelo (1936).
*1 étage, cet étage du Ministre pourrait aussi bien être répété au 10éme étage, 13 août 1936.*
PCMESP V.349 Courtesy of SPHAN.

mezzanine and first floor (Figures 2.12–2.15).[59] He retained the same components as his previous scheme, but as an adaptation to the site in Castelo, proposed a ten-storey block running along the Avenida Graça Aranha on low *pilotis* like those at the Centrosoyuz Building. The auditorium was turned around 90° and linked to the main building through an intermediate block running across the back of the site, which provided a

2.14 Le Corbusier: Project for the Ministry of Education and Health, Rio de Janeiro at Castelo (1936).
*Rez-de-chaussée, 13 août 1936.*
PCMESP V.350 Courtesy of SPHAN.

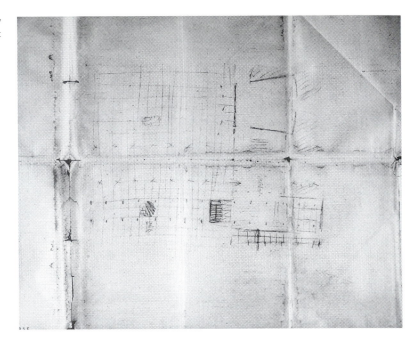

2.15 Le Corbusier: Project for the Ministry of Education and Health, Rio de Janeiro at Castelo (1936).
*Entresol, 13 août 1936.*
PCMESP V.351 Courtesy of SPHAN.

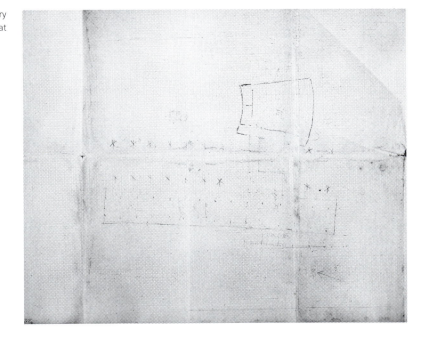

plaza arranged with two rows of palm trees and the seated figure by Celso Antonio. This unhappy orientation of the building meant that the *pan-de-verre* faced north-east, which received most of the hot sun, while the south-west side was partially covered with *brise-soleil* and square windows. Le Corbusier never published his scheme for Castelo, although he published three drawings for the Praia de Santa Luzia scheme in the *Œuvre Complète 1934–38*.[60]

After Le Corbusier's departure, Costa had two projects to work on, and he gave priority to the Cidade Universitária. For the Ministry Building, the team went back to their original scheme, apparently as a stop-gap measure, incorporating some of Le Corbusier's comments, which was approved by Capanema.[61] Costa's true intentions were different; as soon as they had made the submission for the Cidade Universitária on 21 October 1936, they abandoned the approved scheme completely. Costa explained the situation to Le Corbusier:

> The idea of building the 'mummy' after having seen the beautiful things which you did didn't thrill us – we are proposing a new solution of a single block as you advised us – but in the shorter direction on the site (S–S–E) and twice as deep.[62]

By 5 January 1937, they had designed the basis of the final scheme (Figures 2.16–2.19).[63] Presentation drawings of the final version were approved on 22 February (Figures 2.20 and 2.21).[64]

2.16 Lucio Costa and Team: Draft of final project for the Ministry of Education and Health, Rio de Janeiro (1937).
Perspective, view of the north façade.
PCMESP VI.377 Courtesy of SPHAN.

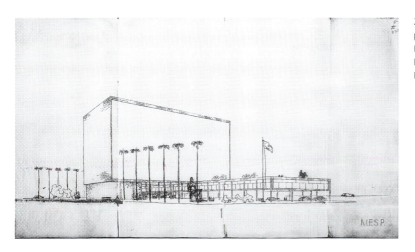

2.17 Lucio Costa and Team: Draft of final project for the Ministry of Education and Health, Rio de Janeiro (1937).
Perspective, view of the south façade.
PCMESP VI.378 Courtesy of SPHAN.

2.18 Lucio Costa and Team: Draft of final project for the Ministry of Education and Health, Rio de Janeiro (1937).
Third floor.
PCMESP VI.381 Courtesy of SPHAN.

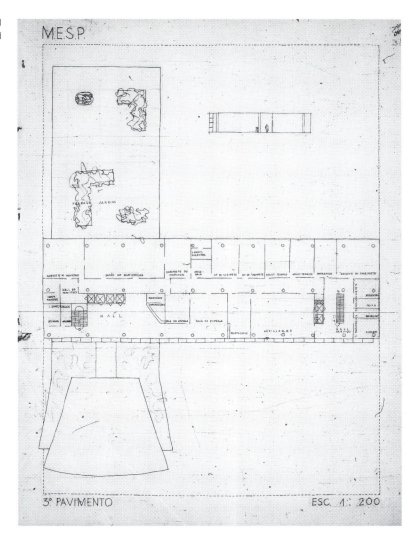

This final design was a radical departure from both the 'múmia' and Le Corbusier's long horizontal block (Figures 2.22 and 2.23). Costa and his team retained the prominent central block of the 'múmia' but increased it in height, which created a more spatially dynamic relationship to the surrounding buildings. The increase in height to 15 floors, which had been desired from the start, emphasised the verticality of the tower.[65] The auditorium and lower exhibition block were moved asymmetrically, as suggested by Le Corbusier, but along the small Rua da Imprensa, forming a plaza to the more important Avenida Graça Aranha; two subsequent extensions of the exhibition hall at the back of the site, each by an extra bay of *pilotis*, enhanced the contrast of the two blocks.[66] That they were fully aware of this more dynamic relationship may be seen in the drawing showing their original and new proposals in the context of the Agache plan [see Figure 2.19]. The *brise-soleils* were changed from the concrete egg-crate type of the 'múmia' – similar to those of the Maison Locative in

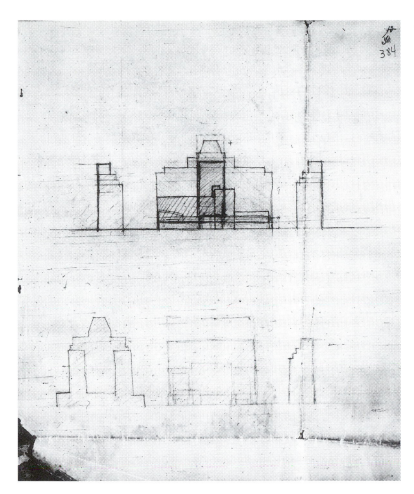

2.19 Lucio Costa and Team: Draft of final project for the Ministry of Education and Health, Rio de Janeiro (1937).
Height study.
PCMESP VI.384 Courtesy of SPHAN.

Algiers – to a series of movable lamina in asbestos cement covering the entire north façade – similar to those of his Lotissement in Barcelona.

The main difference from Le Corbusier's plan was that the buildings formed a dynamic relation to the surrounding urban landscape and contained a sociable urban space at ground level (Plates 4 and 5; Figures 2.24 and 2.25). Le Corbusier's long, low block effectively formed a corridor street on the Avenida Graça Aranha with the plaza terminating in the blank wall of the auditorium. In the final building, the main block was raised on 10-metre-high *pilotis*; the public entrance and a book-shop faced each other under the resulting portico. The colonnade framed the view from the Rua Araújo Porto Alegre to the harbour, and channelled circulation through the site. The sensuous bulge of the auditorium now articulated the main street.

The minister's floor was intended to be a showpiece of Modernism with sumptuous finishes, art and furniture and a tropical garden. The public elevators opened onto an immense reception hall; on the other side of the corridor were meeting rooms, including the anteroom opening onto the roof garden on top of the exhibition hall (Plate 6; Figures 2.26 and 2.27).

2.20 Lucio Costa and Team: Final project for the Ministry of Education and Health, Rio de Janeiro (1937).
MESP 1, site plan.
PCMESP VI.389 Courtesy of SPHAN.

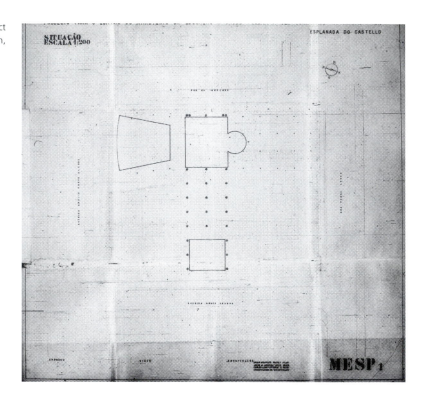

2.21 Lucio Costa and Team: Final project for the Ministry of Education and Health, Rio de Janeiro (1937).
MESP 4, third floor: Minister's quarters.
PCMESP VI.392 Courtesy of SPHAN.

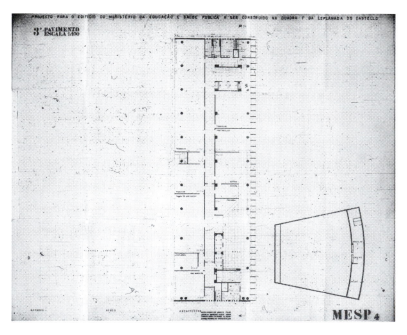

Air conditioning was installed on this floor only, because it could not profit from the cross-ventilation facilitated by low divisions. The Minister's floor was slightly higher than the others with an extra row of *brise-soleils*, which gives a 'base' to the form.

The library, located on the next floor up, was left free of divisions with a seating area by the *pan-de-verre* and book stacks by the *brise-soleil* (Figure 2.28). Part of the roof was occupied by a restaurant, allowing the rest for a terrace overlooking the Bay and Santos Dumont Airport. The machine rooms and water tower were placed on top of the restaurant and consisted of two sculptural shapes covered in blue tiles which delineated and animated the skyline. All remaining floors had the same layout of a central corridor and open areas on either side. The corridors were separated from the offices by permanent two-metre-high divisions which had doors at regular intervals.[67] The generous floor-to-ceiling height of four metres allowed for cross-ventilation. Movable filing cabinets divided the offices, and sockets for light and telephone plugs were placed in the floors at two metre intervals.

The circulation on the site was split between the public entrance and Minister's private entrance on one side of the main block, and the service entrance on the other. This arrangement allowed public and private circulation to be kept separate throughout the building. The public elevators and staircase opened to a public hall at one end of the corridor; at the other, the service elevators and staircase opened to a small service hall where the toilets and kitchens were located. A round staircase led from the entrance hall to an exhibition hall and auditorium. A private entrance for the minister was provided from a driveway under the auditorium, with a secluded access to the platform of the auditorium and to all floors via a

2.22 Philip L. Goodwin: *Brazil Builds* (New York: The Museum of Modern Art 1943) pp.106–7. Offset, printed in black, page sizes 8½ × 11″ (21.6 × 27.9 cm). Photograph © 2000 The Museum of Modern Art, New York. Lucio Costa and Team: Ministry of Education and Health, Rio de Janeiro (1936–45). North façade.

*Here is no merely skin-deep beauty. Each unusual element has resulted from fresh and careful study of the complicated problems of the modern office building.*

*Most startling innovation is the elaborate brise-soleil which shield the glass-walled north facade. This system of sunshades, first of its kind anywhere in the world.*

*Boldly set above the cleanly defined block of offices are freely curving structures containing water tanks and elevator apparatus. These are covered with blue vitreous tile.*

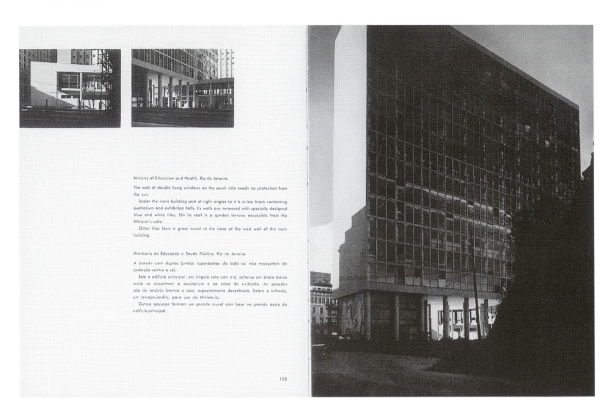

2.23 Philip L. Goodwin: *Brazil Builds* (New York: The Museum of Modern Art 1943) pp.108–9. Offset, printed in black, page sizes 8½ × 11" (21.6 × 27.9 cm).
Photograph © 2000 The Museum of Modern Art, New York.
Lucio Costa and Team: Ministry of Education and Health, Rio de Janeiro (1936–45). South façade.
*The wall of double hung windows on the south side needs no protection from the sun.*
*Under the main building and at right angles to it is a low block containing auditorium and exhibition halls. Its walls are veneered with specially designed blue and white tiles. On the roof is a garden terrace accessible from the Minister's suite.*
*Other tiles form a great mural at the base of the west wall of the main building.*

private elevator. The auditorium was enclosed at ground level to provide a private garage, while the short *pilotis* under the exhibition hall allowed for parking.

The architects were fortunate in having the services of Emilio Baumgart, the exceptional engineer who had designed some of the early reinforced concrete structures in Rio de Janeiro. The structure consisted of rows of columns arranged in a monumental *plan libre*; three rows of *pilotis* rise across the main block and four rows of a smaller diameter across the annex. Baumgart utilised a system of integrated columns and floor slabs with inverted column capitals which gave flat ceilings and allowed services to be run through the floor. One set of corner columns was doubled up to support the greater span across the exhibition hall, which gives a greater sense of definition to the form compared to the more consciously indeterminate structures of Le Corbusier.

At the ground-breaking ceremony, Capanema heralded the birth of the building as:

a great architectural monument in which the design had been studied with consciousness, pertinence, detail and care [...] envisaging the double objective of making a work of art and a house for work.[68]

Capanema's long term in office fortunately allowed him to oversee the construction of the building accurately and in detail. Due to the unusual

2.24  Lucio Costa and Team: Ministry of Education and Health, Rio de Janeiro (1936–45).
Bookshop and service entrance. *Azulejo* panel by Portinari underneath the colonnade.
© Zilah Quezado Deckker.

2.25 Lucio Costa and Team: Ministry of Education and Health, Rio de Janeiro (1936–45).
Sculpture 'Juventude' by Bruno Giorgi. The view through the colonnade originally extended to the harbour, but was blocked by later developments.
© Zilah Quezado Deckker.

2.26 Lucio Costa and Team: Ministry of Education and Health, Rio de Janeiro (1936–45).
Minister's meeting room. Murals by Portinari. Doors to the roof garden over the exhibition hall.
© Zilah Quezado Deckker.

nature of the works, Capanema decided to cancel the Tender procedure which he had initiated immediately after approving the final design and undertook the works by direct labour through the Department of Works of the Ministry.[69] The engineer Eduardo Souza Aguiar, who had been Capanema's assistant on the competition jury, became Head of the

2.27 Lucio Costa and Team: Ministry of Education and Health, Rio de Janeiro (1936–45).
Minister's office. Double columns encased in *sucupira* wood.
© Zilah Quezado Deckker.

2.28 Lucio Costa and Team: Ministry of Education and Health, Rio de Janeiro (1936–45).
Library floor.
© Zilah Quezado Deckker.

Department of Works. The shortage of building materials during the Second World War inevitably caused delays in construction. Brazil was only at the beginning of its industrialisation, and building materials were largely imported; furthermore, mechanical items had to be either imported or specially made. Thus, it was only the close co-operation between engineers, architects and client in solving each problem which made the detailing of the building a success.

Capanema's double objective of 'a work of art and a house of work' led him to commission works of art and furniture specially for the building, and he did not consider the building complete until these had been incorporated.[70] Several young artists who were later to become prominent in Brazil launched their careers with commissions for the Ministry Building. Only one work was by a foreign artist, Jacques Lipchitz (1891–1973), who received the commission for the sculpture hanging on the north façade of the auditorium. All the others were by national artists, with the massive participation of Cândido Portinari (1903–62), with murals in the Minister's quarters depicting Brazilian economic cycles, and monumental *azulejo* panels on the external walls; a sculpture by Bruno Giorgi (b 1905), 'Juventude' was placed in the plaza, and one by Celso Antonio, 'Mulher Reclinada', in the exhibition hall. Desks, chairs, reception counters, and office divisions were all in *sucupira*, a native hardwood. Roberto Burle Marx landscaped the urban plaza, the minister's private roof garden on top of the exhibition hall, and the roof terrace which surrounded the restaurant, with native plants. With the combined efforts of so many and varied talents, the building may be regarded as a true *gesamtkunstwerk* of Brazilian Modernism.

It took eight-and-a-half years until its inauguration on 3 October 1945, although the building was substantially complete by 1942.[71] That day had been specially chosen as it marked the fifteenth anniversary of the 'Revolução de 30' which had, in fact, made the building possible, in spite of the constitution of the Estado Novo in 1937.[72] In the lobby of the building, an inscription carefully composed by Lucio Costa registered the participation of the client, each architect and that of Le Corbusier:

> Under the President of the Republic Getúlio Vargas and the Minister of Education and Health Gustavo Capanema, the construction of this building was ordered for the headquarters of the Ministry of Education and Health, designed by the architects Oscar Niemeyer, Affonso Reidy, Jorge Moreira, Carlos Leão, Lucio Costa and Ernani Vasconcellos, after an original sketch by Le Corbusier 1937–45.[73]

Capanema's role as patron of the arts and his commitment to the Modernist avant-garde was characterised by high intentions and contradictions. He worked closely with his architects and artists and took a lot of care in choosing the final details to perfect the finished product. This was the case of an *azulejo* panel covering the east façade of the functionaries hall – the most important panel underneath the main block opposite the main entrance – which had been designed by Portinari and executed by Rossi; the central part of this panel was removed during the placement of the tiles because the motif – of fish – had been considered aesthetically unsatisfactory and a new design commissioned and executed.[74] However, in the case of Lipchitz's 'Prometheus', Capanema did not display such care when he determined that the sculpture, to be placed on the north façade of the auditorium, should be moulded in bronze at the same size of the model the artist had sent to Rio. At seven feet high, it was one-third of the intended size of 20 feet. The sculpture as it stands today is dwarfed by the size of the blind wall of the auditorium, and was disowned by the artist who considered the event to be the greatest disappointment of his career.[75]

The process which had been so felicitous at the Ministry Building did not have the same result at the Cidade Universitária; several sites and several styles were considered but came to nothing. The academic committee preferred Piacentini to Le Corbusier; Piacentini accepted the site proposed by Agache at the Praia Vermelha, another beach overlooking Guanabara Bay. Costa initially proposed, in June 1936, a site in the lagoon, the Lagoa Rodrigo de Freitas, built over the water to allow the free disposition of roads and buildings.[76] Le Corbusier proposed a site at the Quinta da Boa Vista, which had been suggested originally by the academic committee. The Cité Universitaire was an amalgam of Corbusian building typologies, including pieces from his unsuccessful League of Nations competition entry and a Mundanéum (Figure 2.29). Its main feature, and the principal cause of objection from the academic committee, was an elevated vehicle circulation system of four kilometres of roads and 40,000 square metres of platforms. This design was also published in the *Œuvre Complète 1934–38*.[77]

After Le Corbusier's proposal had been rejected, Costa prepared another plan in which he tried to adapt Le Corbusier's principles to the

2.29 Le Corbusier: Project for the Cité Universitaire du Brésil, Rio de Janeiro at the Quinta da Boa Vista (1936).
Aerial perspective.
© FLC/ADAGP, Paris and DACS, London 2000.

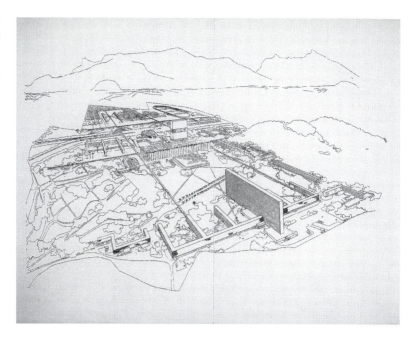

more exacting requirements of the brief (Figure 2.30). Compared to Le Corbusier's more elaborate building types dispersed throughout the site, Costa's plan showed greater emphasis on the urban spaces, such as the entrance plaza dominated by a slab and a central avenue of *palmeiras imperiais*, with rather simpler building forms. One building, the main auditorium, was to be reserved for Le Corbusier. This plan clearly demonstrates Costa's interest in urbanism and the difference between the 'Brazilian Style' and European Modernism.[78]

The new design by the Brazilian group was presented to the Professors on 21 October 1936; on 12 March 1937 it was rejected by the commission with an endorsement by Capanema.[79] Lucio Costa wrote to Le Corbusier describing the events related to the development of the University project:

> The committee of professors – Amaral and Campos in charge – refused, without understanding it, your good design. With regards to us, having two months to present a new solution we have done our best in adapting it to the circumstances which required the site to be cluttered by buildings. But again they were unanimous (and they were 14 on the committee of professors) in rejecting it.[80]

Capanema must have envisaged the difficulties inherent in such an enormous and controversial project, and he appeared to lose interest in it. Lucio Costa wrote to Capanema expressing his resentment upon his refusal of the design:

> Now that everything seems to be well 'arranged', I should tell you how much it hurts to see an idea, high and pure such as the creation of the Cidade Universitária take shape and develop in such a manner [. . .]. The

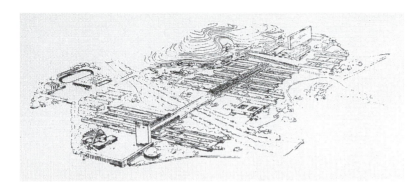

2.30 Lucio Costa and Team: Project for the Cidade Universitária do Brasil, Rio de Janeiro at the Quinta da Boa Vista (1937). Aerial perspective.
*PDF* (May 1937).

saddest thing is that while one perseveres, for years and years, on the building of the wrong thing, there will be lying on some architect's shelves the 'true' solution – the right thing.[81]

The 'right thing' had only been possible in the Ministry of Education Building. Lucio Costa regarded the failure of the Cidade Universitária as the greatest disappointment of his career.[82] Le Corbusier, too, had hoped for this commission as well; after his visit to Brazil, he continued to write enthusiastic letters to both Capanema and Lucio Costa, expressing his interest in continuing to participate on both designs. First, he had hoped that the plans for the Ministry of Education Building at Santa Luzia and the Cidade Universitária would be realised; after he had been informed by Capanema that the definitive site was to be at Castelo and that work had actually started with the new design, he continued to put forward his interest in developing the plan for the Cidade Universitária: 'There remains the University campus. Could I collaborate on it?'[83] Although Capanema's last response to Le Corbusier's queries was dated late 1937, Le Corbusier continued to write to him until late 1939, always reminding him of his continued interest in the project for the Cidade Universitária: 'I have not abandoned the hope of taking up with you again the plans of the campus of the University of Brazil.'[84]

In the Rio de Janeiro of the 1940s, the Ministry Building immediately became a landmark, together with the natural beauties of Pão de Açúcar and Corcovado.[85] Ultimate praise and world-wide fame came with the exhibition 'Brazil Builds' and the publication of its book. Philip Goodwin claimed with enormous enthusiasm that:

It has set the spirit of creative design and put a depth charge under the antiquated routine of governmental thought. While Federal Classic in Washington, Royal Academy Archaeology in London and Nazi Classic in Munich are still triumphant, Brazil has had the courage to break away from the safe and easy path with the result that Rio can boast of the most beautiful government building in the Western hemisphere.[86]

## Notes

1 Lúcia Lippi Oliveira: *Estado Novo: Ideologia e Poder* (Rio de Janeiro: Zahar 1982) p.7.

   *A memória social, representada pela lembrança do homen comum, guarda alguns traços, ainda que contraditórios, do período: a censura; a polícia de Filinto Müller; a construção de Volta Redonda; a legislação trabalhista e as manifestações operárias no estádio do Vasco da Gama; o prédio do Ministério da Educação no Rio de Janeiro; a figura de Villa-Lobos; a Rádio Nacional; Carmen Miranda; Zé Carioca; e, obviamente, Vargas.*

2 The Ministry of Finance by Ari Fontoura Azambuja was started on 1 August 1939 and inaugurated on 10 November 1943.

3 Alfred Agache: *Cidade do Rio de Janeiro: Remodelação, Extensão e Embelezzamento 1926–1936* (Paris: Prefeitura do Rio de Janeiro 1930; French edn *La Remodelation d'une Capitale* Paris: 1932). It was initially the site for the exhibition of The Centenary of Independence in 1922.

4 The site formed a rectangle 91.60 m between the Rua Araújo Porto Alegre and the Rua Pedro Lessa, and 69.00 m between the Rua da Imprensa and the Avenida Graça Aranha.

5 Simon Schwartzman: *Tempos de Capanema* (Rio de Janeiro: Paz e Terra/São Paulo: Editora Universidade de São Paulo 1984) p.13.

   *O edifício do Ministério da Educação no Rio de Janeiro, construido em sua gestão, segundo as linhas modernistas de Le Corbusier, simboliza até hoje a imagem que ficou para muitos de um ministro esclarecido, avançado para a sua época, defensor da cultura e das artes, promotor da educação.*

6 Schwartzman: *Tempos de Capanema* p.24.

   *Capanema [. . .] jamais renunciou explicitamente à sua pretensão intelectual, que mantinha pela preocupação com questões relativas à educação e cultura, pela amizade pessoal que cultivava com escritores, pintores e artistas em geral, e pelo hábito de estudo e leitura. Ele procura ser, sempre, um intelectual no poder.*

7 His involvement was a gesture of fraternity by the Italian Government, which had close diplomatic links with Brazil. His fee was paid by the Italian Government, with a nominal sum from the Brazilian Government.

8 *Diário Oficial* (23 April 1935, 2 and 11 May 1935). PCMESP I.26–7 SPHAN. Instituto de Arquitetos do Brasil (IAB) was founded in 1921 as Instituto Brasileiro de Arquitetura, it became Instituto Central de Arquitetos in 1924 and IAB in 1934.

9 *Diário Oficial*, first prize: $40.000, second prize: $20.000; third, fourth and fifth prizes: $6.000. PCMESP I.26–7 SPHAN. (Exchange value in 1935: $1.000 = US$82.00. Robert Levine: *The Vargas Regime* (New York: Columbia University Press 1970) Appendix D.).

10 'Concurso de Anteprojetos para o Ministério da Educação e Saúde Pública', *PDF* (September 1935) p.515.

11 Salvador Duque Estrada Batalha (IAB), Adolfo Morales de los Rios (Escola Nacional de Belas Artes), and Natal Paladini (Escola Polytechnica). Capanema's assistant was the engineer Eduardo Souza Aguiar (Superintendent of Transport and Works). PCMESP I.52 SPHAN.

12 Competition Results. PCMESP I.100–33 SPHAN.

13 José Roberto Macedo (to Capanema, Rome 14 June 1935) suggested that the Ministry of Aviation in Rome, by Marino Roberto, 1931, was a good example of an office building and added that it was considered the most perfect in Europe. Fernando Lobo (to Gustavo Capanema, Washington, 24 August 1935) recommended the North American mode of office building which included closed offices for the heads and open ones for all other offices. CE: CPC 1.5 and 1.9 CPDOC/FGV.

14 Bill 193, 17 January 1936, revoked by Bill 125, 3 December 1935. PCMESP-SPHAN I.194–6.

15 *Correio da Manhã* (6, 7 and 10 March 1936). CE: CPC 1.21–3 CPDOC/FGV.

16 Archimedes Memória to Getúlio Vargas, 1936. CE: CPC 1.18 CPDOC/FGV.

17 Mauricio Nabuco, 16 March 1936; Domingos da Silva Cunha, 24 March 1936; Saturnino de Brito Filho, 10 March 1936. PCMESP I.168–88 SPHAN.

18 The Instituto Central de Arquitetos, the Sindicato Nacional de Engenharia, and the Clube de Engenharia. PCMESP I.190–3 SPHAN.

19 This initial group of 1935 consisted of Lucio Costa, Angelo Bruhns and Firmino Saldanha. Oscar Niemeyer, Jorge Moreira and Affonso Reidy joined the group in 1936. The engineer was Paulo Fragoso.

20 Capanema to Vargas, 21 November 1936. PCMESP V.365–70 SPHAN. Lucio Costa was nominated by the IAB and Sindicato Nacional de Engenharia. PCMESP I.190–3 SPHAN.

21 Conversation with Lucio Costa, December 1988.

22 Their names are seen in a list of competitors' signatures in support of a request to postpone the deadline of the first phase of the competition. PCMESP I.45–7 SPHAN.

23 *PDF* (September 1935) pp.511–19.

24 PCMESP I.260–1 SPHAN.

25 *Projet d'execution*: *Œuvre Complète 1910–29* pp.210–13; final project *Œuvre Complète 1929–34* pp.34–41.

26 First Project: PCMESP II.205–21 SPHAN.

27 Conversation with Lucio Costa, December 1988.

28 'Memorial Descritivo', 15 May 1936, p.5. PCMESP II.222–32 SPHAN. *'sera a primeira vez que, em toda a cidade, um edificio de vulto attende integralmente ás imposições de uma boa orientação'* [sic].

29 Engineer Saturnino de Brito Filho, 4 June 1936. PCMESP II.238–89 SPHAN.

30 Capanema to Vargas, 29 January 1936. Schwartzman: *Tempos de Capanema* p.98.

31 Monteiro de Carvalho to Le Corbusier, 21 March 1936. FLC I3–3.5. *'viennent d'être chargés de faire le projet pour le nouveau Ministère de l'Instruction Publique'*.

     *Les deux (Lucio Costa et Carlos Leão) ainsi qu'un groupe de camarades modernistes à Le Corbusier, comme Affonso REIDY, Jorge MOREIRA, Oscar NIEMEYER, Ernani VASCONCEL-LOS, etc. pensent que le Ministre pourrait vous faire venir ici pour donner un cours de 2 ou 3 mois à l'Ecole de Beaux-Arts et quand vous serez ici certainement le Ministre demandera aussi votre avis sur la Ville Universitaire et sera plus facile d'arranger les choses pour qui vous puissiez au moins diriger le projet en profitant les jeunes brésiliens.*

32 Le Corbusier to Monteiro de Carvalho, 30 March 1936. FLC I3–3.6. *'idées bien modernes sur la conception d'une cité universitaire'*.

33 Le Corbusier: 'Le Préfet Passos, 12 August 1936' *PDF* (September 1936) p.243. Also mentioned in *The Four Routes* (London: Dennis Dobson 1947) p.36.

34 Le Corbusier to Monteiro de Carvalho, 17 April 1936. FLC I3–3.10. *'je voudrais pouvoir avoir les contacts avec le Président si possible pour la mise à l'étude de mon fameux plan de 1929'*. The only mention of a meeting with Vargas, which, if it took place, had no consequences, is in a letter from Charles Offaire to Le Corbusier, 12 February 1938: *'Capanema croit se souvenir que tu as rencontré le President'*. FLC I3–3.63.

35 Henry-Russell Hitchcock: 'Le Corbusier and the United States' *Zodiac* 16 (1966). Le Corbusier recorded his impressions in *Quand les Cathédrales etaient Blanche* (Paris: Plon 1937).

36 Le Corbusier to Monteiro de Carvalho, 5 May 1936. FLC I3–3.14. *'J'ai eu la douloureuse surprise de ne pas devoir me déclarer satisfait de ce qui m'est arrivé en U.S.A.'*.

37 Le Corbusier to Monteiro de Carvalho, 15 June 1936. FLC I3–3.20. *'ville qui est latine et qui par conséquence, fait partie de la zone où j'aime à travailler: Athènes, Alger, Barcelone, Paris'*.

38 Le Corbusier to Monteiro de Carvalho, 30 March 1936. FLC I3–3.5.

     *Quel plaisir ce serait pour moi de revenir à Rio, la plus belle ville du monde, et d'y trouver cette chaleureux atmosphère d'amitié que je n'ai jamais pu oublier.*

39 Le Corbusier to Monteiro de Carvalho, 17 April 1936. FLC I3–3.10. *'il est indispensable que je puisse rapporter du travail pratique d'un tel voyage, car le métier de prophète commence à me peser lourdement sur les épaules'*.

40 Monteiro de Carvalho to Le Corbusier, 8 April 1936, FLC. I3–39. *'Le projet du Ministère de l'Instruction, ils [Costa and Leão] font déjà'*.

41 Le Corbusier to Gustavo Capanema, 5 May 1936. FLC I3–3.15.

     *Je suis à un âge où je ne peux pas me déplacer si loin pour faire purement et simplement des conférences à des étudiants. Il est indispensable que je trouve à créer des œuvres d'architecture petites ou grandes, mais significatives.*

42 Claude Lévi-Strauss recalled in *Tristes Tropiques* (Paris: Plon 1955; London: Picador 1989) the role that European intellectuals played in Brazil in the 1930s.

43 Facsimile of a letter from Lucio Costa to Gregori Warchavchik, 20 October 1936. Ferraz: *Warchavchik* p.242. (FF86,000 = US$5,850. Rate of exchange: $1.000.000 = US$85, FF1 = 0.800.000$. FLC I3–3.8. Robert M. Levine: *The Vargas Regime* Appendix D).

44 Lucio Costa: 'Presença de Le Corbusier' in *Lucio Costa: registro de uma vivência* (São Paulo: Empresa das Artes 1995) p.144.

45 Official letter from Capanema to Macedo Soares, Minister of Foreign Relations, 19 June 1936, CE: CPC 2.14 CPDOC/FGV.

46 Conversation with Lucio Costa, December 1988.

47  He was apparently not welcome at the Escola Nacional de Belas Artes, where Archimedes Memória was Director.

48  Report from Le Corbusier to Capanema, 10 August 1936. PCMESP V.330–7 SPHAN.

49  MESP 3, 10. PCMESP II.207 and III.214 SPHAN.

50  Report from Le Corbusier to Capanema, 10 August 1936. PCMESP V.330–7 SPHAN. '*Ce projet peut être classé pour sa valeur architecturale parmi les meilleurs qui aient été faits à ce jour dans n'importe quel pays*'.

51  Lucio Costa to Le Corbusier, 26 June 1936. FLC I3–3.21.
    *Encore un môt. Une des vos tâches auprès du Ministre sera de lui faire savoir votre avis sur le projet dont je vous envoi des photos. S'il vous déplait dites-le-nous carrément, mais, je vous en prie, ne dites pas brusquement a Mr Capanema: 'C'est moche . . . ils ne m'ont pas compris' – car alors nous serons sans appel, puisque les 'autres' l'ont déjà condamné, et nous vous prenons à temoin.*

52  Report from Le Corbusier to Capanema, 10 August 1936. PCMESP V.330–7 SPHAN. '*Je propose non pas de remplacer le projet qui est excellent mais de remplacer le terrain qui est mauvais.*'

53  Report from Le Corbusier to Capanema, 10 August 1936. PCMESP V.334 SPHAN.

54  Report from Le Corbusier to Capanema, 10 August 1936. PCMESP V.334 SPHAN. '*J'insiste sur le fait qu'il ne s'agit pas d'un nouveau Palais, mais du même dont les ailes sont simplement déployées.*'

55  Project for Praia de Santa Luzia: PCMESP V.338–46 SPHAN.

56  *Œuvre Complète 1934–38* pp.40–1.

57  Note from Capanema to Le Corbusier, 11 August 1936. CE: CPC 2.25 CPDOC/FGV.

58  Report from Le Corbusier to Capanema, 10 August 1936. PCMESP V.334 SPHAN.
    *Si le Palais se construit au Castelo, l'opinion publique pourra reprocher un jour un tel choix. S'il construit à la Praia de Santa Luzia, l'opinion publique, non seulement celle de Rio, mais aussi celle de tous les étrangers et touristes, sera unanime pour louer une solution qui fait état des splendeurs naturelles de Rio, splendeurs qui sont précisément l'objet de admiration [sic] mondiale, et qui jusqu'ici ont été parfaitement méprisées dans l'édification de la plus grande partie de la ville, sauf par le grand Préfet Passos qui a attaché son nom à la gloire mondiale de Rio.*

59  Project for Castelo: PCMESP V.348–51 SPHAN. Drawings signed and dated 13 August 1936.

60  PM6, PM7, and PM8 PCMESP V.343–5 SPHAN. *Œuvre Complète 1934–38* pp.78–80.

61  Capanema approved the scheme on 19 October 1936 with a series of recommendations. PCMESP V.362–4-SPHAN.

62  Lucio Costa to Le Corbusier, 31 December 1936. FLC I3–3.38.
    *L'idée de faire la 'momie' après qu'on a vu les choses si belles que vous en avez fait ne nous emballe pas – nous lui proposons alors une nouvelle solution en un seul bloc comme vous nous avez conseillé – mais dans le sens le plus court de terrain (S–S–E) et a double profondeur.*

63  Draft of Final Project: PCMESP VI.377–84 SPHAN.

64  Final Project: PCMESP VI.389–400 SPHAN.

65  The extra height was allowed by a change in the flight path to Santos Dumont Airport, which had limited the overall building height in the Agache Plan. Baumgart had calculated the increased loads on the foundations by 22 July 1937; on 26 November 1937, Capanema approved 12 floors with foundations to take 15 floors. PCMESP VIII.77–8 SPHAN. By 16 April 1938, Baumgart had calculated the extra floors; the Serviço de Obras requested a decision on erecting the extra floors on 18 May 1938. PCMESP VIII.170–1 SPHAN.

66  The first extra bay of *pilotis* was granted as a relaxation of the Agache Plan in exchange for allowing a pedestrian passage under the hall, in 1938; the second, which included a fire escape staircase, was facilitated by the rationalisation of the Agache Plan in 1945 after the building was occupied. PRPPC 17 SPHAN.

67  The opposite of Le Corbusier's proposal where the division walls contained files etc. *Œuvre Complète 1934–38* p.79.

68  Gustavo Capanema: 'O Futuro Palácio do Ministério da Educação' *Jornal do Brasil* (25 April 1937). PCMESP VIII.48 SPHAN.
    *um grande monumento arquitetonico, cujo projeto se estudou, com consciencia, pertinacia, minucia e esmero [. . .] visando o duplo objetivo de se fazer uma obra de arte e uma casa de trabalho.* [sic]

69 Capanema to Vargas, 13 April 1937. Vargas approved this on 15 April 1937. PCMESP VIII.44 SPHAN.

70 Total works of art: 12 murals and 9 paintings (Portinari), 21 sculptures (Jacques Lipchitz, Bruno Giorgi, Celso Antonio, and others), 10 *azulejo* panels (Portinari), 3 gardens (Burle Marx), 1 curvilinear carpet (Niemeyer). PRPPC 2 SPHAN *'uma obra de arte e uma casa de trabalho'*.

71 SPHAN took offices there in 1942.

72 Speech delivered by Gustavo Capanema. 'O Palácio do Ministério da Educação' *Revista do Serviço Público* (November 1945) pp.75–6.

73 Inscription in the lobby.

   *Sendo Presidente da República Getúlio Vargas e Ministro da Educação e Saúde Gustavo Capanema, foi mandado construir este edifício para sede do Ministério da Educação e Saúde, projetado pelos arquitetos Oscar Niemeyer, Affonso Reidy, Jorge Moreira, Carlos Leão, Lucio Costa e Ernani Vasconcellos, segundo risco original de Le Corbusier 1937–45.*

74 Capanema Order, 16 May 1942. PRPPC 12 SPHAN.

75 Lipchitz: *My Life in Sculpture* (New York: Viking Press 1972) pp.xxxi–xxxii and pp.164–7. Capanema may not have been committed to carrying out the sculpture because he may have viewed accepting the work of a foreign artist as a compromise.

76 Lucio Costa to Le Corbusier, 26 June 1936. FLC I3–3.21.

77 *Œuvre Complète 1934–38* pp.42–5. Also published in *PDF* (9 July 1937) pp.184–6.

78 Lucio Costa: 'Cidade Universitária' in *Lucio Costa registro de uma vivência* pp.172–89.

79 Schwartzman: *Tempos de Capanema* p.101.

80 Lucio Costa to Le Corbusier, 3 July 1937. FLC I3–3.47.

   *La Commission de professeurs – Amaral et Campos en tête – refuse, sans rien y compren- dre, votre beau projet. Quant'a [sic] nous, ayant deux mois pour présenter une nouvelle solution nous avons fait de notre mieux quoiqu'en nous adaptant aux circonstances puisqu'il fallait encombre le terrain de batisses. Mais encore cette fois ci à l'unanimité (et ils sont 14 à la commission de professeurs) on l'a regeté.*

81 Lucio Costa to Capanema, September 1937. Schwartzman: *Tempos de Capanema* pp.101–2.

   *Agora que tudo já parece bem 'arrumado', venho lhe dizer o quanto dói ver uma idéia alta e pura, como essa da criação da cidade universitária, tomar corpo e se desenvolver assim desse jeito [. . .]. E o mais triste é que enquanto se perseverar, durante anos e anos, na construção dessa coisa errada, estará dormindo em qualquer prateleira de arquivo a solução 'verdadeira' – a coisa certa.*

82 Conversation with Lucio Costa, December 1988.

83 Le Corbusier to Capanema, 21 November 1936. FLC I3–3.36. *'Il reste la Cité Universitaire. Pourrai-je y collaborer?'*

84 Le Corbusier to Capanema, 1 April 1939. FLC I3–3.81. *'Je n'abandonné [sic] l'espoir de reprendre avec vous les plans de la Cité Universitaire du Brésil'.*

85 It appeared in the opening scenes of the film 'Black Orpheus' in which views of Rio de Janeiro are shown. Marcel Camus, 1959. Awarded Grand Prize, and Oscar for the Best Foreign Language Film, at the Cannes Film Festival 1959. Based on the play 'Orfeu da Con- ceição' by Vinícius de Morais, first staged at the Teatro Municipal, Rio de Janeiro, in 1956, with a set by Oscar Niemeyer.

86 Philip Goodwin: *Brazil Builds* (New York: Museum of Modern Art 1943) p.92.

# 3  The Brazilian Pavilion at the New York World's Fair 1939

In 1935, Henry-Russell Hitchcock wrote, in view of the general interest in expositions stimulated by the proposed 1939 New York World's Fair, that:

> Expositions, like skyscrapers, dramatize architecture for the general public. Hence they have an influence upon architectural history far greater than their intrinsic importance. [. . .] Real innovations of structure or design seldom make their first appearance in expositions. But World's Fairs are sounding boards for ideas, both good or bad, which have already taken solid form under more obscure conditions.[1]

If this may be believed, then the Ministry of Education Building may be said to have provided the 'solid form', while the Brazilian Pavilion at the 1939 New York World's Fair represented the 'sounding board'. Designed by Lucio Costa and Oscar Niemeyer after the approval of the final version of the Ministry of Education Building on 22 February 1937, and the rejection of the Cidade Universitária project on 12 March 1937, it was a further development of many of their ideas of what a Modern Brazilian architecture should be.

The 1939 Brazilian Pavilion was intended to be nothing like any previous Brazilian pavilion. Brazilian pavilions had never featured among the buildings of distinction at International Expositions; the Pavilion of 1939 was unprecedented, politically and architecturally. The President of Brazil, Getúlio Vargas, was anxious to promote his country as being a developed nation, and Lucio Costa and Oscar Niemeyer were emerging as architects with a number of prestigious commissions which were later to be recognised internationally as the 'Brazilian Style'.

Although Brazil had participated in International Expositions since 1862, it had tended to rely on foreign architects. Its representation became of increasing concern to the new Republic established in 1889, and it tried to establish an image which reconciled national identity and modernity. For the 1904 Saint Louis Exhibition, an engineer, Francisco Marcelino Souza Aguiar (1855–1935), had designed a Beaux-Arts Pavilion; it was later dismantled and re-erected, to house the Senate, as the Monroe Palace on the Avenida Rio Branco in Rio de Janeiro where it stood until it was demolished in 1981. For the Philadelphia Exhibition of 1926, there had been a competition for the design of the Pavilion, in which Neo-Colonial was the required style; Lucio Costa had won first prize, but the design was not built. There was not, however, a continuous policy of employing Brazilian architects to design pavilions. At the 1937 Paris Exhibition, the Brazilian Pavilion had been a gift from the French government, with the Brazilian government providing the interior decoration and the displays.[2] Designed by a French architect, it was described in the *Guide Officiel* as being '*sobre et moderne*'. In fact, it consisted of a plain façade 30 metres high and 25 metres wide, on which the national arms were reproduced in bas-relief; behind it was a two-storey shed 27 metres long.[3] For the San Francisco Exhibition, which opened a few months before the New York Fair, the design of the Pavilion was left to a local architect, who, seemingly without any knowledge of the country, featured motifs which were more Mexican than Brazilian.[4]

For the New York World's Fair, however, a different procedure altogether was followed; this was by far the largest and most important International Exhibition so far, and Brazil's representation had become an important concern to the Vargas Government during the years of the Good Neighbour Policy. Their Pavilion had an important role to perform, both economically and diplomatically, and they took great care in its making. The Brazilian Pavilion was intended to show to the North Americans and the world that Brazil was not just one more Republic among the many others of the Southern Continent. The special interest shown by President Vargas may be seen by his attendance at the ceremony at which the competition result were announced.[5]

The co-ordinating body for the construction of the pavilion was the Ministry of Labour, Industry and Commerce. The Ministry had assembled a technical commission and announced a competition for the design of the pavilion in late 1937, but the terms of the competition were criticised by the Instituto de Arquitetos do Brasil (IAB), who asserted the presence of several intrinsic faults and argued that it would thus not attract the best architects. Among these alleged faults were: the brief called for a *concorrência*, which implied tendering, and not a competition on the basis of design; the scale of 1:50 for the presentation drawings was considered excessive for the judgement of the designs; the name of jury was omitted; and, no guarantee was given that the architect of the winning scheme would be sent to New York to oversee the execution of the project. In view of these criticisms, the brief was amended conforming to the Institute's guide-lines, and the deadline for submission postponed until 7 March 1938.[6]

The jury consisted of three architects appointed by the IAB (one, Eduardo Souza Aguiar, had been a member of the Ministry of Education competition jury and later Head of the Department of Works for the building; another, Angelo Bruhns, had been nominated for the Cidade Universitária), an architect from the Ministry, and a representative of the Minister as chairman. The jury described the criteria by which they would judge the projects in this way:

The question should not imply a search for traditional or indigenous architectural details, but for an architectural form which would translate the expression of the Brazilian environment; and furthermore, that this architectural form be preferably contemporary, in view that the New York

World's Fair has, as a principle, established a vision of the 'The World of Tomorrow'.[7]

The aspirations of this jury, of 1938, were very different from the ones for the Ministry of Education competition in 1935. The jury consciously searched for a national architecture within a contemporary framework. They seemed to have freed themselves of the desire for historical references, and instead, they were for 'technical standards appropriate to an exhibition pavilion'.[8] It is not surprising, however, that with such ambitious aspirations, the jury did not find any work which fully conformed to both criteria. They selected Lucio Costa's design for first prize, as the one which best displayed '*espírito de brasilidade*', and Oscar Niemeyer's for second prize, for its technical aspects.

Lucio Costa, however, invited Oscar Niemeyer to collaborate with him on a new proposal. In view of this settlement, they never published or made known their competition entries, in spite of the numerous requests made by *Arquitetura e Urbanismo*, the magazine of the IAB, which had followed the competition closely. Through the brief description given by the jury, it is known that, in Lucio Costa's scheme, there was a long exhibition hall with large windows opening onto a patio, with easy access from the street to the patio where beverages were to be served. Oscar Niemeyer's, on the other hand, while completely lacking *espírito de brasilidade*, met the functional requirements of the pavilion with a vast entrance, large halls, and good use of space.

The jury did not make clear what *espírito de brasilidade* really meant. Within the Estado Novo, *brasilidade* implied the adaptation of the general concepts of Modernism to Brazil's specific conditions. In architecture, this meant that the jury wanted to avoid a scheme which was a straightforward exercise in the International Style; they referred complimentarily to the fact that neither design made use of what they considered elements characteristic of it. About Costa's, they commented: 'Your project has a beautiful harmony within the spirit of modernity which takes it away from the preoccupation of imposing certain elements of contemporary techniques of construction', and about Niemeyer's: 'We emphasise yet again the fact of the author not having made use of elements considered indispensable to the new architecture.'[9] The jury was in search of the fusion of 'Modern' and 'national' by which the new architecture in Brazil ultimately came to be known. By joining Costa's *espírito de brasilidade* with Niemeyer's technical abilities, they hoped to achieve this synthesis.

By April 1938, Costa and Niemeyer had gone to New York to elaborate the design of the pavilion in partnership with the American architect Paul Lester Wiener (1894–1967), who handled the structure and contracts and designed the interior decoration and exhibition display. They stayed in New York until at least August 1938. Lucio Costa recounted that their general intentions were based on what a pavilion should be:

An exhibition pavilion should present characteristics of a provisional building instead of artificially simulating a building of permanent character.

In an industrial and culturally developed land like the United States and in a fair in which countries richer and more 'experienced' than ours are taking part, it could not be reasonably thought to stand out through lavishness, monumentality or expertise. We tried to call interest in another way: by making a simple pavilion, unceremonious, attractive and cosy, which would impose itself, not by its scale – the site is not big – nor by luxury – the country is still poor – but through its qualities of harmony and equilibrium and as an expression, as far as possible pure, of contemporary art.[10]

The site of the New York World's Fair, Flushing Meadow, was a swamp three-and-a-half miles long, in the Borough of Queens; the reclamation of the land was part of a plan to provide a public park. A Board of Design was set up to ensure a suitable 'modernity', except, at least, in the Government Zone.[11] The Fair was planned around a Theme Centre and the Trylon and Perisphere (both designed by Wallace K. Harrison (1895–1981)), from which symmetrical axes emerged; it was divided into zones, from the centre outwards: Communications and Business Systems, and Production and Distribution; Community Interests, and Food; Government, and the Amusement Area (Plate 14). The longitudinal central axis of Constitutional Mall extended from the Trylon and Perisphere eastwards to the oval Lagoon of Nations and beyond to the Court of Peace where the foreign pavilions were located, and was terminated by the United States Government Pavilions (Figure 3.1). Both sides of the Court of Peace were reserved for national pavilions built by the Fair; France and Belgium had the most desirable sites overlooking the Lagoon of Nations.

The site of the Brazilian Pavilion was not large but was well located for a national pavilion. On the edge of the Government zone, it was limited to the south by the large Rainbow Avenue, and to the west by the curved Garden Way, which separated the Government zone from the Community Interest zone, and to the north by a river with a walking path along its bank. The large French Pavilion was the neighbour to the east.

The side façade of the French Pavilion was a blind wall which provided the backdrop for the spatial interplay of the Brazilian Pavilion. Setting the

3.1 New York World's Fair 1939. Aerial view.

The theme of the Fair was *The World of Tomorrow*. It was planned around the Trylon and Perisphere. In the foreground are the futuristic pavilions of General Motors and Ford. The longitudinal central axis of Constitutional Mall extended from the Trylon and Perisphere to the Government Zone.

*Official Guide Book.*

building back from the front of the site allowed for an entrance plaza which completely detached the building from the massive neighbouring construction, and aligning the building with the lateral edge of the site allowed a substantial rear garden (Figures 3.2 and 3.3). In describing the main origin of the design, Lucio Costa stated that:

> We had to take into account the existence of the neighbouring building. This explains the line of the building on the extreme edge of the site and the adopted *parti*, light and open, like lace, with the aim of standing out through contrast instead of letting itself be completely dominated by the heavy compact mass, higher and much bigger, of the French Pavilion.[12]

Costa expressed his willingness to distance himself from the strictness of the International Style and made a parallel between it and the Doric order, and his own architecture and the Ionic:

3.2 Lucio Costa and Oscar Niemeyer: Brazilian Pavilion, New York World's Fair (1939).
Front façade.
The south façade was protected by 'egg-crate' *brise-soleils*. A curved ramp led to the main exhibition area on the upper floor. The lower floor was devoted to a restaurant and a cafeteria.
*Album do Pavilhão do Brasil*.

3.3 Lucio Costa and Oscar Niemeyer: Brazilian Pavilion, New York World's Fair (1939).
Rear façade.
View across the Lagoon of Nations. The side which faced the garden had floor-to-ceiling glazing.
*Album do Pavilhão do Brasil*.

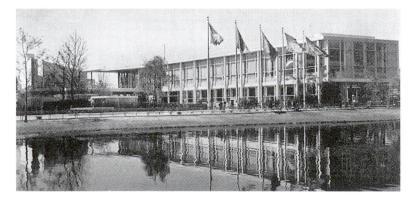

The use of the beautiful curve of the site directed the whole scheme. It is the basic motive which, in degrees more or less accentuated, repeats itself in the canopy, in the auditorium, in the ramp, in the free walls of the ground floor, etc. giving the group grace and elegance, and as such making it correspond, in academic language, to the Ionic order and not the Doric, in opposition to what usually happens to the contemporary architecture.[13]

The Pavilion animated the ground plane in much the same way as the Ministry of Education Building. The ground floor was partially enclosed, occupied by free-standing display stands for national beverages like coffee, *mate* tea, and *guaraná*, and allowing the entrance plaza to progress to the garden through the building; at the far end of the main block there was a restaurant extending to a dance floor. The rear garden had a display of the flora and fauna of the country with a lily pond, a snake pit, an aquarium, an orchid house and an aviary. A large curved ramp led from the entrance plaza to a terrace on the upper floor where an auditorium and the main exhibition spaces, with double height columns and a mezzanine, were

3.4 Lucio Costa and Oscar Niemeyer: Brazilian Pavilion, New York World's Fair (1939).
Terrace.
On the left the entrance to the main exhibition spaces on the upper floor. On the right the curved wall of the Auditorium with a list of famous Brazilians in 'Bodoni Brazil', a typeface specially designed for the Pavilion.
*Album do Pavilhão do Brasil.*

3.5 Lucio Costa and Oscar Niemeyer: Brazilian Pavilion, New York World's Fair (1939).
Exhibition hall.
*Album do Pavilhão do Brasil.*

located (Figures 3.4 and 3.5). The rigid steel structure contrasted with the freedom of the concrete floor slabs which curved around the columns.

The Ministry of Education Building may also be recalled in the treatment of the façades: the main façade of the exhibition space, which faced south, was protected by 'egg-crate' *brise-soleils*; the side which faced the garden had floor-to-ceiling glazing; the other external walls were blind. As in the Ministry Building, works of art received primary attention: three panels by Portinari were placed in the main hall – the 'Good Neighbour Hall', and 'Mulher Reclinada' by Celso Antonio on the terrace. A special lettering – 'Bodoni Brazil' – was designed for the Pavilion.[14]

The confidence with which Costa and Niemeyer developed the Modern architectural language which they had tentatively initiated at the Ministry of Education Building (still under construction) was astonishing. With hindsight, it is obvious that Niemeyer was developing an individual approach to architecture which was to reach a full independent flowering when he returned to Brazil. However, the success in relating the building to its site should be attributed to Costa.

It is easy to see how Costa's and Niemeyer's pavilion could stand out from the others by its openness and lightness. Most of the other pavilions in the fair were fully-enclosed, air-conditioned structures with unbroken exterior surfaces relieved only by murals or sculptures. The Brazilian Pavilion received immediate acclaim, being noted and praised by all the architectural critics who reported on the Fair. In the United States, The *Magazine of Arts* emphasised how the pavilion stood out from the other buildings in the Fair:

The Brazilian pavilion has a purity and style that makes it close to breathtaking. The finesse of subtly curved façade makes the ordinary Fair buildings look almost brutal, the plan is an excellent refutation of the dogmas of the industrial designers, the arrangement on the plot is designed to produce the maximum of enjoyment, the ramps make an evil contrast to Norman Bel Geddes' intestine-like exits from the General Motors Building, and the location of the entire building on posts is just as good economy as it is good design.[15]

*Architectural Forum* selected 18 national pavilions of 'notable interest' out of the 60 nations represented in the Fair, and only two received two pages of illustrations, Brazil and Sweden. Of the Brazilian Pavilion it said:

> Brazil's pavilion was designed by two pupils [sic] of Le Corbusier, and provides a superlative display of his ideas and forms. A magnificent plan for the accommodation of larger crowds, it is almost completely open on the ground floor, equally spacious above. The exhibits are among the best in the Fair for interest, technique of display and quality of execution.[16]

The *Architectural Record* found the solution for light control noteworthy: 'the cellular panel attached to the outer wall of the Brazilian Pavilion is designed to keep out direct sun rays; ample light is admitted and the inside temperature is reduced.'[17]

In Europe, the *Architectural Review* dedicated an issue to the Fair which was highly critical of most of the architecture, considering it to be of a superficial modernity. Of the national pavilions – except the British which was dealt with separately – only nine were studied. The Brazilian Pavilion was again noted for its openness and lightness, which was emphasised by its relation to the neighbouring French Pavilion:

> By its openness of plan, the Brazilian Pavilion achieves a lightness and grace which are usually absent in pavilions of this size.
>
> The complete openness of the ground floor, and the (apparently) informal arrangements of exhibits, gives the whole building a particular quality of subtle design, as fascinating as it is rare.[18]

The Brazilian Pavilion was also noted for its spatial divisions in a section dealing with different details of the pavilions; it was illustrated as an example of Modern exhibition display:

> In the Brazilian pavilion [. . .] there are no definite partitions, the division of space being merely suggested by the form of display stands and ceiling, so that an effect of ample size is achieved in quite a small building.[19]

*Architettura* illustrated the model in 1938 and later dedicated a page to photos of the pavilion,[20] while *Casabella* declared that:

> in some pavilions, such as Brazil's or Sweden's for example, even the architecture of the building, which does not stray into pompous rhetoric, expresses itself with stylistic clarity.[21]

Later, Philip Goodwin compared the Brazilian Pavilion to other buildings at the Fair in *Brazil Builds* (Figure 3.6):

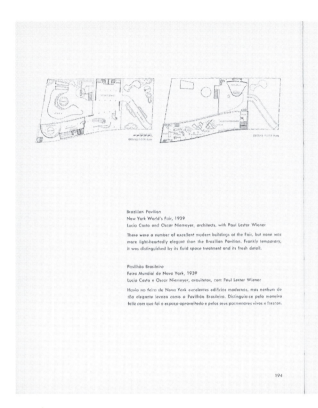

Brazilian Pavilion
New York World's Fair, 1939
Lucio Costa and Oscar Niemeyer, architects, with Paul Lester Wiener

There were a number of excellent modern buildings at the Fair, but none was
more light-heartedly elegant than the Brazilian Pavilion. Frankly temporary,
it was distinguished by its fluid space treatment and its fresh detail.

Pavilhão Brasileiro
Feira Mundial de Nova York, 1939
Lucio Costa e Oscar Niemeyer, arquitetos, com Paul Lester Wiener

Havia na feira de Nova York excelentes edifícios modernos, mas nenhum de
tão elegante leveza como o Pavilhão Brasileiro. Distinguiu-se pela maneira
feliz com que foi o espaço aproveitado e pelos seus pormenores vivos e frescos.

194                195

3.6 Philip L. Goodwin: *Brazil Builds* (New York: The Museum of Modern Art 1943) pp.194–5. Offset, printed in black, page sizes 8½ × 11″ (21.6 × 27.9 cm).
Photograph © 2000 The Museum of Modern Art, New York.
Lucio Costa and Oscar Niemeyer: Brazilian Pavilion, New York World's Fair (1939).
*Ground floor plan/Second floor plan.*
*There was a number of excellent modern buildings, at the Fair, but none was more light-heartedly elegant than the Brazilian Pavilion. Frankly temporary, it was distinguished by its fluid space treatment and its fresh detail.*

none was more light-heartedly elegant than the Brazilian Pavilion. Frankly temporary, it was distinguished by its fluid space treatment and its fresh detail.[22]

## Notes

1  Henry-Russell Hitchcock: 'Exposition Architecture' *The Bulletin of the Museum of Modern Art* (January 1935) p.2.
2  'Pavilhão do Brasil' *Arquitetura e Urbanismo* (November–December 1937) p.334.
3  Jacques Guilbert, architect. *Guide Officiel* Exposition Internationale Arts et Techniques (Paris: 1937) pp.72–3.
4  'O Pavilhão do Brasil na Exposição da California' *Arquitetura e Urbanismo* (March–April 1938) p.98.
5  'Feira Mundial de Nova York' *Arquitetura e Urbanismo* (May–June 1939) p.471.
6  'A Exposição Mundial de Nova York' *Arquitetura e Urbanismo* (January–February 1938) pp.50–1.
7  'Termo do Julgamento do Concurso de Ante-Projetos para o Pavilhão Brasileiro na Feira de New York' *Arquitetura e Urbanismo* (March–April 1938) p.99.
    *A questão não se devia prender ao detalhe dos elementos arquitetônicos, fossem tradicionais ou indigenas, mas se devia ater a uma fórma arquitetônica capaz de traduzir a expressão do ambiente brasileiro; e mais, que essa fórma fosse de preferência atualista, tendo em vista que a Feira Mundial de New York tem, por principio, estabelecer uma visão do 'Mundo de Amanhã'.*
8  *Arquitetura e Urbanismo* (March–April 1938) p.99. 'condições técnicas inerentes a um pavilhão de exposição'.
9  *Arquitetura e Urbanismo* (March–April 1938) p.99.

*O seu conjunto tem uma bela harmonia dentro do espirito moderno que o afasta da pre-ocupação de impôr determinados elementos da técnica moderna de construir* [sic].

*Ressalta ainda o fato de não haver o autor recorrido a elementos construtivos julgados indispensaveis à nova arquitetura* [sic].

10 'O Pavilhão Brasileiro na Feira Mundial de Nova York' *Arquitetura e Urbanismo* (May–June 1939) p.471.

*Um pavilhão de exposição deve apresentar caracteristicas de construção provisoria e não similar artificiosamente obra de carater permanente. Em uma terra industrial e cultural-mente desenvolvida como os Estados Unidos e numa feira em que tomam parte paizes tão mais ricos e 'experimentados' que o nosso, não se poderia razoavelmente pensar em sobre-sahir pelo aparato, pela monumentalidade ou pela técnica. Procurou-se então, interessar de outra maneira: fazendo-se um pavilhão simples, pouco formalistico, atraente e acolhedor, que se impuzesse, não pelas proporções – que o terreno não é grande – nem pelo luxo – que o paiz ainda é pobre – mas pelas suas qualidades de harmonia e de equilibrio e como expressão, tanto quanto possivel pura, de arte contemporanea.* [sic]

11 It was the largest land reclamation project in the eastern United States. The president, Grover A. Whalen, had been head of the local National Recovery Administration under the New Deal. Stanley Applebaum: *The New York World's Fair 1939/1940: in 155 photographs by Richard Wurts and Others* (New York: Dover 1977) pp.ix–xiii.

12 *Album do Pavilhão do Brasil Feira Mundial de Nova York* (1939).

*teve-se que levar em conta inicialmente a preexistencia da construção visinha. Dai o afas-tamento até o extremo limite do terreno e o partido adotado leve e aberto, como que rendado, afim de sobresair pelo contraste em vez de se deixar dominar completamente pela massa compacta pesada, mas alta e muito maior do pavilhão francês.* [sic]

13 *Album do Pavilhão do Brasil Feira Mundial de Nova York* (1939).

*O aproveitamento da curva bonita do terreno comandou então todo o traçado. É o motivo basico que em gráo mais ou menos acentuado se repete na marquize, no auditorio, na rampa, nas paredes soltas do pavimento terreo, etc. dando ao conjunto graça e elegan-cia e fazendo com que assim corresponda, em linguagem academica, á ordem jonica e não a dorica, ao contrario do que sucede o mais da vezes na arquitetura contemporanea.* [sic]

14 *Album do Pavilhão do Brasil Feira Mundial de Nova York.* 'Bodoni Brazil' was an angular version of the 'modern' serif typefaces of Giambattista Bodoni's *Manuale Tipografico* (Parma 1818).

15 F.A. Gutheim: 'Buildings at the Fair' *Magazine of Art* (May 1939) p.316.

16 *Architectural Forum* (June 1939) pp.448–9.

17 *Architectural Record* (August 1939) p.6.

18 *Architectural Review* (August 1939) pp.63–4.

19 *Architectural Review* (August 1939) p.89.

20 *Architettura* (October 1938) p.598; (July 1939) p.407.

21 *Casabella* (September 1939) p.23.

*in alcuni padiglioni, del Brasile e della Svezia ad esempio, anche l'architettura d'edificio, che non si svia in retoriche ampollose, riesce ad esprimersi con una sufficiente netteza stilis-tica.*

22 *Brazil Builds* p.194.

# 4 'A whole new school'*

By 1942, a number of buildings were complete which confirmed Philip Goodwin's view that the Ministry of Education Building was not an isolated example of Modern architecture in Brazil, but that a whole movement was taking shape. Most of these buildings were in Rio de Janeiro, almost all within sight of each other: the Ministry of Education Building, the Brazilian Press Association, Santos Dumont Airport, and the Boat Passenger Station. Not all the Modern buildings were confined to Rio de Janeiro; in Belo Horizonte, there was the Pampulha complex, in São Paulo the 'Sedes Sapientiæ' School and the Edifício Esther, which Goodwin selected as worthy of inclusion in *Brazil Builds*.

Goodwin's view masked the enormous differences between the buildings in Rio de Janeiro and those in São Paulo. Rio de Janeiro was the capital of Brazil and thus received the benefits of patronage from a government anxious to promote itself as progressive by investing in Modern architecture. In São Paulo, with a largely European population, immigrant and commercial, it is perhaps not surprising that the pattern of patronage should have resembled that of similar cities in North America, for instance Chicago, with which it was often compared.[1] The major Modern buildings there were all commissioned by private institutions.

The result of the differing constitutions of the clients and the aspirations of the architects was that the buildings in Rio de Janeiro were more programmatically Modern, especially in their allegiance to Le Corbusier; they formed the major part of what would later be defined as the 'Brazilian Style'. Architecture in São Paulo, with its strong Italian ties, was more eclectic in its allegiances and more pragmatic, and greater care had to be taken to choose examples which conformed to the 'Brazilian Style'.

Among the Modern buildings in Rio de Janeiro, the Brazilian Press Association was almost an exact contemporary of the Ministry of Education. Although strictly speaking a private organisation, the Association was of paramount importance to Vargas, due to the importance of the press as an instrument of state propaganda.[2] Determined to erect a remarkable building, Herbert Moses, the President of the Association, supervised the

*Robert C. Smith: 'Brazil Builds' *The Bulletin of the Museum of Modern Art* (April 1943) p.13.

4.1 Marcelo and Milton Roberto: Competition entry for the Brazilian Press Association, Rio de Janeiro (1936). First prize.
Photomontage.
*Arquitetura e Urbanismo* (March–April 1937).

4.2 Moreira and Vasconcellos: Competition entry for the Brazilian Press Association, Rio de Janeiro (1936).
Perspective.
*PDF* (September 1936).

competition process himself, with a jury compiled mostly of Association representatives and with a few architects appointed by professional bodies.[3] Herbert Moses had become acquainted with architectural developments, when, as a journalist in 1931, he had been the translator of Frank Lloyd Wright's speeches; Wright later wrote that Moses had added 'inflamed' words he himself had not used.[4] The competition started later than the one for the Ministry, but due to the long competition process of the Ministry, the Association was completed earlier. The competition was won by Marcelo and Milton Roberto in June 1936, just before Le Corbusier's arrival in Brazil in July (Figure 4.1).

Among the competition entrants were three teams of Modern architects, including three architects working on the Ministry: Jorge Machado Moreira and Ernani de Vasconcellos, and Oscar Niemeyer (Figures 4.2 and 4.3).[5] Marcelo and Milton Roberto were independent from Lucio Costa's Ministry team but their allegiance to Le Corbusier's ideas is clear. They declared in the Memorial Descritivo which accompanied their competition entry – although without directly mentioning Le Corbusier – that:

> Our work is based on the immutable laws of the Great Architecture of all times, and in the principles of the Modern Architecture, fruits of the Contemporary Technology:
> 'Independent structure
> free plan
> free façade
> roof-terrace'[6]

Marcelo Roberto (1908–64) was the elder of the two brothers; he had graduated from the Escola Nacional de Belas Artes in 1929. After graduating he spent six months travelling in France, Italy and Germany; on his

4.3 Oscar Niemeyer: Competition entry for the Brazilian Press Association, Rio de Janeiro (1936).
Perspective.
*PDF* (September 1936).

return he started to work for a construction company, a post he held until 1936 when he won the competition for the Brazilian Press Association. Milton Roberto joined him after graduating from the Escola Nacional de Belas Artes in 1934; he had been there during Lucio Costa's brief reform of 1930. The Brazilian Press Association was their first large-scale project.

Even though the commission had been won in competition, the architects still had to fight to secure the right to undertake the execution of the works and to carry out the building to completion to ensure the integrity of the design, as may be seen in the correspondence between the architects and Herbert Moses:

> It is impossible today (as in the great epochs, etc.) to separate the work of the architect on the drawing-board, from the work on 'site'.
> Our building is a unity. Its principal characteristic, homogeneity. Like a tree, an egg, a human body. All the elements will have to be accomplished under a single spirit. From the structure to the lettering of the signs, from the system of masonry to the counters and cupboards, the rhythm must be constant.[7]

They were successful in winning Moses' confidence, however: not only did the Robertos complete the Association Building, they later designed a house for him.

The site of the Brazilian Press Association Building was also part of the Agache plan, on the corner of Rua Araújo Porto Alegre and Rua México in Castelo, only a block away from the Ministry (see Plate 1). It was not considered a favourable site, especially in its orientation, by all three of the Modern competition entrants; the two main façades faced north and west, getting the hottest sun; they all displayed solutions to protect both street façades against insolation. Moreira's scheme utilised brise-soleil of the type Le Corbusier had designed for Algiers; they acknowledged that:

> The brise-soleil that Le Corbusier studied and designed for various buildings in Algeria, a country of climatic conditions, in certain aspects, similar to ours, seemed to us the most appropriate solution.[8]

The Roberto brothers' solution was of a similar type, with fixed horizontal and vertical bars, but they specified them in duraluminium, an alloy of aluminium used in aeroplane manufacture, fixed in a concrete frame. Both types created between the glazing and the brise-soleil what the former called a 'protection zone' and the latter a 'heat dispersion zone'. Niemeyer's solution was to break the plane of the façade with concrete fins set at 45°, thus aligning them ideally with the orientation of the sun. The drawback of this solution was that it would disperse the direct rays of the sun but not the heat.

The most remarkable feature of the Roberto brothers' plan was its relation to the site. The building code – defined by Agache in his plan for Castelo – required a clear passage six-and-a-half metres wide running from the Rua Araújo Porto Alegre to the interior of the Quadra, splitting the site. The Robertos located the main entrance on the Rua Araújo Porto

Alegre adjacent to this passage. It allowed for a generous and well-defined entrance, through a row of *pilotis*, to the elevators which opened directly to the street. A row of shops opened to the Rua México, leaving the Rua Araújo Porto Alegre exclusively for the Association's own entrance. The other two schemes did not explore the possibilities of this determining factor; Niemeyer created a symmetrical entrance on the corner of the Rua Araújo Porto Alegre and the Rua México, and Moreira placed the entrance on the Rua México. The Robertos' choice proved to be a happy one when the Ministry of Education was erected on the adjacent Quadra, turning the Rua Araújo Porto Alegre into a more important street than the Rua México.

The headquarters of the Brazilian Press Association was to function both as an office for the Association and as a club for its members, thus demanding a wide variety of types of space. It was designed as a 13-storey reinforced concrete structure. The ground floor was recessed to expose the structural columns. The first seven floors were standardised for office use; the next was double height for an exhibition hall and auditorium. The three floors above formed an irregular set-back structure which allowed for external areas: the first was a lounge for club members, the second a restaurant, and the top a roof garden, designed by Roberto Burle Marx, with a covered area for a bar.

The building was realised almost as originally conceived, with the omission of some facilities such as the swimming pool and gymnasium which had been located in the basement, but with a different design for the *brise-soleil*, which were altered to vertical concrete fins fixed diagonally, separated from the building by a continuous passage. This change altered the external appearance of the building dramatically and contributed to the comments on its heavy appearance. The exterior walls were faced with granite and travertine; the concrete slabs and *brise-soleil* were coated with white render. The interior walls were finished with native Brazilian woods: *sucupira*, *ipé*, *peroba*, and rosewood. The elevator wall to the street was faced with stainless-steel sheets.

The Brazilian Press Association was situated adjacent to the Biblioteca Nacional, a Second Empire style building on the Avenida Rio Branco, in conjunction with which it was shown in *Brazil Builds* to illustrate how well Modern architecture could harmonise with the buildings of the past (Figures 4.4 and 4.5). Goodwin defined the characteristics of the Brazilian Press Association Building with a comparison to the Ministry of Education:

> The formula is not unlike that of the Ministry of Education, but the forms could hardly be different. This building is solid and substantial while the other, though just as well constructed, seems light and airy.[9]

In 1937, the Civil Aviation Department launched competitions for the design of two important buildings for the proposed Santos Dumont Airport in Rio de Janeiro: a large Central Terminal for land-based planes and a Seaplane Terminal. The competition for the Seaplane Terminal was announced in early 1937 and, for the Central Terminal, in mid 1937. Both were organised by the Instituto de Arquitetos do Brasil in collaboration with the Civil Aviation Department; the juries were composed of

4.4 Philip L. Goodwin: *Brazil Builds* (New York: The Museum of Modern Art 1943) pp.112–13. Offset, printed in black, page sizes 8½ × 11″ (21.6 × 27.9 cm).
Photograph © 2000 The Museum of Modern Art, New York.

Marcelo and Milton Roberto: Brazilian Press Association, Rio de Janeiro (1936–8).

*A simple rectilinear block equipped with sunshades and set upon the exposed columns of a recessed ground floor; above, an irregular superstructure, again recessed.*

*The photographs on the left show the pleasant garden terraces on the top floors and the auditorium which is set behind the blank wall at the ninth floor level.*

architects appointed by the IAB and engineers by the Department.[10] Both terminals became regarded as outstanding examples of the 'Brazilian Style'.

The site for the airport was on landfill in the Bay adjacent to the city centre formed by the spoil from the Morro do Castelo. The two types of aeroplane could not share a terminal because the mooring facilities and docks demanded by the seaplanes required a protected area of the Bay while the land-plane traffic demanded a large landing area. The Seaplane Terminal was thus located in the northern sector of the airport and the Central Terminal in the southern sector, closer to the city centre (Figure 4.6). Between the two terminals, four hangars were proposed. The Seaplane Terminal was very modest in scale in relation to the Central Terminal, which was intended to have a far greater volume of traffic; at that time, however, seaplanes were more commonly used and that terminal took priority. The project for the Seaplane Terminal, won by Atilio Corrêa Lima, was completed in 1938, while the Central Terminal project, won by Marcelo and Milton Roberto, was not started until 1944.

Atilio Corrêa Lima graduated from the Escola Nacional de Belas Artes in 1925, followed by studies in urbanism at the Sorbonne. Returning to Brazil in 1931, he was appointed Professor of Urban Planning at the Escola Nacional de Belas Artes and designed the master plan for Goiânia, the new capital for the state of Goiás, in 1933. He entered the competitions for both airport buildings, winning one and receiving second prize in the

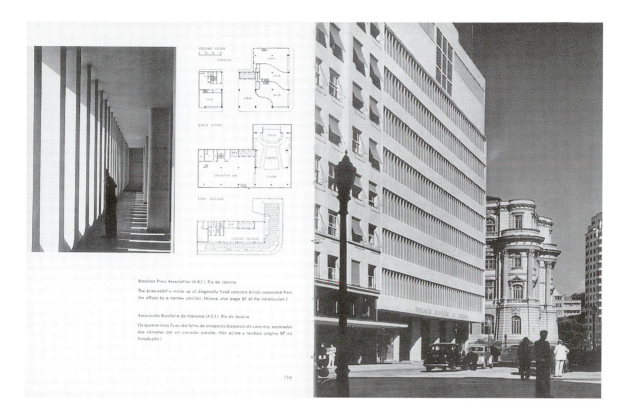

other; he also entered the Ministry of Education competition. His Boat Passenger Station, a ferry terminal for traffic across the Bay, was also illustrated in *Brazil Builds* (Figure 4.7). His sudden death in 1943, the victim of an aeroplane accident on a flight from Rio de Janeiro to São Paulo, ironically 100 metres from his own airport building, cut his career short; the Seaplane Terminal remains his most successful building.

The Seaplane Terminal was a small building 35 m × 35 m and two storeys high (Plate 8; Figures 4.8 and 4.9). On the land side, the lower floor was recessed, leaving the upper floor extending over it, which provided a canopy over the entrance. On the Bay side, an extension of the lower floor provided an embarkation lounge, which was linked to the pier by a covered passage supported by elliptical arches; the extension allowed for an observation platform above. On the ground floor were located all the necessary travelling services: companies, passenger hall, customs, and staff quarters. An enormous map of Brazil showed the Seaplane routes. On the upper floor were located a restaurant and bar around a void to the passenger hall below, and open to a terrace overlooking the landing area. Corrêa Lima made extensive use of travertine and stainless-steel sheets. Attention was given to the landscape around the Terminal with front and rear gardens treated with vegetation typical of different regions of Brazil.

Atilio Corrêa Lima's Seaplane Terminal served both the land and seaplane traffic for several years until the Central Terminal was opened in 1946; a few years later it lost its function as seaplanes went out of use.

4.5 Philip L. Goodwin: *Brazil Builds* (New York: The Museum of Modern Art 1943) pp.114–15. Offset, printed in black, page sizes 8½ × 11" (21.6 × 27.9 cm).
Photograph © 2000 The Museum of Modern Art, New York.
Marcelo and Milton Roberto: Brazilian Press Association, Rio de Janeiro (1936–8).
Ground floor/ninth floor/roof garden.
*The brise-soleil is made up of diagonally fixed concrete blinds separated from the offices by a narrow corridor.*

4.6 Santos Dumont Airport, Rio de Janeiro. Site plan.
Seaplane Terminal was located adjacent to the Bay. The Central Terminal and the four hangars were located on the landfill formed from the spoil of the razed Morro do Castelo.
*Arquitetura e Urbanismo* (July–August 1937).

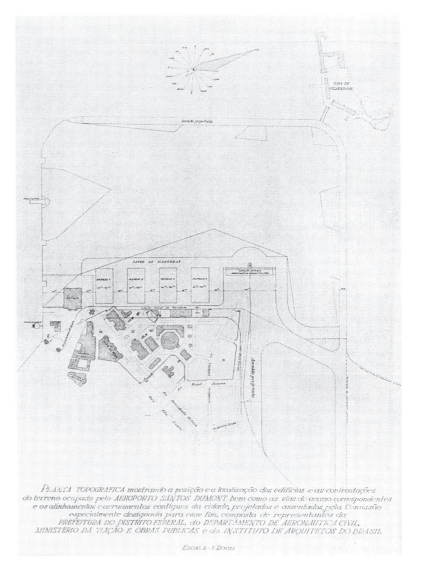

The building was then turned into a club for officials with a playground in place of the tropical garden and a swimming pool in place of the pond. It is now a Museum of Aviation.

While waiting for the Central Terminal to go ahead, the Roberto Brothers were commissioned to design the Hangar No. 1, which was built in 1940. A series of four identical hangars had been projected as part of the original airport plan; Hangar No. 1 was the first to be built, being finished in 1940 (Figure 4.10). It displayed a clear-cut solution to the problem of obtaining the maximum clear floor space and door openings; it had a concrete structure comprising five columns, 100 feet apart, supporting a longitudinal spine, off which pairs of cantilever ribs were hung. This provided a continuous clear space 75 feet deep. An office block was located on the west side, along the access road. The three floors were covered by fixed

Coastal Boat Passenger Station
Rio de Janeiro
Atilio Corrêa Lima, architect, 1940

The two elevations are very different in character. One has thin concrete arches
gaily scalloped across its flat white front. The other, with its rows of movable
louvres, is sober and substantial.

Estação de Barcas
Rio de Janeiro
Atilio Corrêa Lima, arquiteto, 1940

As duas fachadas são de caráter muito diferente. Uma com arcos de concreto
contínuos atravessando alegremente a fronteira branca e lisa. A outra com
filas de quebra-luzes móveis é sóbria e forte.

156        157

brise-soleil of the type used at the Brazilian Press Association. There was, of course, a striking difference between the office block and the hangar behind it.

During the years when the Seaplane Terminal was in full use as the main airport of Rio de Janeiro and Hangar No. 1 was completed, Goodwin considered them:

> models of their kind, surpassing the New York or Washington airport buildings in design, but not in area. Smaller airfields are not yet well equipped with the necessary buildings and those that exist are mediocre, although air travel has special importance in this huge and difficult country.[11]

The competition for the design of the Central Terminal was held in two phases, because the jury considered that none of the designs in the first submission had fulfilled the conditions of the brief. Instead, they selected five candidates to carry their designs forward to a second phase.[12] All the Modern competition entries resembled the *Grande Salle* of Le Corbusier's League of Nations Competition entry, with the juxtaposition of a long rectilinear volume and a smaller sculptural block.[13] For the second phase, the Robertos seemed determined to make an impression, as they presented, in addition to the drawings demanded in the brief, a model and a photomontage which, at that time, was still an unusual form of presentation

4.7 Philip L. Goodwin: *Brazil Builds* (New York: The Museum of Modern Art 1943) pp.156–7. Offset, printed in black, page sizes 8½ × 11" (21.6 × 27.9 cm).
Photograph © 2000 The Museum of Modern Art, New York.
Atilio Corrêa Lima: Boat Passenger Station, Rio de Janeiro (1940).
*The two elevations are very different in character. One has thin concrete arches gaily scalloped across its flat white front. The other, with its rows of movable louvres, is sober and substantial.*

Seaplane Station
Santos Dumont Airport, Rio de Janeiro
Atilio Corrêa Lima, architect, 1940

Situated on filled-in ground at the entrance to Guanabara Bay, this seaplane station will be used for both kinds of planes until the new airplane station by the brothers Roberto is completed.

The building has a reinforced concrete frame and is covered with slabs of yellow travertine imported from Argentina. Inside and outside, elegant spiral concrete staircases lead up to the balcony restaurant.

A light canopy with diagonal steel supports shades the path to the embarkation pier (top left) and the pleasant garden is embellished with a gay little concrete shelter.

Estação para hidro-aviões
Aeroporto Santos Dumont, Rio de Janeiro
Atilio Corrêa Lima, arquiteto, 1940

Situado no aterro sobre a baía Guanabara, este hidroporto será usado por qualquer espécie de aeroplanos até que o novo aeroporto, construído pelos irmãos Roberto, esteja pronto.

O edifício tem uma estrutura de cimento armado e é coberto de lajes de travertino importado da República Argentina. Dentro e fora, uma elegante escada também de concreto e um espiral conduz ao restaurante.

Uma leve cobertura com suportes diagonais de aço protege a passagem para o cais de embarque (à extremo esquerda). O jardim está ornamentado com um pequeno refúgio de concreto.

150

4.8 Philip L. Goodwin: *Brazil Builds* (New York: The Museum of Modern Art 1943) pp.150–1. Offset, printed in black, page sizes 8½ × 11″ (21.6 × 27.9 cm).
Photograph © 2000 The Museum of Modern Art, New York.
Atilio Corrêa Lima: Seaplane Terminal, Santos Dumont Airport, Rio de Janeiro (1937–8).
*This building has a reinforced concrete frame and is covered with slabs of yellow travertine imported from Argentina. Inside and outside, elegant spiral concrete staircases lead up to the balcony restaurant.*
*A light canopy with diagonal steel supports shades the path to the embarcation pier (top left) and the pleasant garden is embellished with a gay little concrete shelter.*

(Figure 4.11). This time the jury seemed completely satisfied with their choice and asserted that:

> With the laudable preoccupation of solving the problem rationally, distancing the artificial and the superfluous, and remaining precisely within his own time, the author of the project under study, showed that a functional utility can be combined with high spirituality and superior emotivity. [...] The new spirit which presided over the organisation of this project harmonises perfectly with its function.[14]

Their statement reveals a commitment to Modernist principles; their desire to mix the functional – *utilitarismo* – and the poetic – *espiritualismo* – reflects Le Corbusier's desire to combine the *objet-type* with the *objet a reaction poétique*.

The Robertos' solution was largely dictated by the conditions of the site and brief. The brief determined an area for the building, all of which was required for the extensive accommodation; it was to be arranged on two floors with a mezzanine, and only the control tower should protrude. The winning scheme added two front wings to this: one, smaller, housing the director's quarters, and the other, larger, housing a conference hall. Both wings were attached to the main block only on the upper two floors, leaving the ground level free for circulation; the large wing formed the sheltered entrance. The building contained a longitudinal hall with a transverse passengers' hall which gave a view straight from the entrance to the airfield. The two upper floors were intended for the offices of the Civil Aviation Administration, with private entrances through the wings. The structure consisted of circular concrete columns and floor slabs; the long façades were entirely glazed, protected on the western side by *brise-soleil*. The upper floors formed a Vierendeel girder to reduce the columns required in the halls.

The Robertos' scheme, although accepted by the jury, underwent several revisions. The scheme which was partly erected in 1944 maintained the original conception, but was confined to a single rectangular block. The roof gardens were reduced to allow for increased office space. These changes, however, were not to the detriment of the project; the airfield façade displayed a full-height colonnade broken only by the control tower, at one end of the building, the volume of the projecting transverse hall, framing the arrival gate, in the centre, and the projection of the restaurant mezzanine at the other end. The façade to the city had a single-storey

4.10 Philip L. Goodwin: *Brazil Builds* (New York: The Museum of Modern Art 1943) pp.154–5. Offset, printed in black, page sizes 8½ × 11" (21.6 × 27.9 cm).
Photograph © 2000 The Museum of Modern Art, New York.
Marcelo and Milton Roberto: Hangar No.1, Santos Dumont Airport, Rio de Janeiro (1940).
*By cantilevering the roof out from paired concrete columns, the designers were able to make their long walls entirely of sliding doors. The roof is suspended from the under side of the concrete trusses. Between the trusses are the windows of second-floor workshops and store-rooms.*
*The rectangular main façade with its rows of sunshades has little to do with the unusual construction behind.*

4.9 Atilio Corrêa Lima: Seaplane Terminal, Santos Dumont Airport, Rio de Janeiro (1937–8).
Interior, ground floor.
Originally the Departure Lounge with a panoramic view of the Bay on the left hand side.
© Zilah Quezado Deckker

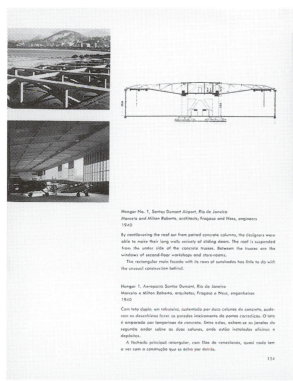

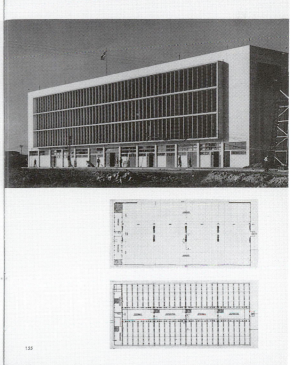

4.11 Marcelo and Milton Roberto:
Competition entry for the Central Terminal,
Santos Dumont Airport, Rio de Janeiro
(1937). First prize.
Model.
*Arquitetura e Urbanismo*
(November–December 1937).

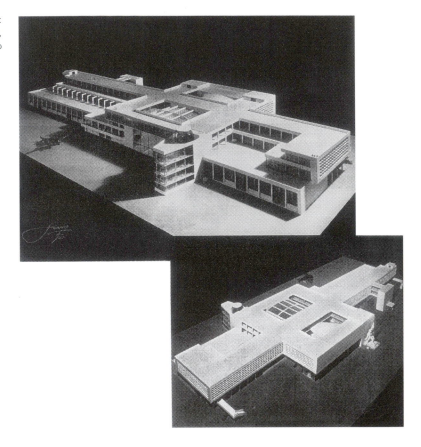

colonnade surmounted by two floors of *brise-soleil*; for several years this
stood as only the concrete frame without the louvres (Plate 7; Figure 4.12).

In spite of the protracted construction process, the airport worked very
well, and for many years formed the aerial gateway to Brazil, showing a
'Modern' face. It was considered by such important visitors as Henry-
Russell Hitchcock, in 1954, 'the most attractive airport in the world'; he
added that both the Seaplane Terminal and Santos Dumont 'remain
notable features of the Rio seafront'.[15]

4.12 Marcelo and Milton Roberto: Central
Terminal, Santos Dumont Airport, Rio de
Janeiro (1937–44).
Interior: embarkation lounge.
© Zilah Quezado Deckker.

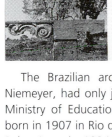

Museum of the Church of São Miguel
Rio Grande do Sul

A few hundred feet away from the ruins of São Miguel, SPHAN has recently built an attractive museum to house the large number of stone and wood carvings found in the church.

The architect of SPHAN's various restorations and constructions is Lucio Costa, well known for his work in modern architecture.

It is refreshing to find a society of this kind which realizes that only honestly contemporary design is suitable for such a museum. The simple glass-walled building provides a pleasantly non-competitive background for the brilliantly arranged sculpture. One of the finest pieces is the wooden figure of St. Catherine (over 6 feet high) shown at right.

Museu da Igreja de São Miguel
Rio Grande do Sul

A poucos centenas de metros das ruínas de São Miguel, o SPHAN construiu recentemente um encantador museu para abrigar o grande número de entalhes de pedra e madeira oriundos da igreja.

O arquiteto das várias restaurações e construções feitas pelo SPHAN é o engenheiro Lucio Costa, muito conhecido pelos seus trabalhos de arquitetura moderna.

É consolador encontrar-se uma instituição desta espécie que compreende que só um plano lídimamente moderno fôra adequada a tal museu. A construção, de simples paredes de vidro, proporciona um fundo agradável que não entra em competição com a escultura brilhantemente disposta. Uma das peças mais finas é a imagem de madeira de Santa Catarina (dois metros de altura) que se vê à direita.

42

The Brazilian architect who was to become most famous, Oscar Niemeyer, had only just emerged as a major talent with his work on the Ministry of Education Building and the Brazilian Pavilion. Niemeyer was born in 1907 in Rio de Janeiro, and graduated from the Escola Nacional de Belas Artes in 1934, thus he was a student during Costa's reforms. He worked as a draughtsman in the office of Lucio Costa and Carlos Leão. According to Costa, Niemeyer had not previously shown any special talent for architecture; his contact with Le Corbusier in 1936 acted as a catalyst for his talents.[16] Niemeyer acted as a draughtsman for Le Corbusier and thus must have drawn the presentation drawings from Le Corbusier's sketches for the Praia de Santa Luzia scheme for the Ministry of Education Building published in the *Œuvre Complète 1934–38*. Le Corbusier later described him to Costa as 'brave Oscar with his beautiful perspecties'.[17] It seems his sense of plastic form and elementary composition emerged on this project, together with Costa's interest in urban planning.

While working on the Ministry of Education Building, Niemeyer received, in 1937, his first private commission, for the Obra do Berço, completed in 1940 (Figure 4.14); this was illustrated in *Brazil Builds* with special attention paid to the vertically-pivoting *brise-soleil*. When SPHAN listed Ouro Preto, the colonial capital of Minas Gerais, in 1940, they decided to build a hotel to attract tourism, for which they commissioned Niemeyer. It was perhaps surprising that the commission did not go to Costa, who was then Director of Research at SPHAN, rather than to Niemeyer; Costa had been the architect of the SPHAN Museum of the Church of São Miguel in 1937, which was praised in *Brazil Builds* (Figure 4.13).[18] The hotel, still wrapped in scaffolding, was illustrated in *Brazil Builds*.

4.13 Philip L. Goodwin: *Brazil Builds* (New York: The Museum of Modern Art 1943) pp.42–3. Offset, printed in black, page sizes 8½ × 11" (21.6 × 27.9 cm).
Photograph © 2000 The Museum of Modern Art, New York.
Lucio Costa: Museum of the Church of São Miguel, Rio Grande do Sul (1937–8).
*A few hundred feet away from the ruins of São Miguel, SPHAN has recently built an attractive museum to house the large number of stone and wood carvings found in the church.*
*The architect of SPHAN's various restorations and constructions is Lucio Costa, well known for his work in modern architecture.*
*It is refreshing to find a society of this kind which realizes that only honestly contemporary design is suitable for such a museum. The simple glass-walled building provides a pleasantly non-competitive background for the brilliantly arranged sculpture. One of the finest pieces is the wooden figure of St. Catherine (over six feet high) shown at right.*

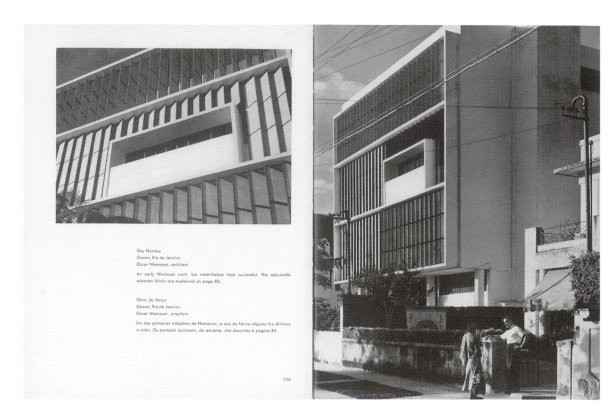

Day Nursery
Gavea, Rio de Janeiro
Oscar Niemeyer, architect

An early Niemeyer work, but nevertheless most successful. The adjustable
asbestos blinds are explained on page 86.

Obra do Berço
Gavea, Rio de Janeiro
Oscar Niemeyer, arquiteto

Um dos primeiros trabalhos de Niemeyer, o que de forma alguma lhe diminue
o valor. Os parasois ajustaveis, de amianto, vão descritos á pagina 86.

136

4.14 Philip L. Goodwin: *Brazil Builds* (New York: The Museum of Modern Art 1943) pp.136–7. Offset, printed in black, page sizes 8½ × 11" (21.6 × 27.9 cm).
Photograph © 2000 The Museum of Modern Art, New York.
Oscar Niemeyer: Obra do Berço Nursery, Rio de Janeiro (1937).
*The building is beautifully planned in relation to both use and climate, and its appearance seems well suited to its function.*

*The cleanliness and authority suggested by flat white stucco walls and precise geometric forms are relieved by the friendly scale p.138.*

*A bank of tall louvers, six feet high by one wide, can be worked by one of the nuns with no more trouble than it takes to turn a door handle. p.86.*

Niemeyer was fortunate to be championed by an exceptional patron, Juscelino Kubitschek (1902–76). Kubitschek had studied Medicine at the University of Minas Gerais before becoming Federal Deputy of Minas Gerais in 1935. He was appointed Mayor of the city of Belo Horizonte in 1940, and decided to expand the city by creating a garden suburb at Pampulha, about six miles from the old centre. Kubitschek had met Niemeyer through Gustavo Capanema, and chose him as architect for Pampulha not only because of his growing international reputation but because of his hotel in Ouro Preto. Kubitschek was later President of Brazil from 1957 to 1961 and commissioned Niemeyer to design the buildings at Brasília.

At Pampulha, an artificial lake was created by damming a river; the remaining alluvial plain became the airport. The focus of development was a series of leisure and cultural buildings around the lake: a casino, a yacht club, a Casa de Baile – a type of outdoor restaurant, and a church, with landscaping by Roberto Burle Marx. The choice of facilities was aimed at the upper echelons of society: physical education and pleasure balanced by spiritual guidance. The success of the scheme wildly exceeded the plan; the infrastructure was already overwhelmed in the early days.

Each structure displayed a different set of concerns. The Casa de Baile, located picturesquely on an island in the lake, had a free-form concrete roof with the cylindrical walls arranged freely in plan (Plate 11; Figure 4.15). It was still under construction when Goodwin saw it; nevertheless, he remarked that 'architecture and nature are delightfully intermingled'.[19]

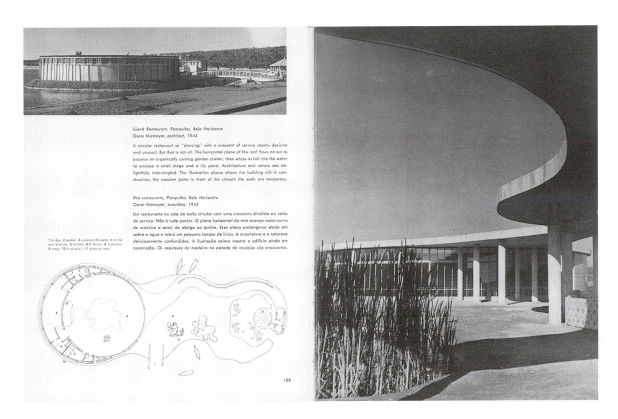

4.15 Philip L. Goodwin: *Brazil Builds* (New York: The Museum of Modern Art 1943) pp.188–9. Offset, printed in black, page sizes 8½ × 11" (21.6 × 27.9 cm).
Photograph © 2000 The Museum of Modern Art, New York.
Oscar Niemeyer: Casa de Baile, Pampulha, Belo Horizonte (1940–2).

The Casino consisted of a set of plain cubic volumes, almost 'International Style' (Plate 10; Figures 4.16 and 4.17). The interior gained a rich effect from quite simple materials, outside the reductivist canons of that style: gold mirrors, onyx floors and walls, and chromium steel columns. The Yacht Club had a butterfly roof (Figure 4.18), derived, perhaps, from Le Corbusier's project for the Errazuris house (1930), a feature also used later at a weekend house Niemeyer designed for Kubitschek nearby (1946).[20] The Church consisted of a series of shell vaults, with murals and *azulejos* by Portinari (Plates 12 and 13). The Church of São Francisco, however, was not completed until 1946, and thus not included in *Brazil Builds*. It caused a scandal among the religious hierarchy and was not consecrated until 1959.

Pampulha quickly became a heavily-populated residential area, but the buildings underwent a period of neglect. The Casino was closed in 1946 following a law prohibiting gambling. It was later converted into an Art Museum, a function it does not perform well, with its large glass surfaces blocked by solid panels and the dancing hall unused. The Casa de Baile was abandoned for many years and its restoration started only in 1990.

Goodwin related his overall impressions of the Pampulha development:

At Pampulha, the new development of the energetic upland city of Belo Horizonte, the municipality has just opened Oscar Niemeyer's delightful

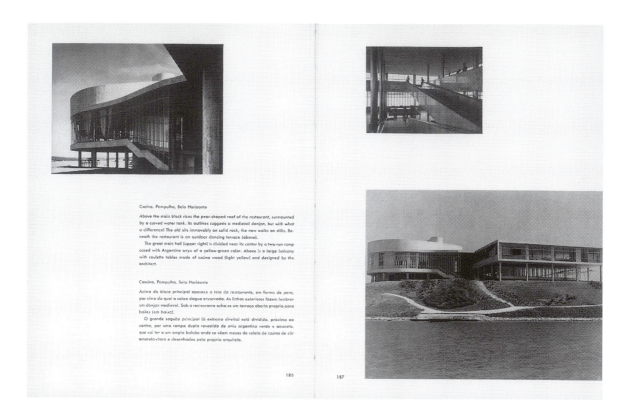

4.16  Philip L. Goodwin: *Brazil Builds* (New York: The Museum of Modern Art 1943) pp.186–7. Offset, printed in black, page sizes 8½ × 11″ (21.6 × 27.9 cm).
Photograph © 2000 The Museum of Modern Art, New York.
Oscar Niemeyer: Casino, Pampulha, Belo Horizonte (1940–2).

*Above the main block rises the pear-shaped roof of the restaurant, surmounted by a curved water tank. Its outlines suggest a medieval donjon, but with what a difference! The old sits immovably on solid rock, the new walks on stilts. Beneath the restaurant is an outdoor dancing terrace (above).*

*The great main hall (upper right) is divided near its center by a two-run ramp cased with Argentine onyx of a yellow-green colour. Above is a large balcony made of caúna wood (light yellow) and designed by the architect.*

casino. On a small promontory in the irregular artificial lake, its low cylindrical tower a landmark for the pleasure-loving public. An airy canopy shelters the big bronze figure of a semi-reclining woman by the sculptor August Zamoiski. Large areas of glass in metal frames make views of the lake and distant mountains a part of the decoration of the spacious interior.

Across the water is an island restaurant or 'dancing', seeming to follow the curves of the shore as it winds along to the yacht club beyond. [. . .] They form a related group, using similar materials even to the blue and white tile walls at their bases. Light supports, open walls, variety of line, cool color, what could be more right for these places of recreation?[21]

While the buildings in Rio de Janeiro and later Minas Gerais were determinedly Corbusian in character, those in São Paulo showed an allegiance to Italian Rationalism. The most prolific architect of the period, Rino Levi, had actually studied in Italy, graduating in 1926. The more positive attitude towards historic building typologies and construction methods within Rationalism meant that the buildings in São Paulo were more traditional in appearance. This may be exemplified by Bernard Rudofsky (1905–88), an Austrian architect who had lived in Italy during the early 1930s and in Brazil from 1938 to 1941. He designed two houses: the Frontini House (1940–1) and the Arnstein House (1941), which, by being planned around courtyards, were more Mediterranean than Brazilian in character.

However, when the 'Brazilian Style' was being formulated, it was their Modern aspects which were accentuated.

The first large scale building in São Paulo to call attention for its deliberate affiliation with Rationalism, the Edifício Esther (Figure 4.19), was commissioned, after a limited competition, by the owner of a sugar refinery as an investment. The site was in a new centre in São Paulo developing around the Praça da República; at that time, it was not known how the city would develop, so the client opted for a mixture of offices and apartments. The headquarters of the refinery was to occupy one of the floors and the remainder were to be rented.[22] The competition was won by Álvaro Vital Brazil and Adhemar Marinho (b 1909). Both had graduated in 1933 from the Escola Nacional de Belas Artes in Rio de Janeiro; they had been there during Costa's reforms. Álvaro Vital Brazil was living in Rio de Janeiro when he won the competition to design the Edifício Esther in 1936 but moved to São Paulo to oversee the works.

The Edifício Esther, completed in 1938, was an 11-storey block which utilised the possibilities of the reinforced concrete structure in a *plan libre*. The architects left the columns free-standing wherever it was acceptable, arguing that:

[we] did not see with this any impediment to forming good rooms for residence, much the opposite, we think that the columns will come to be highly decorative elements.[23]

The ground floor was occupied by shops; the three floors above it were for offices; the remaining eight floors was occupied with various types of

4.17 Oscar Niemeyer: Casino, Pampulha, Belo Horizonte (1940–2). Now Museu de Arte de Belo Horizonte.
Interior.
© Zilah Quezado Deckker.

4.18 Philip L. Goodwin: *Brazil Builds* (New York: The Museum of Modern Art 1943) pp.190–1. Offset, printed in black, page sizes 8½ × 11″ (21.6 × 27.9 cm).
Photograph © 2000 The Museum of Modern Art, New York.
Oscar Niemeyer: Yacht Club Pampulha, Belo Horizonte (1940–2).

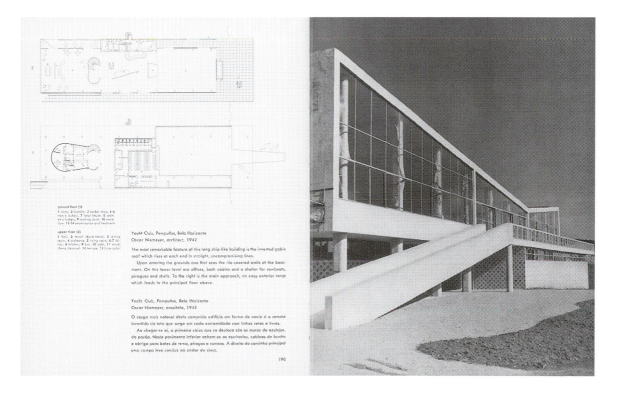

4.19 Philip L. Goodwin: *Brazil Builds* (New York: The Museum of Modern Art 1943) pp.118–19. Offset, printed in black, page sizes 8½ × 11″ (21.6 × 27.9 cm).
Photograph © 2000 The Museum of Modern Art, New York.
Álvaro Vital Brazil: Edifício Esther, São Paulo (1937).
*It would be difficult to find more modern living arrangements than those provided by this handsome São Paulo apartment house.*

apartments, from units of a room with bathroom and one-bedroom apartments on the lower floors, to three-bedroom split-level apartments, to four-bedroom penthouses on the eleventh floor; the basement contained a vast garage.

Because of its elaborate detailing – the brass handrails, numbering and lettering, the symbol of the Refinery on the front door and elsewhere, and the figured green marble covering the ground floor columns – the Edifício Esther may be considered to be an Art Deco design, but the architects did not view the decoration as a means by itself and stated that 'We were not so preoccupied with decorating or making effects, and if we decorated it was the result of "building".'[24] If the detailing of the halls had lost its visual rigour, the overall appearance of the building as well as the interior spaces of the apartments had not. They described their method of working as 'form follows function':

> From the detailed study of each floor and the resulting structure, the elevations or façades flourished naturally. Therefore we did not start from outside to inside, [...] but from inside to outside, because [...] any object should fulfil certain intrinsic functions.[25]

The result was a simple volume, the two front façades with elongated windows and verandas, and the two side façades with square windows and semicircular glass staircase enclosures. The circulation ran longitudinally, with

Vital Brazil Institute, Niterói, Rio de Janeiro
Álvaro Vital Brazil and Ademar Marinho, architects, 1942

In addition to the famous Butantã at São Paulo, Brazil now has this handsome
new laboratory for the preparation of snake bite serum.
The little windows pierced in the north façade are not for the snakes to look
out; they quite prosaically light the corridors behind. The laboratories are on
the south side of the building (left). Projected from the main block is the clearly
defined mass of the stair-hall.

Instituto Vital Brazil, Niterói, Rio de Janeiro
Álvaro Vital Brazil e Ademar Marinho, arquitetos, 1942

Como complemento do famoso Butantã de São Paulo, o Brasil possue agora
este vistoso laboratório para a preparação do soro antiofídico.
As pequenas janelas ao longo da fachada voltada para o norte não são
para as cobras olharem, mas sim para iluminar os corredores que ficam prós. O
laboratório acha-se instalado no lado sul do edifício (à esquerda). Projetando-se
do bloco principal, surge claramente delineado a massa da escadaria do
vestíbulo.

160

staircases at each end, and one in the centre, which served the fourth to the eleventh floors, and five elevators, two serving the office floors and the service entrances of the apartments and three for the residents' entrances. The façade was framed with planes of Vitrolite – a proprietary pigmented glass – attached to the corners, which functioned as an external rainwater pipe. The architects saw a parallel between this use of Vitrolite and the Baroque buildings of Minas Gerais which have the salients protected with stone, in particular with *pedra sabão*, a relatively durable material.[26]

Philip Goodwin, however, ignored this comparison, emphasising instead the Edifício Esther's virtue of providing a modern way of life, and the sun-protection system:

> Each pleasantly proportioned living room and bedroom opens widely to the outside through continuous eye-level bands of horizontally sliding steel sash, protected by roll-up, awning type wooden blinds.[28]

After the Edifício Esther, Vital Brazil moved to Niterói, a city which lay on the other side of the Bay from Rio de Janeiro, and executed a series of works: the Raul Vidal Elementary School and the Instituto Vital Brazil, which appeared in *Brazil Builds*. The Raul Vidal Elementary School consisted of a long, low, block with a hipped roof, on *pilotis*; the north elevation – the corridors – was covered with small square windows and the south – the classrooms – with large windows; the stair hall was a clearly

4.20 Philip L. Goodwin: *Brazil Builds* (New York: The Museum of Modern Art 1943) pp.160–1. Offset, printed in black, page sizes 8½ × 11" (21.6 × 27.9 cm).
Photograph © 2000 The Museum of Modern Art, New York.
Álvaro Vital Brazil: Instituto Vital Brazil, Niterói, Rio de Janeiro (1942).
*In addition to the famous Butantã at São Paulo, Brazil now has this handsome new laboratory for the preparation of snake bite serum.*
*The little windows pierced in the north façade are not for the snakes to look out; they quite prosaically light the corridors behind. The laboratories are on the south side of the building (left). Projected from the main block is the clearly defined mass of the stair-hall.*

articulated block. He justified lifting the building up by saying it provided a view of the Bay and a sheltered play area underneath the building. Vital Brazil used the same *parti* for the Instituto Vital Brazil, a new laboratory for the preparation of snake-bite serum, but with flat roofs and *pan-de-verre* on the south elevation (Figure 4.20).

Another *paulista* building which fitted within Goodwin's precepts was the 'Sedes Sapientiæ' School (Figure 4.21), also an example of a private enterprise. Founded as a private school for girls by the nuns of the Augustinian Order, the nuns decided to expand it in 1933 by offering Higher Education in the areas of Philosophy, Sciences and Letters. They owned a large site in a residential area close to the city centre, and decided to build a complete new building which they saw as a model college of its kind.[29]

The architect commissioned for the work was Rino Levi, who, by 1940, had already developed a solid career in São Paulo. Born in São Paulo in 1901 of Italian parents, Levi had graduated from the Escola Superiore di Roma in 1926. Returning to Brazil that same year, he worked first for a construction company before setting up in practice by himself.[30] Levi had been, like Warchavchik, a student of Piacentini, but they did not meet in Rome, but in Brazil, having worked in the same construction company. He had already built several houses, an apartment building – the Edifício Columbus – and several cinemas.[31] Even though Rino Levi was aware of the revolutionary architecture of the masters – Le Corbusier, having read *Vers une Architecture* when still in Rome, Gropius and Mies van der Rohe – he did not affiliate himself with them in particular:

> As if it could be any different, I suffer the influence of Italian architecture, above all that of Rome. Returning to Brazil, I made a deliberate effort to free myself of these influences.
>
> My interest was equally in all the other movements which reacted against eclecticism and which fought for a renewal of the arts. As such, I think that the influence I suffered came from various sources.[32]

In 1925, when still in Rome, Rino Levi wrote in a São Paulo newspaper expressing his views on architecture, which showed that he did share the interest of the revolutionary *carioca* group in new materials and construction methods:

> Architecture, as mother of the arts, is the one which most is subject to the influx of modernity, and to the new materials available to the artist, to the great progress achieved in the last years in the building techniques, and above all, to the new spirit which reigns in opposition to cold and insipid neo-classicism. Therefore, practicality and economy, an architecture of volumes, straight lines, few decorative elements, but sincere and well-used, not masking the structure of the building to achieve effects which in many cases are disproportional to their end, and which always constitute a false and artificial thing.[33]

He did not share their aesthetic aims, however, and his buildings remain more Moderne than International Style.

The programme for the 'Sedes Sapientiæ' School involved all the usual

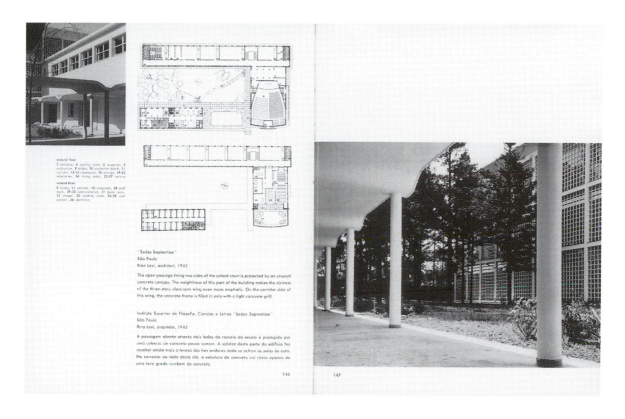

educational facilities, with the addition of residences for the students. The design comprised three distinct blocks: the School, the Auditorium, and the Residences. The School block had classrooms ranged along a corridor, faced with fixed glazing held in concrete frames. The Auditorium block housed an auditorium on the ground floor, with a chapel and library above opening onto a roof terrace. In the Residence block, all the common areas such as the restaurants were located on the ground floor, with two floors of bedrooms above. The *parti* was similar, in fact, to the Bauhaus, Dessau (1925–6) by Walter Gropius, although far more traditional in appearance. The blocks were linked by an unusual corrugated concrete canopy, which contrasted with the plainness of the buildings. However, only the Auditorium block had a flat roof; the others had hipped tiled roofs hidden by concrete cornices. Philip Goodwin, who visited several of Rino Levi's buildings, considered the 'Sedes Sapientiæ' Levi's best.[34] He was attracted by the canopy, which he felt emphasised the 'airiness of the three-storey classroom wing' (Plate 9 and Figure 4.22).[35]

In 1942 these few Modern buildings constituted almost the entire production of European Modern architecture in Brazil. They stood out markedly from contemporary buildings, especially the almost completed Ministry of Education, and were still the subject of criticism and indignation from both architects and the popular press. It was Philip Goodwin's self-appointed task to demonstrate that these disparate buildings had a unified expression with a truly Brazilian flavour.

4.21 Philip L. Goodwin: *Brazil Builds* (New York: The Museum of Modern Art 1943) pp.146–7. Offset, printed in black, page sizes 8½ × 11" (21.6 × 27.9 cm).
Photograph © 2000 The Museum of Modern Art, New York.
Rino Levi: 'Sedes Sapientiæ', São Paulo (1942).
*The open passage lining two sides of the school court is protected by an unusual concrete canopy. The weightiness of this part of the building makes the airiness of the three-storey classroom wing even more emphatic. On the corridor side of this wing, the concrete frame is filled in only with a light concrete grill.*

4.22  Rino Levi: 'Sedes Sapientiæ', São Paulo (1942).
Courtyard.
© Zilah Quezado Deckker.

## Notes

1  Lévi-Strauss: *Tristes Tropiques* p.118.

2  Conversation with Roberto Cerqueira Cesar, October 1988. Roberto Cerqueira Cesar was Rino Levi's partner from 1944. In 1934, Vargas created the Departamento de Propaganda e Difusão Cultural within the Ministry of Justice; in 1939 it became an independent body subordinated directly to the President as the Departamento de Imprensa e Propaganda (DIP). Schwartzman: *Tempos de Capanema*, pp.87–9.

3  'Como Nasceu a Casa do Jornalista' *Boletim da Associação Brasileira de Imprensa* (April 1957) p.5.

4  Frank Lloyd Wright: *An Autobiography* (New York 1932; London: Quartet Books 1977) p.517.

5  Jorge Machado Moreira & Ernani de Vasconcellos: 'Ante-Projeto para a Associação Brasileira de Imprensa' *PDF* (November 1936) pp.334–41. Oscar Niemeyer: 'Ante-Projeto para a Associação Brasileira de Imprensa' *PDF* (September 1936) pp.261–73.

6  'O Edifício da ABI' *Arquitetura e Urbanismo* (September–December 1940) p.269.
   *O nosso trabalho é baseado nas leis imutáveis da Grande Arquitetura de todos os tempos, e nos principios da Arquitetura Moderna, frutos da Técnica Contemporânea:*
   *'Estrutura independente*
   *plano livre*
   *Fachada livre*
   *Této-jardim'.* [sic]

7  'O Edifício da ABI' *Arquitetura e Urbanismo* (September–December 1940) pp.266–8.
   *É impossível hoje (como nas grandes épocas, etc.) superar o trabalho de prancheta do arquiteto, do trabalho do mesmo no 'chantier'.*
   *Nosso edifício é um todo. Sua caracteristica principal, unidade. Como uma arvore, um ovo, um corpo humano. Todos os elementos terão que ser realizados sob um espirito unico. Desde a estrutura até os letreiros indicativos, do sistema de alvenarias aos balcões e armações, o ritmo deverá ser constante.* [sic]

8  'Ante-Projeto para a Associação Brasileira de Imprensa' *PDF* (September 1936) pp.261–73.
   *O 'brise-soleil' que Le Corbusier estudou e projectou para varios edificios na Algeria, paiz de condições climatericas, sob certos aspectos, semelhante ás nossas, nos parece a solução mais indicada.*

9   *Brazil Builds* p.112.

10  Seaplane Terminal: architects Augusto Vasconcellos Junior, Paulo de Camargo Almeida and William Preston; engineers Junqueira Ayres and Alberto de Mello Flores. *Arquitetura e Urbanismo* (March–April 1937) p.99. Central Terminal: architects Nestor de Figueredo, Paulo Santos, Mauricio Joppert, Ricardo Antunes, Augusto Vasconcellos Junior, engineers Junqueira Ayres and Alberto de Mello Flores. *Arquitetura e Urbanismo* (November–December 1937) p.297.

11  *Brazil Builds* p.93.

12  The other four were, in order of final classification: Atilio Corrêa Lima, Renato Mesquita and Paulo Camargo Almeida; José Teódolo Silva; Angelo Bruhns; Benedito de Barros, Gastão Tassano and Flavio Amilcar Reis do Nascimento. 'Aeroporto Santos Dumont' *Arquitetura e Urbanismo* (November–December 1937) p.297.

13  *Œuvre Complète 1910–29* pp.160–73.

14  'Aeroporto Santos Dumont' *Arquitetura e Urbanismo* (November–December 1937) p.295.
    *Com a louvavel preocupação de resolver racionalmente o problema, afastando o artificial e o supérfluo e conservando-se precisamente dentro de sua época, o autor do projeto em estudo, demonstrou que o utilitarismo integral das funções pode ser concebido com elevado espiritualismo e superior emotividade. [. . .] O espirito novo que presidiu á organização deste projeto harmoniza-se perfeitamente com a sua função.* [sic]

15  Henry-Russell Hitchcock, *Latin American Architecture since 1945* (New York: Museum of Modern Art 1955) p.31.

16  Lucio Costa: 'Presença de Le Corbusier' *Lucio Costa: registro de uma vivência* (São Paulo: Empresa das Artes 1995) p.152.

17  Le Corbusier to Lucio Costa, 21 November 1936, FLC I3–3.35. *'brave Oscar avec ses belles perspectives'*.

18  Brazil's finest Jesuit mission church. *Brazil Builds* pp.40–3.

19  *Brazil Builds* p.188.

20  *Œuvre Complète 1929–34* pp.48–51. Stamo Papadaki: *The Works of Oscar Niemeyer* (New York: Reinhold 1950; repr. 1951) p.108.

21  *Brazil Builds* pp.93–4.

22  Álvaro Vital Brazil: *Álvaro Vital Brazil: 50 Anos de Arquitetura* (São Paulo: Nobel 1986) p.21.

23  'Edifício Esther' *Acrópole* (May 1938) p.54.
    *não vimos com isso nenhum impedimento de formar bons salões de habitação, muito pelo contrario, pensamos que as colunas somente vieram a ser elementos altamente decorativos.*

24  'Edifício Esther' *Acrópole* (May 1938) p.54. *'Não tivemos tão pouco a preocupação de decorar ou enfeitar, e se decoramos foi o resultado do "construir"'.*

25  'Edifício Esther' *Acrópole* (May 1938) p.54.
    *Do estudo detalhado de cada plano e da estructura resultante, aflorou naturalmente a elevação ou fachada. Portanto não partimos de fóra para dentro, [. . .] mas sim de dentro para fóra, pois [. . .] qualquer objeto deve cumprir determinadas funcções intrinsicas.* [sic]

26  'Edifício Esther' *Acrópole* (May 1938) p.54.

27  *Brazil Builds* p.118.

28  *Brazil Builds* p.120.

29  Conversation with Roberto Cerqueira Cesar, October 1988.

30  Statement by Rino Levi, 14 August 1964. Rino Levi Archives.

31  Renovation for Casa Silva Teles, 1927; Houses at Rua Mazzini, a group of small houses for rent, 1931; Casa Ferrabino, 1931; Edifício Columbus, 1932; Casa Schiesser, 1934; Casa Santo Amaro, 135; Cine UFA Palace, 1936; Cine Universo, 1936; Cine UFA Palace, Recife, 1938.

32  Statement by Rino Levi, 14 August 1964. Rino Levi Archives.
    *como não podia deixar de ser, sofri influência da arquitetura italiana, sobretudo a de Roma. Voltando ao Brasil, fiz um esforço para me libertar dessa influência.*
    *meu interesse era igualmente por todos os demais movimentos que reagiam contra o ecletismo e que lutavam por uma renovação da arte. Assim, penso que a influência que sofri vinham de vários setores.*

33  Rino Levi: 'A Architectura Moderna' *O Estado de São Paulo* (15 October 1925). Rino Levi Archives.
    *A Architectura* [sic]*, como arte mãe, é a que mais se resente dos influxos modernos e devido aos novos materiaes, á disposição do artista, aos grandes progressos conseguidos*

*nestes ultimos annos na technica da construcção e sobretudo ao novo espirito que reina em contraposição ao neo-classicismo frio e insipido. Portanto, praticidade e economia, architectura de volumes, linhas simples poucos elementos decorativos, mas sinceros e bem em destaque, nada de mascarar a estructura do edificio para conseguir effeitos que na maioria das vezes são desproporcionados ao fim, e que reflectem sempre uma coisa falsa e artificial.* [sic]

34  Conversation with Roberto Cerqueira Cesar, October 1988.
35  *Brazil Builds* p.146.
36  *Brazil Builds* pp.38–9, 182–8.
37  *Brazil Builds* p.111.

# PART III
## THE MUSEUM AND THE WAR

Brazil knows more individual freedom and contentment than most of our European countries. So one of our greatest hopes for future civilisation and peace in our world, which has been destroyed by hatred and madness, rests on the existence of Brazil, whose desires are aimed exclusively at pacific development. Wherever ethical forces are at work, our task is to strengthen those intentions. Wherever in our troubled times we find hope for a new future in new zones, it is our duty to point out this country and these possibilities.

Stefan Zweig: *Brazil: Land of the Future*, 1942

# 5 The Museum of Modern Art, New York, and architecture

When the 'Brazil Builds' exhibition opened at the Museum of Modern Art in New York, Philip Goodwin, the Director of the Architectural Department, announced that The Museum of Modern Art, New York, had undertaken a 'flying trip' to Brazil:

> with a keen desire to know more about Brazilian architecture, especially their solutions for the problem of controlling heat and light on large exterior glass surfaces.[1]

The idea of a Museum being interested in a particular device of architecture and searching for it in, of all places, Brazil, is a striking one. Philip Goodwin's announcement expressed two important points: firstly, that the Museum had a strong commitment to Modern architecture, and, secondly, that there were certain conditions in America which led a museum to be aware that there was architecture of significance in Brazil.

In 1942, the year the 'flying trip' to Brazil was undertaken, the Museum was already well established as a major propagandist of Modernism in various fields of the arts. Their exhibition programme of architecture was intended to propagate and legitimatise Modern architecture in America. This intention had been clear from their first architectural exhibition, 'Modern Architecture: International Exhibition', held in 1932 which coined the term 'International Style'. With the 'Brazil Builds' exhibition, the Museum played a similar role by selecting and presenting as an 'original contribution to Modern Architecture'[2] a group of Modern buildings in Brazil which subsequently came to be regarded as the first 'national style'[3] within the Modern Movement.

Established in 1929 to display the private collections of Modern art of its Founders – Abby Aldrich Rockefeller (1874–1948, the wife of John Davison Rockefeller jr (1874–1960)), Mary Quinn Sullivan, and Miss Lizzie (Lillie) Bliss (1864–1931) – and Trustees, the Museum of Modern Art was soon propelled into a more radical programme.[4] They appointed Alfred Barr (1902–81), an associate professor of History of Art and already known as a 'young radical', to be its first Director. Barr had graduated from Princeton and Harvard, and had gone on to teach at Wellesley

College, then a fashionable ladies' College outside Boston. His course there in Modern Art was radical for the time, consisting of studies of film, photography, music, theatre, architecture, and industrial design, apart from the usual painting and sculpture. His recommendations for the multi-departmental organisation of the Museum paralleled his Wellesley course:

> in time the Museum would probably expand beyond the narrow limits of painting and sculpture in order to include departments devoted to draw- ings, prints and photography, typography, the arts of design in com- merce and industry, architecture (a collection of *projets* and *maquettes*), stage designing, furniture and decorative arts. Not the least important collection might be the *filmotek*, a library of films.[5]

The marriage of Barr and the formidable Committee was a happy one. The Trustees were all heirs to immense fortunes; they collected traditional as well as Modern art. They were not the pioneer collectors of Modern art in America, nor did the Museum hold the pioneering show of Modern art in New York.[6] The Museum was intended to provide public vindication of their taste in Modern art; the financial benefits were of secondary import- ance. The bulk of the acquisitions were donations from the Trustees; they took advantage of the law which allowed income tax exemption at market rates, rather than purchase price, for donations of works of art to museums and educational institutions.[7] For relatively small investments, they could benefit enormously from the increase in value of works of art engendered by the success of the Museum. Purchases were not, therefore, a cost-effective way of acquiring works, and the purchase budget was almost nil. The operating costs were paid by the Trustees; Philip Johnson (b. 1906) later recalled that three things – 'money, money, and money' – were required to maintain a position as Trustee.[8] This meant that the Museum was continually looking to share costs by preparing travelling exhibitions and seeking government sponsorship. Wages for staff were low; the staff needed to work to a large extent 'for love' and many were fortunately able to do so. The compensation, or rather the magnet, for many – Barr included – was the unprecedented opportunity and support, and the enthusiasm of the Trustees, for a Museum devoted to Modern Art.

In contrast to a conventional museum, the permanent collection was small and of relatively minor importance; publicity was therefore an important factor in the Museum and was self-consciously pursued. In 1933 they employed a full-time publicity manager. Publications, too, were an important part of the Museum's character. In the early days, catalogues had been free for members and 'at cost' for sale copies, in the belief that they were of important propaganda value. In 1939, as part of the reorgan- isation of the new President of the Museum, Nelson Rockefeller (1908–79; the second son of Abby Aldrich Rockefeller), Monroe Wheeler (1899–1988) was brought in to supervise the publications, previously entirely within Barr's jurisdiction. Even before he took over, the publica- tions of the Museum had already established a reputation for the excel- lence of their design. They were more than exhibition catalogues: most were monographs on their subjects, aimed at both scholars and the general public. Under Wheeler's control, sales increased dramatically: he reported a 300 per cent increase between 1942 and 1945.[9]

In its third season the Museum ventured into a new field by opening its first exhibition of architecture: 'Modern Architecture: International Exhibition' (Figure 5.1). The possibility of holding an exhibition of Modern architecture at the Museum was due to Barr's desire for a Museum covering all modes of art, and the desire of its organisers, Henry-Russell Hitchcock (1903–87) and Philip Johnson, to display in America the advanced architecture they admired in Europe. In 1931, Hitchcock and Johnson had travelled throughout Europe, photographing buildings which they regarded as good examples of Modern architecture; to these, they added other buildings in the United States to form the basis for an exhibition on Modern architecture.

Hitchcock was at the beginning of his career as an architectural historian, having graduated from Harvard in 1927; he had already published several works on Modern architecture.[10] Philip Johnson had studied Classics and Philosophy at Harvard, and after graduating in 1930, he volunteered his services to the Museum. Without any formal training as an architect, he extended his interests not only to architecture, but also design.

The 'Modern Architecture: International Exhibition' set the pattern for the format and content of future architectural exhibitions at the Museum. It ran from 9 February to 23 March 1932; in it were displayed models, photographs and drawings of work by 40 architects in the style dubbed 'International' by its organisers. The show was split into three parts: a survey of the extent of Modern Architecture, a closer examination of the leaders, and a section on housing. A catalogue, variably called *Modern Architecture* or *Modern Architects*, but with the same contents, accompanied the exhibition.

Hitchcock's and Johnson's emphasis upon aesthetics and style, and deliberate avoidance of social issues, could also be taken as the policy of the Museum in general. A left-wing political orientation would not have been acceptable to the Trustees, nor would it have been appealing to most of the American public. When the Mexican painter Diego Rivera was commissioned by John D. Rockefeller to paint a mural, 'Man at the Crossroads Looking towards His Future', in the great hall of the RCA Building in 1932, which included a portrait of Lenin, he was not allowed to complete the mural; it was covered up and later destroyed.[11]

In New York the exhibition received extensive publicity: an audience of 33,000 attended the exhibition in the Museum; its influence was further enhanced, firstly, by being available to a much larger public on tour, and, secondly, by the simultaneous publication of *The International Style: Architecture since 1922* by the same authors. The exhibition travelled for two years in its original form to ten museums and one department store, which had subscribed to its cost, and, for six years, in a smaller version, to schools and colleges. It set a pattern for travelling exhibitions which later became a norm; the Department of Circulating Exhibitions was set up on the basis of its success.[12]

The impact of this exhibition on the architectural scene in America and the establishment of the 'International Style' as the approved image of the

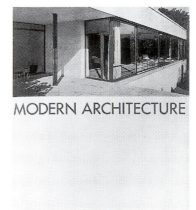

MODERN ARCHITECTURE

MUSEUM OF MODERN ART

5.1 *Modern Architecture* (New York: The Museum of Modern Art 1932). Offset, printed in colour, page sizes 10 × 7½" (25.4 × 19.1 cm). The Museum of Modern Art Library, The Museum of Modern Art, New York.
Photograph © 2000 The Museum of Modern Art, New York.

twentieth century has been a matter of controversy ever since.[13] For the Museum, the show proved to be a successful entry onto unfamiliar ground and opened the possibility for future innovations. It led to the immediate formation of a Department of Architecture, with Philip Johnson as chairman.

The Department of Architecture quickly expanded into other fields, with shows of furniture and decorative arts curated by Philip Johnson: 'Objects 1900 and Today' (1933), 'Walker Evans: Photographs of Nineteenth Century Houses' (1933) and 'Machine Art' (1934). 'Machine Art' displayed products of industrial design which were all in mass-production and were intended as a 'shopping guide' for the public as much as an exhibition of good design. Johnson was also involved in another exhibition: 'America Can't Have Housing?' (1934). This exhibition was on the benefits that public housing policies might bring in alleviating the terrible housing conditions brought about by the Depression, and included the reconstruction in the Museum of a typical New York slum dwelling, complete with live cockroaches.[14]

In 1935, Johnson became involved in right-wing politics and left the Museum;[15] Philip Goodwin, a Trustee since 1934 and practising architect, was appointed Chairman of the Architectural Committee, with Ernestine Fantl (1907–83) as Curator. John McAndrew took over as Curator in 1937, until his departure in 1940. Elizabeth Mock (b. 1911) joined as a freelance staff member in 1937; she had been a Taliesin Fellow and was very active in the Museum until 1946.

The Department of Architecture produced many exhibitions specifically on Modern architecture, some of which met with enormous success and became landmarks in their subject. Three main trends can be identified in their pre-war programme: the historical basis, the works of the masters, and the confirmation of the widespread acceptance of Modernism.

The first trend included exhibitions of the work of nineteenth-century and early-twentieth-century architects who could be described as precursors or pioneers of Modernism. These exhibitions were planned by Hitchcock and Johnson and made apparent a line of investigation which they adopted after 'Modern Architecture', in which they tried to identify the roots of Modern architecture in the United States. They travelled around the Mid-West collecting photographs for 'Early Modern Architecture: Chicago 1870–1910' which opened in January 1933. Particular emphasis was given to the work of Henry Hobson Richardson, Louis Sullivan and Frank Lloyd Wright.[16] Hitchcock's interest in the work of these architects prompted an exhibition and book 'The Architecture of Henry Hobson Richardson and His Time' (1936) in which he was portrayed as 'the great pioneer of American Architecture',[17] and an exhibition 'Louis Sullivan 1856–1924' (1948), in which he was portrayed as the originator of the Modern skyscraper.[18]

The second trend was the investigation of the work of the masters of Modern Architecture. This can be seen as a continuation of the Museum's commitment to the particular brand of Modernism it had identified in the first exhibition. It led to a series of one-man or one-building exhibitions on the work of the figures shown at the 'Modern Architecture' exhibition: 'The Philadelphia Savings Fund Society Building by Howe and Lescaze'

(1934); 'Recent Works by Le Corbusier' (1935), which was opened by the architect himself followed by a lecture tour of the United States arranged by the Museum; 'A New House by Frank Lloyd Wright: Fallingwater' (1938), 'Bauhaus 1919–28' (1938), which brought Walter Gropius to prominence, 'Architecture and Furniture by Alvar and Aito Aalto' (1938), 'The Architecture of Eric Mendelsohn 1914–40' (1941), and 'Mies Van der Rohe' (1947). Hitchcock later asserted that the individual shows were the result rather than the cause of their subjects' fame; they had been brought to prominence by the 'Modern Architecture' exhibition.[19]

A third tendency was that the Museum looked at the work of Modern architects in the United States and other countries to prove an international acceptance of Modernism. These included 'Modern Architecture in California' (1935), which gave emphasis to the works of Richard Neutra; 'Modern Exposition Architecture' (1936), which traced the development of Modern exhibition pavilions from Paxton's Crystal Palace, through Le Corbusier's Pavillon d'Esprit Nouveau, Mies van der Rohe's Barcelona Pavilion, and Gunnar Asplund's Stockholm Exhibition; 'Modern Architecture in England' (1937) and 'T.V.A. Architecture and Design' (1941–2).

With the outbreak of war, the Museum turned to the United States, and to neutral countries like Sweden and Brazil, which had not suffered destruction, for subject matter. The exhibitions 'Stockholm Builds' and 'Brazil Builds' followed in 1940 and 1943 respectively, and 'Built in USA: since 1932' in 1944. At the end of the Second World War, the success of the Museum's self-declared policy of 'the discovery and proclamation of excellence'[20] in the arts was clearly recognised by its contemporaries:

> The record of the Museum is an astonishing and enviable one for any institution which has existed a brief decade and a half. In that time it has achieved both national leadership and international fame. Neither is easily won. Both are well-deserved rewards of a wisely flexible policy, generous private support, and the unremitting intellectual labour of a brilliantly endowed staff.[21]

## Notes

1  *Brazil Builds:* p.7.
2  *Brazil Builds:* p.7.
3  Reyner Banham: *Guide to Modern Architecture* (London: Architectural Press 1962) p.36.
4  Russell Lynes: *Good Old Modern: An Intimate History of the Museum of Modern Art* (New York: Atheneum 1973) p.14. The Trustees also included the important American collectors A. Conger Goodyear, Chester Dale, Duncan Philips and Paul Sachs.
5  'A New Art Museum', brochure issued in July 1929. *MoMA: The History and the Collection* (London: Thames and Hudson 1984) p.12.
6  The first show of Modern art in New York had been the Armory Show in 1913.
7  Lynes relates that they received, therefore, a public subsidy far in excess of any European museum. *Good Old Modern* p.314.
8  Lynes: *Good Old Modern* p.435. In 1939, the costs for the fiscal year 1940 were estimated at $500,000, and the revenue at $200,000.
9  Lynes: *Good Old Modern* p.218.
10  Introduction to *Frank Lloyd Wright, Maître de l'Architecture Moderne I*, Paris 1928; *Modern Architecture: Romanticism and Reintegration* (New York 1929); *J.J.P. Oud* (Paris 1931).
11  Myer Kutz: *Rockefeller Power* (New York: Simon and Schuster 1974).

12  Henry-Russell Hitchcock and Philip Johnson: *The International Style: Architecture since 1922* (New York: W.W. Norton 1932; repr. 1966). *The Bulletin of the Museum of Modern Art* (Summer 1954) p.4.

13  See Terence Riley: *The International Style: Exhibition 15 and The Museum of Modern Art* (New York: Rizzoli 1992).

14  A. Conger Goodyear: *The Museum of Modern Art: The First Ten Years* (New York: [the author] 1943) p.113.

15  Lynes: *Good Old Modern* p.92.

16  'Early Modern Architecture: Chicago 1870–1910' Catalogue, Museum of Modern Art, New York (1933).

17  *The Bulletin of the Museum of Modern Art* (October 1934). Henry-Russell Hitchcock: *The Architecture of Henry Hobson Richardson and his Time* (New York: Museum of Modern Art 1936; repr. Cambridge MA: MIT Press 1966).

18  'Louis Sullivan 1856–1924' Catalogue, Museum of Modern Art, New York (1948).

19  'Le Corbusier and the United States' *Zodiac* 16 (1966) p.10.

20  Philip Goodwin, Preface, in *Built in USA: since 1932* (New York: Museum of Modern Art 1945) p.8.

21  Agnes Mongan, Curator of the Fogg Museum, *Art News* (August 1944). Lynes: *Good Old Modern* p.257.

# 6  'America for the Americans'

It was more than the availability of subject matter which led the Museum of Modern Art, New York, to Brazil, however. The increase in interest by the Museum reflected the growing importance, brought about by the war, of the other American nations to the United States. Philip Goodwin revealed the reasons behind *Brazil Builds* in his foreword:

> The Museum of Modern art, New York and the American Institute of Architects in the spring of 1942 were both anxious to have closer relations with Brazil, a country which was to be our future ally.[1]

Goodwin's statement indicates that, besides the Museum's 'keen desire' to pursue Modernism in general, it had ulterior motives in its interest in Brazil in particular.

Relations between the United States and Latin America had developed from the early nineteenth century and had passed through three distinct phases before the end of the Second World War, dependent on their relative economic strengths and their relations to global economic and political circumstances.[2]

In the first phase, from 1823 to 1880, the United States, itself a newly-created republic, became a symbol of post-colonial success for the Latin American nations which were also emerging from European colonisation. Although the United States did not yet have the means of becoming a hemispheric power in the early nineteenth century, it attempted to assert its leadership in the Americas with the 'Monroe Doctrine', promulgated in 1823, which was intended to exclude Europe from the New World. It declared that:

> The American continents, by the free and independent condition which they have assumed and maintained, are henceforth not to be considered as subject for colonization by an European powers [sic].[3]

The 'Monroe Doctrine' met with considerable sympathy in Latin America and popularity in the United States but, in the early nineteenth century, it remained more a set of ideas than a functioning inter-American system based upon a community of interest. In spite of the United States' early attempts to create Pan American integration, the first Pan American Conference was not held until 1889; during most of the nineteenth century, Europe remained Latin America's greatest influence, with Britain exercising the predominant market role and France influencing the cultural scene. France had coined the name Latin America in 1860 to assert the primacy of its influence there; the term Latin referred to France, not to Iberia. Nevertheless, the 'Monroe Doctrine' became an important part of United States–Latin America policy for the next century. The United States later called upon the doctrine to justify both its military interventions in other American Republics and the defence of the hemisphere against non-American nations.

The second phase, from 1880 to 1933, was marked by increased investment in Latin America in general, and military interventions to support its own interests, in Central America in particular. By 1880, economic growth and industrial development in the United States had led to a new type of interest in Latin America, as North American industrialists looked to their immediate neighbours in the south for the supply of raw materials and for markets for their goods. Economic expansion was followed by political imperialism, which led to the creation of several 'protectorate states' in Central America – Cuba, Haiti, Panama, Dominican Republic, and Nicaragua. As the century came to an end, the United States could claim that it was: 'practically sovereign on this continent, and its fiat is law upon the subject to which it confines its interposition'.[4]

The third phase, from 1933 to 1945, was marked by a redefinition of United States policy to Latin America, one that stressed the importance of 'good neighbourhood' among hemispheric nations while refraining from direct intervention. This new approach was brought about by the Depression and the coming of the Second World War, and was parallel to the domestic policies of the 'New Deal' which President Franklin Roosevelt announced when he took office in 1933; Roosevelt immediately instituted programmes of Government intervention such as the Agricultural Adjustments Act, the National Industrial Recovery Act and the Tennessee Valley Authority. The 'Good Neighbour' policy was also announced in 1933; through this policy, the United States gave up direct intervention in favour of more subtle forms of domination, with the intention of creating confidence among Latin Americans. Roosevelt expressed his intentions as:

> a new approach that I am talking about to these South American things. Give them a share. They think they are just as good as we are, and many of them are.[5]

The United States was, in fact, seeking more than neighbourliness: it was seeking economic and political hegemony over its neighbours.

In South America, however, the United States had to rely more on diplomacy than force. The First World War brought South America into the United States' economic orbit: on one hand, it closed off European markets, and on the other, it brought forward the United States as an economic power. The need for markets on both sides bound the United States and South America into closer economic relations.

Initially, the 'Good Neighbour' policy emphasised the need for economic reciprocity between the United States and the other American
nations. This was viewed with scepticism by Brazil which had been profit-
ing from trade with Germany. Coming out of the Depression, Germany's
search for new markets led it to be interested in Brazil, because, as they
both lacked hard currency, they could operate a barter system of trade.
This made German goods cheaper and more accessible than American
ones, thus making trade with Germany easier and more profitable than
with the United States.[6]

Viewed from the 1930s, without the benefit of hindsight, the compet-
ing efforts of Germany and the United States to assist nationalist programmes must have looked equally inviting. President Getúlio Vargas
played one off against the other between 1935 and 1941 to gain advantages for his nation.[7] Even after the British naval blockade stopped commercial traffic with Germany, the Nazis continued to promise huge
commodity deals to Brazil, and the Brazilians continued to bargain with
them to win concessions from the North Americans.

As the war broke out across Europe and the struggle for the Latin
American market took on ideological overtones and greater strategic
significance, the United States focused its attention on the threat of Nazi
penetration in the Americas, and the 'Good Neighbour' policy came to
mean a commitment to the Allied cause. While Germans troops advanced
in Europe, Roosevelt began to prepare the continent for defence. The
necessity of preparing to meet the German advances acted to catapult the
United States out of its policy of non-intervention and into a frenzy of
activity. A nationwide radio broadcast in the spring of 1938 by Fiorello
LaGuardia, Mayor of New York City, warned:

> For the maintenance of our economic well-being, for the preservation of
> peace, it is vital that we take immediate steps to eliminate this new
> growing sore on the soil of the Western Hemisphere. In this way, we may
> lay the foundation of peace and security for our world of the future. A
> united people in the Western Hemisphere, without invasion of the
> sovereign rights of any government. The Americas for the Americans.[8]

The concern about Nazi infiltration in the Americas was greatly justified.
Southern Brazil possessed a large population of German immigrants who
maintained their cultural identity through schools, newspapers, radio
broadcasts and social organisations; this population sympathised with
developments in Germany, and pro-Nazi organisations were active in
Southern America, whose members played a major role in the German
espionage network throughout the American continent. The German
government heavily subsidised sympathetic newspapers and the Condor
airline.[9] It was believed that Nazi propaganda might lead to the establishment of German military bases there; these would not only threaten the
United States directly but pose a hazard to shipping in the South Atlantic.

The United States relied on Brazil for the supply of natural resources
such as rubber and quartz, but their main strategic concern was the
'Brazilian Bulge', the most easterly point of the American continent which
made possible the air routes across the Atlantic.[10] At that time, aeroplanes

6.1 'The Brazilian Bulge'.
*THE BRAZILIAN BULGE is a major geographical asset. Without it, the air routes to the Middle and Far East would be impossible. With it, the 'Dakar Strait' is a potential invasion route toward Vichy Africa and Rommel's rear.*
*Fortune* (November 1942).

could not fly to Europe across the North Atlantic; they had to fly south to Brazil and cross the South Atlantic to Africa (Figure 6.1). From there, the planes could reach the fronts in the Western Desert, Southern Europe, or cross to India and Burma. An article in the *New York Herald Tribune* described the position:

> Natal [Northeast Brazil] is the middle-point, and perhaps the keypoint, in the United States' long chain of air bases over which bombing and transport planes and supplies are fed to Allied forces halfway around the globe.[11]

The Japanese bombing of Pearl Harbor and the subsequent United States declaration of war against the Axis in 1941 forced the neutral nations to make a decision about their loyalties. The United States called a conference of all the American nations, which took place from 15 to 28 January 1942 in Rio de Janeiro. At the Rio Conference, all but two countries signed the pact breaking with the Axis, which was considered by Roosevelt and his office a triumph for hemispheric solidarity.[12] *Fortune* reported the curious way in which the alliance was formed: when General Góes Monteiro (1889–1956), the Brazilian Chief of Staff, had visited Washington in 1939 as part of the United States Government programme of impressing influential foreigners, he had been unimpressed with American military power except high-level precision bombing; at the Rio Conference, the American diplomats had been impressed with Brazilian schoolgirls: 'a certain bright, unconquerable jauntiness, the look of a free people.'[13] The

Alliance was further strengthened after Brazil's Declaration of War against Italy and Germany on 12 August 1942, after German submarines torpedoed five Brazilian ships off the coast. Brazil sent an expeditionary force, the Cobra Squadron, to the Italian Front.

In return for military support, the United States supplied technical backing for a programme of industrialisation in Brazil, in particular the creation of the steel mills at Volta Redonda, the first time that the United States had contributed public funds to industrialisation in a developing country.[14] Concurrent with these changes came a subservience to, if not a dependence on, the United States.[15] The pursuit of the 'Good Neighbour' policy led the United States to include culture and education as instruments of foreign policy. Cultural co-operation came to be seen by the United States as a powerful means of increasing the ties between the American nations.

Until the Second World War, Americans from the North and South continued to look across the Atlantic, maintaining closer cultural ties with Europe than with each other. In fact, the Latin American elites regarded North Americans as less culturally sophisticated than they were, and bitterly resented their economic superiority. The influence of the United States was restricted to the writings of leading figures of American independence like Benjamin Franklin and Thomas Jefferson upon Latin American revolutionaries. Some had travelled to the United States to observe the new democracy; the Emperor of Brazil, Pedro II, a moderate reformer, toured the United States in 1876. These were, however, individual initiatives.

In the 1930s the popular culture of North America had enormous influence largely through Hollywood films which became popular throughout Latin America. However, the elite and intellectuals continued to look to Europe for sources of culture. French was the most widely-spoken foreign language and Paris was the point of reference for artists and writers in Latin America. When the University of São Paulo was founded in 1934, it sent a delegation to France, and a mission of leading scholars in social sciences, which included Claude Lévi-Strauss, Jacques Lambert and Pierre Monbeig, was sent to Brazil, while a fellowship programme for study in France was established.[16]

During the early 1930s, the United States Government dismissed the need for cultural interchange with its neighbours, while European governments were maintaining well-financed bodies to promote cultural operations. Both the Italian and German communities in South America developed networks financed by their governments to propagate their cultures. Germany, in particular, worked firmly towards the preservation of 'Germanism' abroad.[17] The acceptance of European cultural influences extended to the totalitarian political beliefs of Germany and Italy.

It was only in the late 1930s, when the increasing German interest and activity in Brazil and Spanish America caused anxiety in Washington, that the State Department began to consider its own role in cultural diplomacy. Private and government agencies began to co-operate in their effort to promote inter-American cultural interchange to drive the 'totalitarian menace' from the hemisphere. Carl Ackerman, Dean of Colombia University, reported, after a trip to Latin America, the large acceptance of European totalitarianism and warned of the need to counteract it:

The nations of South America are endangered both from within and without by the philosophy of dictatorship with the result that we are witnessing today the test of Pan American solidarity. [. . .] The scientific world of the US must be made aware of opportunities in Latin America. College graduates must realize that they may look to the East and West to see the past but to the South to see the future. The next two years will determine whether South America is to remain American or become Italo-Germanized. We must provide recognition for South America in the news, in education, in science and in literature.[18]

Roosevelt initially approved the creation of a Division of Cultural Relations within the Department of State in July 1938 to foster intellectual co-operation, and announced that the Division's establishment was to meet the challenge of Nazi infiltration in the Americas. The Division promoted exchange programmes of professors and student training in the United States, encouraged the translation of North American publications into Spanish, and established cultural institutes in several Latin American countries which provided English language classes and aid to libraries. Other measures of improving relations included the transmission of shortwave radio programmes to Latin America in Portuguese and Spanish, and the inauguration of a regular passenger steamship service to Rio de Janeiro and Buenos Aires with governmental subsidy.[19]

The government programme of cultural diplomacy reached fever pitch under the Office of Inter-American Affairs. This new agency was created by Roosevelt in August 1940 with Nelson Rockefeller as Co-ordinator, and was based on Rockefeller's Memorandum on 'Hemispheric Economic Policy' which called for a vigorous programme for improving cultural, scientific and educational relations between the Americas, as well as trade connections, through 'an organisation which would not be hampered by the limitations of traditional diplomacy in the promotion of goodwill among the Latin America Republics'.[20] The Co-ordinator was responsible directly to the President and:

was charged with the formulation and the execution of a program in cooperation with the State Department which, by effective use of governmental and private facilities in such fields as the arts and sciences, education and travel, radio, the press and cinema will further national defense and strengthen the bonds between the nations of the Western Hemisphere.[21]

Under Nelson Rockefeller's supervision, the Office of Inter-American Affairs opened press, radio, and movie sections. These provided features on North American subjects for Latin American newspapers and subsidies to keep up the circulation of friendly newspapers, expanded United States shortwave radio broadcasting, and prepared and selected films. The OIAA also supported the Arts by sending ballet groups and opera companies to Latin America, and helping museums to send out exhibitions; in June 1943, it had 16 art exhibitions, including 'Brazil Builds', under its control, to be distributed throughout the Americas.[22] The Co-ordinator also maintained a private diplomatic service with offices in many cities reporting directly to

Washington; the OIAA subsequently became known as the 'Rockefeller Office'.[23]

These government agencies were responsible for the waves of good-will missions which broke over Brazil between 1940 and 1943. Americans poured in to Rio from Pan-American planes and Moore-McCormack ships. Men from the National Research Council inspected Brazil's laboratories and talked about United States–Latin American co-operation. A representative of the US Weather Bureau arrived to study Brazil's meteorological equipment. Two women from Washington's Children's Bureau arrived to help organise one in Brazil. Film star Douglas Fairbanks Jr visited as a special representative of Roosevelt. Leopold Stokowski and Arturo Toscanini came with their orchestras.[24] Film director Orson Welles caught the Rio Carnival of 1942 for a good-will movie which constituted the first major report on it. Walt Disney came in search of new characters for good-will roles, and came out with 'Zé Carioca', a parrot personifying the gay witty Brazilian, showing Donald Duck the sights of Rio. Zé Carioca became a regular in Disney films of the period (Plate 15).[25]

Brazilian Chancellor Oswaldo Aranha (1894–1960) is credited with exclaiming: 'one more good-will mission and Brazil will declare war on the USA', a joking statement that expresses, however, the sudden and violent courtship of Brazil by the United States. Aranha himself would have preferred more favourable trade terms.[26] The missions usually did all of South America in one whirlwind trip, and the majority of them did little to revolutionise cultural relations. Some verged on the ridiculous: Hollywood's misportrayal of Latin America caused outrage at the time.[27] Others, like 'Brazil Builds', had a long-range influence and became landmarks of the era.

As the Second World War reached its final stages, the United States turned its attention to the problem of the devastation in Europe, and largely abandoned its emphasis on hemispheric solidarity. The post-war emphasis on globalism and the Cold War lessened the importance of Latin America; the Truman Doctrine of 1947 identified Communism as the main threat to the United States. The two prime ingredients which had made the Good Neighbour policy possible no longer applied: firstly, the Depression and World War II, and, secondly, Roosevelt's Presidency. With hindsight, Good Neighbour diplomacy and the Roosevelt Presidency had become synonymous. Over a span of 12 years the Good Neighbour policy had created confidence among the American nations and Roosevelt remains to this day the United States President who enjoyed the most prestige among Latin Americans. For Brazil, the honeymoon was over.

## Notes

1 *Brazil Builds* p.7.

2 Thomas E. Skidmore and Peter H. Smith: *Modern Latin America* (New York: Oxford University Press 1984; 2nd edn 1989) pp.335–71.

3 President Monroe, Declaration. Skidmore: *Modern Latin America* p.338.

4 Secretary of State Richard Olny to Lord Salisbury in 1895. David Green: *The Containment of Latin America: A History of the Myths and Realities of the Good Neighbor Policy* (Chicago: Quadrangle Books 1971) p.5.

5 President Franklin Roosevelt, 12 January 1940. Green: *The Containment of Latin America* p.38.

6  The United States required irrevocable credits in dollars. 'The Wooing of Brazil' *Fortune* (October 1941) pp.97–116. German exports increased from 12.7 per cent of the Brazilian market in 1929 to 25 per cent in 1938. United States exports were reduced from 30.1 per cent to 24.2 per cent and British exports were nearly halved from 19.2 per cent to 10.4 per cent. John D. Wirth: *The Politics of Brazilian Development 1930–1945* (Stanford: Stanford University Press 1970) p.20.

7  Vargas sent his eldest son to study at the Medical School of the University of Berlin while his other son was studying Chemical Engineering at John Hopkins. Frank D. McCann: *The Brazilian–American Alliance 1937–1945* (Princeton: Princeton University Press 1973) p.179.

8  Irwin F. Gellman: *Good Neighbor Diplomacy: United States Policies in Latin America, 1933–1945* (Baltimore: John Hopkins University Press 1979) pp.107–8.

9  The German Embassy apparently spent US$2,500,000 per month on *Meio Dia*, one of three newspapers it controlled. 'Brazil's Year of Change' *Inter-American Monthly* (May 1943) pp.27–9.

10  Newspapers frequently reported with amazement that the whole of Brazil lay east of New York City. 'Brazil the New Ally' *Fortune* (November 1942) p.105.

11  'Natal Feeds U.S. Bombers to Fighting Fronts' *New York Herald Tribune* (24 January 1943).

12  'Brazil the New Ally' *Fortune* (November 1942) pp.105–8. Chile broke with the Axis in early 1943, but Argentine remained neutral throughout the war and considered the 'bad neighbour' by United States officials.

13  *Fortune* (November 1942) p.105.

14  Skidmore: *Modern Latin America* p.164.

15  McCann: *The Brazilian–American Alliance* p.5.

16  For an account of the influence of French intellectuals in Brazil, see Lévi-Strauss: *Tristes Tropiques*.

17  Ruth McMurry and Muna Lee: *The Cultural Approach, Another Way in International Relations* (Chapel Hill: 1947) p.54.

18  Gellman: *Good Neighbour Diplomacy* pp.143–4.

19  McMurry: *The Cultural Approach* pp.216–17.

20  Nelson Rockefeller: 'Hemispheric Economic Policy', 14 June 1940. Nelson Rockefeller's qualification for the job was said to be experience as Director of the Creole Petroleum Company in Venezuela. Myer Kutz, *Rockefeller Power* (New York: Simon and Schuster 1974) p.201.

21  Washington: Executive Order 8840 of 30 July 1941. McMurry: *The Cultural Approach* p.213.

22  Madaline W. Nichols: 'Cultural Relations' *Inter-American Affairs* 3 (1943) pp.180–2. The Office of Inter-American Affairs spent $140,000,000 on its programmes between 1941–5. Kutz: *Rockefeller Power* p.202.

23  Initially called the Office of Coordination of Commercial and Cultural Relations Between the American Republics, in 1941 it changed to Office of the Coordinator of Inter-America Affairs, and later shortened to Office of Inter-America Affairs but was commonly referred to as the Coordinator's or Rockefeller's Office. Kutz: *Rockefeller Power* p.202.

24  'The Wooing of Brazil' *Fortune* (October 1941) p.100.

25  Other films from this trip included: 'Lake Titicaca': Donald Duck touring the Bolivian Andes; 'Pedro': a babyplane's first adventurous flight over the Andes; 'El Gaucho Gofy': an Argentine Gaucho; and 'Malaria and Mosquito': an educational film for the OIAA's public health programme. Disney also made war propaganda films: 'Donald Duck in Nutziland', as a worker in Nazi-Germany, and 'Education for Death', on Nazi Youth-training. 'Walt Disney: Great Teacher' *Fortune* (August 1942) pp.91–5, 154–6; 'Walt Disney Goes to War' *Life* (31 August 1942) pp.61–8.

26  'The Wooing of Brazil' *Fortune* (October 1941) p.100, 115.

27  Movies specifically aimed at Latin America were considered misrepresentative: *Flying Down to Rio* showed the tango and rumba as Brazilian dances; *A Night in Rio* was considered 'ignorant and foolish'. 'Hollywood's Carioca Fans' *Inter-American Monthly* (September 1943) pp.28–30.

# 7 'the MUSEUM and the WAR'

The Museum of Modern Art, New York, although a private enterprise, had been involved, since its inception, with government programmes in the Arts. In collaboration mainly with the Works Progress Administration, it promoted exhibitions of housing programmes, non-western and primitive art, photographs from the Farm Security Administration, and Government Posters. Its interest in promoting Modernism was happily in agreement with many of the policies of the 'New Deal'. Roosevelt's policies of social reform became inextricably linked to Modernism, as had similar policies in Europe.

In an address delivered by Roosevelt in a nation-wide broadcast which marked the opening of the Museum's new building on 8 May 1939, the President stressed the political role of the Museum:

> As the Museum of Modern Art is a living museum, not a collection of curious and interesting objects, it can, therefore, become an integral part of our democratic institutions – it can be woven into the very warp and woof of our democracy.[1]

The Museum defined its aims in a similar fashion:

> Does it seem strange to you to think of a museum as a weapon in national defense? [...] [A museum could] educate, inspire, and strengthen the hearts and wills of free men in the defense of their own freedom.[2]

American Museums collectively resolved to be 'prepared to do their utmost in the service of the people of this country during the present conflict'.[3]

During the war, the Museum maintained close links with official policy through the involvement of its Trustees and staff in government agencies. The Rockefellers had come to dominate the Museum: Nelson, John D. III (1906–78, Nelson's brother) and Blanchette (b. 1909, John D. III's wife) were all Trustees or Chairman; they had donated the entire new site of the

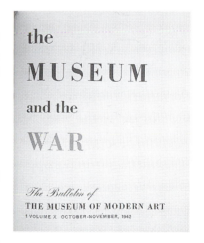

7.1 *The Bulletin of the Museum of Modern Art* (New York: The Museum of Modern Art October–November 1942) Cover. Offset, printed in black and red, page sizes 9⅛ × 7" (23.2 × 17.8 cm). The Museum of Modern Art Library, The Museum of Modern Art, New York.
© 2000 The Museum of Modern Art, New York.

Museum and had contributed substantially to the building funds. They also mixed in politics: Nelson's political interests coincided with Roosevelt's and he became prominent during the war years. He had been President of the Museum since 1939, but resigned in 1941 to become the Co-ordinator of the Office of Inter-American Affairs. Wallace K. Harrison, who had been a Trustee since 1939, became Assistant Co-ordinator from 1941 to 1943 and then Consultant to the OIAA until it closed in 1946. Among the Museum staff, Monroe Wheeler became a part-time consultant to the Co-ordinator's Office; Stephen C. Clark, Chairman of the Board of Trustees, became Chairman of the Advisory Committee on Art of the Division of Cultural Relations; Eliot Noyes, Director of the Department of Industrial Design, went to the Pentagon to design gliders.

In 1941, the Museum set up the Armed Services Program. By the end of the war, the Museum had executed 38 contracts with the Office of Inter-American Affairs, the Library of Congress, and the Office of War Information. Exhibitions included 'Britain at War' (1941), 'Camouflage for Civilian Defense' (1942), 'Useful Objects in Wartime' (1942), 'Road to Victory' (1942), 'Airways to Peace' (1943), 'Norman Bel Geddes' War Manoeuvre Models' (1944) and 'The Lesson of War Housing' (1945). There were unofficial links, too: an International Rescue Committee was set up to bring artists from Europe to the United States: both Alfred Barr and Philip Goodwin contributed their own money to sponsor artists, including the sculptor Jacques Lipchitz.[4]

The Museum's policy changed to presenting itself as an 'American' Museum, by preparing exhibitions and making acquisitions of not only North American but also of Central and South American art. This should be seen as more than expediency but as marking a sharp shift from European Modernism to Pan-Americanism. Before the war years, the Museum had not been committed to showing American art, not least the American avant-garde; American shows had not proved a critical or popular success.[5] In 1942, however, a series of exhibitions was initiated which presented American artists who were mainly representatives of Abstract Expressionism, for instance: 'Americans 1942: Eighteen Artists from Nine States', 'Americans 1943: Realists and Magic Realists' and 'Fourteen Americans' (1946). The commitment to American art also included an interest in its primitive arts which was expressed in two major shows: 'The Wooden House in America' (1941) and 'Indian Art of the United States' (1941).

The concerted effort to acquire and display Latin America art gathered force in 1940. There had been an exhibition of works by the Mexican painter Diego Rivera in 1931, and an exhibition of Inca, Maya and Aztec art in 1933, but these were isolated events. The first was due to the artist having been fashionable in America rather than an interest in Mexican art as a whole; the second was part of an exhibition entitled 'American Sources of Modern Art' (1933), which looked at Ancient American art to identify possible sources of Modern Art. There was also a small exhibition entitled 'Three Mexican Artists' in 1938.

The 1940–1 season of the Museum was proliferous in shows of Latin America art: inaugurating the series was 'Twenty Centuries of Mexican Art', a large exhibition which consisted of about 6,000 individual pieces covering Mexican art from Pre-Colombian times, 500 BC, to 1940. In conjunction with this exhibition, the Mexican muralist José Clemente Orozco was commissioned to paint a series of six movable panels in the Museum which enhanced the importance of the event.[6] The exhibition was sent on tour throughout the United States in two, smaller, versions: 'The Popular Art of Mexico' (1940–2) and 'Modern Mexican Paintings' (1940–1). A catalogue was written in both English and Spanish, in collaboration with the Mexican Government, whose Department of Foreign Affairs stated that:

Nothing does more to strengthen the bonds between peoples than the mutual understanding and appreciation of their spiritual values; and there is no clearer exponent of the human spirit than art in its diverse manifestations. Conscious of this, the Museum of Modern Art is carrying on an effective and invaluable labour of culture, friendship, and better international relations.[7]

Another major exhibition the same year was on the work of the Brazilian painter Cândido Portinari, which was also the first exhibition of South American art (Figure 7.2). A 'Festival of Brazilian Music' was held at the same time in the auditorium, in which works by Heitor Villa-Lobos and Camargo Guarnieri were played.[8] The exhibition 'Cândido Portinari of Brazil' was shown in the Museum from October to November 1940, and in a smaller version, 'Murals by Cândido Portinari', circulated around the United States during 1941. The accompanying catalogue included an article on Portinari's work by Robert Chester Smith (1912–75) who, in his concluding sentence, put forward the idea of the pursuit of an art representative of the Americas:

Upon such a firm basis Brazilian Painting should continue to grow in importance and to play an increasingly significant role in the future art of Pan-America.[9]

A number of exhibitions followed these two: a large one such as 'Brazil Builds', in 1943 the first show ever of Latin American architecture; 'Faces and Places in Brazil: Photographs by Genevieve Naylor', shown at the same time as 'Brazil Builds' in the auditorium foyer; and 'Modern Cuban Painters', in 1944. Other smaller but widely-circulated shows were 'Latin America Contemporary Art' (1942–3), 'Rivera, Orozco, Siqueiros' (1942–5), 'Paintings from Ten American Republics' (1943–4), 'Cuban Paintings Today' (1944–6), 'Fifteen Latin American Painters' (1944–6), 'Modern Painters of Brazil' (1944), 'Watercolours and Drawings by Six Cuban Painters' (1944–6), 'Graphic Arts from Mexico and Argentine' (1943–6), 'Latin America Colonial Art' (1942–4) and 'Latin America Pre-Colombia Art' (1942–4).

   The collection of works from Latin America by the Museum had begun in 1935 with a donation from Abby Rockefeller of paintings by the Mexicans Orozco, Rivera and Siqueiros. The first purchase by the Museum of a work by a Latin American artist took place in 1939, 'Morro' by Portinari, which was also the first work to be acquired by the Museum from a non-Mexican Latin American artist. Acquisitions were meagre until 1942 when Nelson Rockefeller donated an 'Inter-American Fund' for this purpose.[10]

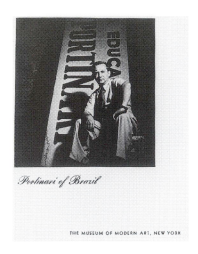

7.2 'Portinari of Brazil'
*The Bulletin of the Museum of Modern Art*
(New York: The Museum of Modern Art
October 1940) Cover. Offset, printed in
black, page sizes 9⅛ × 7" (23.2 × 17.8 cm).
The Museum of Modern Art Library, The
Museum of Modern Art, New York.
© 2000 The Museum of Modern Art, New
York.

7.3 'United Hemisphere Posters Competi-
tion'
*The Bulletin of the Museum of Modern Art*
(New York: The Museum of Modern Art
October-November 1942) p.12. Offset,
printed in black, page sizes 9⅛ × 7"
(23.2 × 17.8 cm). The Museum of Modern
Art Library, The Museum of Modern Art,
New York.
© 2000 The Museum of Modern Art, New
York.

Lincoln Kirstein (1907–96) went to South America and Alfred Barr to Mexico and Cuba for purchases and in 1943 the Museum was able to open the exhibition 'The Latin America Collection of the Museum of Modern Art'. A book of the same name by Lincoln Kirstein constituted the first survey in English of Latin American art from the colonial period to date, with emphasis on the Modern works recently acquired by the Museum.[11] A foreword by Alfred Barr explained their interest:

> Thanks to the second World War and to certain men of good will throughout the Western Hemisphere, we are dropping those blinders in cultural understanding which have kept the eyes of all the American republics fixed on Europe with scarcely a side glance at each other during the past century and a half.[12]

The standard of these works caused Barr to wonder:

> Whether we should make allowances for the general mediocrity or back-wardness of any national school or whether we should set a standard similar, say, to that which we maintain for American painting.[13]

New works continued to be acquired, however, and an updated show called 'Paintings from Latin America in the Museum Collection' was again assembled in 1945.

Among the various activities undertaken was an 'Industrial Design Competition for 21 American Republics', meant to select good design for mass production, with separate prizes for Latin America and United States. Eero Saarinen and Charles Eames were the prize winners for the United States, and Bernard Rudofsky for Brazil. The results were shown in the 'Organic Design in Home Furnishings' exhibition and catalogue in 1942.[14] The 'United Hemisphere Posters' was a competition 'to enable artists of all the Americas to play a role in tightening the bonds of hemispheric culture and defence' (Figure 7.3).[15] The winning designs were to be used by government agencies for reproduction throughout the country. They were shown at the Museum during October 1942, and travelled to other cities in Latin America.

Other undertakings directly concerned with the war effort were a series of educational exhibitions prepared for the OIAA in 1942; 'The Americas Co-operate', for instance, informed its audiences that 'Latin American Raw Materials are Essential to United States War Production'.[16] A series of educational and documentary films, in Spanish, Portuguese and French, as well as English, were carried out by the Film Library under a contract with the OIAA.[17]

There was also a series of exhibitions of American Art specially prepared to circulate outside the United States, in particularly to the countries of Latin America. 'La Pintura Contemporanea Norteamericana' (1941) was a large exhibition prepared in conjunction with four other American Museums to circulate to ten capital cities in Latin America.[18] It was accompanied by a comprehensive catalogue published by the Museum and was intended to be the first of a series of art collections to be exhibited throughout the Americas. In the foreword the committee stated:

Art is, without doubt, the best ambassador which we can send to express our feelings towards our own country and the vast social, intellectual, and economic problems which face all the countries of the world today.[19]

Although the feelings were certainly genuine, they declined to comment on the 'vast problems' and how they were related.

The frenzy of interest in Latin America passed with the war. The OIAA closed on 20 May 1946. The appointment of new Directors of the Museum – René d'Harnoncourt (1901–68), in 1949, and of the Department of Architecture – Philip Johnson, in 1949, and Arthur Drexler (1925–87), in 1954 meant a change in the approach of the Department of Architecture from didactic Modernism to a more inclusive approach to architecture.[20] The economic supremacy of the United States after the war gave it a world-wide field of action.

Conscious of its new global position, the Museum opened a new department for International Programs in 1953 under Porter McCray, with a five-year grant from The Rockefeller Brothers Foundation. The International Program prepared exhibitions of American Art to show in Europe and the Far East, such as 'Built in USA: Post-War Architecture' (1953) and 'The Skyscraper USA' (1953); it also presented 'Architecture of Japan' (1953), 'The Modern Movement in Italy' (1954), 'German Art of the Twentieth Century' (1957) and 'Prints from Europe and Japan' (1955) in the United States. On Latin American subjects, only architecture was thought worth reporting on: 'Latin American Architecture Since 1945' (1955), was an isolated attempt to maintain contacts. The Museum stated that it was participating in the post-war mood of 'stimulating understanding and respect among nations through a mutual awareness of their creative accomplishments'.[21]

## Notes

1 Published in *The Bulletin of the Museum of Modern Art* (Summer 1945).

2 'The latest and strangest recruit in Uncle Sam's defense line-up is – the museum!' Central Press Release, 20 June 1941. Lynes: *Good Old Modern* p.233.

3 'Usefulness in war is aim of Museums' *New York Times* (22 December 1941). The Museum of Modern Art Archives, NY: Alfred H. Barr, Jr. Papers [AAA: 2167; 0970].

4 Lynes: *Good Old Modern* pp.231–2.

5 Goodyear: 'Early Exhibitions' *The First Ten Years* pp.19–28.

6 *The Bulletin of the Museum of Modern Art* (August 1940).

7 Foreword in *Twenty Centuries of Mexican Art* (New York: Museum of Modern Art 1940) p.10.

8 'A Festival of Brazilian Music' Notes and Programme, Museum of Modern Art, New York (October 1940).

9 Robert C. Smith: 'The Art of Cândido Portinari' *The Bulletin of the Museum of Modern Art* (October 1940) p.12.

10 Lynes: *Good Old Modern* p.224.

11 Lincoln Kirstein: *The Latin American Collection of the Museum of Modern Art* (New York: Museum of Modern Art 1943).

12 Alfred Barr, Foreword in Kirstein: *The Latin America Collection* p.3.

13 Alfred Barr to Stephen Clark, 21 October 1942 MoMA Archives, NY: AHB [AAA: 2167; 0143].

14 *The Bulletin of the Museum of Modern Art* (February–March 1941).

15  *The Bulletin of the Museum of Modern Art* (February 1942). *United Hemisphere Posters* (New York: Museum of Modern Art 1942). The exhibition attracted a large interest with 855 posters received – 473 from Latin America, 34 prizes and 19 honourable mentions.
16  *The Bulletin of the Museum of Modern Art* (October–November 1942).
17  *The Bulletin of the Museum of Modern Art* (June–July 1941).
18  The others were: The American Museum of Natural History, The Brooklyn Museum, The Metropolitan Museum of Art and The Whitney Museum of America Art. From May to December 1941 it travelled from New York to Mexico City, Havana, Caracas, Bogota, Quito, Lima, Rio de Janeiro, Santiago, Montevideo and Buenos Aires.
19  *La Pintura Contemporanea Norteamericana* (New York: Museum of Modern Art 1941) p.5.
    *El arte es, sin duda, el mejor embajador que os podemos enviar para que os diga nuestro sentir acerca de nuestro proprio país y de los vastos problemas sociales, intelectuales y económicos a que hacen frente hoy todas las naciones del mundo.*
20  Anthony Alofsin has dealt with the changing roles of the Museum in the post-war years in an unpublished paper, 'Reflections of cultural change: the architectural exhibitions of the Museum of Modern Art', delivered at the 37th Meeting of the Society of Architectural Historians, 1984. Summarised in a letter to the author, 28 April 1989.
21  *The Bulletin of the Museum of Modern Art* (Summer 1954) p.13.

# PART IV
## THE EXHIBITION AND THE BOOK

And then, finally arriving in Rio, I received one of the most powerful impressions of my whole life. I was fascinated, and at the same time deeply moved. For what lay before me here was not merely one of the most magnificent landscapes in the world – a unique combination of sea and mountain, city and tropical scenery – but quite a new kind of civilisation. Contrary to all my expectations, it was an entirely individual picture, with its orderly clean-lined architecture and city planning; there were courage and generosity in all the modern things, and with all the traces of a well-preserved ancient culture. There were colour and movement which fascinated and never tired the eye; and wherever one looked there was a pleasant surprise. I was overwhelmed by a rush of joy and beauty. My emotions were aroused, my nerves braced, my heart warmed, my mind stirred – and the more I saw the more I wanted to see.

Stefan Zweig: *Brazil, Land of the Future*, 1942

# 8 The planning of the exhibition 'Brazil Builds'

The idea of holding an exhibition of Brazilian architecture at the Museum of Modern Art in New York resulted in equal measure from the Museum's commitment to the 'International Style' of architecture which it had promoted since 1932, and its involvement with the United States Government policy of promoting Pan-Americanism. Philip Goodwin summed up these reasons and gave an insight into the initial interest in the new Brazilian architecture:

> We went down partly on a good will mission and partly to investigate the advanced modern architecture of which photographs had been coming to this country for several years.[1]

Brazilian buildings had already been included in some early surveys of Modern Architecture, but these were not the 'advanced' buildings which were to attract wider international attention.[2] The first photographs of the 'advanced modern architecture' in Brazil were by Bernard Rudofsky, then living in São Paulo; his photographs of the buildings for the Ministry of Education and the Brazilian Press Association, still under construction, had been published in *Casabella* in 1939.[3] The Brazilian Press Association appeared in *Architectural Record* upon its completion.[4] Le Corbusier had promoted the most striking new construction in Brazil, the Ministry of Education, through the publication of his sketches and a photograph of the model of the final building in the *Œuvre Complète 1934–38*.[5] Most significant for American observers, however, was the one actual example of Modern Brazilian architecture which had arrived in New York in 1939 to feature in the New York World's Fair: the Brazilian Pavilion.

The Brazilian Pavilion at the New York World's Fair, designed by Lucio Costa and Oscar Niemeyer, constituted a show-piece of the work being done in Brazil. Unlike the photographs, the Pavilion could be easily visited and experienced, and as such, it did more than anything else to draw attention to the architecture recently being built in Brazil. It also marked the initial contact of Lucio Costa and Oscar Niemeyer with American architects such as Paul Lester Wiener and Wallace K. Harrison. The pavilion was widely published and praised; the American periodical *Magazine of Arts* pointed out its role in revealing the new Modern architecture of Brazil:

> The greatest architectural surprises to most people will be those produced by the South Americans. The rising importance of modern architecture in this part of the world has long been heralded, but few have seen the new buildings in Buenos Aires and Rio.[6]

The Museum of Modern Art acquired the model of the building for the collection of the Department of Architecture, which marked the start of the Museum's interest in Brazilian architecture.[7]

The staff of the Department of Architecture had been 'talking about' an exhibition on Brazilian Architecture since 1939, but the preparations for an exhibition did not start until early 1942. The Rio Conference from 15 to 28 January 1942, which brought Brazil's strategic importance to the forefront of political discussions, undoubtedly brought the matter to a head at the Museum. Janet Henrich, then Acting Curator of Architecture, wrote to Elodie Courter (1911–94), Director of the Department of Circulating Exhibitions, about the Brazilian exhibition on the same day as the opening of the Rio Conference on 15 January 1942.[8]

Initially, the Museum thought of making a show on South America in general, but they admitted ignorance of any built work of quality except the Brazilian Pavilion in New York and the Ministry of Education in Rio de Janeiro. Their discussions were based on whether there would be enough material for a show on Brazilian architecture, based on the example of 'Stockholm Builds' (1940). Monroe Wheeler, Director of Publications, was firmly in favour of restricting the show to Brazil only, and he again pressed Elodie Courter to consider using the same format for an exhibition on Brazil: 'People keep telling me how extraordinary Brazilian architecture is, and I still think you should have a show like "Stockholm Builds" on Brazil.'[9] 'Stockholm Builds', however, had been a relatively simple show to organise: it had been based on the photographic material that George Everard Kidder-Smith (1913–97) had gathered during a trip to Scandinavia as a Fellow of the American Scandinavian Foundation, but with background information provided by Elizabeth Mock with research done in the United States. South American buildings, on the other hand, were barely known and research *in situ* would have had to be undertaken.[10]

The Museum's main source of information on architecture in Brazil was Paul Lester Wiener, who had worked with Lucio Costa and Oscar Niemeyer on the Brazilian Pavilion and had since been a Visiting Professor at the Federal University in Rio de Janeiro. They also knew of Brazilian Baroque architecture through the studies of Robert C. Smith, Associate Director of the Hispanic Foundation of the Library of Congress.[11] Wiener, however, was able to provide first-hand information: he assured them that there was enough Modern architecture for an interesting show and also some good record material on Colonial architecture. There was, however, no record material on Modern architecture, and not only would photographs have to be taken, but also all the data would have to be obtained from the architects themselves.[12]

The cost of such an enterprise was of great concern for the Department

8.1 Philip. L. Goodwin and Elizabeth Mock, planning the exhibition 'If You Want to Build a House', January 1946.
Photograph Courtesy Photographic Archives, The Museum of Modern Art, New York.

of Architecture, and discussions revolved around the ways of making a trip to Brazil possible. The Department of Architecture was then going through some financial difficulties; recent budget cuts had left it in constant danger of disappearing. These cuts were part of the reforms Nelson Rockefeller made when he assumed the Presidency of the Museum in 1939; he apparently believed that 'Architecture shows did not make money', despite the presence of Wallace K. Harrison as a Trustee.[13] The number of staff was cut down, and John McAndrew, the Director of the Department of Architecture and Industrial Design since 1937, had been forced to resign late in 1940, without being replaced.[14] The result was that, during the war years, the Department of Architecture had no formal administration and had to rely on a scant budget and the individual efforts of Philip Goodwin – its chairman, Elizabeth Mock – a freelance assistant, and Alice Carson – Acting Curator (Figure 8.1). This meant that the Museum had to look for external funding to accomplish the Brazilian exhibition project. They initially thought of a grant from the Co-ordinator of the Office of Inter-American Affairs to send Kidder-Smith to collect material by himself.[15] By then, however, Nelson Rockefeller was willing to subscribe to the cost of an exhibition of Brazilian architecture at the Museum in his capacity as the Co-ordinator of the Office of Inter-American Affairs, when he realised that shows of architecture could be an instrument for promoting Pan-American friendship. The Department did not initially get a grant from the Co-ordinator; the funding came after the trip.

By March 1942, the Museum had prepared a statement of intentions and needs for a Brazilian show, as well as sample questionnaires to collect the data:

> If material of sufficient quality can be obtained, the Museum of Modern Art – in cooperation with the Pan American Committee of the American Institute of Architects – would propose to hold in New York and circulate throughout the country an exhibition of Brazilian Architecture – Colonial and Modern.

In order to prepare such an exhibition it would be necessary to obtain 200–300 photographs of which approximately half would be selected for inclusion in the exhibition.

> The photographs should be, at the discretion of the person who selects them, $\frac{1}{3}$ to $\frac{1}{2}$ Colonial and the remainder modern. Based on interest and quality of design as the first requisite, it is hoped that the selection would include a cross-section of building types – Government and religious, office buildings, schools, houses, etc. In addition it is believed that material on recent public works (engineering) and on regional or city planning will be found to be of considerable interest.[16]

The statement did not mention who was to undertake the project, but it is clear that the matter had already been formally decided: 'I am so delighted to hear that you definitely can go to Brazil,' wrote Alfred Barr to Philip Goodwin on 20 March 1942.[17] Goodwin replied to Barr summarising his agreement and outlined his plans:

> The Museum of Modern Art, in collaboration with the American Institute of Architects is sending me and Kidder-Smith to Brazil some time in May, in order to collect data on colonial and modern buildings in that country, for an architectural travelling show. [. . .] It is proposed that we should start as soon as passports and places on the plane can be secured, within six weeks if possible, remaining in Brazil not more than two months.[18]

With neither any previous interest in Brazil, or Latin America for that matter, nor any knowledge of Portuguese or Spanish, Goodwin's involvement can only be understood, as he described later, as having been 'taken on the spur of the moment'.[19] Goodwin must have found the subject stimulating enough; he not only took a particular interest in the Brazilian exhibition but also bore the entire expense of the expedition personally. Since early 1941, Goodwin had discussed with other Trustees his particular interest in the subject:

> As I told Mr. Moe a year ago, it would seem to me a time to study the question of heat and light on large glass surfaces, as experienced in modern buildings in Brazil. This question has been one of great moment to Americans, who have lately borrowed the idea of these large glass surfaces from northern European sources. Northern Europeans sources are not a good guide for Brazil nor for us, to any great extent, and it would be interesting to compare our experiments with theirs.[20]

Born in 1885 in New York City, Goodwin was not from the same generation as the bright young men who had organised the 'Modern Architecture: International Exhibition', with a youthful enthusiasm to investigate Modern architecture in foreign countries, nor was he an architectural critic or historian with a Harvard degree as were the intellectual forces in the Museum. He was a practising architect who had a BA from Yale and had studied architecture at Columbia, 1909–12, and at the Fontainebleau School in Paris, 1912–14. Goodwin began his architectural career in the

New York firm of Delano & Aldrich, later forming a partnership – Goodwin, Bullard & Woolsey – before establishing his own practice in New York in 1921. His work consisted mainly of large houses.[21] He also wrote a book on the chateaux of Touraine, *French Provincial Architecture*, and a monograph on 'French Architecture as Source Material'.[22] He lived in a replica of a French chateau outside New York.

Goodwin's association with the Museum was not as an architect, however, but through his activity as a collector of art. His collection was considerably large and important, and when Goodwin died in 1958, he left the major part of it to the Museum, who held a special exhibition of it.[23] He became a Trustee of the Museum in April 1934, and was made Chairman of its Architecture Committee in 1935.

When the Trustees decided to build the Museum's permanent home on West Fifty-third Street in 1936, they intended that it 'would serve as a three-dimensional demonstration of all that the Museum stood for'.[24] The Trustees preferred that the Museum should be designed by an American, and so it was to Philip Goodwin, the only architect on the Board, that the Building Committee turned to, firstly, for advice, and finally, as the architect of the new building. Goodwin was obviously not likely to be able to design the Modern building that the Trustees desired; he was, however, known for his sense of detail: 'he stubbornly resisted being hurried into second-rate design or inferior execution.'[25] For the Modern design, Wallace K. Harrison recommended Edward Durrell Stone, then working on the Radio City Music Hall and the Century Theater, to Nelson Rockefeller.[26] Stone claimed that the Museum was the first International Style building in New York.[27] The union of Goodwin and Stone was a happy one; they later collaborated on other projects including the Food Building at the New York World's Fair in 1939.

After his experiences with the Museum project, Goodwin's houses displayed a more rational idiom without departing entirely from a 'historical' approach. A house in Florida with the minimal use of large windows, and large covered porches and roof overhangs, which were justified by the intense natural light, was published by *Architectural Forum* as an example of regional expression in contemporary work.[28] This approach reveals Goodwin's preoccupation with an architecture adapted to the conditions of climate, in particular his self-declared preoccupation with 'the problem of controlling heat and light on large exterior glass surfaces', which was a factor in his subsequent interest in the new Brazilian architecture.[29]

There was an element of personal experience in the reason Goodwin felt this 'technical device' was so important: the façade of the Museum of Modern Art had been largely covered by a translucent material called Thermolux – a sandwich of spun glass between two sheets of clear glass – which was then a very unusual material. The Thermolux panels, intended to light the exhibition halls, had proved too bright in practice – they faced due south – and were later covered internally.[30] More important, perhaps, was the experience with Le Corbusier's buildings. The *pan-de-verre* had failed at the Armée du Salut (1929–32) and the Pavillon Suisse (1930–2) in Paris: the problems of solar gain and lack of ventilation experienced there would have made conditions intolerable in the tropics, or indeed the United States with its much higher standards of comfort. Philip Goodwin had arranged Le Corbusier's exhibition and lecture tour of the United States in 1935, so he must have been familiar with Le Corbusier's work. It might have been the refusal to retreat over the supposedly scientific, but primarily aesthetic, use which had led to the search for a solution. And, after all, Modern architecture was supposed to be 'functional'.

Kidder-Smith himself recounted that his involvement had been because he had just done 'Stockholm Builds'; Goodwin wanted an architect who could take photographs to accompany him.[31] As it was to him that the Museum had first turned to undertake the trip, he was the natural choice when the project was taken over by Goodwin. In fact, all in the Museum seemed to be in agreement: Barr thought that 'Kidder-Smith would be a wonderful photographer to take along'.[32] At the age of 29, Kidder-Smith was a young architect when he undertook the excursion to Brazil; after the exhibition and the widespread publishing of his photographs, he built a reputation as an outstanding architectural photographer. Although he set up an architectural practice in 1946, he continued to be active as an architectural photographer and writer. Exploiting the success of *Brazil Builds*, he used the same framework for a further series: *Switzerland Builds* (1950), *Italy Builds* (1955), and *Sweden Builds* (1957).[33]

Like explorers, Goodwin and Kidder-Smith travelled across the country for two months, covering not only the two major cities of Rio de Janeiro and São Paulo, but also the northern cities of Salvador and Recife, with stops in smaller cities where examples of 'great architecture', new or old, were to be found. Although the success of his trip would depend on personal contact with the architects to obtain information on the buildings, Goodwin went with only an introduction from the Brazilian ambassador, Carlos Martins, to Gustavo Capanema; he described Goodwin's objectives as 'collecting material for an exhibition to take place in the United States about the Colonial and Modern architecture of Brazil'.[34]

For Goodwin, an urbane New Yorker, the first contact with Brazil must have been a novel experience. He immediately set out to record his impressions in great detail in a series of ecstatic letters to Alfred Barr. Many of these comments later found their way directly into *Brazil Builds*. His first letter described the aeroplane journey, which must have been an experience in itself:

> Four days in a plane and three nights on land, at Ciudad Trujillo (Sto Domingo), Trinidad and Belém. The high spots were a storm over Haiti, a view on Devil's Island (Cayenne) and the rather awful grandeur of the mouth of the Amazon as night was falling. The river is immense and the sense of limitless wastes very impressive. We landed in the dark and saw little of Belém as of course we always started at 4 a.m. in the morning. Just before Rio we flew over Bello Horizonte [sic] (Minas Geraes) [sic] and saw the plan of the city, skyscrapers and a huge artificial lake shaped like an octopus.[35]

Goodwin stayed at the sumptuous and highly fashionable Copacabana Palace Hotel, which he described as 'something of a centre for lots of people'; he certainly made it so: he held a lunch for 14 people soon after his arrival including Lincoln Kirstein, Cândido Portinari, Marcelo Roberto, Oscar Niemeyer, Corrêa Lima, and Lucio Costa.[36] He relied on his Brazilian

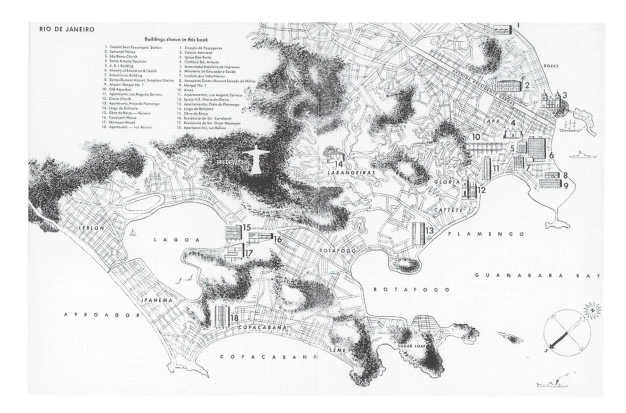

contacts to show him the buildings (Figure 8.2);[37] he communicated easily with them in French.[38] Lincoln Kirstein, who was in Rio collecting works of art for the Museum, took him to see Portinari, but was otherwise not too valuable: 'Lincoln Kirstein has been most kind and helpful but I think has not unearthed a great deal that is new.'[39] Costa was no longer involved on the Ministry of Education Building, but as Director of Research at SPHAN was able to give photographs and drawings of numerous Colonial buildings – many recently discovered – which Goodwin and Kidder-Smith were not able to visit:

> Lucio Costa, another very able designer took us on a day's sightseeing to Niemeyer's own house, small and unfinished but good, a nursery [. . .], refuge for poor people, and his own Serviço Patrimonio Historico where he has hundreds of photos of old work.[40]

Goodwin praised the work of SPHAN and was impressed with the Colonial architecture: 'Gloria chapel is a gem',[41] and 'Daniel by Aleijadinho a wonder!' (Figure 8.3).[42]

Goodwin seemed to have enjoyed Rio de Janeiro, and made a comment about the city more perceptive than usual: 'The weather is pleasingly warm – the city is quite lovely in a Paris-cum-Los Angeles way' (Figures 8.4 and 8.5). As soon as he landed, he remarked on the Seaplane Terminal, then being used as the main terminal. The Ministry Building was the first to be visited:

8.2 Philip L. Goodwin: *Brazil Builds* (New York: The Museum of Modern Art 1943) pp.82–3. Offset, printed in black, page sizes 8½ × 11" (21.6 × 27.9 cm).

Photograph © 2000 The Museum of Modern Art, New York.

Map of Rio de Janeiro showing the buildings in the book.

*1 Coastal Boat Station. 2 Itamarati Palace. 3 São Bento Church. 4 Santo Antonio Fountain. 5 Brazilian Press Association. 6 Ministry of Education and Health. 7 Industriarios Building. 8 Seaplane Station, Santos Dumont Airport. 9 Hangar No. 1, Santos Dumont Airport. 10 Old Aqueduct. 11 Apartment House. 12 Gloria Church. 13 Apartment House. 14 Largo do Boticario. 15 Obra do Berço Nursery. 16 Private House. 17 Private House. 18 Apartment House.*

8.3 Philip L. Goodwin: *Brazil Builds* (New York: The Museum of Modern Art 1943) pp.34–5. Offset, printed in black, page sizes 8½ × 11″ (21.6 × 27.9 cm).
Photograph © 2000 The Museum of Modern Art, New York.
Photographs of Fazendas from SPHAN.

Rio has at least sixty buildings in construction, some very large indeed but the most interesting is the Education Building which we have visited with Oscar Niemeyer and Reide [sic] the architects. [. . .] The Le Corbusier influence is strong in this building but it is perhaps the best in Rio and better than most in the U.S.A. The *brise-soleils* are painted blue [illegible] and on the North only. The windows fine big iron double hung. Native granite and blue and white tile designed by Portinari (who has also done some murals) give great interest to the E. + W. sides.[43]

He immediately became involved in the discussions about the sculpture for the auditorium of the Ministry Building: 'The idea is apparently a Victory of Samothrace up to date.'[44] He used the opportunity to promote Jacques Lipchitz, acting as an intermediary between Capanema and Lipchitz, and sending Lipchitz photos of the wall and details.

Goodwin found his study of Brazilian architecture *in situ* was 'a somewhat difficult undertaking under war conditions', but most of the hindrances met on the trip would have been due less to the war than to the conditions of travelling in Brazil in the early 1940s.[45] When Goodwin and Kidder-Smith arrived in May, Brazil had not yet entered the war, which was declared, after they had left, on 22 August 1942. Even after the declaration of war, life in the rest of the country went on much as it had before. Only the shortage of gasoline and the imposition of rationing, and later the black-out at night, reminded people that there was a war. In fact, Goodwin did not even experience the black-out:

8.4 Philip L. Goodwin: *Brazil Builds* (New York: The Museum of Modern Art 1943) pp.26–7. Offset, printed in black, page sizes 8½ × 11″ (21.6 × 27.9 cm).
Photograph © 2000 The Museum of Modern Art, New York.
Rio de Janeiro.
*The original beauty of Rio seems to have suffered remarkably little during the four centuries of building activity. Even where man has built most boldly or, from the point of view of modern city-planning, least sensibly, he has often contrived to enhance the natural splendor of the city.*

*At Copacabana beach, beloved by tourist and Cariocans alike, the surf sweeps in over a wide curve of dazzling white sand surrounded by a promenade of black and white blocks laid in serpentine mosaic. The edge of the great ellipse is punctuated by the regularly spaced verticals of lofty hotels and apartment buildings.*

At night the curving line of the street lamps along the bays and the well-lighted parks and avenues recall the title Paris once held of the Ville-Lumière, a title to which Rio has some right in these days of general gloom.[46]

Nevertheless, a series of bureaucratic procedures had to be followed on account of the state of emergency, such as registering with the Police and obtaining permits from the Department of Press and Propaganda, a government agency instituted during the Estado Novo.[47] This was, presumably, to avoid any question of espionage while Kidder-Smith was taking photographs.[48]

The conditions of travelling, however, would have demanded a great effort of will. Brazil in the early 1940s was not a modern, industrialised, urbanised country. Outside the key cities along the coast, which had experienced enormous growth since 1930, two-thirds of the country was still classified as rural. Approximately 42,000,000 inhabitants populated Brazil in 1942, but 90 per cent of this population was clustered along the 3,517-mile-long Atlantic Coast, from Amapá to Rio Grande do Sul, leaving the rest of the country virtually uninhabited.[49] Brazil had not yet developed a network of railways or roads for serving the coastline, let alone the interior, remaining dependant on shipping for its internal communication. Airlines for passenger transportation were in the midst of expansion during the 1940s. Although Goodwin and Kidder-Smith flew to the major cities,

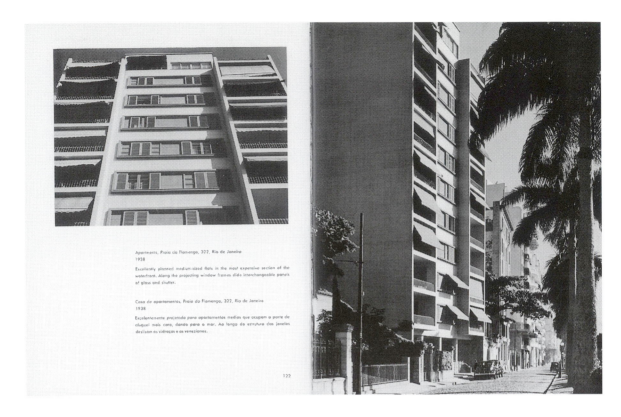

Apartments, Praia do Flamengo, 322, Rio de Janeiro
1938
Excellently planned medium-sized flats in the most expensive section of the
waterfront. Along the projecting window frames slide interchangeable panels
of glass and shutter.

Casa de apartamentos, Praia do Flamengo, 322, Rio de Janeiro
1938
Excelentemente projetado para apartamentos medios que ocupam a parte de
aluguel mais caro, dando para o mar. Ao longo da estrutura das janelas
deslisam as vidraças e as venezianas.

122

8.5 Philip L. Goodwin: *Brazil Builds* (New York: The Museum of Modern Art 1943) pp.122–3. Offset, printed in black, page sizes 8½ × 11″ (21.6 × 27.9 cm).
Photograph © 2000 The Museum of Modern Art, New York.
Apartment blocks.
*Excellently planned medium-sized flats in the most expensive section of the waterfront. Along the projecting window frames slide interchangeable panels of glass and shutter.*

they still faced a harsh trip across country when visiting the small towns. Goodwin recalled:

> As for the connecting roads between centres, Brazil is extremely backward. The chief difficulties are red clay, torrential rain at times, and the most irritating mountains an engineer could find. The new road between São Paulo and Santos will not be finished for several years, nor the long and difficult link to Rio. One of the few modern roads in the entire country leads from Rio to Petrópolis and eventually to Therezopolis.[50]

The rationing of gasoline seems to have made travelling a little difficult, and Goodwin was forced continually to revise his plans: 'We are revolving things a little as gas is being scarce and we don't know how long we can use our car',[51] and later, he reported that 'we have switched our tour a little on account of gas scarcity'.[52] When thanking his hosts and guides he not only thanked them for their time and knowledge, but for their gasoline.[53] In the end, he spent a week in Belo Horizonte and Ouro Preto (Figure 8.6), returning to Rio de Janeiro to go to São Paulo, and returning again to await clearance to travel north along the coast to Salvador and Recife (Figure 8.7); he found the distances huge.[54] Despite any hardships of travelling, Goodwin seemed to find the journey quite pleasant: 'we are enjoying it here a lot'.[55]

Goodwin must have been aware of the quality and importance of the

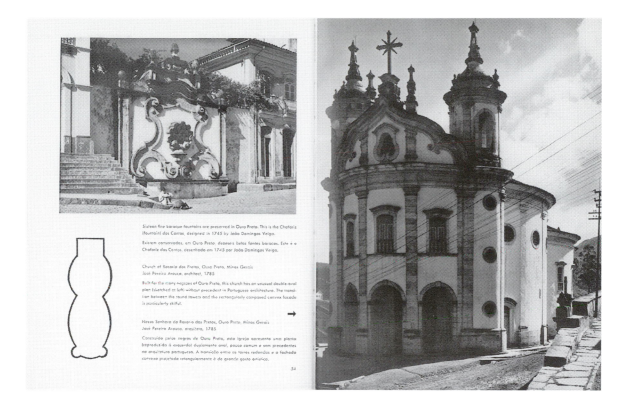

material he had collected even before he had left, as he wrote to Barr: 'Let us hope that the Architecture Department can be prolonged until the Brazil exhibitions are finished.'[56] Kidder-Smith, later recalling his pioneering experience in Brazil in the 1940s, retained his fond impressions of the country and its architecture: 'We were both thrilled by what we saw.'[57]

On their return, Goodwin's report on the Brazilian trip was met with enthusiasm by the Museum. Barr wrote to Goodwin:

> We are delighted with the excellent reports you bring us of the Brazilian Architecture photographs. Given the general interest in Latin America and the fact that no Latin America indigenous modern architecture has as yet received such serious attention, we all think that it will be a very successful and influential show.[58]

Aware of the quality of the material, Barr, to secure the originality and impact of the show, stated that:

> all negatives and publication rights of photographs made on this expedition are the property of the Museum of Modern Art and will remain in our negatives files under the care of our Photography Registrar. Mr. Kidder-Smith may of course use the negatives whenever he likes but all publication rights must of course be cleared with the Department of

8.6 Philip L. Goodwin: *Brazil Builds* (New York: The Museum of Modern Art 1943) pp.54–5. Offset, printed in black, page sizes 8½ × 11" (21.6 × 27.9 cm).
Photograph © 2000 The Museum of Modern Art, New York.
Ouro Preto.
*Sixteen fine fountains are preserved in Ouro Preto. This is the Chafariz dos Contos, designed in 1745 by João Domingos Veiga.*
*Church of Rosario dos Pretos, José Pereirra Arouco, 1785.*
*Built for the many negroes of Ouro Preto, this church has an unusual double-oval plan (sketched at left) without precedent in Portuguese architecture. The transition between the round towers and the rectangular composed convex façade is particularly skilful.*

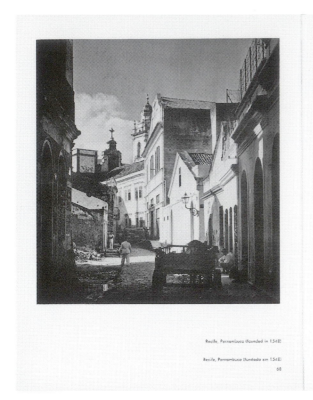

Recife, Pernambuco (founded in 1548)

Recife, Pernambuco (fundada em 1548)

68            69

8.7 Philip L. Goodwin: *Brazil Builds* (New York: The Museum of Modern Art 1943) pp.68–9. Offset, printed in black, page sizes 8½ × 11″ (21.6 × 27.9 cm).
Photograph © 2000 The Museum of Modern Art, New York.
Colonial Towns.
*Recife, Pernambuco (founded in 1548).*

Publications and the Publicity Department. It is naturally very important that key pictures in the exhibition should not be published before the exhibition opens.[59]

Thus, when a magazine offered to pay for the colour plate, Barr chose the Industrial School in Rio de Janeiro rather than a more exciting building like the Ministry of Education. In fact, the Museum was not the only Institution with an interest in Brazil. Even before Goodwin's return, the Museum started to be sought out about the material he would be bringing home:

> The Pan-American Society of Massachusetts is making out its program for next winter. We have heard of Philip Goodwin's expedition in Brazil. [. . .] We would like to have an exhibition of the baroque architecture of Brazil either in November or February. [. . .] I know I can borrow some things from Robert Smith of the Hispanic Foundation, Library of Congress, but I would like to keep these as supplementary material to the new things brought home by Mr. Goodwin, if we may borrow Goodwin's stuff.[60]

In an 'Agenda' prepared to present to the Brazilian Architecture Exhibition Committee meeting on the 11 August 1942, Goodwin described the nature of the collected material and listed various points concerning the exhibition, the publications to be made from it, and people in charge. The material consisted of 650 black and white photographs and 250 Kodachromes taken by Kidder-Smith, plus 200 black and white photographs from the Instituto de Arquitetos do Brasil and SPHAN archives, original tracings by Oscar Niemeyer, prints and photographs of several other sketch drawings, a few actual sketch drawings and sample *azulejos* from the Ministry Building.

The Museum had found that the material collected was of such outstanding quality that it was decided that the exhibition should feature as a major event, and the entire ground floor was reserved for its presentation in January. This meant that new funds from outside the Museum had to be found. A Memorandum was sent to Nelson Rockefeller, the Co-ordinator of the OIAA, which stressed the propaganda value to the OIAA:

The six hundred photographs he [Kidder-Smith] made in Brazil, together with the documentation and plans assembled by Mr. Goodwin, form ideal material for a comprehensive exhibition and publication on the subject. [. . .] The Museum and Mr. Goodwin, who bore the entire expenses of the expedition, cannot underwrite both the exhibition and a book based upon it, and I would like to know whether the Coordinator would care to share the cost of both in order that they may be produced simultaneously, and in the finest conceivable manner.

Architecture books are extremely costly to produce, and the Museum budget, recently curtailed, cannot absorb the cost of this one. Although an authoritative book on Brazilian modern architecture, issued in New York, would be most felicitous from the point of view of inter-American relations and very influential because of significant treatment and innovations developed in Brazil, it would entail very heavy losses as a publishing venture.

The Museum estimated a cost of $12,500 for the exhibition and a publication of approximately 150 pages, and proposed that the Co-ordinator share the cost by purchasing copies of the book for distribution in Brazil, for which they argued the importance of this publication to the policies of the OIAA:

It would be possible to issue this publication in a complete and appropriate manner which will reflect great honour upon our new ally. Without special subsidy it will be impossible to issue a book at all, which would, we feel be highly regrettable in view of the importance of the material assembled and its relation to the cultural development of one of the greatest countries of the new world.[61]

They asked for $11,000, most of which would be spent on 3,000 copies of *Brazil Builds*.

Another statement from the Museum to the OIAA argued further in favour of the project:

It is a common complaint of the progressive nations of South America that the United States fails to appreciate their contributions to contemporary thought and modern living, and that we only stress those picturesque aspects of their countries that are in their own minds more often associated with their remote past or with their more backward regions.

The modern architecture of Brazil is an achievement in terms of the most advanced thought of the twentieth century that is without parallel on this hemisphere. It is the aim of this project to give recognition to Brazil for its leadership in a field of modern endeavour and to demonstrate our appreciation of her outstanding contributions to progress.

This exhibition offers an opportunity to demonstrate to the people of Brazil that the United States is fully aware of and appreciates the great contribution that Brazilian architects have made to contemporary living and contemporary art.[62]

By September, Goodwin was ready to go to Washington to ensure the support of the Co-ordinator by personally presenting the material. Wallace K. Harrison and Nelson Rockefeller approved the project in principle, and Goodwin felt confident to go ahead without a formal decision.[63] By October the exhibition had taken a busy turn of activity and the small Architecture Committee required extra staff. Elodie Courter, Kidder-Smith, Philip Goodwin, and Alice Carson met to pick out the photographs and devise a layout; Elizabeth Mock was called to work on the book and labels.[64] Although she preferred to remain freelance, she was heavily involved in the Museum; she worked with Philip Goodwin on *Brazil Builds*, *Built in USA: since 1932*, and *What is Modern Architecture?*

By the time the exhibition was set up, the book was, in fact, already complete, and the text of the labels of the photographs in the exhibition were taken directly from Goodwin's comments and referred to pages in the book. Barr thought that the exhibition might be considered 'a kind of magnificent poster for the book'.[65]

'Brazil Builds' seemed to many to be the natural title for the exhibition as a follower to 'Stockholm Builds'. However, Philip Goodwin found some drawbacks with it:

> With regard to the title of the exhibition although 'Brazil Builds' is succinct and clear, it is the same as 'Stockholm Builds' and it does not suggest, to my mind, that the photographs would cover the 18th century, part of the 19th as well as the 20th.[66]

He suggested other titles: 'Brazilian Buildings – 1700–1900', 'Brazilian Buildings – Old Gold, New Concrete', 'Building in Brazil From Gold to Concrete', but 'Brazil Builds' stuck.

## Notes

1 Philip Goodwin: 'Modern Architecture in Brazil' in Elizabeth Wilder (ed): *Studies in Latin American Art*, Proceedings of a Conference held in The Museum of Modern Art, New York, 28–31 May 1945 (Washington: American Council of Learned Societies 1949) p.89.
2 The first houses by Gregori Warchavchik had been featured in Alberto Sartoris: *Gli Elementi dell'Architettura Funzionale* (Milan: Hoepli 1932; 2nd edn 1935) pp.121–7, which included 625 illustrations of buildings from 25 countries; *Cahiers d'Art* (1931) pp.102–9; *L'Architet-*

*tura* (May 1932) p.322; *Domus* (April 1933) p.177. Some early works by Rino Levi had been published in *L'Architettura* (May 1938) pp.275–86; *L'Architecture d'Aujourd'hui* (September 1938) pp.62–4, (February 1939) pp.26, 29.

3  Bernard Rudofsky: 'Cantieri di Rio de Janeiro' *Casabella* (April 1939) pp.12–17.

4  'ABI Building: From New Techniques Spring New Forms' *Architectural Record* (December 1940) pp.74–9.

5  *Œuvre Complète 1934–38* pp.78–81.

6  F.A. Gutheim: 'Buildings at the Fair' *Magazine of Arts* (May 1939) pp.289, 316.

7  *The Year's Work June 1940–July 1941* (New York: Museum of Modern Art 1941).

8  Janet Henrich to Elodie Courter, 15 January 1942. The Museum of Modern Art Archives, NY: Records of the Department of Circulating Exhibitions, II.1/41 (5).

9  Monroe Wheeler to Elodie Courter, 11 February 1942. The Museum of Modern Art Department of Registration, NY: Brazil Builds, Exhibition No. 213.

10  'Stockholm Builds: an Exhibition of Modern Swedish Architecture Opens at the Museum of Modern Art', Press Release. MoMA Archives, NY: CE, II.1/104(4). No catalogue was produced.

11  Robert C. Smith: 'Colonial Architecture of Minas Gerais' *Art Bulletin* (June 1939) p.110–59. This was his first publication on Brazilian Colonial architecture, he later published extensively on the subject.

12  Record of Conversation with Paul Lester Wiener, re Brazilian Architecture material [before 4 March 1942]. MoMA Department of Registration, NY: Brazil Builds, Exhibition No. 213.

13  Lynes: *Good Old Modern* p.221.

14  After the departure of John McAndrew, the Department was split into Architecture and Industrial Design. Eliot Noyes became Director of the Department of Industrial Design for a brief period, leaving during the war.

15  Monroe Wheeler to Elodie Courter, 11 February 1942. MoMA Department of Registration, NY: Brazil Builds, Exhibition No. 213.

16  Statement, March 1942. MoMA Department of Registration, NY: Brazil Builds, Exhibition No. 213. The Division of Pan American Affairs of the American Institute of Architects was created in June 1942. *Inter-American Affairs* 2 (1942) p.211.

17  Alfred Barr to Philip Goodwin, 20 March 1942. MoMA Archives, NY: AHB [AAA: 2167; 0368].

18  Philip Goodwin to Alfred Barr, 1 April 1942. MoMA Archives, NY: AHB [AAA: 2167; 0366].

19  Goodwin: 'Modern Architecture in Brazil' in *Studies in Latin American Art* p.89.

20  Philip Goodwin to Alfred Barr, 1 April 1942. MoMA Archives, NY: AHB [AAA: 2167; 0366].

21  'House in West Hartford Connecticut: Philip Goodwin' *Architectural Forum* February 1934 pp.158–60.

22  *French Provincial Architecture* (New York 1924); 'French Architecture as Source Material', *The Tuileries Brochure, a series of monographs on European Architecture*, ed. by William Dewey Foster (Chicago: Ludovici-Celadon 1931–2); *Rooftrees: The Architectural History of an American Family* (Philadelphia: Lippincott 1933).

23  *The Bulletin of the Museum of Modern Art* (Fall 1958).

24  'The Museum of Modern Art, New York' *Architectural Forum* (August 1939) p.116.

25  Lynes: *Good Old Modern* p.191.

26  Lynes: *Good Old Modern* p.191.

27  Edward Stone: *The Evolution of an Architect* (New York: Horizon 1962) p.36.

28  'House in Winter Park, Florida' *Architectural Forum* (June 1940) pp.428–9.

29  *Brazil Builds* p.7.

30  Lynes: *Good Old Modern* p.195.

31  Letter from Kidder-Smith, 12 April 1990.

32  Alfred Barr to Philip Goodwin, 20 March 1942. MoMA Archives, NY: AHB [AAA: 2167; 0368].

33  He followed these with *The New Architecture of Europe* (1961) and *The New Churches of Europe* (1964). Two surveys of American architecture: *The Pictorial History of Architecture in America* and the massive three-volume *The Architecture of the United States*, were published in 1981.

34  Ambassador Carlos Martins to Gustavo Capanema, 28 April 1942. CE: CPC 3.25 CPDOC/FGV.

35  Philip Goodwin to Alfred Barr, 26 May 1942. MoMA Archives, NY: AHB [AAA: 2167; 0360-3]. The 'octopus' lake was Pampulha.

36 Philip Goodwin to Alfred Barr, 3 June 1942. MoMA Archives, NY: AHB [AAA: 2167; 0354-5].

37 Conversation with Roberto Cerqueira Cesar, October 1988, and Lucio Costa, December 1988.

38 Philip Goodwin to Alfred Barr, 26 May 1942. MoMA Archives, NY: AHB [AAA: 2167; 0360-3].

39 Philip Goodwin to Alfred Barr, 26 May 1942. MoMA Archives, NY: AHB [AAA: 2167; 0360-3].

40 Philip Goodwin to Alfred Barr, 26 May 1942. MoMA Archives, NY: AHB [AAA: 2167; 0360-3].

41 Philip Goodwin to Alfred Barr, 26 May 1942. MoMA Archives, NY: AHB [AAA: 2167; 0360-3].

42 Philip Goodwin to Alfred Barr, 18 June 1942. MoMA Archives, NY: AHB [AAA: 2167; 0351-3].

43 Philip Goodwin to Alfred Barr, 26 May 1942. MoMA Archives, NY: AHB [AAA: 2167; 0360-3].

44 Philip Goodwin to Alfred Barr, 3 June 1942. MoMA Archives, NY: AHB [AAA: 2167; 0354-5].

45 *Brazil Builds* p.8.

46 *Brazil Builds* p.95.

47 *Brazil Builds* p.8.

48 This actually happened to a SPHAN photographer, who was questioned while taking photographs in Petrópolis during the war, and to Claude Lévi-Strauss in Salvador, just before the war. Lucio Costa, Preface, in *Rodrigo e seus Tempos* p.9; Lévi-Strauss: *Tristes Tropiques* pp.33–4.

49 Census of September 1940: 41,565,083 inhabitants. *Inter-American Affairs* 2 (1942).

50 *Brazil Builds* p.96.

51 Philip Goodwin to Alfred Barr, 26 May 1942. MoMA Archives, NY: AHB [AAA: 2167; 0360-3].

52 Philip Goodwin to Alfred Barr, 3 June 1942. MoMA Archives, NY: AHB [AAA: 2167; 0354-5].

53 *Brazil Builds* p.8.

54 Philip Goodwin to Alfred Barr, 26 May 1942. MoMA Archives, NY: AHB [AAA: 2167; 0360-3].

55 Philip Goodwin to Alfred Barr, 3 June 1942. MoMA Archives, NY: AHB [AAA: 2167; 0354-5].

56 Philip Goodwin to Alfred Barr, 18 June 1942. MoMA Archives, NY: AHB [AAA: 2167; 0351-3].

57 Letter from Kidder-Smith, 20 March 1990.

58 Alfred Barr to Philip Goodwin, 30 July 1942. MoMA Department of Registration, NY: Brazil Builds, Exhibition No. 213.

59 Alfred Barr to Philip Goodwin, 30 July 1942. MoMA Department of Registration, NY: Brazil Builds, Exhibition No. 213.

60 Agnes Mongan, Curator of the Fogg Museum, to Monroe Wheeler, 16 July 1942. MoMA Department of Registration, NY: Brazil Builds, Exhibition No. 213.

61 Memorandum: Monroe Wheeler to Nelson Rockefeller, 26 August 1942. MoMA Department of Registration, NY: Brazil Builds, Exhibition No. 213.

62 Statement, 'Purchase of 3000 copies of Brazil Builds'. MoMA Department of Registration, NY: Brazil Builds, Exhibition No. 213.

63 Philip Goodwin to Monroe Wheeler, 2 September 1942. MoMA Department of Registration, NY: Brazil Builds, Exhibition No. 213.

64 Alice Carson to Elizabeth Mock, 9 October 1942. MoMA Department of Registration, NY: Brazil Builds, Exhibition No. 213. She was employed on a freelance basis for $1.00 an hour.

65 Alfred Barr to Philip Goodwin, 7 October 1942. MoMA Archives, NY: AHB [AAA: 2167; 0347-8].

66 Philip Goodwin to Monroe Wheeler, 2 September 1942. MoMA Department of Registration, NY: Brazil Builds, Exhibition No. 213.

# 9  The 'Brazil Builds' exhibition

The 'Brazil Builds' exhibition opened on 13 January 1943 in the Museum's new building on West Fifty-third Street and remained on view until 28 February (Figures 9.1 and 9.2). The exhibition occupied the entire main hall and ground floor gallery of the Museum (Figures 9.3 and 9.4). It was composed of photographic enlargements, architectural plans, models, maps and a continuous slide show. The installation of the exhibition was designed by Alice M. Carson. Barr described the opening as 'all very gay and festive' to which he jokingly added 'P.L.G. [Goodwin] contributed vast pots and tubs of tropical plant life which made some of us wonder whether it was a flower show or an architectural exhibition.'[1] 'Faces and Places in Brazil: Photography by Genevieve Naylor' was also showing in the Museum, in the foyer to the auditorium.

The exhibition was split into two parts, one devoted to the old architecture, which embraced a period of 280 years from 1652, and the second showing the Modern buildings which had been erected in the previous decade. The focus of the exhibition, however, was placed firmly on Modern architecture. The Museum's interest in the old architecture and its subsequent inclusion in the exhibition can also be seen as an attempt to legitimatise Modern architecture by drawing parallels with the architecture of certain periods of the past, and to reconcile the earlier 'heroic' phase of Modernism to differing climatic and cultural contexts. They described it themselves in a Bulletin:

> 'Land of contrasts' is a stock description of Brazil. This cliché has some validity, being as applicable to architecture as to climate and landscape. Yet old and new in Brazilian architecture are not completely dissimilar, for both have brilliantly met the unique demands of climate and geography and both reflect the living preferences and aesthetic convictions which have not altogether changed over two hundred odd years.[2]

These views could be held with some conviction because it was very much how the architects themselves, in particular Lucio Costa, saw Modern architecture in Brazil.

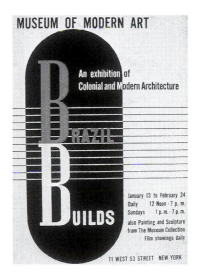

9.1 Announcement card of the exhibition 'Brazil Builds'. The Museum of Modern Art, New York, January 1943. Offset, printed in colour, 10⅛ × 7¼″ (25.7 × 18.4 cm). The Museum of Modern Art Library, The Museum of Modern Art, New York.
© 2000 The Museum of Modern Art, New York.

9.2 Invitation to the opening of the exhibition 'Brazil Builds'. The Museum of Modern Art, New York, 12 January 1943. Offset, printed in colour, 4½ × 6¼" (11.4 × 15.9 cm). The Museum of Modern Art Archives: Monroe Wheeler Papers, Museum Invitations vol. 1.
© 2000 The Museum of Modern Art, New York.

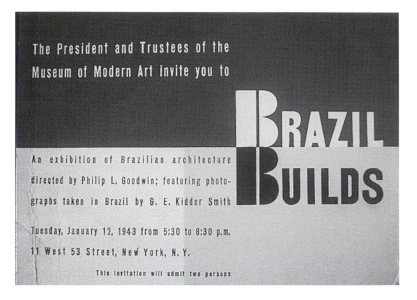

In the main hall of the Museum, a wooden map of Brazil was superimposed on the outline of South America painted on the wall. Cities and States shown in the exhibition were indicated on the map and aerial views of the Brazilian coastline bordered it. Next, the visitor to the exhibition was greeted by a screen on which 48 colour slides of Brazil were continuously projected. It is worth noting that a slide show would have been a great attraction, because Kodachrome colour slide film had just been made commercially available. A special slide projector had to be hired from E. Leitz Scientific Instruments at almost the same cost that the Museum rented the whole exhibition.[3]

The first section, which comprised just less than a third of the whole show, were dedicated to Colonial architecture. The second part, dedicated to Modern architecture, was divided into sections loosely based on building types. A bold colour scheme was used throughout the exhibition to evoke a feeling of the period – gold and rose in the Colonial galleries, and cool blues and light terracottas in the Modern [Appendix: 'Brazil Builds' Exhibitions: Large Version].

The visitor entered the exhibition through a gallery, painted grey and gold, devoted to the architecture of Bahia and Minas Gerais (Figure 9.5); he then passed into another gallery with buildings from Rio de Janeiro and Pernambuco, facing a wall of buildings from Belém (Figure 9.6). The first glimpse of a Modern building was an enormous photograph and model of the Ministry of Education Building, framed in the doorway to the Modern section (Figure 9.7). This gallery also contained the Brazilian Press Association Building. The next gallery was devoted to education: the School in Niterói, 'Sedes Sapientiæ', and Industrial Schools. Behind, a long wall with illustrations of Transportation Buildings: the Seaplane Terminal, Hangar No. 1 of Santos Dumont Airport, and the Boat Passenger Station; this wall ended in models of the *brise-soleils* from the Ministry of Education, the Brazilian Press Association, and the Yacht Club at Pampulha (Figure 9.8), which shielded these galleries from the large windows opening onto the

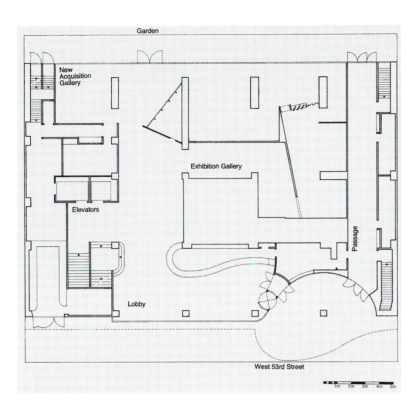

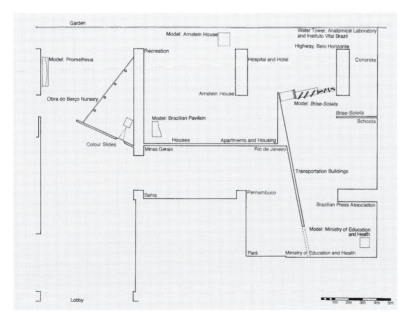

Museum's gardens. Three large galleries opened onto the gardens (Figure
9.9): a section containing a group of miscellaneous Modern buildings
which demonstrated the wide application of Modern architecture in Brazil;
a section on Recreation buildings showed the Pampulha complex and the
Brazilian Pavilion, followed by sections on hotels, apartment buildings and

9.5 Installation view of the exhibition 'Brazil Builds'. The Museum of Modern Art, New York, 13 January–28 February 1943. Photograph © 2000 The Museum of Modern Art, New York.
Colonial galleries: the architecture of Bahia and Minas Gerais.

The right-hand wall showed the Baroque architecture of Minas Gerais.

The wooden map of Brazil in the entrance hall showed the places illustrated in the exhibition.

9.6 Installation view of the exhibition 'Brazil Builds'. The Museum of Modern Art, New York, 13 January–28 February 1943. Photograph © 2000 The Museum of Modern Art, New York.
Colonial galleries: the architecture of Rio de Janeiro, Pernambuco and Belém.

The left-hand wall showed the Baroque architecture of Pernambuco.

private houses (Figure 9.10). Another two models were shown: the Brazilian Pavilion, and the Arnstein House by Bernard Rudofsky.

The visitor exited the exhibition into the main hall of the Museum. Facing him was a plaster sketch of Lipchitz's sculpture of Prometheus proposed for the auditorium wall of the Ministry of Education Building, attached to a model of the wall to display the original proportions. Finally, there was a panel suspended from poles which contained photographs of the Obra do Berço by Niemeyer.

While the choice of models in an exhibition may reveal the importance of a particular building, and in fact the Ministry of Education Building and the New York Pavilion were the most remarkable ones in the show, it was also a question of the availability of the models for the exhibition. The transportation of a model from Brazil to the United States, under war-time conditions, was difficult and expensive. Only the Ministry of Education

9.7 Installation view of the exhibition 'Brazil Builds'. The Museum of Modern Art, New York, 13 January–28 February 1943. Photograph © 2000 The Museum of Modern Art, New York.
Entrance to the Modern galleries.

Photograph, 8 × 12 feet, and model of the Ministry of Education, framed in the doorway from the Colonial Galleries.

The foreground wall showed the Colonial architecture of Rio de Janeiro.

9.8 Installation view of the exhibition 'Brazil Builds'. The Museum of Modern Art, New York, 13 January–28 February 1943. Photograph © 2000 The Museum of Modern Art, New York.
Modern galleries: models of the *brise-soleils* from the Ministry of Education, the Brazilian Press Association and the Yacht Club at Pampulha.

The *brise-soleils* shielded this gallery from the large windows opening onto the Museum's garden. The left-hand wall displayed Transportation buildings; the right-hand wall School buildings.

model had been thought worth the trouble of bringing to New York, for which insurance of US$750 was needed.[4] The other two models were included because they were already in the United States: the Pavilion already belonged to the Museum's collection and the Arnstein House by Bernard Rudofsky had been made specially for the exhibition and provided by the architect himself, who by then was living in New York.[5] The model of the sculpture of Prometheus, at the correct scale, had been commissioned by Goodwin himself specially for the exhibition.[6]

The modest publicity in the Museum *Bulletin* about the exhibition did not reflect its popularity. Goodwin had wanted coverage in the *Bulletin* as well as a book, because the *Bulletin* would go to many more members, but Barr disagreed; it was Museum policy to use the *Bulletin* for exhibitions which did not have accompanying catalogues or books.[7] Therefore 'Brazil Builds' did not make the cover of the *Bulletin* for that season: 'Arts in

9.9 Installation view of the exhibition 'Brazil Builds'. The Museum of Modern Art, New York, 13 January–28 February 1943. Photograph © 2000 The Museum of Modern Art, New York.
Modern galleries: Apartments and houses, opening onto the Museum's garden.

9.10 Installation view of the exhibition 'Brazil Builds'. The Museum of Modern Art, New York, 13 January–28 February 1943. Photograph © 2000 The Museum of Modern Art, New York.
Modern galleries: Private houses. Model of the Arnstein House.
© The Museum of Modern Art, New York.

Therapy' was the subject matter of that *Bulletin*, while the contemporary 'Brazil Builds' and 'Americans 1943: Realists and Magic Realists' were only mentioned briefly in the section 'Museum Notes'; 'Brazil Builds' got a one-page illustration.[8] Favourable comments in the Press were, however, recorded in the *Bulletin*.

There are no formal attendance records in the Museum's archives for 'Brazil Builds' alone, but for the first two months of 1943, during the showing of 'Brazil Builds', 'Twentieth Century Portraits', 'The Arts in Therapy', and 'Americans 1943', 59,633 people visited the museum, which was a high attendance for war-time and a marked increase over the previous year's attendance of 36,419 for the same period.[9] Taking into consideration the location and size of the 'Brazil Builds' exhibition, which occupied almost the entire ground floor of the Museum, a considerable percentage of general visitors must have had at least a sight of it.

So popular was the exhibition that the Museum quickly produced several versions for touring. After closing at the Museum on 28 February, 'Brazil Builds' circulated to museums and galleries around the United States, as well as Toronto and Mexico City, until April 1945 [Appendix: 'Brazil Builds' Itineraries: Large Version]. Special editions were prepared for showing in Brazil, at the request of the Office of Inter-American Affairs, and London, at the request of the Brazilian Embassy.[10] By the end of February, the Museum was overwhelmed with requests for the exhibition.[11] The Department of Circulating Exhibitions prepared a small version comprising 60 photographs for colleges and small galleries, which travelled from February 1944 to May 1946 [Appendix: 'Brazil Builds' Exhibitions: Small Version, 'Brazil Builds' Itineraries: Small Version]. A slide show of 86 slides was put together, which travelled around the United States and Canada from November 1943 to December 1947 [Appendix: 'Brazil Builds' Itineraries: Slide Show]. Later, in 1944, the Museum was able to report in the *Bulletin* that '*Brazil Builds* has been enormously popular here and abroad'.[12]

In Brazil, the exhibition was first shown at the Ministry of Education and Health on 23 November 1943, where it was installed by Oscar Niemeyer and opened by Gustavo Capanema (Figure 9.11). It then went to São Paulo where it was shown at the Galeria Prestes Maia; from there it circulated to various cities in the State of São Paulo and neighbouring States. The Office of Inter-American Affairs maintained an efficient network of agents in Brazil to implement and report on the success of the Office initiatives; Carleton Sprague-Smith accompanied the tour to several places as the representative of the Museum of Modern Art.[13] Presentation copies of the book were distributed to influential people, with personalised dedications; invitations were sent by messenger; posters were printed with the cover of the book; extensive publicity material and photographs were released to newspapers; attendances were counted – 66,388 came in São Paulo [Appendix: 'Brazil Builds' Itineraries: Brazil Version].[14]

The Museum became a major source of information on Brazil in the United States, and even on subjects not directly linked to architecture. For example, the Library of Congress obtained photographs for its archives; the *Encyclopaedia Britannica* requested a picture of the Ministry of Education for the 1944 Year Book; an educational publisher requested photographs for a high-school textbook. The New York Botanical Garden wanted information on plant life in Brazil.[15]

In short, 'Brazil Builds', unusually for an exhibition with architecture as its subject, was a popular success, being widely seen in New York and other American cities, as well as in Brazil. It had overtaken its model, 'Stockholm Builds', in size and popularity; although the result of a goodwill mission, it did not suffer the usual fate of such initiatives. Barr's prophecy about the Brazilian show was fulfilled:

I want to say again how delighted and excited I was about the Brazilian photographs. I think they will cause a sensation among American architects and that to an unusual extent the public will also be interested.[16]

## Notes

1  Alfred Barr to Kidder-Smith, 18 January 1943. MoMA Department of Registration, NY: Brazil Builds, Exhibition No. 213.

2  *The Bulletin of the Museum of Modern Art* (April 1943) p.14.

3  At $35 for the first week and $15 per week subsequently. E. Leitz Inc. to L. Anne Tredick (Assistant Department of Architecture), 11 December 1942. MoMA Department of Registration, NY: Brazil Builds, Exhibition No. 213. The exhibition was $75.00 for 3 weeks (see Appendix: 'Brazil Builds' Itinerary Large Version p.223).

4  Gustavo Capanema to Alfred Barr, May 1942. CPC–CPDOC/FGV doc.3.26.

5  Alice Carson to Sarah Newmeyer, 17 December 1942. MoMA Department of Registration, NY: Brazil Builds, Exhibition No. 213.

6  *The Bulletin of the Museum of Modern Art* (November 1944) p.9.

7  Alfred Barr to Philip Goodwin, 7 October 1942. MoMA Archives, NY: AHB  [AAA: 2167; 0347-8].

8  *The Bulletin of the Museum of Modern Art* (February 1943) pp.22–3.

9  *The Bulletin of the Museum of Modern Art* (April 1943) p.13.

10  The Museum sent the negatives for printing in London. As an exhibition was never arranged, the Embassy made the negatives available for publication.

11  Alice Carson to Elodie Courter, 26 February 1943. MoMA Department of Registration, NY: Brazil Builds, Exhibition No. 213.

12  *The Bulletin of the Museum of Modern Art* (November 1944) p.5.

13  Memorandum: OIAA, BD 3874, 3 July 1944. MoMA Archives, NY: CE, II.1/41(5).

14  Memorandum: OIAA, 204/SP, 12 April 1944. MoMA Archives, NY: CE, II.1/41(5).

15  Alice Carson to Robert C. Smith (Library of Congress), 5 October 1942; Encyclopaedia Britannica to MoMA, 8 December 1943; L. Ginn & Co. Educational Publishers to Elizabeth Mock, 8 December 1943; New York Botanical Garden to MoMA, 25 September 1944. MoMA Department of Registration, NY: Brazil Builds, Exhibition No. 213.

16  Alfred Barr to Philip Goodwin, 7 October 1942. MoMA Archives, NY: AHB  [AAA: 2167; 0347-8].

# 10  *Brazil Builds: Architecture new and old 1652–1942*

The book *Brazil Builds* had originally been published by the Museum as the catalogue of the exhibition, but due to its popularity was reprinted three times. It consisted of 200 pages with 300 illustrations, including four in colour. The text was written by Philip Goodwin; the editing and lay-out was largely credited to Elizabeth Mock; the cover and dust jacket were by E. McKnight Kauffer (1890–1954), a Modern illustrator and poster designer who had already designed several book covers.[1] The colours – brilliant green and yellow – were the colours of the Brazilian flag (Plate 16). It was written in parallel English and Portuguese texts (Figure 10.1).

It was left to Goodwin again to organise the production of the book, about which, it seems, he did not have any special knowledge. The printers, William E. Rudge's Sons, initially quoted for the printing of 3,200 copies of the book,[2] and separately for the colour plates and jackets.[3] Goodwin selected the paper, which was not without problems due to war-time conditions:

> 22,000 or 23,000 sheets of $38 \times 50$, basis $25 \times 38$ – 100/500, No. 2 Coated, grain the 50″ way, in ten days [. . .]. You are familiar enough with the paper situation to appreciate this is very rapid delivery.[4]

Goodwin also commissioned two leather-bound albums to be presented to the President of Brazil, Getúlio Vargas, and the Minister of Education, Gustavo Capanema, with the warning that he was 'trying to do a particularly handsome job' and hoped that the binders would 'take every care to see that these two albums are a success'.[5] They obviously were: Nelson Rockefeller thought that they were 'one of the best publications I have ever seen'.[6] The cost of these albums had been budgeted at $150.00 each in a petition for funds to the Office of Inter-American Affairs.[7]

The success of the book was totally unexpected by the Museum. In February 1943, Wheeler had authorised the dismantling of the block type by William E. Rudge's Sons.[8] By May 1943 *Brazil Builds* was out of print,[9] and Wheeler was debating whether to reprint it. He received some encouraging news from George Wittenborn, a major distributor of books on art in New York:

We have heard that you are considering a reprint of BRAZIL BUILDS – news that interests us very much. Due to its inclusion in our lists we receive almost daily requests for this book and we are sure there is a large, untapped market for this work even should the Museum be forced, through rising production costs, to increase the price.[10]

Wheeler wrote back asking advice on the possible price increase; he required to sell the second edition for between $7.00 and $7.50 as his costs would be around $4.00 per copy without subsidy.[11] This was a considerable increase over the original price of $3.75 to members and $5.00 to non-members,[12] which had been heavily subsidised by the Office of Inter-American Affairs. Wittenborn thought that $7.50 would be no hindrance to sales.[13] Fortunately, William E. Rudge's Sons had not broken up the blocks of type, and by the beginning of June had quoted for the work.[14] The price of the second edition of September 1943 was kept to $6.00 per copy.[15] *Brazil Builds* was reprinted twice more, with a third edition in November 1944 and a fourth in May 1946, although on lighter paper.

*Brazil Builds* was an example of the early style of book publication of the Museum of Modern Art, it brought together a variety of talents to produce a thoroughly convincing production [Appendix: *Brazil Builds*]. It continued the style set by *The International Style* with shiny-coated paper which enhanced the quality of black-and-white illustrations, plenty of white space on the page and blank pages to assist the narrative flow. A large photograph usually occupies the whole of the right-hand page and small photographs with explanatory notes in English and Portuguese on the facing page. The large photographs are usually bled all around to further heighten the impact. Within the main texts, small photographs and drawings illustrate points made in the text. Not all of the Museum's architectural catalogues were produced to this standard: many were simply typed sheets – 'Le Corbusier' and 'Modern Architecture in California', for example.

Kidder-Smith's photographs of Brazil were an attraction in themselves. He listed details of his equipment with pride in the preface to *Brazil Builds*: 'A Zeiss Juwel A camera, with Carl Zeiss Tessar and other lenses, a Zeiss Contax for the Kodachrome film, and a series D Graflex for the scenic shots.'[16] The black and white pictures were unusual in being very high quality and high contrast;[17] furthermore, Kodachrome colour slide film had just become commercially available. Kidder-Smith was careful to include context: old buildings and streets, landscape and foliage, and people for local colour and scale, and equally careful to exclude undesirable details, such as pitched roofs.

Goodwin's book followed the same organisation as the exhibition. The first part, comprising one-third of the book, was dedicated to historical architecture and the second to the Modern architecture, which was, in fact, the main purpose of the book [Appendix: *Brazil Builds*: Buildings]. Each part has an introduction in both English and Portuguese, running in parallel columns on each page, so that the nine pages in 'Introduction I' and 23 in 'Introduction II' are in fact no more than five and 12 pages of text respectively. In spite of both Introductions being quite short,

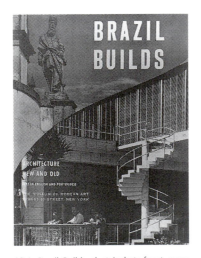

10.1 *Brazil Builds*, dust jacket: front cover in English (New York: The Museum of Modern Art, 1943). Offset, printed in colour, 11¼ × 8⅝" (28.6 × 22 cm). The Museum of Modern Art Library, The Museum of Modern Art, New York.
Photograph © 2000 The Museum of Modern Art, New York.

they are highly informative and critical of their subject. The remaining pages are filled with photographs with aphoristic notes which greatly complement the text; they describe individual aspects of the buildings. These notes included information on historic, economic and social conditions, and descriptions of settings, as well as Goodwin's own criticisms and appreciations.

Being primarily a picture book, and attempting to cover 300 years of architectural history, *Brazil Builds* did not allow for a detailed consideration of the various periods and places. Generalisations between various cities which were, in fact, very diverse in character and thousand of miles apart, gave, at times, the wrong impression of uniform development in all parts of the country. In particular, the difference between Rio de Janeiro and the more Italian and German character of the emerging industrial centre of São Paulo was glossed over.

Goodwin introduced the subject to the readers through an aerial view, as he had done to Barr in his first letter. As he described the views from his flight from Belém, in the north of the country, to Rio de Janeiro, in the south-east, he suggested that: 'In an aeroplane one can see hundreds of years of a nation's building in a few days.'[18] Referring to aeroplanes seems to have been a popular mode at that time, doubtless brought about by the greatly increased availability of flight. Other contemporary authors conjured up poetic descriptions of the views from an aeroplane to introduce their subjects such as John Summerson (1904–92) in *Georgian London*[19] and Le Corbusier in *Précisions*.[20]

In *Georgian London*, Summerson suggested a similar aerial introduction to London 'to watch the development of two hundred years in three and a half minutes'.[21] The similarity of the style of their writings is remarkable as they conjure up poetic descriptions of the views from an aeroplane. Goodwin of Brazil:

A shining silver aeroplane rushes over the great river Amazon, endless miles of rivers winding among marshes and islands far to the west.[22]

Summerson of London:

Below us the inconstant ribbon of the Thames curving backwards and forwards among marshes and meadows.[23]

Le Corbusier had also fully appreciated the value of the aerial view on his visit in 1929 to Rio de Janeiro:

when, by plane, everything becomes clear, and that topography – so animated and complex – has been understood [. . .] you have entered into the heart and soul of the city.[24]

His pilot, Antoine de Saint-Exupéry, was at that time engaged in writing *Night Flight*, his own work about flight in South America.[25]

Goodwin looked at the buildings of Brazil both as examples of the Modern style and as a product of the building industry and urbanisation process. His first aerial description revealed his interest in the pattern of

10.2 *Brazil Builds*, dust jacket: back cover in Portuguese (New York: The Museum of Modern Art, 1943). Offset, printed in colour, 11¼ × 8⅝″ (28.6 × 22 cm). The Museum of Modern Art Library, The Museum of Modern Art, New York. Photograph © 2000 The Museum of Modern Art, New York.

urban development in Brazil; he described that from Belém there were only 'desolate wastes of green hills, not a village or human trace in sight', until one got to the coast where 'the earth becomes a place for humans again', and to Rio de Janeiro 'there it lies, thin lines of high buildings circling long loops of surf' (see Figure 8.4).[26]

In 'Introduction I', Goodwin identified three influences which had affected architecture in the Colonial period, from 1520 to 1807: the 'Church, gold, and the Negro slave'.[27] Although these three influences constituted an extreme generalisation of a very long and diverse period (for instance, gold had not been discovered in Brazil before the eighteenth century), this revealed Goodwin's approach to context in the analysis of architecture: the three factors were seen as representative of the patron, economics, and the social conditions. To these, Goodwin added the 'constant factors of the land and the climate' and included a description of the climate in each of the various regions of the country.

Goodwin based his analysis of the architecture of the colonial period on the work of Robert C. Smith, an authority on Portuguese art and the related art of Colonial Brazil. Smith had put forward the idea that Colonial architecture in Brazil, such as in Salvador, the first capital of Brazil, remained essentially Portuguese; the similarity of climate and building materials was seen as the reason for it not differing from the architecture of the mother country (unlike the colonists of New England who had met a very different set of building conditions, and therefore developed a different architecture). In fact, only the eighteenth-century architecture of the mining towns shows a certain independence from the Portuguese Baroque style, and is seen as having a genuine national character; most of the examples illustrated in *Brazil Builds* were from this period (see Figure 8.6). Some earlier examples were shown, such as the São Bento Monastery in Rio de Janeiro of 1652, which was taken as the starting date for the book. The façade of this church and monastery was considered to be 'severe and unremarkable';[28] only the interiors were of interest for being of 'extraordinary richness'.[29] A few forts from the sixteenth century were also included.

The illustrations demonstrated a wide range of interest, as they showed examples of rural buildings – in *fazendas* (see Figure 8.3), the urban setting (see Figure 8.7) – in warehouses, town houses, and town villas, and vernacular buildings – such as the fishermen's huts in Pernambuco. Goodwin's book is essentially a Modernist text in its displeasure for the architecture of the nineteenth century. He dealt with it swiftly, from the French Mission of 1816 to the buildings on the Avenida Rio Branco in Rio de Janeiro of the early twentieth century. He concluded that:

> One fashion quickly followed another in the late 19th century. [. . .] The less said about them the better. Imposing they are, or mean to be, like the many clumps of monumental statuary which surround them [. . .]. Academic correctness was confused with living, breathing architecture, and the dreary pretentiousness of the result was equalled only by its sterility.[30]

Goodwin embodied the contemporary vision of the nineteenth century as a period of decline and confusion in architecture, and he put forward the doctrine that the Modern Movement had come as a redemption. He gave an introduction to the second part of the book by stating the good news that:

> The story has a happy ending. A few more years pass and almost overnight the lovely capital city was cured of its disease and began to reconsider its architectural possibilities in terms of modern building techniques.[31]

In the second part, Goodwin dealt with the subject he was, in fact, really concerned with: the 'advanced architecture'. Only built examples were included in *Brazil Builds*. Many were unfinished, still wrapped in scaffolding; few interiors could be shown. In 'Introduction II', he started by listing the three factors he believed made the Modern Movement possible in Brazil: the patronage of the state, the building boom, and Le Corbusier. Firstly, he stated that: 'Even before the advent of the Vargas government in 1930 there were Brazilian experiments in modern architecture',[32] he made it clear that the Vargas government had been responsible for the real advent of Modern architecture in Brazil, due to remarkable personalities such as Gustavo Capanema, who had commissioned the Ministry of Education building, and the Mayor of Belo Horizonte, who had commissioned the Pampulha complex.[33] These patrons had not only commissioned young Modern architects but also Modern artists, and had even been responsible for inviting Le Corbusier to Brazil. Other, anonymous, Government initiatives had resulted in Modern schools, hospitals and libraries.

Secondly, Goodwin considered the economic factor: 'From modest beginnings, the movement, happening to coincide with a building boom, spread like brushfire.'[34] Although 'coincide' might not be the appropriate word, Goodwin revealed that there was a new economic wealth in the country which had brought about a building boom which had encouraged experiments in modern architecture.

Lastly, he concluded that 'Le Corbusier had proved to be particularly sympathetic to young Brazilian architects' because of the large influence of French culture in Brazil. While it might be true that, because of French influence, architects could read Le Corbusier in the original, it should be added that Le Corbusier had a complete set of theories – social, technical, and artistic – which he propagated widely, and which were widely taken at the time to be the epitome of a rational industrial society. Other influences were German and Italian, due to the number of immigrants 'who came to Brazil already equipped with the new aesthetics'. The influences from the United States, Goodwin affirmed, were not aesthetic, but practical devices such as 'the elevator which made the skyscraper feasible, and it was the skyscraper which had changed the face of the great cities of São Paulo and Rio de Janeiro.'[35]

Goodwin's emphasis on context was doubtless due to his experience as a practising architect, which required a similar grasp of the necessities of patronage and construction, rather than concentrating on an essentially visual approach of contemporary historians. Goodwin focused on the buildings and on the processes which had made them possible, rather than on the individuals who had designed them. This approach was used in his analysis of both the old and the new architecture. In fact, the instigation of their expedition had been the 'keen desire' to know more about a very practical and technical device of architecture: 'the control of heat and light on large external glass surfaces'.[36] Goodwin was not interested in promoting the pioneers of Modern architecture in Brazil; he had been taken by both Warchavchik in São Paulo, and the Robertos in Rio de Janeiro, to their early Modernist houses, but he did not find much suitable for inclusion.[37] He included only one photograph of a house in the Rua Bahia (1931) by Warchavchik, and small illustrations of an apartment building and another house from his later, less heroic phase, which he referred to as 'a simple new house'.

A few architects had been overlooked by Goodwin; Roberto Burle Marx did not receive much coverage in *Brazil Builds*. He was mentioned by Goodwin only for his gardens at the Fazenda Garcia and Pampulha.[38] Burle Marx had designed the gardens for the Ministry of Education Building, but it is likely that they were not ready during Goodwin's visit as he did not show any photographs or remark on Burle Marx's involvement, although the Minister's roof garden appears on the plans.[39] He also designed the roof-top gardens of the Brazilian Press Association, but these, too, were not credited. Affonso Reidy was largely overlooked, being only mentioned as a participant in the Ministry group, even though he had been a very active Modern architect and had actually built one striking Modern building, the Albergue da Boa Vontade (1931), a hostel for the homeless which Goodwin had been taken to visit by Costa.[40]

On the other hand, Goodwin did show several buildings which he found suitably Modern, but were anonymous (Figure 8.5). He found several small scale buildings that he found worthy of inclusion such as the Water Tower (1936–7) in Olinda and the Anatomical Laboratory (1936–7), a Mortuary, in Recife which he used to demonstrate the wide extent of the Modern idiom and the 'fine contrast' of the new architecture against the old in these colonial towns.[41] Both buildings were by Luiz Nunes, but Goodwin left the former anonymous and credited the latter to Nunes' collaborator Fernando Saturnino de Brito, doubtless because Luiz Nunes had died in 1937.

In the same way that, in the Baroque period, Brazilian churches were influenced by Portuguese models but displayed a flavour of their own, Goodwin affirmed that in the twentieth century, 'While the first impetus came from abroad, Brazil went ahead on her own'.[42] For Goodwin, it was the determinants of climate and land which had led Brazil to develop a Modern architecture of her own. It was due to the tropical heat and intense sunlight that architects sought to find solutions to the problem of protecting large glass surfaces from the sun, one of the many encountered by early International Style buildings. Their solution of applying *brise-soleils* to the exterior of the façades he considered to have been 'Brazil's great original contribution to modern architecture', which he discussed in detail.[43] Le Corbusier was credited with having first used them for an unexecuted project in Barcelona, but the Brazilians with having put them into practice, and developing it into various types. All the Modern buildings Goodwin showed in the book displayed some type of *brise-soleils* from roll-up wooden blinds to the sophisticated system of the Ministry, which was considered the most successfully integrated with the architecture.

Goodwin described in some detail the materials used and their sources. He was greatly impressed by the large-scale use of reinforced concrete; he was astonished to find 'fifty tall buildings of reinforced concrete rising in one city, as was the case in Rio in 1942.'[44] He found many unusual materials and features which contributed to the originality of the buildings. Among them were *azulejos* – decorated glazed tiles – which he thought most suitable for Brazil, both historically and climatically; others were the well-related sculpture, mural painting and landscaping. Goodwin was particularly impressed by the great variety of colours in Burle Marx's landscape designs.[45]

Once the main architectural standards had been established, the buildings were judged as successes or failures by their ability to achieve them. Goodwin's judgements on both buildings and personalities are brief, firm and clear. He delighted in what he appreciated, mainly the Ministry of Education, the Brazilian Press Association, and the Pampulha complex. One apartment building in Rio de Janeiro was illustrated as an example of a failure in Modern design;[46] Pampulha was not considered a total success due to 'the weakness of colour, smallness of design and antique look of the tiles, so unrelated to the buildings they cover'.[47] There were inconsistencies: he showed an exaggerated interest in Bernard Rudofsky's houses, which, by being planned around courtyards, were more Mediterranean than Brazilian in character; he must have realised that the inclusion of São Paulo's Public Library, which was a Moderne design, was not really consistent with his appreciation of the other Modern buildings: it appeared in *Brazil Builds* covered in foliage. With what he disapproved of, he could be very direct: for instance, the Ministry of Finance being built next door to the Ministry of Education was regarded as 'a monster construction',[48] and apart from the Seaplane Terminal and Santos Dumont Airport in Rio de Janeiro, all the airport buildings were considered 'mediocre'.[49]

As Goodwin discussed the buildings, he also gave accounts of the social conditions in Brazil, which constitute a lively description of Brazil in the early 1940s. For instance, in his description of São Paulo's new Public Library and the new Modern schools, he reported that 'The upper class reads enormously but the many times larger lower class almost not at all', and that schools were most needed in the interior and north of the country.[50]

The book was intended for a North American audience, and North American buildings and conditions were used directly as standards for comparison. For instance, the new airport in Rio de Janeiro was held to have surpassed those of New York and Washington, not in scale, but in design;[51] Detroit and Houston were credited with not having grown like Rio de Janeiro and São Paulo;[52] Rio de Janeiro was compared to Manhattan in the restricted space in the centre – one on an island, the other sandwiched between mountains and the ocean; São Paulo's mayor, who was an engineer, was 'a combination of Moses and LaGuardia'.[53] Brazilian apartment houses were acknowledged to have good and simple taste in the use of colour, a taste which was difficult to find in Park Avenue;[54] and, the 'contemporary colonial style' houses were found to be as popular in Brazil as they were in the United States.[55]

Although briefly dealt with, due to the size of the book, various facets of the practice of architecture were included: the conditions of the profession, the average building costs, town planning, and housing. He addressed the latest developments of the new road system in São Paulo and the new tunnels in Rio de Janeiro, and criticised the old-fashioned plans of the new cities of Belo Horizonte and Goiás. Slum clearance and property development were examined.

*Brazil Builds* contains elements of formal criticism from three most important histories which had established the theoretical principles of the Modern Movement: *Pioneers of the Modern Movement* by Nikolaus Pevsner (1902–83), *Space, Time and Architecture* by Siegfried Giedion (1888–1968), and *The International Style* by Hitchcock and Johnson. From Giedion, Goodwin took the thesis of the 'constituent and transitory facts' in architecture.[56] The use of external blinds and decorated tiles in external walls was considered a recreation of the colonial *rótulas* and *azulejos*.

From Hitchcock, Goodwin took the view that Modern architecture was the triumph of a certain ideological formulation: Modernism. Like Hitchcock in *The International Style*, Goodwin glossed over the differences between the various buildings, especially between São Paulo and Rio de Janeiro, to show a uniform movement. He asserted that the Modern Movement had spread to all parts of the world, and sought to prove that it had triumphed in Brazil:

Whatever criticism has been levelled at the outstanding examples of buildings in the contemporary idiom – and much has been written and spoken against them – has failed to suggest any reasonable alternative.

It is hardly conceivable that young designers would be satisfied to make endless variations on such themes as the colonnaded addition to the Itamarati Palace, the Parisian fashions of the Avenida Rio Branco [. . .]. The new architecture has come to stay in Brazil.[57]

From Pevsner, Goodwin took the assumption that Modernism was the only possible alternative for the twentieth century; seeking to prove the Modern Movement as historically inevitable, Goodwin stated that:

Brazil has launched out into an adventurous but inevitable course. The rest of the world can admire what has been done and look forward to still finer things as time goes on.[58]

Where Goodwin differed from Giedion, Hitchcock and Pevsner is his appreciation that buildings were a product of many other factors, and not only of an aesthetic discourse; what he considered most remarkable in the new architecture in Brazil were its regional characteristics:

Firstly, it has the character of the country itself and the men there who have designed it. Secondly, it fits the climate and the materials for which it is intended. In particularly, the problem of protection from heat and glare has been courageously attacked and often brilliantly solved.[59]

## Notes

1 E. McKnight Kauffer worked extensively in advertising in the United Kingdom; his trademark consisted of a mixture of photographs and bold typography superimposed on blocks of colour. He returned to the United States and worked for MoMA. MoMA held an exhibition of his posters in 1937.

2 William E. Rudge's Sons to Monroe Wheeler, 12 November 1942. MoMA Department of Registration, NY: Brazil Builds, Exhibition No. 213.

3 William E. Rudge's Sons to Ione Ulrich, 16 November 1942. MoMA Department of Registration, NY: Brazil Builds, Exhibition No. 213.

4 Stevens-Nelson Paper Corporation to Monroe Wheeler, 13 November 1942. MoMA Department of Registration, NY: Brazil Builds, Exhibition No. 213.

5 Philip Goodwin to Brewer-Cantelmo Company, 21 January 1943. MoMA Department of Registration, NY: Brazil Builds, Exhibition No. 213.

6 Nelson Rockefeller to Monroe Wheeler, 15 February 1943. MoMA Department of Registration, NY: Brazil Builds, Exhibition No. 213.

7 Statement, 'Purchase of 3000 copies of Brazil Builds'. MoMA Department of Registration, NY: Brazil Builds, Exhibition No. 213.

8 William E. Rudge's Sons to Monroe Wheeler, 7 June 1942. MoMA Department of Registration, NY: Brazil Builds, Exhibition No. 213.

9 Information for Annual Report, 1943. MoMA Department of Registration, NY: Brazil Builds, Exhibition No. 213.

10 Wittenborn and Company, Books on the Fine Arts, to Monroe Wheeler, 10 August 1943. MoMA Department of Registration, NY: Brazil Builds, Exhibition No. 213.

11 Monroe Wheeler to Wittenborn and Company, 24 August 1943. MoMA Department of Registration, NY: Brazil Builds, Exhibition No. 213.

12 *The Bulletin of the Museum of Modern Art* (April 1943).

13 Wittenborn and Company to Monroe Wheeler, 28 August 1943. MoMA Department of Registration, NY: Brazil Builds, Exhibition No. 213.

14 William E. Rudge's Sons to Monroe Wheeler, 7 June 1942. MoMA Department of Registration, NY: Brazil Builds, Exhibition No. 213.

15 Brochure for *Brazil Builds* 2nd edn. MoMA Department of Registration, NY: Brazil Builds, Exhibition No. 213.

16 *Brazil Builds* p.7.

17 Kidder-Smith had been specially commissioned because existing photographic material of Brazilian architecture was considered poor. Record of conversation with Paul Lester Wiener, re Brazilian Architecture material [before 4 March 1942]. MoMA Department of Registration, NY: Brazil Builds, Exhibition No. 213.

18 *Brazil Builds* p.17.

19 John Summerson: *Georgian London* (London: Peregrine 1944; 3rd edn 1978) p.18.

20 Le Corbusier, *Précisions*, p.235–6. Le Corbusier published his own eulogy to flight in *Aircraft* (London: Studio 1935).

21 Summerson in *Georgian London* p.5.

22 *Brazil Builds* p.17.

23 Summerson: *Georgian London* p.18.

24 Le Corbusier: *Précisions* p.235–6.
    *Quand, par l'avion, tout vous est devenu clair, et que cette topographie – ce corps si mouvementé et si complexe – vous l'avez apprise [. . .] vous êtes entré dans le corps et le coeur de la ville.*

25 Antoine de Saint-Exupéry: *Vol de Nuit* (Paris: Gallimard 1931). He had also written *Flight to Arras* (1926) and *Southern Mail* (1929).

26 *Brazil Builds* p.17.

27 *Brazil Builds* p.18.

28 *Brazil Builds* p.32.

29 *Brazil Builds* p.17.

30 *Brazil Builds* p.25.

31 *Brazil Builds* p.25.

32 *Brazil Builds* p.81.

33 The Mayor of Belo Horizonte was Juscelino Kubitschek, later President of Brazil and responsible for commissioning Brasília. Goodwin did not name him.

34  *Brazil Builds* p.81.
35  *Brazil Builds* p.81.
36  *Brazil Builds* p.92.
37  *Brazil Builds* pp.99, 118, 179.
38  *Brazil Builds* pp.38–9, 194.
39  *Brazil Builds* p.111.
40  Philip Goodwin to Alfred Barr, 26 May 1942. MoMA Archives, NY: AHB [AAA: 2167; 0360–3].
41  *Brazil Builds* pp.158–9.
42  *Brazil Builds* p.81.
43  *Brazil Builds* pp.81. 84–89.
44  *Brazil Builds* p.97.
45  *Brazil Builds* p.101.
46  *Brazil Builds* p.117.
47  *Brazil Builds* p.90.
48  *Brazil Builds* p.92.
49  *Brazil Builds* p.93.
50  *Brazil Builds* p.93.
51  *Brazil Builds* p.93.
52  *Brazil Builds* p.95.
53  *Brazil Builds* p.94.
54  *Brazil Builds* p.97.
55  *Brazil Builds* p.100.
56  Siegfried Giedion: *Space, Time and Architecture* (Cambridge MA: Harvard University Press 1941; 5th edn 1967) p.15. The 'constituent facts' are those which, when suppressed, would inevitably reappear; the 'transitory facts' would fail to attach themselves to a new order.
57  *Brazil Builds* p.103.
58  *Brazil Builds* p.103.
59  *Brazil Builds* p.103.

# PART V
## THE 'BRAZILIAN STYLE'

From Europe our view of the new architecture of Brazil is almost as misty and romantic as was our forefathers' of Hy Brazil, that vast and legendary glass tower off the coast of Galway, inhabited by fabulous creatures. To the European architect, few creatures could look as fabulous as his Brazilian counterpart as he appears in the stories which filter back from Rio – of men with Cadillacs, super-charged hydroplanes, collections of modern art to make the galleries blush, bikini-clad receptionists and no visible assistants – nor could any glass towers of medieval imagination appear as improbable as skyscrapers which are reported to have been returned to the vertical by hydraulic jacks resting on refrigerated quicksands.

'Report on Brazil' *Architectural Review* (October 1954)

14 New York World's Fair 1939. General plan.
Violet: Government (around the oval Lagoon of Nations). G3 Brazilian Pavilion.
Orange: Community interests.
Pink: Food.
Green: Communications and business systems.
Blue: Production and distribution.
Yellow: Amusement area around Fountain Lake.
Brown: Transportation.
*Official Guide Book.*

15 'Zé Carioca' showing Donald Duck the sights of Rio.
© Disney Enterprises, Inc.

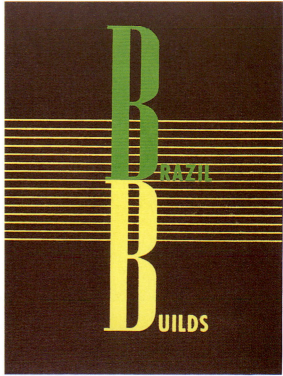

16 *Brazil Builds* (New York: The Museum of Modern Art 1943).
Cover by E. McKnight Kauffer. Holüstan Roxite Buckram black with yellow and green ink stamping, 8¾ × 11" (22 × 27.9 cm).
Photograph © 2000 The Museum of Modern Art, New York.

17 View of the Parque Glória-Flamengo, Rio de Janeiro (1952–c.1969), from Pão de Açucar. Landscaping by Roberto Burle Marx. The Hotel Gloria is on the extreme left; the Museu de Arte Moderna (1954–60) by Affonso Reidy is opposite, almost exactly on the site chosen by Le Corbusier for his first design for the Ministry of Education on the Praia de Santa Luzia. The Ministry of Education (1936–42) by Lucio Costa is no longer visible immediately behind the Museum; the Central Terminal of Santos Dumont Airport (1937–44) by M.M. Roberto is just out of sight to the right.
© Zilah Quezado Deckker.

18 Oscar Niemeyer with Zenon Lotufo, Helio Uchôa and Eduardo Kneese de Mello: Exhibition Building, Parque do Ibirapuera, São Paulo (1951–4).
Interior.
© Zilah Quezado Deckker.

19 Oscar Niemeyer: Niemeyer House, Gávea, Rio de Janeiro (1953).
© Zilah Quezado Deckker.

20 Lucio Costa with Le Corbusier: Maison du Brésil, Cité Universitaire, Paris (1957–9).
Interior: Entrance hall.
© Zilah Quezado Deckker.

21 Lina Bo Bardi: Museu de Arte de São Paulo (1957–68).
Interior: temporary exhibition space underneath the podium.
© Zilah Quezado Deckker.

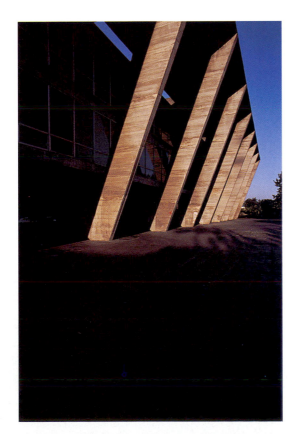

22 Affonso Eduardo Reidy: Museu de Arte Moderna, Rio de Janeiro (1954–60).
The site of Le Corbusier's proposal for the Ministry of Education at the Praia de Santa Luzia.
© Zilah Quezado Deckker.

23 Vilanova Artigas and Carlos Cascaldi: Faculdade de Arquitetura e Urbanismo da Universidade de São Paulo, São Paulo (1961).
Interior.
© Zilah Quezado Deckker.

24 Lucio Costa, urban design and Oscar Niemeyer, architect: Congresso Nacional, Brasília (1957–60).
View of the Congresso Nacional from the Esplanada dos Ministérios.
© Zilah Quezado Deckker.

26 Lucio Costa, urban design and Oscar Niemeyer, architect: *superquadras*, Brasília (1957–60).
An original *superquadra* with landscaping by Roberto Burle Marx.
© Zilah Quezado Deckker.

25 Lucio Costa, urban design and Oscar Niemeyer, architect: Tribunal Superior de Justiça, Praça dos Três Poderes, Brasília (1957–60).
© Zilah Quezado Deckker.

27 Oscar Niemeyer: Panteão da Pátria, Praça dos Três Poderes, Brasília (1987).
© Zilah Quezado Deckker.

28 Roberto Burle Marx: gardens of the Ministério do Exército, Brasília (1970).
© Zilah Quezado Deckker.

# 11  *Brazil Builds* and the press

The opening of the exhibition 'Brazil Builds' catapulted Brazil, which previously had been virtually unknown in architectural circles, into the forefront of the world of Modern architecture. The architectural press reviewed the exhibition and the book with admiration. 'Brazil Builds' received immediate coverage in the popular press as well. Reports had begun to appear from October 1942 before the exhibition opened and frequent notices continued into 1946 as the exhibition travelled around the United States.

On 13 January 1943, the Art sections of the New York newspapers featured photographs of the Ministry of Education Building announcing the opening of the show. The opening itself was a social event with political overtones: Maria Martins (1900–73), a well-known Surrealist sculptor and wife of the Brazilian ambassador, was photographed with Philip Goodwin against the large panel of the Ministry Building (Figure 11.1).[1] The headlines in the New York newspapers in January 1943 displayed the same enthusiasm for Brazil's involvement in the war, 'Natal Feeds U.S. Bombers to Fighting Fronts: Base in Brazil Is Key Point in Ferry Service'[2] as to its architecture, 'Brazilian Architecture: Our Progressive Neighbour to the South Shows Us How'.[3]

11.1 *'Brazil Builds'.*
*Herald Tribune*, New York, NY (17 January 1943).
*The South American nation's great progress in modern architecture is being demonstrated at an exhibition being conducted at the Museum of Modern Art, 11 West Fifty-third Street, until March 7* [sic. actually 23 February], *when it will begin a tour of American schools and colleges. Left: Mme Carlos Martins, wife of Brazil's Ambassador to the United States, is conducted through the exhibit by Philip L. Goodwin, director.*

On Goodwin's return from Brazil, the Museum of Modern Art had acted to restrict the publication of material before the opening of the exhibition. The first photographs had appeared in October 1942 in *Life*, where Brazil was declared to be 'a paradise for young architects'.[4] Nevertheless, the Museum was reliant on publicity, and was naturally anxious to promote the exhibition. Its press releases repeated the key points of Goodwin's text:

> The Brazilian Government leads all other national governments in the Western Hemisphere in its discriminating and active encouragement of modern architecture. [...] Rio de Janeiro has the most beautiful government building in the Western hemisphere, the new Ministry of Education and Health. [...] The capitals of the world that will need rebuilding after the war can look to no finer models than the modern buildings of the capital city of Brazil.[5]

As Director of the exhibition, Goodwin contributed to relations with the public in a decisive way: his statements resonated with the cadences of Scripture. Goodwin's claim that the Brazilian government was taking the lead in modern architecture in the Western hemisphere, and that, because of the war, this position was pre-eminent in the world, was echoed by the press which put forward a new role for Brazil:

> A current exhibition in the Museum of Modern Art in New York will cause visitors and others to realize that not all progress is confined to the U.S. Some of it is made in the United States of Brazil. [...] Some of them can make even a New Yorker gape in admiration and envy. [...] Brazil is now seen as something more than a producer of coffee. It is seen as a land of progress and unlimited opportunity.[6]

> Along with coffee, cotton, canned meat, hides and skins, cocoa, carnauba wax, castor beans and rubber, Brazil may be exporting to North America – when happier days of peace are won – ferro-concrete architecture with the welcoming addition of the 'sun break'.[7]

Brazil was held up as an example for the post-war reconstruction of Europe:

> When bombed cities of Europe start rebuilding after the war, they may find in Brazil many ideas for their new structures.[8]

> The exhibition has a very direct bearing on post-war reconstruction. Brazil has much to offer in this respect and what has already been achieved there deserves to be studied with the greatest attention.[9]

Elizabeth Mock, who had been responsible to a large degree for the editing of the book, was chosen by the Museum as the best person to write about Brazilian architecture for the lay reader.[10] She extended the same line as Goodwin in articles for the popular press:

Some of the world's boldest and most successful innovations in Architecture are taking place on an impressive scale in a sub-tropical Portuguese-speaking country which North Americans have too often ignored.[11]

She also developed the theme that these Modern features were a continuation of the colonial and Baroque architecture of the seventeenth and eighteenth centuries: the *brise-soleil* was said to be the reappearance of a historical feature in both its functional and aesthetic qualities:

> For centuries Brazilians had shaded their houses with covered verandas and projecting eaves, with lattice-work and shutters.
>    The same insistence on façade though in very different terms is found in the bold outlines and elaborately sculptured fronts of Brazil's eighteenth century baroque churches.[12]

The use of reinforced concrete which allowed the building to be raised from the ground on *pilotis* was also said to have a past precedent:

> The open loggia [. . .] provides welcome shelter from the sun and the frequent rains. What is more, it insulates the main part of the building from the damp ground. For the same good reason, the living quarters of many of the old houses of this region were placed above a high basement.[13]

And lastly, the finishing materials and related works of art also found historical justification:

> The popularity of blue and white tile work goes back to the early eighteenth century, when the fashion was imported from Portugal, and frequently the tiles themselves. Brazilian churches at that time were often embellished with tile murals of classic or Biblical scenes, as [. . .] in the case of Bahia. In a tropical climate their cool, washable surface has always been appropriate.
>    The effect of richness and elegance is often enhanced by well-related sculpture, mural painting and landscaping. Here again one finds ample historical precedent. Consider the famous eighteenth century pilgrimage church of Bom Jesus in the hill town of Congonhas do Campo. The front of the church and the beautiful terraced garden are decorated with marvellous baroque carvings and vigorous statues by Aleijadinho, the master sculptor.[14]

The much vaunted contrast of new and old, which was such a feature of Kidder-Smith's photographs, was not appreciated by all:

> Portuguese baroque and 'functional' modern do not often blend. There is a sharp line of demarcation. This becomes conspicuously evident as we study the handsome modern home of the Brazilian Press Association at Rio; as we study it in relation to some of the architecture that surrounds it. Most startling of all is a photograph in which the severely designed water tower at Olinda, Pernambuco, rises close beside a Portuguese baroque church. The juxtaposition is most unhappy.[15]

*Time*, however, considered Brazil's architecture 'one of the artistic glories of the Western hemisphere' and agreed that 'the baroque is now neighbour to the modern'.[16]

That the American press was ready to marvel at the Ministry of Education as the best building in their hemisphere despite the accomplishments of the Rockefeller Center and Radio City Music Hall was quite extraordinary, and there was some irony in the enthusiasm:

> all these cultural expeditions have been going the wrong way. They should have been coming north instead of going south. We are the benighted ones; not the Brazilians.
>
>  Did you imagine, for instance, that our Radio City buildings were the very last word in elegance and utility? Well, how ridiculous that turns out to be. You were completely misinformed.[17]

Another writer, although admitting that the utilitarian aspects of the Ministry of Education and Health were of a high order, pointed out that it was more a European than a native Brazilian architecture:

> As for the modern architecture, it can be said that it looks towards Europe for its sources rather than to the native background. It is, therefore, more of a unity with the sophisticated life of São Paulo and Rio de Janeiro than with any totality of native life and culture.[18]

Questions were occasionally raised specifically on the point that the exhibition dealt with only one facet of architecture in Brazil. An attack that the Museum's approach showed too restricted a view on such an inclusive title, prompted a defensive article by Catherine Bauer, who had written on housing for the Museum, stating that it was not the intention to include, in a small exhibition and book, an encyclopaedic survey of Brazilian history, architecture, economy, and politics; instead it was meant to have 'opened up and high-lighted a field too long ignored by most North Americans'.[19] Others, however, considered Goodwin's approach to have contributed to a better understanding of the subject; he had:

> Not written a mere exercise in style and technique or even an arid comparative study. His book is organized to make the most of architecture's many facets, and through it we come to a better understanding of Brazilian life than might be gained from a longer, more literary, or more critical work.[20]

Elizabeth Wilder, Editor of *Studies in Latin American Art*, attempted to put the architectural achievement into the social context of contemporary Brazil:

> It is only just to balance this enthusiasm by the observation that most of Brazil is still badly housed, that most of the country is without schools or hospitals of any sort, and that outside the few cities represented here functionalism has hardly been heard of. In short, the architects are ahead of social planners; they ought to be set to work on small hospitals for provincial towns, day nurseries, community centers, and subsistence

housing for the people who now live between banana thatch and bamboo floor. Brazil needs all these things desperately, needs them rather than casinos and hotels.[21]

However, the Ministry of Education and Health Building was seen as a portent of a bright future:

Looking at the new Ministry of Education and Health, however, one expects Brazil to proceed to these problems: one cannot but have faith in a country which produces such public building instead of a Roman temple.[22]

It is interesting to note that the New York press was not equally enthusiastic about most of the shows of Latin American art. In fact, the popular press had been very critical of the sudden wave of Latin American subjects in New York galleries:

This year, egged on by Europe's war and talk of Pan-American solidarity, U.S. art galleries have plastered their walls with Latin American art. But though an unprecedented quantity of pictures and sculpture from south of the Rio Grande is being exhibited from coast to coast, Latin American art plays to a poor box office. [. . .] Main reason for the gallery-goers' apathy: most of the contemporary Latin American art shown has looked like the post cards tourists send home.[23]

The reservations were overwhelmed by assertive approval. For the great majority of critics in the United States, 'Brazil Builds' was a new world of excitement, as shown in some of the headlines: 'Brazil Builds For The Future',[24] 'Brazil Blazes Modern Trail In Architecture',[25] 'Brazil Replaces Windows with Sun-Reflecting Panels',[26] 'Brazil has much to offer U.S.',[27] 'Brazil leads U.S. in Modern Architecture',[28] 'Brazil Goes Ultra-Modern' (Figure 11.2),[29] and 'Brazil Builds For Peace' (Figure 11.3).[30] Misunderstandings, of course, occurred: one newspaper reported that 'Brazil Blazes Modern Trail in Agriculture'.[31]

'Brazil Builds' quickly became a fashion item: *Women's Wear Daily* depicted that 'Exhibition of Architecture of Brilliant South American City is Reminder of Growing Appreciation of Good Clothes that will Provide Postwar opportunities for New York Style Leadership'.[32] *Mademoiselle* included the Casino at Pampulha in its section 'What is new in . . .' in March, and in April showed the Ministry of Education as a background for 'The New After Dark Look' (Figure 11.4).[33] *Home and Food* featured a fashion Hats Collection with the photographs of Brazilian buildings providing the background (Figure 11.5).[34]

Subject matter from 'Brazil Builds' was incorporated into a variety of different interests. 'Brazil Uses Imagination in School Construction' was the headline of a periodical dedicated to school management.[35] Photography magazines used photographs of the Ministry of Education for experiments in composite pictures.[36]

The publication *Brazil Builds* itself received substantial praise. The *American Printer* listed it in its '50 Best Books of the Year'.[37] It was a 'Book

11.2 *Brazil Goes Ultra Modern.*
*Press*, Pittsburgh, PA (31 January 1944).
*For more than a decade Brazil has been experiencing a building boom in its key cities, Rio de Janeiro and São Paulo. But instead of erecting standard conservative structures, Brazil has developed a new modern architecture which is unusual because most governments are conservative when it comes to architecture and prefer classic designs.*

*After the war, when the capitals of the world start rebuilding, they perhaps should look to Brazil for new ideas. The modern trend is portrayed in these pictures taken from a Brazilian architecture exhibit at New York's Museum of Modern Art.*

Clinic Selection' of *Book Binding and Book Production* [Appendix: Specification *Brazil Builds*] which praised its Modern style:

> Worthy of its contents, the format of this collection of pictures and text is no less modern than the 20th-century buildings it depicts. It was inevitably a Book Clinic Selection, from its brilliant binding stamped in parrot greens and yellows to the 4-colour and black-and-white bleed plates, sanserif types, and dynamic layouts within. [. . .] The result is a splendidly unified text that may well set a style.[38]

For the professional press, too, 'Brazil Builds' was a new world of excitement. It initiated a period when Brazilian buildings featured frequently in architectural journals. Kidder-Smith's photographs of the new work in

11.3 *Brazil Builds for Peace.*
*Citizen*, Columbus, OH (23 November 1945).
*Exhibition at Art Gallery Depicts Progress Made In Modern Architecture by Southern Republic.*

Brazil appeared in architectural publications even before the exhibition opened. The Museum had decided to release photographs of minor works to the widely-circulated *Architectural Record*, rather than to the rival *Architectural Forum*, with whom they had been 'somewhat allied' in the past, because they believed that they would receive 'more careful treatment and space'.[39] The *Architectural Record* covered the Roberto brothers' Hangar No. 1 at Santos Dumont Airport intensively over four pages in December 1942.[40]

The first reports on the exhibition itself appeared in *Architectural Record* and *Pencil Points* concurrently with its opening in January 1943. The coverage in *Architectural Record* constituted almost a special issue on Brazil. Under the title 'Architecture of Brazil' they showed several photographs of historic buildings, as well as reproducing every Modern building

11.4 *The New After Dark Look*.
*Mademoiselle* (April 1943).

from *Brazil Builds* except the Ministry of Education and Health Building.[41] *Pencil Points*, in an article 'Brazilian Architecture: Living and Building Below the Equator', concentrated on the use of *brise-soleils* and conditions of professional practice.[42] The following month, *Architectural Forum* featured the Ministry of Education and Health Building in great detail in 'Office Building for Ministry of Education and Health, Rio de Janeiro', including Le Corbusier's sketches, the design drawings, and working drawings of the *brise-soleils*. It seems that there had been an agreement between the two leading American journals that the Ministry of Education was worth all the other buildings. The editor of the *Architectural Forum* argued that:

> The Ministry of Education and Health, now approaching completion, is probably the most exciting example of modern architecture in the Western Hemisphere. [...] It demonstrates more forcibly than any of its predecessors that contemporary architecture contains within itself

11.5  Hats Collection.
*Home and Food* (April 1943).

the seeds of a beauty and richness that is different from, but in no way inferior to the building of past ages. It shows, too, that the modern architect, even when commissioned to do a single building, is acutely conscious of the new requirements of city planning.[43]

*California Arts & Architecture*, then about to embark on the Case Study house programme under John Entenza, had a policy of reprinting articles from MoMA catalogues, although its coverage of 'Brazil Builds' was not extensive. It published a general review of *Brazil Builds* in February 1943;[44] in September, Ray Eames (1916–88) used the Ministry of Education Building in a spread with other icons of Modernity such as the Willys Jeep, Picasso's 'Guernica', an Eames chair, Lehmbruck's 'Kneeling Woman', and an electricity pylon (Figure 11.6).[45]

In all the subsequent coverage in architectural periodicals, the Ministry of Education and Health received the most scrutiny and was the most praised building. Philip Goodwin's succinct description of its importance as the first office building fully committed to European Modernism by a government enterprise was emphasised by all the critics who reported on the show. The Ministry Building fuelled the contemporary debate on the aesthetic merit of Modernism as the newly-completed building was seen as a strong case in its favour.

Perhaps most astonishing for the North American architect was that this 'ultra-modern' architecture was taking shape in, of all places, Brazil. The critics readily emphasised this point:

To the untutored among us who consider Brazil or any other nation to be backward because conditions are unfamiliar, this may come as a shock.[46]

11.6 Layout by Ray Eames for *California Arts and Architecture* (September 1943). Images include: the Ministry of Education, the Willys Jeep, Picasso's 'Guernica', an Eames chair, Lehmbruck's 'Kneeling Woman', and an electricity pylon.

The comparison with conditions in the United States, and other countries where Modern architecture was said to lack State patronage, accentuated the uniqueness of the Brazilian situation:

> But the boom, and even the coincident existence of a body of architectural ability, would not have been enough alone. Similar conditions have at times existed in the United States and other countries, with results by no means as impressive.[47]

The results were the more remarkable, as was unanimously pointed out, in a country which was larger than the United States and had a landscape of varied topography and sharp contrasts. The most striking characteristic of Brazil's old and modern buildings was considered by the critics to be their adaptation to the climate and land. Typically enthusiastic was the assessment by the editor of the *Architectural Record*:

> Brilliant contrasts give character to Brazilian life and Brazilian architecture – sunlight and shadow, broad sea and rugged hills, lazy siestas and progressive activity – and, in architecture, picturesque, traditional Colonial, of Portugal, and the most modern Twentieth Century design. Some of the modern work is brilliant, some distinguished, some exotic, but all is interesting. Through all the building of Brazil, ancient or modern, one finds the imprint of the character of the country, the climate, and its people.[48]

Concurrent with the opening of the exhibition at the Boston Museum of Fine Arts in March 1943, a symposium on Brazilian architecture was held and brought together the only three persons who had any previous knowledge of Brazilian architecture in the North American architectural circle: Paul Lester Wiener, Robert C. Smith and Bernard Rudofsky. They found no cause to disagree with Philip Goodwin's views; instead they contributed to his credit. In his talk 'Background to Brazilian Architecture', Wiener gave the testimony of one familiar with the buildings:

> Brazil is the country where the impact of Europe and America meet. The new architecture is a synthesis of this impact. It is not a copy of European or American, but creatively synthesizes some Corbusier ideas by using the new 'thinking' and new technique for the problem of Brazil.
>
> By meeting climatic conditions and functions, the Ministry of Education building arrives at something quite Brazilian. If you study it on the site as I have done with Oscar Niemeyer, you will find a generosity of space, an openness of plan and a boldness of architectural solutions that somehow results in an atmosphere of grace and gentility which are true reflections of the Brazilian character.[49]

Robert C. Smith was recognised as the leading authority on Portuguese art and the related art of colonial Brazil. He wrote in *Art News*, highly praising the exhibition:

> It makes known a whole new school of modern architecture [. . .] the only study to date of this remarkable achievement. [. . .] Coming at a moment when in Brazil as elsewhere all such building work must be suspended because of the war, the Museum of Modern Art's exhibition is a timely tribute as well as an invaluable service for the recording of architectural history.[50]

Smith's accounts of Colonial architecture complemented Goodwin's descriptions as he gave further insights into the related Portuguese architecture. In dealing with Modern architecture, he again shared most of Goodwin's views, especially in finding it closely related to the colonial architecture of the seventeenth and eighteenth centuries. He added to this point by identifying other elements:

> Another characteristic of modern Brazilian design is the use of a single sloping roof, inspired perhaps from the old colonial roofing *de uma agua* [. . .]. In his Cavalcanti House at Rio this sloping roof is combined with rough stone masonry that recalls the construction of Minas Gerais and before them the granite farmhouses and granaries of the Oporto region of Portugal. The eighteenth century Luso-Brazilian fondness for the sparingly used curve as the principal decorative note in a formal design reappears in striking form in such Brazilian inventions as the subtle breaks in the roofline of connecting passageways in the 'Sedes Sapientiæ' the suggestion of a triple barrel vault at the entrance of the Rio Boat Station, the flaring wings of the New York pavilion, and the portal of the Pampulha casino.[51]

Bernard Rudofsky, who had lived in Brazil from 1938 to 1941, was then living in New York and was associate editor of *Pencil Points*. He was thus able to publish his talk as well as his two houses shown in the exhibition in great detail.[52] In his article 'On Architecture and Architects', Rudofsky concentrated on answering the question of how those Modern buildings appeared in Brazil. He considered a string of questions in an attempt to decipher such a phenomenon:

> Who are these people who work quietly, without annoying the rest of the world with tales of their deeds? What drives these Brazilian builders and architects, and why has their government not failed them? And why was Brazil qualified to carry European ideals to fruition when the light went out in their home country?[53]

For Rudofsky, the answer lay in a purity of life which he believed was still to be found in Brazilian society, which, reflected in the architectural profession, meant that:

> The Brazilian architect likewise prides himself on having helped to maintain the purity of his vocation. His profession has not yet been infected by the pest of decorators, designers, or architectural design factories. His success is seldom expressed in terms of money or bulk of production.[54]

He considered, furthermore, that the profession in Brazil had not succumbed to cultural homogenisation:

> In Brazilian architecture one finds a wealth of native peculiarities which eloquently dispose of the insinuation that the architects follow a formula imported from abroad. However, forces are at work today which pave the way for standardization which might result in dulling the people's sensitivities.[55]

The reception *Brazil Builds* received from the English architectural periodicals confirmed the 'unrivalled' aspect of the Brazilian buildings. Reviewers all agreed that *Brazil Builds* was beautifully produced and well illustrated:

> The book is superbly produced. The text is scholarly and brief, the photographs good in the taking and in the reproduction.[56]

> The book is delightful in every way, with a lively text by Mr. Goodwin and brilliant photographs by Mr. Kidder Smith. The colour photograph of a church at Salvador, with gold ornament, writhing over everything like some fantastic ivy, is a regular knock-out.[57]

A reviewer in the *Journal of the Royal Institute of British Architects* remarked that the Brazilian architecture represented a new, and local, variation, of earlier Modernism:

> In some ways this recent modern building in Brazil is even more significant than the pre-war modern building in Switzerland, Czechoslovakia or Sweden because, coming later than the modern movement in those countries, it has swung into the social pattern with an impressive self-

confident bravado, and it may be found [. . .] that it has become sincerely integrated with the social and political aspirations of the Brazilian people.[58]

John Summerson, in the *Architectural Review*, weighed up in favour of the conditions of patronage in Brazil, compared to England:

To look through this book is to be reminded under what peculiar psychological conditions modern architecture labours here in England, where a few private houses and a playground for quaint birds are almost the only representatives of advanced architectural thought.

He asked why modern buildings had 'sprung up quickly and naturally' in Brazil: 'Is the answer climate or tradition?'. He believed that 'probably climate' was determinant in Brazilian architecture, as much in contemporary times as in the Baroque period: 'A Brazilian sky tempts men to build fantastically, and the fantasy of functionalism succeeds quite naturally the fantasy of Baroque.'[59]

Henry-Russell Hitchcock, on the other hand, reviewing *Brazil Builds* for *Art Bulletin*, seemed to have placed the reason on tradition – specifically the tradition of importing French models and adapting them to local conditions; France had been, of course, the major cultural influence on Brazil throughout the nineteenth century. He found a better clue for understanding contemporary work in a few nineteenth-century monuments, and explained that some of the buildings of the mid nineteenth century in Brazil by, for example, José Maria Jacinto Rebelo (1821–71) and Louis Vauthier (1815–1901), were emulations of the French Restoration style which had suffered some 'loss of distinction in proportion and precision of composition' from the French original in favour of 'gay colour and handsome local materials', and that a similar development had occurred with the contemporary buildings which were Corbusian in character but varied and enlivened by the use of 'native stones and even the traditional painted and glazed tiles'.[60]

The first special issue on Brazil in an architectural journal outside the United States appeared in the April 1944 issue of the *Architectural Review* (Figure 11.7).[61] The presentation was sensational: in the old large format of the *Architectural Review*, it allowed for enlarged illustrations from *Brazil Builds*. Joaquim de Souza Leão, a Counsellor at the Brazilian embassy in London and notable collector of Colonial art, gave background information on Brazilian history; Kidder-Smith revealed his personal views in 'The Architects and the Modern Scene'; the English writer Sacheverell Sitwell (1897–1988) emphasised the uniqueness of Brazilian architecture, both new and old, by christening it the 'Brazilian Style'.[62] Sitwell put forward the view of Brazil as a country of the future:

The beauties of Rio are its sea and mountains and its modern buildings. [. . .] Nothing old in Rio de Janeiro can compete for our interest with the beauties of Nature, which are eternal, and with what is new and of our time. Rio is a city of the present and the future. What is past, comparatively, is dead and faded.[63]

After the cessation of hostilities, countries such as France and Italy which had been cut off by the war, but had cultural links with Brazil, started to report on the situation there. In September 1947, *L'Architecture d'Aujour-d'hui* dedicated an issue mainly to the buildings included in *Brazil Builds* with a particular interest in showing many of the interiors which had not been completed during Goodwin's visit (Figure 11.8); it also showed Niemeyer's Church of São Francisco at Pampulha and the Central Terminal of the Santos Dumont Airport, then almost completed. It included a historical introduction, a section on *azulejos*, a brief history of *brise-soleils* according to Le Corbusier, and an article on Niemeyer.[64] In 1948, *Domus* published an article on the 'Brazilian Style',[65] and *Werk* published one on the Ministry of Education and Health.[66] *Werk* did not have a special issue until 1953, when there was renewed interest in the new works of Niemeyer, Reidy, and Burle Marx.[67]

Out of these reactions a pattern of criticism emerged: the illustrations had made more impact than the written word, and images and details had been assimilated more readily than text. Kidder-Smith's photographs were the main source of illustrations and Goodwin's text the basic source of information on the subject. In spite of Goodwin's caution not to label it, the 'Brazilian Style' came to be known through the illustrations in 'Brazil Builds'; its seemingly regional image was seen as the expression of necessity. *Brise-soleils*, *pilotis*, *azulejos*, and the tropical landscape became the

11.8  Cover of Spécial Brésil.
*L'Architecture   d'Aujourd'hui* (September
1947).

icons of the style. According to most contemporary interpretations, the
'Brazilian Style' expressed a stage forward in the maturity of the Modern
Movement.

## Notes

1  'Brazil Builds' *New York Herald Tribune* (17 January 1943).
2  *New York Herald Tribune* (24 January 1943).
3  *Sun*, New York NY (15 January 1943). The Museum of Modern Art Archives, NY: Public
   Information Scrapbook, 60.
4  'Modern Brazil' *Life* (26 October 1942) p.132.
5  Press release: 'Brazilian Government Leads Western Hemisphere in Encouraging Modern
   Architecture' (1943). MoMA Archives, NY: CE, II.1/41(5).
6  'Interest in Brazil' *Telegram*, Worcester MA (14 January 1943). MoMA Archives, NY: PI, 60.
7  'Architecture of Brazil in Modern Museum' *Sunday Union and Republican*, Springfield MA
   (17 January 1943). MoMA Archives, NY: PI, 60.
8  'Brazil's Contribution to Modern Building Design' *Post Dispatch*, St Louis MO (31 January
   1943). MoMA Archives, NY: PI, 60.
9  Edward Alden Jewell: 'Brazil Builds Anew' *New York Times* (17 January 1942). MoMA
   Archives, NY: PI, 60.
10  MoMA to The Committee on Cultural Relations with Latin America, 1 February 1943.
    MoMA Department of Registration, NY: Brazil Builds, Exhibition No. 213.
11  Elizabeth B. Mock: 'Building for Tomorrow' *Travel* (June 1943) p.26.
12  Mock: *Travel* (June 1943) p.29.
13  Mock: *Travel* (June 1943) p.29.

14  Mock: *Travel* (June 1943) p.32.

15  Jewell: *New York Times* (17 January 1942). MoMA Archives, NY: PI, 60.

16  *Time* (15 February 1943). MoMA Archives, NY: PI, 60.

17  'Brazilian Architecture: Our Progressive Neighbor to the South Shows Us How' *Sun*, New York NY (15 January 1943). MoMA Archives, NY: PI, 60.

18  Barry Byrne, *America* (27 February 1943). MoMA Archives, NY: PI, 60.

19  *Task Magazine*, New York NY (Spring 1943). MoMA Archives, NY: PI, 60. Catherine Bauer had contributed to the 'Architecture in Public Housing' exhibition (1936) and the 'Modern Architecture in England' exhibition (1937). She was Elizabeth Mock's sister.

20  F.A. Gutheim: 'Eye-Filling Satisfaction' *Inter-American*, Washington DC (April 1943). MoMA Archives, NY: PI, 60.

21  Elizabeth Wilder: 'Architecture of Brazil' *Nation*, New York NY (7 March 1943). MoMA Archives, NY: PI, 60.

22  Wilder: *Nation* (7 March 1943). MoMA Archives, NY: PI, 60.

23  *Time* (12 August 1940) p.37. MoMA Archives, NY: PI, 60.

24  *Pan American* (February 1943). MoMA Archives, NY: PI, 60.

25  *Virginia Pilot*, Norfolk VA (25 June 1944). MoMA Archives, NY: PI, 60.

26  *Plain Dealer*, Cleveland OH (25 June 1944). MoMA Archives, NY: PI, 60.

27  *Philadelphia Bulletin* (9 February 1943). MoMA Archives, NY: PI, 60.

28  *Inquirer*, Owensboro NY (25 June 1944). MoMA Archives, NY: PI, 60.

29  *Press*, Pittsburgh PA (31 January 1944). MoMA Archives, NY: PI, 60.

30  *Citizen*, Columbus OH (23 November 1945. MoMA Archives, NY: PI, 60.

31  *Advertiser*, Montgomery AL (25 May 1944). MoMA Archives, NY: PI, 60.

32  'War Boom in Beautiful Rio Points to Creative Future' *Women's Wear Daily* (20 January 1943). MoMA Archives, NY: PI, 60.

33  *Mademoiselle* (March 1943, April 1943). MoMA Archives, NY: PI, 60.

34  *Home and Food* (April 1943). MoMA Archives, NY: PI, 60.

35  *School Management* (May 1943). MoMA Archives, NY: PI, 60.

36  *Popular Photography* (May 1943); *Camera Fan*, Indianapolis IN (18 April 1943). MoMA Archives, NY: PI, 60.

37  *American Printer* (March 1944). MoMA Archives, NY: PI, 60.

38  *Book Binding and Book Production* (June 1943). MoMA Archives, NY: PI, 60.

39  Philip Goodwin to Monroe Wheeler, 11 September 1942. MoMA Department of Registration, NY: Brazil Builds, Exhibition No. 213. Robert Stern thought that the *Architectural Record* was 'unquestionably the most innovative among the American professional journals'. *Journal of the Society of Architectural Historians* (March 1965) p.9.

40  'Cantilever Hangar, Santos Dumont Airport, Rio de Janeiro' *Architectural Record* (December 1942) pp.41–4.

41  'Architecture of Brazil' *Architectural Record* (January 1943) pp.34–56.

42  'Brazilian Architecture: Living and Building Below the Equator' *Pencil Points* (January 1943) pp.54–61.

43  'Office Building for Ministry of Education and Health, Rio de Janeiro' *Architectural Forum* (February 1943) p.37.

44  *California Arts & Architecture* (February 1943) pp.20–3.

45  *California Arts & Architecture* (September 1943) p.16. Reprinted in Elizabeth A.T. Smith: '*Arts & Architecture* and the Los Angeles Vanguard' *Blueprints for Modern Living: History and Legacy of the Case Study Houses* (Los Angeles: Museum of Contemporary Art 1989) p.146.

46  'Brazilian Architecture: Living and Building Below the Equator' *Pencil Points* (January 1943) p.61.

47  *Pencil Points* (January 1943) p.54.

48  'Architecture of Brazil' *Architectural Record* (January 1943) p.35.

49  Paul Lester Wiener, lecture notes 'Backgrounds for Brazilian Architecture'. MoMA Archives, NY: CE, II.1/41(5).

50  Robert C. Smith, 'Brazil Builds on Tradition and Today' *Art News* (February 1943) pp.14–15.

51  Smith, *Art News* (February 1943) p.33.

52  'Notes on Patios', 'Three Patio Houses' *Pencil Points* (June 1943) pp.44–65.

53  Bernard Rudofsky, 'On Architecture and Architects' *Pencil Points* (April 1943) p.62.

54  Rudofsky, *Pencil Points* (April 1943) p.63.

55  Rudofsky, *Pencil Points* (April 1943) p.64.

56  *Journal of The Royal Institute of British Architects* (May 1943) p.158.

57  John Summerson, 'The Brazilian Contribution' *Architectural Review* (May 1943) p.135.

58  *Journal of the Royal Institute of British Architects* (May 1943) p.155.

59  Summerson, *Architectural Review* (May 1943) p.135.

60  Henry-Russell Hitchcock, Review of *Brazil Builds*, *Art Bulletin* (December 1943) p.385.

61  *Architectural Review* Special Issue on Brazil (March 1944). J. Sousa-Leão: 'The Background' pp.58–64. Sacheverell Sitwell: 'The Brazilian Style' pp.65–8. 'Modern Buildings' pp.69–77. G.E. Kidder-Smith: 'The Architects and the Modern Scene' pp.78–84.

62  Sitwell was considered the major authority in England on Baroque art through the publication of *Southern Baroque Art* (London: 1924). He included Brazil and Mexico in a revised edition *Southern Baroque Art Revisited* (London: 1967).

63  Sitwell: 'The Brazilian Style' *Architectural Review* (March 1944) p.65.

64  *L'Architecture d'Aujourd'hui* Spécial Brésil (September 1947).

65  L.C. Olivieri: 'Brasile – da Le Corbusier architetto allo "Stile Le Corbusier" ' *Domus* (January 1948) pp.1–4.

66  'Ministerium für Erziehung und Gesundheit in Rio de Janeiro' *Werk* (January 1948) pp.1–5.

67  'Moderne Architektur und Kunst in Brasilien' *Werk* Special Issue (August 1953).

# 12 The 'Brazilian Style' observed

The first articles on 'Brazil Builds' in the architectural press had been decisive in establishing the reputation of the Brazilian Modern architecture in international architectural circles; they repeated the sense of surprise and discovery with which those buildings had been viewed by Goodwin during his trip. The book *Brazil Builds*, which reached a wider audience, was reviewed in the same tone; it inaugurated a period in which Brazilian architecture played a significant part in the international architectural scene.

Although the initial interest in Brazil had come from the United States, later, as North American interests diverged from the policies of Pan Americanism, and the spread of 'Miesiean Style' architecture signalled the end of an interest in European Modernism, so the number of articles on Brazilian buildings in the North American press diminished. The number of reports on Brazilian architecture naturally remained much greater in Europe, carried out mainly by the *Architectural Review* and *L'Architecture d'Aujourd'hui* which provided recurrent reports on Brazilian architecture with a full coverage of subsequent developments. These magazines continued to follow the careers of those architects who had been brought to prominence by 'Brazil Builds': mainly Oscar Niemeyer, Lucio Costa, M.M. Roberto, Affonso Eduardo Reidy and Rino Levi, in articles such as 'From the Drawing Boards of Affonso Eduardo Reidy and Oscar Niemeyer' and 'Brazilian Preview'.[1] These architects enjoyed great international esteem and were frequently invited to take part in architectural events abroad; Niemeyer participated in the United Nations project in New York in 1947 and the Interbau exhibition in Berlin in 1955; Costa was a member of the panel of judges for the UNESCO building in Paris in 1952.

Interest in the major architects was also expressed through the publication of monographs. In 1950, the Reinhold press of New York published the first monograph on Oscar Niemeyer, *The Works of Oscar Niemeyer*, edited by Stamo Papadaki, followed by *Oscar Niemeyer: Works in Progress* in 1956 and Oscar Niemeyer in 1960. *The Works of Affonso Eduardo Reidy*, edited by Klaus Franck with an introduction by Siegfried Giedion, was published in both English and German editions, and *Rino Levi* was published in Italy.[2] Brazilian architecture received further coverage in 1956 in *Modern Architecture in Brazil*, by Henrique Mindlin, with editions in English, French, and German (see Figure 14.5).[3]

After 1951, exchanges with Brazil became more frequent; Brazilian architecture became increasingly well known, partly through the direct experience of visitors who came to see the new architecture. Many foreign critics, architects and artists visited Brazil at the invitation of the committee of the Bienais de São Paulo. The prizes mixed Brazilian Modern architects with their foreign contemporaries, including Le Corbusier, Mies van der Rohe, Aarne Ervi (1910–77), Sven Markelius (1889–1972), Maxwell Fry (1899–1987), Robert Matthew, and Percy Johnson-Marshall. At the first Bienal in 1951, the jury was Siegfried Giedion, Junzo Sakakura, and Mario Pani; at the second in 1953, Walter Gropius, Alvar Aalto (1898–1976) and Ernesto Rogers (1909–69).

Following the second Bienal in 1953, the *Architectural Review* published comments by five visitors in a 'Report on Brazil': Walter Gropius, Ernesto Rogers, Max Bill (1908–94), Peter Craymer and Hiroshi Ohye. This article marked a second phase in the coverage of Brazilian architecture: after the initial euphoria, reactions among reviewers to developments in Brazil were mixed. Reports varied from sympathy with the Brazilian situation, from Rogers, to generalisations, from Gropius, to antagonism, from Bill. Bill criticised four features of the 'Brazilian Style' as evidence of a new academic spirit: free forms, all-glass walls, *brise-soleils*, and *pilotis*:

I do not want to shy off from telling you this: architecture in your country stands in danger of falling into a parlous state of anti-social academicism.[4]

Bill's controversial statements were given at a lecture and subsequently widely publicised; he went further in statements for the popular press:

Portinari's 'azulejos' break the harmony with the whole. They are useless, and so should not have been used. I am against wall painting in modern architecture [. . .]. Wall painting has lost its primary function of education and so it is useless and uselessness is anti-architectural.[5]

Niemeyer, however, noticed that people visiting Brazil felt free to make critical comments when 'their own work hardly justified their criticism'.[6] He started a policy of publishing the work of his critics in *Módulo*, of which he had been one of the founders.[7]

From the mid-1950s, while magazines continued to report on new Brazilian buildings, familiarity with the later work brought some unfavourable reactions. In 'Latin American Architecture since 1945', an exhibition and book which appeared in 1955, the Museum of Modern Art tried to continue from where 'Brazil Builds' had left off in Brazil, and, further, to include the whole of Latin America. This exhibition was organised by Henry-Russell Hitchcock, who visited 11 Latin American countries. *Latin American Architecture since 1945* never achieved the popular or critical success of *Brazil Builds*. The formula of criticising buildings as success or failures of an aesthetic formulation had become uninteresting and even irrelevant, due to the diversity of contemporary architecture, and indeed the exhibition had hardly any impact. The photographs, specially commissioned from Rosalie McKenna, were particularly criticised, both in the United States:

> The old fashioned treatment of a building as an abstract entity, without even a hint of its orientation and setting, deprives the exhibition of half its educational value. In a show supervised by such a learned scholar and critic as Professor Hitchcock, this is a great disappointment, especially because the Museum went to the expense of sending a photographer to South America to get fresh pictures of the buildings.[8]

and in Brazil:

> That which I distinguished as Brazilian and Mexican is bad, not only the photographic part, but also the choice of angles and details.[9]

Hitchcock concluded, however, that the Ministry of Education was 'still perhaps the finest single modern structure in Latin America' and devoted a panel to it in the exhibition.[10]

Criticism of Brazilian architecture became blatantly divided during the construction of Brasília. While William Holford and J.M. Richards wrote favourable articles in the *Architectural Review* in 1957 and 1959, Sybil Moholy-Nagy directed savage criticism against both the urban design and architecture of Brasília in *Progressive Architecture* in 1959.[11] In 1960, according to the *Architect's Journal*, in Pampulha, only the Church, and in Rio, only the Ministry of Education, were worth the time and trouble of a visit.[12]

After the inauguration of Brasília in 1960, there were few serious critical articles on Brazilian architecture. A report in *Progressive Architecture* in 1966 took an ironic stance that verged on ridicule. The article implied that, Le Corbusier having just died, Latin American architects would lose direction. In fact, Latin American architecture was considered simply out of date:

> In the U.S., we know precious little about the recent architecture of South America – perhaps because we have built up several resistances to the work there. For one thing, the character of their architectural photography is alien to our eyes [. . .]. Another, doubtless more perverse reason on our part – and the fact that we expect all South America to look like Le Corbusier may be due to it – is that all the tropical planting that exists there in such abundance was so popular in the 40's and 50's, when the work of South American architects was first becoming known to us.[13]

They still considered the Ministry of Education Building, however, to be the most important work not only in Brazil but in South America, and still thought it worth remarking upon the allegiance to, and transformation of, the principles of Le Corbusier:

After the international acclaim of the Ministry of Education building in Rio in the early 40's, the great number of Le Corbusier's disciples in South America initiated and inspired the greatest amount of Corbusian design approach anywhere [. . .]. This was not done without transforming his style, but it was done with an embracing recognition of the affinity between his Mediterranean sensibility and that of the Latin Americans.[14]

The regional nature of Brazilian Modern architecture had been established by the major polemicists of the Modern Movement, such as Siegfried Giedion and Henry-Russell Hitchcock. Giedion in *Space, Time and Architecture* designated Brazil and Finland as the countries that had made the first 'regional' contributions to modern architecture:

Structures imbued with creative force suddenly arose, first in Finland and then in Brazil. Each country made its own regional contribution. Strongly democratic Finland showed how contemporary architecture can be simultaneously relaxed, regional and universal. Brazil, constantly menaced by Latin American upheavals, introduced a grandeur of line and form in a series of glittering façades and impressive projects.[15]

By referring to the architecture as 'regional', Giedion was linking it to its political and social context. Giedion, however, would have been unwilling to call it 'national' because of his belief that the new architecture should be international. He identified an inherent trend in contemporary architecture toward satisfying 'cosmic' and 'terrestrial' conditions and the 'habits which have developed naturally out of them'; in this context, he justified these regional contributions as being within the 'spirit of the age':

This explains why the forms of Brazilian architecture and Aalto's work in Finland, though so different, are both imbued with the spirit of the age. Both are regional contributions to a universal architectural conception. This attempt to meet cosmic, terrestrial and regional conditions may be termed the new regional approach.[16]

Giedion, as general secretary of CIAM, was instrumental in promoting Brazilian architecture abroad in the immediate post-war years. He corresponded with several of the Brazilian architects who were members of CIAM and included several of their buildings in the CIAM survey *A Decade of New Architecture*. He also took an active part in the Bienais de São Paulo as a member of the architectural jury and wrote prefaces to *Modern Architecture in Brazil* and *The Works of Affonso Eduardo Reidy*.

Hitchcock also viewed the 'Brazilian Style' as a continuation of the Modern Movement. His ideas of Brazilian architecture within an international context were better displayed in *Architecture: Nineteenth and Twentieth Centuries*, of 1958 than in *Latin American Architecture since 1945*. He included architecture in Brazil not only in the chapters on the later works of the Modern Movement, but also in that on the first half of the nineteenth century. Of the nineteenth-century Brazilian architects, he selected Grandjean de Montigny, the French architect who had emigrated to Brazil in 1816, together with his pupils Rebelo and Vauthier, as the architects who had developed a true French style in Brazil. He concluded that architecture in Brazil lacked an 'autochthonous character' in this period:

> The establishment of a Latin American architecture of really autochthonous character, as distinguished from the continuance of various local vernacular building traditions, had to await the mid twentieth century.[17]

In the twentieth century, however, Brazilian buildings were included twice: firstly in the 1930s, in conjunction with Le Corbusier, and again by type in the 1950s. The Ministry of Education was credited with having inspired the adaptation of Modern architecture to the more rigorous tropical climate.

> In most Latin American cities all-glass walls are impractical because of the heat and the glare from the sun. As a result, architects there developed various versions of the sunbreak system introduced twenty years ago on the first tall modern building to be erected in that part of the world, the Ministry of Education in Rio.[18]

Numerous popular architectural historians recognised that the 'Brazilian Style' was among the first national variations of European Modernism. All included the Ministry of Education and ranked it as among the most important buildings of the period. Some, such as J.M. Richards in *An Introduction to Modern Architecture*, were favourable to the architecture.[19] Others, such as Nikolaus Pevsner in *An Outline of European Architecture*, regarded the architecture as 'frivolous'.[20] Within Latin America, historians stressed historical continuity. Leopoldo Castedo, an authority on Latin American Art, concentrated on defining a 'Baroque' connection in *The Baroque Prevalence in Brazilian Art*:

> A Baroque prevalence in the forms of modern Brazil is perhaps best epitomized by the country's unique contribution to Modern art – its architecture, more specifically that exciting conjunction of audacity and unfettered imagination, of richness and variety, of lyricism and love for the curve.[21]

Architectural histories written from the perspective of the immediate postwar period and even up to the 1960s could present the 'Brazilian Style' as part of an ongoing process of Modernism. The regional variation of Modernism was initially seen as its most significant feature; this allegiance was later seen as a disadvantage and a legacy which overshadowed the architecture completely. After the 1960s, however, there were no attempts to include the 'Brazilian Style' or Brazilian architecture in architectural histories, for reasons connected both with the decline of Modernism in general and with the end of the conditions which had supported the 'Brazilian Style'. The military coup in 1964 effectively brought to an end the government which had initiated and supported the 'Brazilian Style'. By this time, a definite reaction against the canon of Modernism had emerged among architects: the later work of Le Corbusier – such as the

Capitol at Chandigarh (1951–9), Alison and Peter Smithson in Britain – such as the Economist Building, London (1963–4), and Louis Kahn in the United States – such as the Capitol at Dacca (1964–83), which challenged the concepts of Modernism so fundamentally that the essentially pre-War European Modernism of the 'Brazilian Style' looked distinctly old-fashioned.

At the Museum of Modern Art, New York, the appointment of Arthur Drexler as Director of the Department of Architecture in 1954 caused a major shift in its policy towards architecture and exemplified the critical decline of Modernism. Exhibitions moved away from promoting the International Modernism of the founding days towards displaying alternative approaches to Modernism and even anti-Modern themes. In 1964, of the people still at the Museum who had been involved in 'Brazil Builds', Elizabeth Mock (then Elizabeth B. Kassler) curated 'Modern Gardens and the Landscape' and Bernard Rudofsky 'Architecture without Architects'.[22] Mock showed not only Modern Brazilian gardens such as those by Burle Marx at the Ministry of Education and Rudofsky at the Arnstein House but also featured the work of Gunnar Asplund (1885–1940) and Luis Barragan (1902–76). The same year, there was an exhibition of the 'Development by Louis I. Kahn of the design for the Second Capital of Pakistan at Dacca'.[23] In 1966, the Museum published its first Paper on Architecture *Complexity and Contradiction in Architecture* by Robert Venturi, credited as the first theoretical treatise against Modernism.[24] By the 1970s, the Museum had published works on Luis Barragan and the École des Beaux-Arts.[25] Of the Brazilian architects, only Burle Marx continued to be promoted by the Museum.[26]

Architectural historians writing from the point of view of the 1980s, such as William Curtis in 1980 and Kenneth Frampton in 1982, were less convinced of the value of the 'Brazilian Style'. The rupture with Modernism that occurred during the 1970s brought about a new appreciation of regional specificity distinct from the universal and technological imperatives of pre-war European Modernism. For Curtis and Frampton, Brazilian architecture seemed to be a continuation of the International Style rather than forming a specifically post-war programme.

Curtis, in *Modern Architecture since 1900*, discussed 'Brazilian Style' buildings in the chapter on 'The Problem of Regional Identity'. He acknowledged that Brazil had produced an early variant of the Modern Movement which, in the post-war years, had grown into greater diversity. However, Curtis did not view the Ministry of Education Building in the same perspective as contemporary authors, as having inaugurated a regional expression of International Modernism; instead, he placed it, unfavourably, in the context of later developments such as those of Louis Kahn at Dacca or William Wurster in San Francisco. He concluded that in the Ministry of Education Building:

> The slab was elegantly modified by sun louvres for shade – but these slender and movable relatives of the brise-soleil hardly constituted an all-out attempt at designing a tropical regionalist architecture.[27]

Frampton, however, in *Modern Architecture: a Critical History* did not

place the 'Brazilian Style' in the chapter on 'Regionalism and Cultural Identity' which dealt with more recent architecture, but in the chapter on 'The
International style: theme and variations 1925–65'.[28] In this context, he
gave a brief, but well placed historical account of Brazilian architecture
from the partnership of Lucio Costa and Gregori Warchavchik in the mid
1930s to Brasília.[29] He endorsed the connection between early Modern
architecture and the eighteenth-century Brazilian Baroque:

> The young Brazilian followers of Le Corbusier immediately transformed
> these Purist components into a highly sensuous native expression which
> echoed in its plastic exuberance the 18th-century Brazilian Baroque.[30]

Frampton recognised that Brazil had started a regional architecture with
the Ministry of Education Building, but one which did not develop into the
later phase that he described as 'critical regionalism', independent of Modernism.

For architectural historians, Brazilian architecture was the period from
the Ministry of Education Building to Brasília. Although their period of dis-
cussion went far beyond the 1960s, they ignored developments in Brazilian architecture after the completion of the initial phase of Brasília. Reyner
Banham, for instance, did not include any of the São Paulo *concretão* –
*beton brut* – buildings, such as the Faculdade de Arquitetura e Urbanismo
da Universidade de São Paulo (1961) by João Vilanova Artigas (1915–85) or
the Museu de Arte de São Paulo (1957–68) by Lina Bo Bardi (1914–92), in
*The New Brutalism*, in spite of the obvious congruities with the canons of
the style.[31] It is not certain whether they ceased to look at Brazil or whether
they regarded the recent architecture in Brazil as not worth considering.

When 'Brazil Builds' had opened in 1943, the optimism towards the
role that Brazilian architecture was going to play in the post-war world
was part of the general optimism towards what was regarded as a new
power. *The Times* and the *Architectural Review* both reported the views of
the United States Assistant Secretary of State:

> Brazil, he said, had doubled her population in less than a quarter of a
> century. Brazil alone, therefore, in the next generation, will be not merely
> a great South American country, but a world Power if she so chooses.[32]

It seems that Brazil did not choose to be a world power as he had so opti-
mistically predicted, or perhaps international conditions did not allow for
new-comers to the ranks of world power nations. As Brazil's prominence
in the world diminished, so did its architecture in the international scene.
Brazilian architecture had, effectively, ceased to exist.

**Notes**

1  *Architectural Review* (October 1950) pp.221–32; (July 1953) pp.10–15.
2  Stamo Papadaki: *The Works of Oscar Niemeyer*, Preface by Lucio Costa (New York: Reinhold
   1950; repr. 1951); *Oscar Niemeyer: Works in Progress* (New York: Reinhold 1956); *Oscar
   Niemeyer*, Masters of World Architecture Series (New York: Braziller 1960). Klaus Franck:
   *The Works of Affonso Eduardo Reidy*, Introduction by Siegfried Giedion (Stuttgart: Gerd
   Hatje; New York: Praeger 1960). *Rino Levi* (Milan: Ed. Comunità 1974).

3  Henrique Mindlin: *Modern Architecture in Brazil* (Rio de Janeiro, Amsterdam: Colibris; London: Architectural Press; New York: Reinhold; Paris: Vincent Fréal; Munich: Callwey 1956).

4  Max Bill: 'Report on Brazil' *Architectural Review* (October 1954) p.239.

5  Interview: 'Max Bill, o inteligente iconoclastra' *Habitat* (September 1953) (first publ. in *Revista Manchete*).

6  Rupert Spade: *Oscar Niemeyer* (London: Thames and Hudson 1971) p.16.

7  'Crítica – Auto-Crítica' *Módulo* (August 1955) p.66. 'Noticiário' *Módulo* February 1957.

8  Lewis Mumford: 'Review: Latin American since 1945' *The New Yorker* (4 February 1956).

9  English Translation of Niomar Moniz Sodré opinion in the article 'Arquitetura Latino-Americana em Nova York' *Correio da Manhã* (30 November 1955). MoMA Archives, NY: CE, II.1/69(1).

10  Hitchcock: *Latin America Architecture since 1945* pp.30–1.

11  William Holford: 'Brasilia: a new Capital City for Brazil' *Architectural Review* (December 1957) pp.394–402. J.M. Richards: 'Brasília' *Architectural Review* (February 1959) pp.94–104. Sibyl Moholy-Nagy: 'Brasília: Majestic Concept or Autocratic Monument?' *Progressive Architecture* [*Pencil Points*] October 1959 pp.88–9.

12  C. Handisyde: 'Brazil' *Architect's Journal* (14 April 1960) pp.572–83.

13  C. Ray Smith: 'In South America: After Corbu, What's Happening?' *Progressive Architecture* (September 1966) p.141.

14  *Progressive Architecture* (September 1966) p.141.

15  Giedion: *Space Time and Architecture* p.xxxxviii.

16  Giedion: *Space Time and Architecture* p.549.

17  Henry-Russell Hitchcock: *Architecture: Nineteenth and Twentieth Centuries* (Harmondsworth: Penguin Books 1958; repr. 1971) p.140.

18  Hitchcock: *Architecture: Nineteenth and Twentieth Centuries* p.561.

19  J.M. Richards: *An Introduction to Modern Architecture* (Harmondsworth: Penguin Books 1940; repr. 1953).

20  Nikolaus Pevsner: *An Outline of European Architecture* (Harmondsworth: Penguin Books 1943; repr. 1985) p.426–7.

21  Leopoldo Castedo: *The Baroque Prevalence in Brazilian Art* (New York: Charles Frank 1964) p.14.

22  Bernard Rudofsky: *Architecture without Architects* (New York: Museum of Modern Art 1964); Elizabeth B. Kassler (ed): *Modern Gardens and the Landscape* (rev. edn New York: Museum of Modern Art 1964; repr. 1984).

23  The first exhibition dedicated to the work of Louis Kahn (1901–74) at the Museum took place in 1961: 'Louis I Kahn Architect: Alfred Newton Richards Medical Research Building'.

24  Robert Venturi: *Complexity and Contradiction in Architecture* (New York: Museum of Modern Art 1966).

25  Emilio Ambasz (ed): *The Architecture of Luis Barragan* (New York: Museum of Modern Art 1976); Arthur Drexler (ed): *The Architecture of the École des Beaux-Arts* (New York: Museum of Modern Art and London: Secker and Warburg 1977).

26  William Howard Adams: *Roberto Burle Marx: The Unnatural art of the Garden* (New York: Museum of Modern Art 1991).

27  William Curtis: *Modern Architecture Since 1900* (Oxford: Phaidon 1982; 2nd edn 1987) p.333.

28  Kenneth Frampton: 'The International style: theme and variations 1925–65' *Modern Architecture a critical history* (London: Thames and Hudson 1980; 2nd edn 1985) pp.254–7.

29  Frampton says from the 'mid-twenties', but the partnership of Lucio Costa and Gregori Warchavchik was, in fact, for a brief period in the early 1930s.

30  Frampton: *Modern Architecture* p.254.

31  Reyner Banham: *The New Brutalism, Ethic or Aesthetic?* (London: Architectural Press 1966).

32  A.A. Berle, United States Assistant Secretary of State. *The Times* 8 February 1944. Special Issue: 'Brazil' *Architectural Review* (March 1944) p.59.

# 13 Le Corbusier and the 'Brazilian Style'

Of all the 'Brazilian Style' buildings, the Ministry of Education became the most influential outside Brazil after the Second World War. Its clear form, dynamic relationship to the surrounding urban landscape and its evident regional adaptation of European Modernism made it extremely popular among architects. It became the prototype for the prismatic tower on *pilotis* in a plaza with a contrasting low block which proliferated in post-war Europe and America. Siegfried Giedion considered that it

> not only marked an important point in the development of South American architecture, it has also had a far-reaching influence on the design of large buildings all over the world.[1]

The most immediate application of the design of the Ministry of Education Building was at the United Nations Headquarters in New York (1947–50) (Figure 13.1). It brought together Le Corbusier and Oscar Niemeyer again on the design of a building and its authorship proved to be equally controversial. Nelson Rockefeller had donated the site in Manhattan on 1st Avenue, between 42nd and 48th street in 1947, a former abattoir, after almost a year spent searching for sites in the United States. Wallace K. Harrison was simultaneously appointed as Director of Planning by the Design Committee.[2] He formed a team from his office to execute the building and invited an international team of architects to advise on the initial stages of design, mainly for political reasons.

Harrison, although trained in the Beaux Arts manner, had already become interested in the aesthetics of European Modernism while an architect at the Rockefeller Center (1932–40). The Rockefeller Center, which extended to several blocks of mid-town Manhattan, was relatively sober and with more abstract forms than were common in New York; the central slab, especially, was quite different to the usual tower form of New York skyscrapers. Two unusual features – the rectilinear form and the urban plaza – were widely praised, not least by Elizabeth Mock, who had been assistant to Philip Goodwin on the 'Brazil Builds' exhibition (it was plainly visible from the upper windows of the Museum).[3] Harrison initially set up his design office in the Rockefeller Center.

Harrison was already familiar with Niemeyer's work. He had met Niemeyer while both were architects at the New York World's Fair in 1939. As Assistant Co-ordinator of the Office of Inter-American Affairs he had advised Nelson Rockefeller favourably on the grant in 1942 to the 'Brazil Builds' exhibition at the Museum of Modern Art, of which he was a Trustee. It was this familiarity with his work which led him to invite Niemeyer to join the team for the United Nations Headquarters.

The inclusion of Le Corbusier was natural given his enormous fame, but it was certainly a problematic choice given his well-known difficult temperament. There was a further reason why the inclusion of Le Corbusier was controversial. By the end of the Second World War, Le Corbusier had moved decisively away from his Purist phase; he was then working on his first Unité d'Habitation (1946–52) in Marseilles. He had abandoned pure forms and technological materials in favour of *beton brut* and *brise-soleils*. Such ideas were not likely to find favour in the United States, with sophisticated manufacturing and efficient air-conditioning. Conversely, Le Corbusier was unlikely to endorse a return to the Purist phase, complete with what was effectively a *pan de verre*.

It appears that in New York, as he had done in Rio de Janeiro, Le

13.2 Oscar Niemeyer: Project '32' for the United Nations, New York (1947). Papadaki: *The Works of Oscar Niemeyer*.

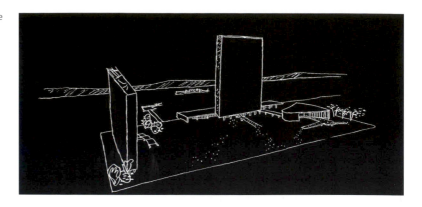

Corbusier concentrated his design effort on buildings for another site. The buildings he proposed included a Unité d'Habitation, a trapezoidal tower for the Secretariat based on a proposal for Algiers of 1939–42, and a General Assembly with internal auditoriums which prefigured that which he would shortly propose for Chandigarh.[4] While Le Corbusier was proselytising these unrealisable proposals, Harrison had started to develop the basis of the final scheme, which was felt by all to be rather awkward.

According to Harrison, it was Niemeyer's model, '32', which provided the key to solving the design problem. This model sprang from studies he had made of a low transversal block, fan-shaped auditorium, and prismatic tower set in an urban plaza which had, by then, become characteristic of the 'Brazilian Style'. Le Corbusier, however, asked him to make a compromise solution in which the spatial definition of the plaza was effectively destroyed by moving the auditorium into the middle of the plaza, apparently for 'scientific' reasons. This was presented as another model, '32–23'.[5] Because of this compromise solution, Niemeyer published his original drawings and model fully in *The Works of Oscar Niemeyer* (Figure 13.2).[6] With characteristic modesty, and in marked contrast to Le Corbusier, Niemeyer refused to make any definitive credits for the authorship of the building.

Le Corbusier's subsequent model, '23A', made when design work was well advanced, was, as admitted by Le Corbusier himself, based on the type first used at the Ministry of Education:

> In 1936 a team of Brazilian architects and Le Corbusier had together constructed a similar building for the Ministry of National Education and Public Health in Rio de Janeiro. [. . .] The office block, that is the Secretariat itself, became a vertical instead of a horizontal mass, with glass walls and brise-soleils, which were here used for the first time.[7]

It should be remembered that it was Costa and Niemeyer who had proposed the vertical block; Le Corbusier had proposed a horizontal block and only knew of the final scheme through Costa's drawings. While Le Corbusier's agreement on the design of the United Nations Headquarters was essential, if only for political reasons, his own contribution was neither original nor decisive.

The final building, however, was far from satisfactory, not least because the design team contained architects of so varied interests and experiences that a compromise was inevitable. The compromise solution lost the formal elegance of Niemeyer's scheme. The omission of the second transverse block compromised even further the spatial definition of the plaza initiated by the awkward relationship of the auditorium to the main block. Unlike the plaza at the Ministry of Education, that at the United Nations Building does not form a public space integrated with the urban grid. The formality and monumentality of the final design prefigure Harrison's increasingly Beaux-Arts-inspired work at the Metropolitan Opera House, New York (1959–66), and the Albany Mall (1972–4). Only the prismatic tower stands as a rather distant gesture of European Modernism.

The direction in which tall buildings developed in the United States was quite different from Brazil, however. The work of Le Corbusier had never been popular among architects in the United States before the Second World War, although his work had been heavily promoted by the Museum of Modern Art, including a lecture tour sponsored by Philip Goodwin in 1935. Neither the social nor technical aspects were felt to be relevant to conditions there. European Modernism was actually a diverse and heterogeneous movement before the war, however; from it, the architect whose work became most influential after the war was Mies van der Rohe. As the architectural historian William Jordy pointed out, the 'Miesiean Style' spread so widely in the United States in the 1950s that it constituted almost a Second International Style.[8]

Mies van der Rohe moved away from a European Modern manner to a distinctly American manner soon after his arrival in the United States in 1937. This development may be seen in the two stages of his project for the Campus for the Illinois Institute of Technology in Chicago. In his original project of 1939, Mies van der Rohe arranged low horizontal blocks within the site, with auditoriums resembling those at the Ministry of Education articulating the central public space (Figure 13.3). For the final

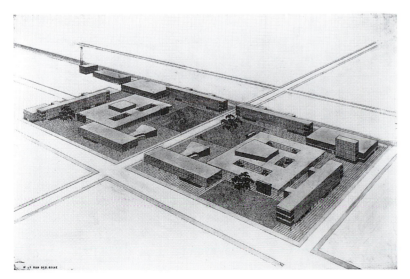

13.3 Mies van der Rohe, Ludwig. Illinois Institute of Technology, Chicago, Illinois (1939–41). Aerial Perspective. Preliminary Version. Pencil, conté crayon on illustration board, 40 × 51″ (101.5 × 129.5 cm). The Mies van der Rohe Archive, The Museum of Modern Art, New York. Gift of the architect.
© 2001 The Museum of Modern Art, New York.

13.4 Skidmore, Owings and Merrill: Lever House, New York (1951–2). © Zilah Quezado Deckker.

stage, in 1940, he developed this into a more abstract spatial composition, with internal auditoriums and uniformly-gridded façades. It was a manner that he developed in the twin residential towers at 860 Lakeshore Drive in 1948 and the Farnsworth House, Plano, Illinois (1945–50) and later in the Seagram Building in New York City in 1958. It was this phase which was to be so influential in the United States.

Lever House, New York (1951–2), by Skidmore, Owings and Merrill was one of the few major office buildings to be completed in the United States before the spread of the 'Miesiean Style' (Figure 13.4). It was started soon after the completion of the United Nations Headquarters (on which Louis Skidmore was a consultant), and is generally regarded as one of the most successful of the post-war office buildings in the United States. Its resemblance to the Ministry of Education and the United Nations Headquarters is quite obvious; the *parti* follows that of the Ministry of Education: a tall dynamic slab and a plaza.[9] There are significant differences, however; the continuous curtain wall and abstract form of the plaza are distinctly American. Lever House was widely imitated, but design standards subsequently dropped sharply. The indiscriminate use of plazas and towers was felt to be particularly corrosive of urban space, not least by its architects.[10]

In Britain, the Second World War defined a sharp cut-off point in practice; young architects simply emerged into designing huge building projects after being excluded first by the conservatism of the establishment and then by the war. For these architects, Le Corbusier was as important as he was in Brazil; many schemes copied the image, if not the content, of Le Corbusier's work. Given such a background, young architects looked for confirmation of the successful large-scale application of Modern principles.[11] Howard Robertson, writing in *The Architect and Building News*, recognised the possibility that *Brazil Builds* would be used as a crib book; he considered the integration of the buildings to the local conditions to be an example to architects in England but warned about the dangers of 'imitations of radiant Rio along the Thames Embankment'.[12] Ironically, the Thames Embankment was to be the site of two major post-war Modern buildings: the Royal Festival Hall and the Churchill Gardens Housing (Figure 13.5).[13] While neither stems directly from *Brazil Builds*, the swelling volume of the auditorium of the Royal Festival Hall and the oval water towers on the roofs of the Churchill Gardens housing blocks recall the exuberance of the Ministry of Education.

The essentially pre-war Modernism of the Ministry of Education fell out of favour among architects during the 1950s and 1960s as it was to do among historians in the 1970s. The numerous imitations of the tower and plaza called into question the value of this type. The demise of this type may be exemplified by one office building in London – State House by Trehearne and Norman, Preston and Partners (1956) (Figure 13.6). Although the architects of State House followed the *parti* of the Ministry of Education in general, the brutal form and finishes and lack of public uses in the plaza show how in London, as in New York, the design ideals of the Ministry of Education could not provide a universal solution to the design of office buildings. Its demolition in 1998 was no real loss to High Holborn. The Ministry of Education itself, however, remains a successful part of the urban landscape of Rio de Janeiro.

13.5 Powell and Moya: Churchill Gardens Housing, London (1946–62).
© Zilah Quezado Deckker.

The success of the Ministry of Education caused an immediate problem, however. The buildings shown in 'Brazil Builds' were clearly based on Le Corbusier's architectural principles, but, because the exhibition displayed the Brazilian work as a coherent movement, Brazilian architects initially received far more attention and praise than Le Corbusier. The Corbusian motifs in Brazilian architecture came to be considered more Brazilian than Corbusian. Le Corbusier's contribution to the Brazilian work had always being recognised by the architects themselves and critics alike. From the engraved plaque on the Ministry to Philip Goodwin's comments in *Brazil Builds*, Le Corbusier's name had never failed to be mentioned. Numerous articles mentioned Le Corbusier as the father of the new architecture in Brazil. However, while Brazil was enjoying a prestigious place in the architectural press, the originality of the Brazilian architects was enhanced and Le Corbusier's influence diminished. Later, as Brazil's importance in the architectural scene faded in the 1970s, the Ministry Building became increasingly linked to Le Corbusier rather than to the Brazilian architects.

With the international fame of the Ministry of Education Building, the problem of its authorship came to prominence and was to prove a continual irritation between Le Corbusier and the Brazilian architects. The relationship was a difficult one: on the one hand, Costa acknowledged that Brazilian Modernism came of age due to the experience gained first-hand from Le Corbusier, but on the other, he found that Le Corbusier distorted the events of 1936.

In the *Œuvre Complète 1934–38*, Le Corbusier had published his schemes for the Ministry of Education at the Praia de Santa Luzia and the Cidade Universitária.[14] In the five years covered by this volume, Le Corbusier had done little work: only the villa at La Tremblade (1934), the Maison de Week-end (1935), and the Pavillon des Temps Nouveau (1937) had been executed, and he must have been glad of the opportunity to publish the Brazilian projects. For the Ministry of Education, he did not publish his own scheme for the site at Castelo, however; doubtless he

13.6 Trehearne and Norman, Preston and Partners: State House, London (1956).
© Zilah Quezado Deckker.

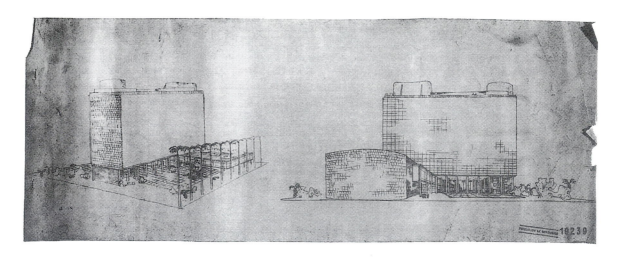

13.7 Final Project for the Ministry of Education and Health (1937).
Heliographic copy 80 cm wide x 31 cm high. FLC 19239.
© FLC/ADAGP, Paris and DACS, London 2000.

Drawing sent by Lucio Costa to Le Corbusier, August 1937.

This drawing shows the building as 10 storeys high, before the official approval of the intended height of 15 storeys on 18 May 1938.

recognised that it had little merit. He showed, instead, a photograph of a model and two sketches which he labelled as 'adaptation on the site adopted at the last minute [Castelo] of the layout of the project on page 78 [Santa Luzia]'. These were not drawings of his own hasty adaptation of the Praia de Santa Luzia scheme for Castelo, however; they were tracings – almost exact – of drawings of the final scheme which Costa had sent to him in July 1937 (Figures 13.7 and 13.8).[15] By 1939 Costa had felt it necessary to publish an explanatory article in *Arquitetura e Urbanismo* showing Le Corbusier's sketches for Castelo and the differences between them and the final project.[16]

With the outbreak of the Second World War contacts between Le Corbusier and his Brazilian friends necessarily became scarce. It was not until after the liberation of France in 1945 that contacts were re-established. Letters from Lucio Costa and Oscar Niemeyer reported on the success of the Ministry and praised the precious teaching received from Le Corbusier. In the *Œuvre Complète 1938–46*, Le Corbusier showed 11 pages of photographs and drawings of the Ministry of Education, again including his sketch which he claimed to be the final design for Castelo (Figure 13.9).[17] The plans and many of the photographs were reproduced directly from *Brazil Builds*, including the original texts in Portuguese. In fact, Goodwin had included four drawings which showed the evolution of the projects for Castelo in *Brazil Builds*, from the closed Agache block, through the 'múmia' and Le Corbusier's scheme for Castelo, to the final building.[18] Le Corbusier kept a well-thumbed copy of *Brazil Builds* in his library.[19]

This volume, too, was short of built work: only the Unité d'Habitation in Marseilles, then under construction, was illustrated. Le Corbusier devoted a further 13 pages to the problem of insolation, showing the *brise-soleils* of the Ministry of Education Building and the projects for Algiers and Barcelona, and the *mur neutralisant* of the Centrosoyuz Building, the Armée du Salut and the Pavillon Suisse.[20] Several of these photographs, too, were taken directly from *Brazil Builds* (Figure 13.10), and he quoted extensively from 'Sir Philip Goodwin' [sic].[21]

Le Corbusier could never come to terms with the international recogni-

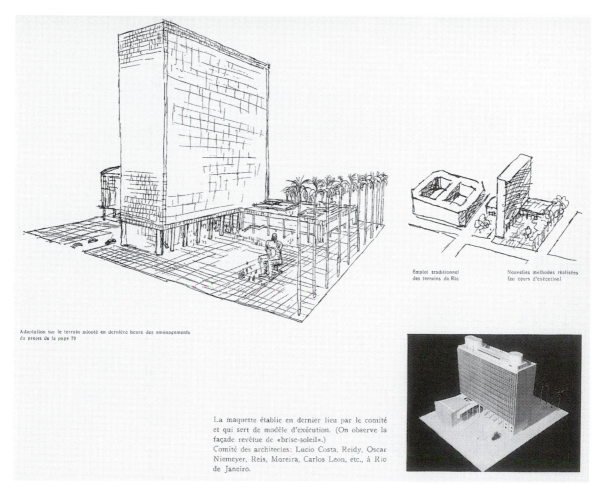

Adaptation sur le terrain adopté en dernière heure des aménagements
du projet de la page 78

Emploi traditionnel
des terrains de Rio

Nouvelles méthodes réalisées
(en cours d'exécution)

La maquette établie en dernier lieu par le comité
et qui sert de modèle d'exécution. (On observe la
façade revêtue de «brise-soleil».)
Comité des architectes: Lucio Costa, Reidy, Oscar
Niemeyer, Reis, Moreira, Carlos Leon, etc., à Rio
de Janeiro.

13.8 Le Corbusier: *Œuvre Complète 1934–38*, p.81.
© FLC/ADAGP, Paris and DACS, London 2000.
Left: *Adaptation sur le terrain adopté en dernière heure des aménagements du projet de la page 78*.
This sketch appears to be based on the drawing sent by Costa to Le Corbusier in August 1937 (see Figure 13.7).
Right: *Emploi traditionnel des terrains de Rio*. This sketch shows the final Costa project with an ideal Agache block from the Esplanada do Castelo, not a typical block from Rio de Janeiro, and appears to be based on Costa's Height Study (see Figure 2.19).
Bottom: *La maquette établie en dernier lieu par le comité et qui set de modèle d'exécution*.
This photograph of a presentation model of the final Costa project appears to have been sent by Costa at the same time as the drawings in August 1937 as it still shows the main block as 10 storeys high.

tion gained by the Brazilian architects. He felt he had been treated unfairly for not having been asked to carry out any work in Brazil (although on what grounds he did not make clear), and found it difficult to accept the quick fame and enormous professional activity of his former disciples. This must have been accentuated when, in 1949, the Brazilian Embassy in Paris organised an exhibition of Brazilian architecture at the Ecole des Beaux Arts.[22] *Pilotis* and *brise-soleil* were put forward as 'Brazil's own invention', as recalled by Le Corbusier, who attended the opening:

I was present at his side greatly enjoying myself to see such a striking nationalisation of my thoughts. I said to the lecturer: 'You have interested me prodigiously'. He took that as a compliment.[23]

Faced with what he considered a humiliation, Le Corbusier's original friendly attitude towards the Brazilians changed into an aggressive and accusative manner. He recalled several points of contention concerning his involvement with Brazil in 1936. Le Corbusier's complaints were first expressed in a letter to Reidy of 6 April 1949, with whom he had started

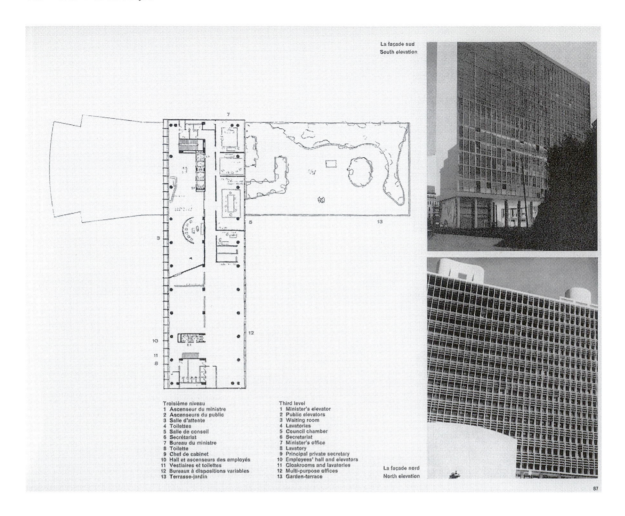

La façade sud
South elevation

Troisième niveau
1  Ascenseur du ministre
2  Ascenseurs du public
3  Salle d'attente
4  Toilettes
5  Salle de conseil
6  Secrétariat
7  Bureau du ministre
8  Toilette
9  Chef de cabinet
10 Hall et ascenseurs des employés
11 Vestiaires et toilettes
12 Bureaux à dispositions variables
13 Terrasse-jardin

Third level
1  Minister's elevator
2  Public elevators
3  Waiting room
4  Lavatories
5  Council chamber
6  Secretariat
7  Minister's office
8  Lavatory
9  Principal private secretary
10 Employees' hall and elevators
11 Cloakrooms and lavatories
12 Multi-purpose offices
13 Garden-terrace

La façade nord
North elevation

13.9 Le Corbusier: *Œuvre Complète 1938–46* p.87.
© FLC/ADAGP, Paris and DACS, London 2000.
Plan: Minister's quarters from *Brazil Builds*.
Top: photograph from *Brazil Builds*.

corresponding with the prospect of collaborating on his plan for Rio. He argued that Brazil had a debt to him which could only be repaid by a commission for a building.

> I consider that the Brazilians have a debt to me. I did not receive one cent for the Ministry of National Education and Public Health which is truly extraordinary. I have talked to the Brazilian Ambassador, who made beautiful promises but nothing changed.[24]

Later in the year, Pietro Maria Bardi (1901–99), the Director of the Museu de Arte de São Paulo, wrote to Le Corbusier inviting him to the opening of his exhibition 'The New World of Space', at the Museum.[25] Bardi had been an art critic in Italy in the 1930s, and had met Le Corbusier at the 1933 CIAM. He left Italy in 1947 to help create the Museu de Arte de São Paulo. Le Corbusier did not feel that an exhibition of his work was sufficient homage. He refused the invitation and took the opportunity to voice his complaints; he felt that he should receive payment for his work on the design for the Ministry of Education and for his consultation on the Cidade

Clive Entwistle, architecte à Londres, auteur d'un projet remarquable au concours pour la reconstruction du Crystal Palace, Londres, 1945/46, et traducteur de plusieurs des livres de Le Corbusier actuellement à l'impression écrit ceci à ce dernier le 5 août 1946:

« Je saisis cette opportunité pour vous remercier de la part de tous les jeunes d'ici, de votre dernier don à l'architecture: le brise-soleil, élément splendide, clef des combinaisons infinies. Maintenant, l'architecture est prête à prendre sa place dans la vie. Vous lui avez donné un squelette (ossature indépendant), ses organes vitaux (les services communs du logis); une peau fraîche luisante (le pan de verre); vous l'avez mise debout sur ses jambes (les pilotis); posé un joli chapeau sur sa tête (les arabesques du toit-jardin). Et maintenant vous lui donnez des vêtements magnifiques s'adaptant aux divers climats! Évidemment, vous devez être un père fier! …»

Clive Entwistle, an architect in London, author of a remarkable competition project for the reconstruction of Crystal Palace, London, 1945/46, and translator of several of Le Corbusier's books actually in print, addressed the following to him on 5 August 1946:

'I take this opportunity to thank you on behalf of all young people here, for your latest gift to architecture: the brise-soleil, a splendid element, the key to infinite combinations. Now architecture is ready to take its place in life. You have given it a skeleton (independent structure), its vital organs (the communal services of the building): a fresh shining skin (the curtain wall); you have stood it upon its legs (the pilotis), And now you have given it magnificent clothes adaptable to all climates! Naturally you must be a little proud! …'

1936–1945  Le ministère de l'Education nationale et de la Santé publique à Rio de Janeiro.
Le brise-soleil de la façade nord
The Ministry of National Education and Public Health at Rio de Janeiro,
The sun-breaker on the north elevation

113

Universitária.[26] Bardi had recently arrived from Italy and was unfamiliar with the events concerning Le Corbusier's involvement. Bardi promised to assist him and asked how much his fees should have been. Le Corbusier asked for 20 per cent of the architects' fees, which would have been, by his calculations, 1.2 per cent of the total cost of the building.[27]

Le Corbusier was deliberately distorting the events of 1936, for while he had not been paid a consultancy fee for his work as an architect, he had agreed to receive an exaggerated fee for his lectures to cover it, an arrangement which had applied to other consultants.[28] In fact, this fee seems to have been extraordinarily generous. Lucio Costa intervened: 'Your present interpretation of the facts according to what I was told is no longer the one of 1939', and he was quite clear over the issue of payment:

But if it is the fees which are still bothering you, let me remind you that during the three months of your stay here you received more than the rest of us during the six years that the business lasted, because we were six architects, and, although the individual contributions were unequal, the fees were always split equally among us.[29]

13.10 Le Corbusier: *Œuvre Complète 1938–46* p.113.
© FLC/ADAGP, Paris and DACS, London 2000.
Problèmes de l'ensoleillement.
Photograph from *Brazil Builds*.
*I take this opportunity to thank you on behalf of all young people here, for your latest gift to architecture: the brise-soleil, a splendid element, the key to infinite combinations. Now architecture is ready to take its place in life. You have given it a skeleton (independent structure), its vital organs (the communal services of the building): a fresh shining skin (the curtain wall); you have stood it upon its legs (the pilotis). And now you have given it magnificent clothes adaptable to all climates!*
(Address by Clive Entwistle).

He was equally direct over the provenance of the sketches in the *Œuvre Complète 1934–38*:

> The sketch made afterwards, based on the photos of the finished building, and which you have published as if it was the original proposal, have given us all a bad impression.[30]

Le Corbusier tried to explain the issue, but did not leave it clear; he said that he had been in hospital after a boating accident and had been unable to correct the proofs.[31] In addition, Le Corbusier wanted to display the controversial sketch with a special label relating the facts as seen by him at his exhibition in São Paulo in 1950. Bardi's efforts to patch things up only made matters worse: he explained that the Brazilians copied European ideas unconsciously, without recognising their paternity.[32] Costa insisted that the sketch be pulled down.[33]

Brazilian architects made several attempts to present the real sequence of events and authorship of the Ministry. Niemeyer tried to distance himself from the Corbusian scheme; in *The Works of Oscar Niemeyer*, he published a set of drawings showing the differences between Le Corbusier's sketches and the final version, and finished with a drawing showing what surely was intended to be an ironic representation of a 'master' and 'pupil'.[34] (Figure 13.11). They showed that, in several important respects, the Ministry of Education Building departed from the Corbusian precedents: the 10-metre high *pilotis*, the vertical orientation of the block and the dynamic relationship to the surrounding buildings were all shown as the creations of the Brazilian team. Henrique Mindlin, in *Modern Architecture in Brazil*, showed a sequence of sketches of the four phases of the Ministry project including Le Corbusier's sketch for Castelo; three of the sketches also appeared on the cover (Figure 13.12; see Figure 14.5).[35]

Le Corbusier continued to see the work of other Brazilian architects, such as Reidy's Museu de Arte Moderna in Rio de Janeiro (1954–61), as derivative of his own: 'I noticed that Reidy used these plans [Maison de la Culture at Firminy] to make his Museum in Rio de Janeiro (very nicely).'[36] The opposite was, in fact, more likely, as the Museum was virtually complete before the Maison de la Culture had started: Le Corbusier's original design for the Maison de la Culture, commissioned in 1956, showed a columnar structure until 1960, when it was abandoned in favour of a suspended structure similar to that of the Museu de Arte Moderna, at the insistence of the Mayor of Firminy, Eugène Claudius-Petit; construction work on the Museu de Arte Moderna was already almost complete by 1960 when the monograph on Reidy appeared.[37] Le Corbusier must have paid particular attention to the Museu de Arte Moderna for another reason: its site was on almost the exact site of his proposal for the Ministry of Education Building on the Praia de Santa Luzia.

The friendship between Le Corbusier and the Brazilian architects survived all the disagreements, however. The Brazilians attempted to repair their friendship through several acts of homage. Bardi purchased his sketches made during the 1936 lecture tour, and a painting for the collection of the Museu de Arte of São Paulo, and tried to launch a book, *Le Corbusier e o Brasil*, on his lecture tour of 1936.[38] Lucio Costa proposed Le

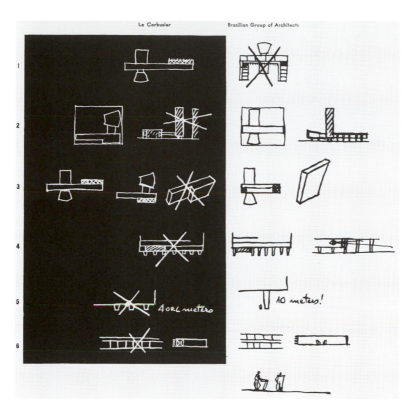

13.11 Oscar Niemeyer: Sketches showing the differences between Le Corbusier's and Costa's proposals.
The bottom figure may be an ironic representation of a master and pupil.
Papadaki: *The Works of Oscar Niemeyer*.

Corbusier as a candidate for the Nobel Peace Prize in 1950.[39] At the first Bienal de São Paulo, in 1951, he was awarded the highest prize, the Grande Prêmio Internacional de Arquitetura.

Le Corbusier continued to be approached by Brazilian friends and architects with the prospect of commissions, and to each he would reply enthusiastically. Firstly, there was a possibility of working with Reidy on his projects for Rio de Janeiro, specifically the incorporation of Le Corbusier's Mundanéum on a site of another razed hill, the Morro de Santo Antonio. Unfortunately the project was only partially realised and did not allow for Le Corbusier's participation. Another possible – though highly unlikely – commission was a Unité d'Habitation for São Paulo.[40] Drawings of his earlier urban plans were sought by Hugo Gouthier, the Brazilian Consul in New York, for a historical reference work during the preliminary discussions on the design of Brasília; with astonishing opportunism, he chose to interpret this as an invitation to act as consultant to a group of Brazilian architects.[41] Kubitschek wanted none of this idea nor of Le Corbusier; he wanted the project to be completely Brazilian and dissolved the commission.[42] Le Corbusier was also involved in the design of both, briefly, the Swiss, and, more conclusively, the French (1964–5; unbuilt), Embassies in Brasília.

Le Corbusier and Costa did collaborate again, though, on the Maison du Brésil (1957–9) at the Citè Universitaire in Paris (Figure 13.13). Costa intended that Le Corbusier's collaboration in the Maison du Brésil be in

13.12 Lucio Costa: Sketches
*The evolution of the design for the Ministry of Education and Health, Rio de Janeiro, 1936–37.* a *Brazilian group of architects.* b *Le Corbusier's scheme for the site near the airport.* c *Le Corbusier's scheme for the present site.* d *Final scheme by the Brazilian group.*
Mindlin: *Modern Architecture in Brazil.*

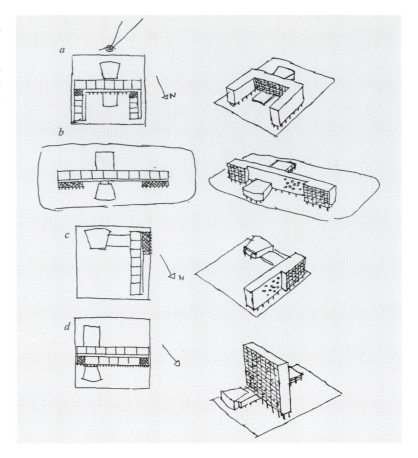

return for his involvement in the Ministry. Le Corbusier was to be the executive architect, and Costa was to supply the initial sketches, a reverse of the situation in 1936. It was characteristic of his adherence to pre-war Modernism that Costa chose the Pavillon Suisse as a model, but while Le Corbusier retained the initial *parti* he changed the appearance of the building by adding elements of his post-war vocabulary, such as the *beton brut* of the structure and balconies derived from the Unité d'Habitation in Marseilles. However, the extensive public facilities on the ground floor, which form a counterpoint to the heavy block above, were part of Costa's initial proposal and typical of his approach to site planning (Figure 13.14; Plate 20).

Although Le Corbusier's Cartesian rationality and technological vision, as well as his aesthetic sensibilities, profoundly influenced a whole generation of Brazilian architects, Le Corbusier's trips to Brazil had a reciprocal influence upon him. His two trips to Brazil, in 1929 and 1936, both marked turning points in his thoughts. Pevsner speculated on the possible influence of Brazil on Le Corbusier:

it is conceivable that the country had an effect on him of forcing into the open the irrational traits of his character and that he then passed on his impulsive enthusiasm to his young admirers.[43]

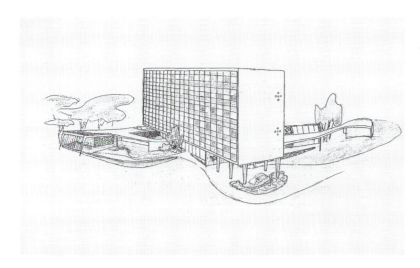

13.13 Lucio Costa: Original sketch for Maison du Brésil, Cité Universitaire, Paris (1953).
Costa: *Lucio Costa registro de uma vivencia.*

13.14 Lucio Costa with Le Corbusier: Maison du Brésil, Cité Universitaire, Paris (1957–9).
Exterior.
© Zilah Quezado Deckker.

In 1929, it seems that the sensuousness of Brazil, and especially Rio, seduced him, accentuating and confirming his erotic interests. It was at this time that he was developing his *objet à réaction poétique* in opposition to the Purist *objet-type*. The 1936 trip marked a shift away from the technological solutions of the *mur neutralisant* towards the passive ones of the *brise-soleil*. The climate and social customs in Brazil, which allowed an association between inside and outside, may have led Le Corbusier to believe that the hermetic environment of the *mur neutralisant* was neither ideal nor desirable. He acknowledged in the *Œuvre Complète 1938–46* that Centrosoyuz would have been better with *brise-soleil*; these were added to the Armée du Salut in 1946, along with new glazing systems to Centrosoyuz and the Pavillon Suisse to make them habitable. His post-war buildings had pronounced *brise-soleil* and balconies which extended the living spaces, starting with the Unité d'Habitation in Marseilles in 1948, and an emphasis on materials used 'as found', an interest first manifest with the Errazuris House in 1930.

In 1962, Le Corbusier went to Brazil to view the site for the French Embassy. It was his third and last visit to Brazil and gave him the opportunity to see the completed Ministry of Education Building. He wrote of his last visit:

> Brasília is built; I have seen the new city. It is magnificent in its invention, courage and optimism; it speaks from the heart. It is the work of two friends and (through the years) battle companions: Lucio Costa and Oscar Niemeyer. In the modern world Brasília is unique. In Rio there is the Ministry 1936–45 (Public Health and National Education). There are the works of Reidy, there is the monument to those who died in the war. There are many other testimonials. My voice is that of a traveller in the world and in life. Permit me, friends in Brazil, to say thank you to you![44]

## Notes

1   Siegfried Giedion: *A Decade of New Architecture* (Zurich: Girsberger 1951) p.134.

2   See Victoria Newhouse: *Wallace K. Harrison, Architect* (New York: Rizzoli 1989). The team of architects under Harrison included Oscar Niemeyer, Le Corbusier, N.D. Bassov, Ernest Cormier, Sven Markelius (who had designed the Swedish Pavilion at the New York World's Fair, 1939), Howard Robertson, G.A. Soilleux, Ssu-ch'eng Liang and Julio Vilamajo.

3   Elizabeth Mock (ed.): *Built in USA: since 1932*, Preface by Philip Goodwin (New York: Museum of Modern Art 1944).

4   Le Corbusier: *The UN Headquarters* (New York: Reinhold 1947); *Œuvre Complète 1938–46* pp.194–5.

5   Oscar Niemeyer: *As Curvas do Tempo: Memórias* (Rio de Janeiro: Revan 1998) pp.105–8.

6   Stamo Papadaki: *The Works of Oscar Niemeyer*, Preface by Lucio Costa (New York: Reinhold 1950; repr. 1951) p.174–81. Note that figure 111 in Newhouse: *Wallace K. Harrison, Architect* p.126 is not Niemeyer's original model, '32' but the compromise model, '32–23'.

7   *Œuvre Complète 1946–52*, p.38.

8   William H. Jordy: *The Impact of European Modernism in the Mid-Twentieth Century* (New York and Oxford: Oxford University Press 1969) p.221, p.228.

9   *The Architecture of Skidmore, Owings and Merrill* Introduction by Henry-Russell Hitchcock (Stuttgart: Gerd Hatje 1962; London: Architectural Press 1963). Significantly, Hitchcock credits the Ministry of Education to Costa and Niemeyer and the United Nations Headquarters to Harrison, p.9.

10  Jordy: *The Impact of European Modernism in the Mid-Twentieth Century* p.221.

11  See Adrian Forty: 'Le Corbusier's British Reputation' in *Le Corbusier: Architect of the Century* (London: Arts Council 1987) pp.35–41.

12  Howard Robertson: 'Building in Strong Sunlight' *The Architect and Building News* (16 April 1943) p.46.

13  Royal Festival Hall, London County Council, Robert Matthew, London 1948–51. Churchill Gardens Housing, Powell and Moya, London 1946. See John Summerson: Introduction, *Ten Years of British Architecture: 1945–55* (London: Arts Council 1956).

14  *Œuvre Complète 1934–38* pp.42–5, 78–81.

15  *Œuvre Complète 1934–38* p.81. 'adaptation sur le terrain [Castelo] adopté en dernière heure des aménagements du projet [Santa Luzia] de la page 78'. Lucio Costa sent the drawings to Le Corbusier by hand through Monteiro de Carvalho. Lucio Costa to Le Corbusier, 3 July 1937. FLC I3–3.47. Costa's drawings show 10 floors; fifteen floors were not approved until November.

16  'Edifício do Ministerio da Educacao e Saude' *Arquitetura e Urbanismo* (July–August 1939) pp.543–51.

17  *Œuvre Complète 1938–46* pp.80–90.

18  *Brazil Builds* p.92.

19 This may be seen in his library at the Fondation Le Corbusier.

20 *Œuvre Complète 1938–46* pp.103–15.

21 *Œuvre Complète 1938–46* p.87 (top right), 113.

22 A small exhibition of the Brazilian work was previously put together by *L'Architecture d'Aujourd'hui*, which opened in Paris in the summer of 1947 at the Galerie Maeght. *L'Architecture d'Aujourd'hui* (June 1947).

23 Le Corbusier to Affonso Reidy, 13 June 1949. FLC T2–13.53. *'l'invention propre du Brésil'*. Le Corbusier to P.M. Bardi, 18 October 1949. C1–18.67–69.
   *Je suis présent à côté de lui m'amusant follement de voir une si foudroyante nationalisation de ma pensée. Je dis au conferencier: 'Vous m'avez prodigieusement interessé'. Il prend cela pour un compliment.*

24 Le Corbusier to Reidy, 14 April 1949. FLC T2–13.48.
   *J'estime que les Brésiliens ont une dette à mon egard. Je n'ai pas touché un centime pour Le Ministère de l'Education Nationale et de la Santé Publique et ceci est vraiment extravagant. J'en ai parlé à l'Ambassade du Brésil, on m'a fait de belles promesses et rien n'a changé.*

25 P.M. Bardi: *Lembrança de Le Corbusier, Atenas, Itália, Brasil* (São Paulo: Nobel 1985). The exhibition was originally prepared for Boston, and travelled around the United States before showing in São Paulo and Buenos Aires. *Le Corbusier: New World of Space* (Boston: Institute of Contemporary Art 1948).

26 Le Corbusier to Bardi, 18 October 1949. FLC C1–18.67–69.

27 Le Corbusier to Bardi, 28 November 1949. FLC C1–18.64–66.

28 A telegram from Le Corbusier to Capanema acknowledged receipt of payment, 2 December 1936. FLC I3–3.37. The final amount was US$5,850, plus travel expenses, accommodation, and an official automobile.

29 Lucio Costa to Le Corbusier, 27 November 1949. FLC E1–17.21–22. *'votre interpretation actuelle des faits à ce qu'un me dit n'est plus celle de 1939'*.
   *Mais si c'est d'honoraires qu'il s'agit, permettez de vous faire savoir que pendant les trois mois de votre séjour ici vous avez touche [sic] d'avantage que nous autre pendant les six années que l'affaire à durer [sic], car nous étions six architectes et quoique les contributions individuelles fussent inégales, les honoraires ont toujours été partagés également parmi nous.*

30 Lucio Costa to Le Corbusier, 27 November 1949. FLC E1–17.21–22.
   *L'esquisse faite après coup, basée sur des photos du batiment construit, et que vous avez publiée comme s'il s'agissait d'une proposition originale, nous a fait, à tous, une pénible impression.*

31 Le Corbusier to Lucio Costa, 12 December 1949. FLC E1–17.23–25.

32 P.M. Bardi: *The Arts in Brazil* (Milan: Edizioni del Milioni 1956) p.80.

33 Conversation with P.M. Bardi, October 1988.

34 Papadaki: *The Works of Oscar Niemeyer* p.50.

35 Mindlin: *Modern Architecture in Brazil* cover and p.9.

36 Le Corbusier to Lucio Costa, 15 September 1964. FLC E1–17.42. *'J'ai vu que Reidy a employé ces plans pour faire son Musée de Rio de Janeiro (très joliment).'*

37 Klaus Franck: *The Works of Affonso Eduardo Reidy* (Stuttgart: Gerd Hatje; New York: Praeger 1960).

38 Bardi gave up the idea due to Le Corbusier's conditions of copyright. Bardi: *Lembrança de Le Corbusier* p.107.

39 Bardi: *Lembrança de Le Corbusier* pp.107–8.

40 Correspondence Le Corbusier and Prince Sanguszko, September–November 1952. FLC I3–3.108–17.

41 Correspondence April–June 1955. FLC I1–1.XX.1–7.

42 Kubitschek, Foreword in Willy Stäubli: *Brasília* (London: Leonard Hill 1966) p.7.

43 Pevsner: *An Outline of European Architecture* p.429.

44 *Œuvre Complète 1957–65* p.8.

# 14 *Construção Brasileira*: the 'Brazilian Style' in Brazil

In Brazil, Goodwin's statements about the Brazilian buildings contributed to change the opinion of the popular press in a decisive way. In the middle of 1942, the almost-completed Ministry of Education Building was under attack in the local newspapers, being condemned for its high cost: '*Palácio de Luxo*' [Palace of Luxury] and '*Mania de Grandeza*' [Mania of Magnificence],[1] and prolonged construction: '*O Edifício mais complicado do Brasil*' [Brazil's Most Complicated Building],[2] '*Quando será terminado o Edifício do Ministério da Educação? a passos lentos marcham as obras*' [When will the Ministry of Education be Completed? The building work plods along].[3]

While the Ministry of Education was only one of the several Government buildings being erected at that time, it had been singled out for criticism because of its avant-garde design. It was only when Goodwin and Kidder-Smith reported with unprecedented enthusiasm on its excellence during their trip that the local press reviewed its opinion. When Goodwin commented that the Ministry of Education was the most advanced building in America, his words made newspaper headlines: '*O Edifício mais Avançado da América*' [The Most Advanced Building in America],[4] which was followed by others in favour of the building: '*Uma Obra Notável da Arte Brasileira Moderna*' [A Remarkable Work of Modern Brazilian Art],[5] '*Uma Obra Notável da Arquitetura Moderna*' [A Remarkable Work of Modern Architecture] (Figures 14.1–14.3).[6]

José Mariano, who had written the article in favour of the neo-Colonial style in '*The Times* Brazil Number' in 1927, remained an isolated voice against 'Brazil Builds' and wrote several articles criticising it in the Rio de Janeiro press. He insisted that it was '*Publicidade Suspeita*' [Suspect Publicity] and was particularly against the claims that the Ministry of Education was well suited to the Brazilian climate: '*Pode ser tudo menos tropical*' [It could be anything but tropical].[7]

Newspapers in Brazil, upon receiving news of the success of the exhibition in New York in 1943, immediately reported it, and Gustavo Capanema received several congratulatory letters from Government and architectural bodies alike, including one which commented that the Ministry of Finance should be demolished because Goodwin considered it '*um monstrengo junto ao Ministério da Educação*' [a monster beside the

Ministry of Education].[8] Capanema was made an honorary member of the Instituto de Arquitetos do Brasil, and the Ministry of Education Building was listed in 1948.

Following the opening of the exhibition in the Ministry of Education Building on 23 November 1943, and the distribution of the book to renowned Brazilian political and social leaders, 'Brazil Builds' received full coverage in local newspapers. These included the prestigious Rotogravure section of *O Estado de São Paulo*,[9] and reviews by important critics and writers such as Mario de Andrade and Paulo Menotti Del Picchia who had both been prominent figures in the 'Semana de 22'.

Menotti Del Picchia commented on the quality and innovation of the publication, as well as its importance to Brazilian self-esteem, on several occasions:

14.2 *Uma Obra Notável da Arte Brasileira Moderna.*
*A Manhã*, Rio de Janeiro (14 June 1942).

It is the finest graphical document organized and printed to date about Brazilian architecture, old and modern, an architecture which, by the way, quite deserves being complimented.

A Brazilian begins to realize what he was and what he is capable of doing in this civilized art of building as he starts running over the marvellous pages of this book. On closing the volume, he feels proud of being a Brazilian and mutters to himself: 'Say, I didn't know we could do this, and so well too'.

This is certainly a masterpiece of publicity for our beloved Brazil of which the rushing 'Yankee' hardly knew more than about its coffee, rubber, its gaudy parrots and decorative orchids. We are the possessors of a great and typical school of music, a good backlog of literature, and as shown here an admirable and original inventive mind for architecture, adapting to the tropics those universal principles belonging to this art,

14.3 *Uma Obra Notável da Arquitetura Moderna.*
*Correio da Manhã*, Rio de Janeiro (19 June 1942).

modernized by Corbuzier [sic] and other masters. Such things – apart from 'business' – are what require being shown since it is through the understanding of the human being and not through the clashing of interests that good friendship is born.[10]

Another critic commented that the portrayal of Brazil in *Brazil Builds* was so flattering that it might have been publicity for the United States itself:

By means of these pictures which the Americans took and commented upon in such a kind and keen spirit of observation, just as if it were intended for publicity of the United States, Brazil appears exactly as she is: a civilized, cultured land, where originality and intelligence overflow, a land rich in undertakings and in creative imagination.
  And the soul of the Brazilian people who visit the exhibit draws untold

comfort, principally and at least in this instance, out of the fact that Brazil is presented to the outside world no longer as a land of savages and miserable huts, as so many European countries have insisted on picturing us, but as a nation having a certain appointed site in the geography of this world, and, furthermore, a place – and of the noblest – in the sphere of achievements which materialize the elevation of the mind and the strength of the civilizing power.[11]

Mario de Andrade confirmed the importance of the exhibition to Brazilians themselves:

I believe that this is the most fruitful gesture of humanity that the United States has ever performed towards us, the Brazilians. Because it will come, has already come, to regenerate our confidence in ourselves, and diminish the disastrous inferiority complex of mixed race which harm ourselves so much. I have already heard many Brazilians, not only astonished, but even annoyed, in face of this book which proves that we possess a modern architecture as good as the most advanced countries of the world.[12]

The Brazilian architectural magazine, *Acrópole*, thought that the importance of the exhibition was that it gave credence to the Modern architects to Brazilians themselves:

['Brazil Builds'] had among other advantages that of showing to ourselves, Brazilians, that the work of our modern architects is neither a simple exoticism nor the desire to be different, but a confident and secure art.

*Acrópole* also tried to prove that *Brazil Builds* was not simply a good-will initiative:

It is not the case, as it may seem, the mere kindness of good neighbours; the Museum of Modern Art is a private institution which has attempted to bring together the best modern art in the world.[13]

As a 'good will' trip, Goodwin and Kidder-Smith's visit was far more consequential to Brazil than most of the 'good-will missions' which visited the country between 1940–3. These trips, most of which were sponsored by the Office of Inter-American Affairs, usually stopped for a week in Rio de Janeiro, on their way to or from Buenos Aires while doing the whole of South America. In contrast, Goodwin's trip was exclusively to Brazil and had a long-lasting influence on Brazilian architecture, and, for that matter, on Brazil itself:

It is often said in Brazil that the country was discovered twice: once in 1500 by Pedro Alvares Cabral, the Portuguese Navigator; the second time in 1942 by Philip Goodwin.[14]

The importance of *Brazil Builds* to the Brazilian establishment was shown in homages given to Philip Goodwin and Kidder-Smith. They were both decorated with the Ordem Nacional do Cruzeiro do Sul [Order of the Southern Cross], a national tribute granted to distinguished foreigners *dignos de gratidão brasileira* [worthy of Brazilian gratitude].[15] Goodwin was also made an honorary member of the Instituto de Arquitetos do Brasil.

International recognition was a very important factor for the acceptance of new ideas by the public in Brazil, due to its colonial complex, as it provided a kind of proof of merit. Heitor Villa-Lobos, for example, had been first praised by the French composer Darius Milhaud and the pianist Artur Rubinstein;[16] Cândido Portinari received the Carnegie International Prize in 1935;[17] and, when Juscelino Kubitschek commissioned Pampulha, Oscar Niemeyer had already been praised internationally for the Brazilian Pavilion at the New York World's Fair. 'Brazil Builds' provided a critical warranty for the new Brazilian architecture in general. Architecture became a source of national pride; it came to be considered Brazil's main contribution to the Arts:

> It is in architecture, in fact, that Brazil, reciting the creed introduced by Le Corbusier, but in the language of a traditional experience rich in native idiom and modes of expression assimilated from Portuguese Baroque, has astonished the world.[18]

Brazilian architecture was recognised as an important contribution to Brazilian art in the Bienais de São Paulo. The Bienais had been created in 1951 by the industrialist Francisco Matarazzo Sobrinho (1898–1977) to hold international shows of contemporary art (Figure 14.4).[19] The prizes came to be considered the principal international awards in architecture in the early 1950s.[20] The prizes in the large number of categories reserved for Brazilian architects were a seal on the success of the 'Brazilian Style'.

14.4 Cover of *Arquitetura na Bienal de São Paulo* (1951).

The success of *Brazil Builds* caused both a rise in the prestige of architects and an increase in interest in architecture in Brazil. During the 1940s and 1950s, architectural magazines proliferated in Brazil. These included *Acrópole* (São Paulo 1938–71), *Ante-Projeto* (Rio de Janeiro 1945–9), *Arquitetura Contemporânea* (Rio de Janeiro 1953–8), *Arquitetura e Engenharia* (Belo Horizonte 1947–65), *Brasil Constroi* (Rio de Janeiro 1947–53), *Habitat* (São Paulo 1950–65) and *Módulo* (Rio de Janeiro 1955–65; 1975–87). The teaching of architecture became autonomous. The Faculdade Nacional de Arquitetura do Brasil took over architectural education from the Escola Nacional de Belas Artes in 1945 and the Faculdade de Arquitetura e Urbanismo da Universidade de São Paulo became independent of the Escola Politécnica in 1948. Other architecture schools were created around the country.

The critical success of Modernism encouraged the use of the style during a phase of hectic building activity during and after the Second World War. Oscar Niemeyer observed:

> The success of Modern architecture in Brazil has been such, that in a very short time it has become the normal and popular taste, with everyone, from government officials to private citizens, wanting modern buildings because of the attention paid to them both here and abroad.[21]

When Hitchcock went to Brazil in 1955 to review the contemporary architectural scene, he remarked that, since the completion of the Ministry of Education, it could almost be said that no major Brazilian building had been completed without Portinari's *azulejos* and Burle Marx's gardens. Hundreds of buildings, private or public, for residential or commercial use, were built on *pilotis*. The façades displayed *brise-soleil* and *pan-de-verre*.[22]

The designs were not always comparable to the standards set up in 'Brazil Builds', however; the critic Geraldo Ferraz pointed out that by the time the Ministry Building was completed, in 1945, the battle was no longer that of establishing Modern architecture, but that against undermining the quality of the architecture due to an indiscriminate use of the Modern idiom:

> The new architecture had become fairly popular in Brazil, to the extent that sincere and qualified professionals were hard put to restrain the activities of their unscrupulous, incompetent competitors who destroyed the spirit of functional architecture.[23]

The reasons for this he found in a certain complacency of the architects enjoying their fame:

> owing to a certain lack of self-criticism and sometimes a disinclination to work out for themselves the real points and purpose of the new architecture. [. . .] The original urge to create in the desert had naturally waned, especially among the pioneers; it was much more important in a country invaded by the horrors of so-called 'futurism', to check excesses, enlighten the public and build honestly and as well as possible.[24]

In fact, after the initial period of euphoria following the publication of *Brazil Builds*, some architects and writers in Brazil became increasingly critical of contemporary architectural production. With hindsight, the buildings portrayed in *Brazil Builds* came to be seen as the zenith of Brazilian Modernism. In a lecture given as the Lethaby Professor of Architecture at the Royal College of Art in London in 1961, the architect Henrique Mindlin (1911–71) summed up his feelings and explained their context:

> A great deal of bad work has been done, because of the very large amount of work promoted by the speculative conditions fostered by inflation, and because of the insufficient number of good professionals. As a matter of fact, in the middle fifties, after twenty years of impressive output, there was a general feeling that perhaps the whole movement had reached a routine period, if not a downward phase, that the summits attained in the most famous buildings were not to be achieved any more.[25]

He reported in that lecture that Lucio Costa, who helped him in the final selection of buildings to be included in *Modern Architecture in Brazil*, in 1956, had asked at the end: 'Is that all?' (Figure 14.5). This rather dejected question expressed that perhaps too much enthusiasm might have generated an overestimation of the achievements of Modern Architecture in Brazil. Lucio Costa himself confirmed this rather pessimistic view:

> At first one is happy with the feeling of variety within the basic unity of intention, revealing maturity and style; then soon the subconscious hints at the fact that, in spite of the hostility of the time (aggressive as in no other country), the initial start with the Brazilian Press Association, the Ministry of Education, the Seaplane Terminal, the Pavilion at the World's Fair in New York, Pampulha – all these marked, from the beginning, the high point of the new architecture; this attitude of disbelief is followed by a promising euphoria when one is faced with the high quality, the inventive content and the size of the work done later by so many architects, including those of the initial phases; however as the pessimist says 'the state of health is a transient state that only foreshadows the worst', and the feeling of doubt and apprehension returns, because, in spite of the ingenious solutions and formal innovations, everything turns, in the last analysis, around the same well-known points and one comes to the sad conclusion that Brazilian architecture has already done its job.[26]

In the 12 years between the publication of *Brazil Builds* and Costa's statement, Brazil had changed a great deal: the population had grown from 42,000,000 to 53,000,000;[27] the large-scale industrial expansion initiated in the 1930s and 1940s had continued with the growth of heavy industries such as steel and automobile production. By 1960 industrial production amounted to more than 25 per cent of the gross domestic product. These economic changes brought about far-reaching transformations in Brazilian society, in particular, urbanisation: the urban population increased from 25 per cent in 1920 to 60 per cent in 1980.[28]

14.5 Cover of *Modern Architecture in Brazil*.

Henrique E. Mindlin, Preface by Siegfried Giedion. Published simultaneously in New York, London, Rio de Janeiro, Amsterdam, Paris and Munich in 1956.

Photographs show the School of Aeronautics, São José dos Campos by Oscar Niemeyer, Parque Guinle, Rio de Janeiro by Lucio Costa, the Banco da Lavoura, Belo Horizonte by Álvaro Vital Brazil, and sketches by Lucio Costa showing 3 of the 4 stages of the Ministry of Education Building, Rio de Janeiro (see Figure 13.12).

The period following *Brazil Builds* was richer both in variety and quantity of buildings, but critics considered that certain original qualities had been lost in the later buildings.[29] For *Modern Architecture in Brazil*, Mindlin had initially intended only to include developments after *Brazil Builds*, but found that the most significant examples of Brazilian Modern architecture were from that time; the Ministry of Education, the Brazilian Press Association, the Seaplane Terminal, Pampulha, the Edifício Esther, and the New York Pavilion were all included.

Most of the architects who had worked on the Ministry of Education Building launched their careers on the strength of their involvement in it, Niemeyer in particular. The greater fame of his work led to a general belief that what had been quickly labelled the 'Brazilian Style' could be defined by his work alone, forgetting, however, that many of its distinctive features, such as paraboloid shell vaults, 'butterfly' roofs, sloping building façades, and various types of grids for sun control had been developed in common.

Niemeyer came to be regarded as Brazil's foremost architect, and thereafter never lacked commissions either in Brazil or abroad. After his collaboration with Costa on the Ministry of Education and the Brazilian Pavilion, Niemeyer exploited the freedom of form inherent in the style:

> Architecture in Brazil, overcoming the stage of orthodox functionalism, is now in search of plastic expression. It is the extreme malleability of present construction methods together with our instinctive love for the curve – real affinity with the Baroque of our colonial times – which suggests unfettered forms of a new and amazing plastic vocabulary.[30]

Niemeyer's search for plastic expression meant that he left many technical details to his collaborators, which may explain his enormous output and the diagrammatic quality of much of his work. This working method was certainly appropriate to the conditions of building in Brazil, however, far from the sophisticated manufacturing and professional services in Europe and the United States. On the other hand, it meant that he could concentrate on the poetic aspects of architecture often missing from the more technological work in the United States and Europe.

Niemeyer's major works of this period show a development of the style of the Ministry Building: the Banco Boavista (1946); Ibirapuera Exhibition Buildings (1951–4) (Plate 18); and his own house at Gávea (1953–4) (Plate 19). This house, with a free-form concrete roof over a sinuous curved plan, was considered by Hitchcock to be 'the most extreme statement of his special cariocan lyricism'.[31] Niemeyer was fortunate to be championed by Stamo Papadaki, who published all his work in a series of monographs which further heightened his international profile.

Lucio Costa built little after the Ministry Building, as he became more involved with his work at SPHAN and the protection of old buildings. His influence, however, can not be over-emphasised. He had been responsible more than any other architect for the creative turn which Brazilian architecture took in the late 1930s. With his great knowledge of historical architecture, he was not ready to assimilate the new without question. The two most important buildings by which the 'Brazilian Style' was usually

14.6 Lucio Costa: Parque Guinle Apartment Buildings, Rio de Janeiro (1948–1954).
Edifício Nova Cintra from Edifício Bristol. West and north façades covered with *cambogé* – a pierced pre-cast concrete sunscreen.
Costa: *Lucio Costa: registro de uma vivência.*

defined – the Brazilian Pavilion and the Ministry of Education – had been under Costa's charge. His apartment blocks in Parque Guinle (1947–53) are illustrative of his work after the completion of the Ministry Building (Figure 14.6). These were eight-storey-high blocks on *pilotis* with façades composed of *cambogé* – a pierced pre-cast concrete sunscreen. Costa had planned six blocks but built only three; these received a prize at the first São Paulo Bienal in 1951. Hitchcock considered them to be 'one of the most characteristic and successful examples of Cariocan architecture'.[32] Costa's major achievement, and the one by which he is now best remembered, is the plan for Brasília.

Affonso Reidy had a prolific career and was to become one of Brazil's foremost architects. Reidy had been appointed Head of the Department of Architecture of the Prefecture of Rio de Janeiro in 1932, where he was engaged in both urban proposals and the designs of buildings. The Pedregulho Residential Neighbourhood in São Cristovão in the centre of Rio de Janeiro was a 260 m long serpentine block of housing for municipal workers which incorporated community facilities such as a Primary School and Gymnasium; the housing block was completed in 1947, and the facilities in 1950. It can be seen as a development of Le Corbusier's 1929 plan for Rio de Janeiro, but wrapping around the contours of the hill on which it is placed, leaving the flat plain for the public facilities. This complex won a first prize at the first São Paulo Bienal in 1951. In 1952, he used a similar design for the Gávea Residential Neighbourhood.

Reidy's last, and before his sudden death in 1964, most famous project, was for the Museu de Arte Moderna in Rio de Janeiro (1954–61). It consisted of a structural frame of 28 splayed concrete ribs which supported and suspended the large glassed-in exhibition area. It showed a marked change from his previous buildings towards a more Brutalist aesthetic of expressive structure and exposed concrete finishes (Plate 22). The Museu de Arte Moderna was on almost exactly the same site chosen by Le Corbusier for his first design for the Ministry of Education, which since 1952 had formed part of the Parque Glória-Flamengo, designed by Burle Marx on infill along the beaches into the Bay of Guanabara (Plate 17).

Roberto Burle Marx became a highly regarded landscape architect of international stature. He continued to be honoured by the Museum of Modern Art, New York with exhibitions and publications.[33] Burle Marx had been born in São Paulo in 1909 but had subsequently lived in Rio de Janeiro and Germany, where he encountered native Brazilian plants in the botanical garden at Dahlem. He had been a student of Fine Art at the Escola Nacional de Belas Artes in 1930; Costa had given him his first commission for a garden at the Schwartz house in 1932. In 1934 he went to Recife to become Director of the Departamento de Parques e Jardims. Burle Marx returned to Rio de Janeiro in 1937 to establish his own practice. It was then that he received his commissions for the gardens at the Brazilian Press Association and the Ministry of Education. After the Second World War, Burle Marx designed several public gardens such as the Parque Glória-Flamengo in Rio de Janeiro (1952–c.1969) (Plate 17) and the pavement in Copacabana (1970) on the *aterro* as well as many notable private gardens. In 1957 he was asked by Costa to design the landscaping for Brasília; he designed the park-like settings of the *superquadras* (Plate 26) and various gardens such as those of the Ministério do Exército (1970) (Plate 28) and the Parque da Cidade (1974). The ecological approach which increasingly characterised his work was most apparent in his country estate, the Sitio Santo Antônio da Bica in the state of Rio de Janeiro.

Jorge Moreira became the chief architect of the Cidade Universitária, which started in 1954. Its definitive site was the Ilha do Fundão, a largely artificial island in the Bay of Guanabara. The most faithful of its authors to the spirit of the Ministry Building, Moreira attached himself firmly to the formula developed there of independent prismatic block. The first buildings of the campus were the Instituto de Puericultura (1953), the Faculdade de Arquitetura e Urbanismo, and the Politécnica (both 1960) (Figure 14.7). Unfortunately the colossal scale of the campus precluded a

14.7 Jorge Machado Moreira: Faculdade de Arquitetura e Urbanismo, Cidade Univer-sitária, Rio de Janeiro (1957).
Podium with connecting passages.
© Zilah Quezado Deckker.

sensitive handling of the site, leaving the main buildings somewhat isolated.

Of the remaining architects who had formed the team for the Ministry Building, two did not continue in practice. Carlos Leão designed several houses after his collaboration on the Ministry, but later, in 1965, retreated to his farm outside Rio de Janeiro and dedicated himself to drawing, and is now better known in Brazil in this capacity rather than as an architect. This was also the case of Ernani Vasconcellos, who devoted himself to painting.

Marcelo and Milton Roberto, who had won the competitions for the Brazilian Press Association in 1936 and Santos Dumont Airport in 1937 and built the Hangar No. 1 in 1940, continued to maintain a prominent practice; they built a great number of apartment buildings in Rio de Janeiro, including two at Parque Guinle in 1960. They did not match the delicacy of Lucio Costa's work at the same complex; their work continued the more solid manner established at the Brazilian Press Association. A third brother, Mauricio (b. 1921), joined the office in 1944; since the mid-1950s the office has been under his leadership, after the death of Milton in 1953 and Marcelo in 1964.

14.8 Álvaro Vital Brazil: Banco da Lavoura (centre), Belo Horizonte (1946–51).
© Zilah Quezado Deckker.

Álvaro Vital Brazil built prolifically; he executed a series of banks for the Banco da Lavoura, but his earlier work, such as the Banco da Lavoura in Belo Horizonte (1946–51), remains his best (Figure 14.8).[34] It received a first prize at the first São Paulo Bienal.

Rino Levi was one of few *paulista* architects to have been included in *Brazil Builds*, although he had no affiliation to the work of Le Corbusier. Levi developed a large practice after the Second World War; his Instituto Central do Câncer of 1954 in São Paulo was regarded as a model hospital. He became more influenced by North American practice; his last work, the Banco Sul Americano of 1962 in São Paulo, in particular, was based on Lever House, although it made extensive use of *brise-soleils*. Rino Levi died in 1965, but his practice, Rino Levi Associados, continued under his partners Roberto Cerqueira Cesar (b. 1917), since 1941, and Roberto Carvalho Franco (b. 1926), since 1951.

While 'Brazil Builds' had displayed the new Brazilian architecture as a coherent movement, there was even then a divergence in approach between the work done in São Paulo and Rio de Janeiro which was to emerge even more strongly later. In 1955, Hitchcock, realising the divergences between the work in Rio de Janeiro and São Paulo, chose to restrict the use of the term 'Brazilian Style' to Rio de Janeiro, and used 'Carioca School of Architecture' instead to define the work of Costa, Reidy, Moreira and Niemeyer. The *paulista* architecture, he wrote, was less Brazilian in flavour. Hitchcock was justified in his judgement: not only did São Paulo have a large European immigrant population, but architects came from a Polytechnic School and had the title of *engenheiro-arquiteto*.

It would be easy to overestimate the influence of Le Corbusier on Brazilian architecture in this period; in fact, much of the *paulista* architecture shown by Mindlin in *Modern Architecture in Brazil* did not look particularly Corbusian. São Paulo was much more North American in outlook and its architecture reflected this. The naturalised American architect Richard Neutra (1892–1970), for example, had visited Brazil in 1945 at the invitation of the United States State Department; he had undertaken genuine research into schools, hospitals and housing in hot climates, stimulated both by his adopted city of Los Angeles and his war-time work in Puerto Rico, and had written a book especially for Brazilian architects.[35] This was in marked contrast to Le Corbusier, much of whose technical solutions were dubious and whose principle attraction was his expressive qualities. It was a paradox, therefore, that while North American influences governed the practices of the major architects in São Paulo, they decried it in print.

The state of São Paulo, which was anyway the most advanced state economically, grew increasingly further from the other states after the end of the war.[36] Intellectuals there viewed North American intrusion into Brazil as cultural and economic imperialism, even as it was becoming more dominant in Brazil in these areas. Architects in São Paulo regarded the 'Brazilian Style' as an expression of subservience to this imperialism due to its promotion by North Americans. Furthermore, they resented the fact that the 'Brazilian Style' was defined by the Modern architecture of Rio de Janeiro. Ironically, it was the São Paulo Bienais which were celebrating the Brazilian Style; not only did they award numerous prizes to buildings such as Costa's Parque Guinle and Reidy's Pedregulho Residential Neighbourhood, but they commissioned the Pavilion in the Parque Ibirapuera from Niemeyer specifically for the 1953 Bienal.

The spokesman for this stream of thought was the architect João Vilanova Artigas, who published successive articles in which he directly attacked the 'Brazilian Style':

> Today, Brazilian Modern Architecture is progressing in such a way as to serve as propaganda for any commercial villainy [. . .], while at the same time reinforcing the penetration of imperialism, giving it cover to enter without being noticed through the doors of cultural movements.[37]

Artigas found that the 'Brazilian Style' served the aims of American imperialism in Brazil. On the one hand, it had first been discovered and promoted by the Americans while serving their own interests:

Because of the participation of Brazil in the war against Nazism, the Americans took advantage to deepen their roots in our country. Cultural missions of every type came here to perform the first manoeuvre of larceny. They discovered the 'Brazilian Style' which became the path to put Brazil culturally on an equal level, 'shoulder to shoulder', with the most cultured people of the world, Yankees included.[38]

On the other hand, Artigas saw it as being affiliated to Le Corbusier, whom he attacked on the same grounds of serving American imperialism. Artigas saw Le Corbusier's Modulor as an attempt to compromise the metric system by accepting the use of the imperial system, preserved by the English and the Americans:

For the progressive architects in Brazil, the language of Le Corbusier, in this book, is the language of the worst enemy of our people, American imperialism. It is up to us to reject it.[39]

However, while Artigas was writing these texts he was still designing buildings within the 'Brazilian Style'; several privates houses, including his own, and a bus station were illustrated in *Modern Architecture in Brazil*.[40]

Artigas' later work was quite distinct and highly influential: it was characteristic of Brutalism – rough concrete walls and sharply geometrical shapes – although not included by Banham in *The New Brutalism* in 1966. The influence of Artigas through his rhetorical discourse and activities at the Faculdade de Arquitetura e Urbanismo in São Paulo, which he designed in 1961, was enormous (Plate 23). He influenced a whole generation of architects, who came to dominate the architectural scene in São Paulo and the rest of Brazil.

Even the highly individual *paulista* architect Lina Bo Bardi worked in a Brutalist manner. Lina Bo Bardi was born in Rome; she studied architecture at the Escola Superiore under Marcello Piacentini and worked for Gio Ponti

14.9  Lina Bo Bardi: SESC–Pompéia Cultural Centre, São Paulo (1977).
View from the towers over the roofs of the restored factory sheds.
© Zilah Quezado Deckker.

(1891–1979). She came to Brazil in 1947 with her husband, Pietro Maria Bardi, who had been appointed Director of the Museu de Arte de São Paulo. She was equally happy designing new buildings such as the Museu de Arte de São Paulo (1957–68) (Plate 21) as renovating historic ones such as the SESC-Pompéia Cultural Centre (1977) (Figure 14.9).

The political, and architectural, inheritance of the 'Revolução de 30' lasted until 1964. Vargas was deposed by military coup in 1945 due to his increasingly populist measures, among them the release from prison of Luís Carlos Prestes (1898–1990), the head of the Brazilian Communist Party, who had been imprisoned in 1938. Vargas had taken these measures as a reaction to the post-war popular opposition to the fascist complexion of the Estado Novo. However, Vargas rebuilt his campaign and returned to the Presidency at the next election in 1951, remaining until his suicide in 1954. The next civilian President was Juscelino Kubitschek, who set a Target Programme of economic development. During his four years of tenure, industrial output grew by an astonishing 80 per cent, laying the foundations of the myth of the 'Brazilian miracle'.[41]

Kubitschek continued his policy, started at Pampulha, of sponsoring the 'Brazilian Style', in the new capital city: Brasília. Kubitschek appointed Niemeyer Director of the Department of Architecture of the Companhia de Urbanização da Nova Capital (NOVACAP), and a competition was announced in September 1956 for the plan of the city. The competition attracted 26 Brazilian architectural practices, including most of the major Modern practices, including Rino Levi Associados and M.M.M. Roberto. All the competition entries had one point in common: they assumed the separation of the functions of the city according to *La Charte d'Athènes*, into dwelling, work, leisure, and circulation. Only Costa's plan was felt by the jury to specifically represent a 'capital' city rather than aspire to the open-ended or universal solution of the *Charte*.[42] Only Costa's plan could be said to involve a development of the 'Brazilian Style'; the other architects had already departed markedly from the canons of the style.

Niemeyer and Costa had not collaborated since the Brazilian Pavilion in 1938, even though they remained close friends, and Niemeyer would have certainly recognised Costa's hand in the competition. In Brasília they had the opportunity to display the virtues of the 'Brazilian Style' on a civic scale. The dynamic urban landscape which Costa and Niemeyer had initiated in the Ministry of Education and the Cidade Universitária was transformed into a colossal ceremonial and symbolic space, the Esplanada dos Ministérios [Esplanade of the Ministries] terminated by the Congresso Nacional [Congress] and the Praça dos Três Poderes [Plaza of the Three Powers] (Plates 24, 25). Niemeyer's work, while recognisably a continuation of the 'Brazilian Style', had developed into a new phase of plastic freedom. The *superquadras*, derived from Costa's Parque Guinle, contained housing blocks and cultural and leisure facilities – churches, cinemas, schools, libraries and sports centres – set in a park-like landscape (Plate 26).[43] A part of that landscape was to be designed by Roberto Burle Marx.

After Kubitschek, the next significant President was João Goulart (1918–76), who had been Minister of Labour under Vargas, and who was strongly left wing. The unworkability of his policies in conjunction with the still-powerful military and aristocratic oligarchy led to his deposition by a

14.10 Oscar Niemeyer: Parti Communiste Français, Paris (1967–80).
© Zilah Quezado Deckker.

coup in 1964. Although inflation caused by the development of Brasília is often cited as the reason for the coup, the socialist direction of the government and Brazil's international position offer a more realistic explanation. Kubitschek had withdrawn Brazil from the International Monetary Fund in 1959 and, in 1961, Goulart had awarded the Ordem Nacional do Cruzeiro do Sul to 'Ché' Guevara. Intense diplomatic pressure, as well as more covert support by the CIA, gave the military confidence to act.

The following 21 years were under a military government. There can be no doubt that both the foreign and domestic policies of this regime were a disaster; not only did foreign indebtedness increase but social inequality was also exacerbated.[44] The military government encouraged the establishment of foreign manufacturers, which effectively killed Brazilian industry; with the collusion of the International Monetary Fund, it embarked on a series of projects, such as the colonisation of the Amazon and the Itaipu dam, which were intended to provide the foundations for industrial development, but had appalling social and environmental consequences with little apparent benefit.[45]

The military regime moved decisively against the use of the 'Brazilian Style', largely because of its close links with the previous government. Even though the Vargas regime and its political heirs had never sought to impose an aesthetic of ideological representation, the 'Brazilian Style' had become inextricably linked to their policies. Lucio Costa virtually withdrew from public life. Oscar Niemeyer spent most of the years 1964–83 abroad; as a Communist, he was invited to design the headquarters of the Parti Communiste Français (1967–80) in Paris (Figure 14.10), among many other prestigious commissions in France, Italy, and Algeria. The end of the self-conscious attempt to define an autonomous Brazilian culture, and the absorption of a North American one, resulted in a loss of self-confidence in almost all fields of the Arts. The reduction of academic freedom, especially the removal of university professors politically opposed to the regime,

14.11 Oscar Niemeyer: Memorial da America Latina, São Paulo (1987). © Zilah Quezado Deckker.

resulted in the loss of a critical discourse of architecture. The considerable number of architectural magazines, which had opened in the wave of enthusiasm after *Brazil Builds*, closed.

With the fall of the military government in 1985, Niemeyer was welcomed back to Brazil as a symbol of democracy. He carried out a number of renovation works to his buildings in Brasília, such as adding stained glass to the Cathedral and removing the marble cladding from the arcade of the Ministério da Justiça, and designed several new buildings such as the Panteão da Pátria (1986) in Brasília (Plate 27), and the Memorial da America Latina (1987) in São Paulo (Figure 14.11). The Ministry of Education Building was restored as the Palácio Capanema. These were, however, isolated and largely symbolic gestures, and did not form a return to the conditions under which the 'Brazilian Style' had flourished. Niemeyer's last works, too, could hardly be thought of as a continuation of the 'Brazilian Style': he had developed the plastic freedom initiated in his first independent work at Pampulha into new concepts of architectural form, but without acknowledging any of the criticisms of Modernism which had brought it into disfavour. In the Brazil of the 1990s, the 'Brazilian Style', as much as the 'Revolução de 30', appeared as a relic of a bygone era.

## Notes

1  *A Notícia* (29 June 1942). CE: CPC 3.23 CPDOC/FGV.
2  *O Radical* (2 March 1941). CE: CPC 3.21 CPDOC/FGV.
3  *A Noite* (27 February 1942). CE: CPC 3.23 CPDOC/FGV.
4  *A Notícia* (2 July 1942). PCMESP X SPHAN.
5  *A Manhã* (14 June 1942) p.3. PCMESP X SPHAN.
6  *Correio de Manhã* (19 June 1942). PCMESP X SPHAN.
7  *Folha Carioca* (12 July 1944, 26 July 1944). CE: CPC 3.55, 3.56 CPDOC/FGV.
8  Cesar Vieira to Capanema, 15 March 1943. CE: CPC 3.32 CPDOC/FGV.
9  *O Estado de São Paulo* (28 March, 4 April 1944). Memorandum: OIAA – 157/SP, 22 March 1944. MoMA Archives, NY: CE, II.1/41(5).

10  English Translation of an article by Anhanguera, pen-name of Menotti Del Picchia, in *A Noite* 29 March 1944. MoMA Archives, NY: CE, II.1/41(5).

11  English Translation of article by Raul de Polillo: 'The Brazil Builds Exhibit in the "Prestes Maia" Gallery' *Folha da Noite* 29 March 1944. MoMA Archives, NY: CE, II.1/41(5).

12  Mario de Andrade: 'Brazil Builds' *Folha da Manhã* (23 March 1944). CE: CPC 3.43 CPDOC/FGV.

>  Eu creio que este é um dos gestos de humanidade mais fecundos que os Estados Unidos já praticaram em relação a nós, os brasileiros. Porque ele veio virão, veio, regenerar a nossa confiança em nós mesmos, e diminuir o desastroso complexo de inferioridade de mestiços que nos prejudica tanto. Já escutei muito brasileiro, não apenas assombrado, mas até mesmo estomagado, diante desse livro que prova possuirmos uma arquitetura moderna tão boa como os mais avançados países do mundo.

13  ' "Brazil Builds" e os Edifícios Públicos Paulistas' *Acrópole* (May 1944) p.23.

>  ['Brazil Builds'] teve entre outras vantagens a de mostrar a nós mesmos, brasileiros, que a obra dos nossos arquitetos modernos não é simples exotismo ou desejo de ser diferente, mas obra de arte segura e bem orientada.

>  Não se trata, como pode parecer, simples amabilidade de bons vizinhos; o Museu de Arte Moderna é uma instituição privada que tem procurado reunir tudo o que de melhor se tem feito no mundo no domínio da arte moderna.

14  Henrique Mindlin: 'Brazilian Architecture' Lethaby Lectures, Royal College of Art, London 1961 (Rome: Brazilian Embassy 1961?).

15  Letter from Kidder-Smith, 12 April 1990.

16  Heitor Villa-Lobos met Darius Milhaud in Rio de Janeiro in 1917 and through him Artur Rubinstein who launched Villa-Lobos internationally.

17  Cândido Portinari's 'Coffee' received a second honourable mention.

18  P.M. Bardi: *Profiles of the New Brazilian Art* (Rio de Janeiro: Kosmos 1970) p.44.

19  His company supplied *azulejos* for many modern buildings including the Ministry of Education.

20  Hitchcock: *Latin American Architecture since 1945* (New York: Museum of Modern Art 1955) p.30.

21  Oscar Niemeyer: 'Considerações sobre a Arquitetura Brasileira' *Módulo* (February 1957) pp.5–10.

22  Hitchcock: *Latin American Architecture since 1945* p.36.

23  Ferraz: *Warchavchik* p.262.

24  Ferraz: *Warchavchik* p.262.

25  Mindlin: *Brazilian Architecture* p.36.

26  Lucio Costa in Mindlin: *Modern Architecture in Brazil* p.37.

27  Census of 1940: 41,236,315; 1950: 51,944,397; 1960: 70,191,370; 1970: 93,139,037. *Almanaque Abril 1990* p.133.

28  Skidmore: *Modern Latin America* pp.153–4.

29  Ferraz: 'Arquitetura Moderna no Brasil: Review of *Modern Architecture in Brazil*' *Habitat* (July–August 1957) pp.30–4.

30  Oscar Niemeyer: 'Forma e Função na Arquitetura' *Módulo* (December 1960) pp.3–7.

31  Hitchcock: *Latin America Architecture Since 1945* p.170.

32  Hitchcock: *Latin America Architecture Since 1945* p.154.

33  William Howard Adams: *Roberto Burle Marx: The Unnatural art of the Garden* (New York: Museum of Modern Art 1991).

34  Álvaro Vital Brazil: *Álvaro Vital Brazil, 50 Anos de Arquitetura* (São Paulo: Nobel 1986) pp.55–9.

35  Richard Neutra: *Arquitetura Social em Paises de clima Quente/Architecture of Social Concern in Regions of Mild* [sic] *Climate* (São Paulo: Gerth Todtmann 1948?).

36  In 1920 São Paulo was producing 30–40 per cent of Brazil's national output; in 1940, 50 per cent. Skidmore: *Modern Latin America* pp.153, 157.

37  Vilanova Artigas: 'Os Caminhos da Arquitetura Moderna' *Caminhos da Arquitetura* (São Paulo: Fundação Vilanova Artigas/Pini 1986) p.79 (first publ. in *Fundamentos* January 1952).

>  Hoje a Arquitetura Moderna Brasileira, progride no sentido de servir de cartaz de propaganda para tudo quanto é malandragem comercialescas [. . .], ao mesmo tempo que concorre, para reforçar a penetração do imperialismo, dando-lhe cobertura para entrar despercebido pelas portas dos movimentos culturais.

38  Artigas: *Caminhos da Arquitetura* p.78.

*Da participação do Brasil na guerra contra o nazismo, aproveitou-se o imperialism ameri-cano para aprofundar suas raízes em nossa pátria. Missões culturais de toda sorte aqui vieram para encobrir as primeiras manobras de rapinagem. Descobriram a Arquitetura Moderna Brasileira, que passou a ser a habilidade que punha culturalmente o Brasil em igualdade de condições, 'ombro a ombro', com os mais cultos povos do mundo, os ianques inclusive!*

39  Artigas: 'Le Corbusier e o Imperialismo' *Caminhos da Arquitetura* p.61 (first publ. in *Fundamentos* January 1951).

*Para os arquitetos progressistas do Brasil, a linguagem de Le Corbusier, neste livro, é a linguagem do pior dos inimingos do nosso povo, o imperialismo americano. Cumpre-nos repudiá-la.*

40  Mindlin: *Modern Architecture in Brazil* pp.34–6, 94–5, 228–9.

41  Some industries grew at over 300 per cent. Skidmore, *Politics in Brazil* p.164.

42  William Holford: 'Brasília' *Architectural Review* (December 1957) pp.397–8.

43  See Thomas Deckker: 'Brasília: City versus Landscape' in Thomas Deckker (ed.): *The Modern City Revisited* (London: Spon Press 2000).

44  Skidmore: *Modern Latin America* p.180.

45  Jane Jacobs has remarked that such policies of development had already been tried by the Tennessee Valley Authority and had actually led to a decrease in the standard of living in the TVA region. They had the same result in Brazil. 'Capital for Regions Without Cities' *Cities and the Wealth of Nation* (Harmondsworth: Penguin Books 1986) pp.105–23.

# Conclusion

The exhibition and book *Brazil Builds* helped to create a consensus among architects and historians of what the new architecture in Brazil actually consisted; as suggested by a contemporary critic: 'no English modern architect, or United States architect either, would have thought to include Brazil among the pioneer countries of modern architecture before the publication of this book.'[1]

The immediate importance of *Brazil Builds* lay in it being a confirmation of the wide acceptance of Modernism and a demonstration of a development of Modernism which assimilated cultural characteristics and regional requirements. In reviews and reports of the exhibition there was great emphasis on the continuity of cultural identity, and on technical devices such as those dealing with intense heat and light.

It could perhaps be said that the more outstanding buildings like the Ministry of Education would have become known internationally without the publicity of the exhibition and the book; nevertheless, without a comprehensive survey it would have been seen as an isolated example without any cultural significance. By being presented as the masterpiece of a whole movement it gained further credibility. *Brazil Builds* presented Brazilian Modernism as a coherent movement and a widespread phenomenon, glossing over the differences between the various buildings and ignoring that the overwhelming majority of contemporary buildings were based largely on traditional models. Despite the differences between the many Modern buildings, it was their common points that became apparent and were acclaimed.

The Museum of Modern Art, New York, had championed International Modernism with 'Modern Architecture: International Exhibition' in 1932. In 1943, it attempted to usher in a new national phase of Modernism with 'Brazil Builds'. The Museum pursued the same policy in both *The International Style* and *Brazil Builds* of showing the movements as *faits accomplis* – as actual buildings shown in excellent photographs as solid proof that the styles existed.

The policies of the Museum of Modern Art mirrored the concerns of the United States Government during the Second World War. The United States felt that it had a community of interest with its hemispheric neighbours, as American nations both united against European fascism, and economically interdependent; the New Deal and the 'Revolução de 30' had much in common. Although 'Brazil Builds' was part of the United States 'Good Neighbour' policy, it went far beyond being a mere instrument of propaganda. As far as it was a result of a good-will mission, it achieved a life of its own and had a far-reaching influence on architecture.

*Brazil Builds* was in accordance with the Vargas Government's ambition of being seen as a progressive nation, and with the views of the architects themselves. It was also a time of enormous cultural self-confidence in Brazil. The reception its architecture received in North America and Europe reflected the general hope, during the Second World War, in Brazil as a 'Land of the Future' – a land of racial harmony and progress. The Modern architecture shown in *Brazil Builds* could only serve to confirm this belief.

The 'Brazilian Style' was forgotten for a variety of reasons both within Brazil and abroad. One of the reasons may be that Brazil did not fulfil the promise of the Vargas years; another may lie with the evolution of post-war architecture. Viewed against the volume and diversity of post-war architecture, Brazilian architecture appeared neither as impressive in quantity nor as stylistically unique as it once seemed. Only the construction of Brasília provided a respite from the decline, and became seen as the swansong of the 'Brazilian Style'. The 'Brazilian Style' became irrevocably linked to the Vargas era and its political inheritance, which lasted until the coming of the military government in 1964.

*Brazil Builds* was a chapter in the history of Modern architecture, not only in Brazil, but of the Modern Movement as a whole. Brazil's return to democracy provides an opportunity for the re-examination of that time when Brazilian architecture was shown abroad, radiant with promise.

## Note

1   *Journal of the Institute of British Architects* (May 1943) p.155.

# Appendix: Brazil Builds

## Specification of *Brazil Builds*

$8\frac{3}{4} \times 11$
Publisher: MoMA
Printer: Wm. E. Rudge's Sons
Binder: Russell-Rutter Co.
Type: Inter. Futura Med. 12/16 31 $\times$ 56$\frac{1}{2}$
Stock: Cantine No. 2 Coated
Cloth: Holüstan Roxite Buckram, black
Stamping: yellow and green ink
Designers: format E. Mock; cover E. McKnight Kauffer

Worthy of its contents, the format of this collection of pictures and text is no less modern than the 20th-century buildings it depicts. It was inevitably a Book Clinic Selection, from its brilliant binding stamped in parrot greens and yellows to the 4-colour and black-and-white bleed plates, sanserif types, and dynamic layouts within. The text is bilingual, and there are twin title pages, the Spanish [Portuguese] one being a mirror-like reflection of the English. The latter is at the left, and the colour frontispiece which separates them is printed to face it. Similarly all other full-page plates and all groups of large halftones are given recto positions. While the text proper is set out 2 columns [sic]. The 10pt. legends are set 27 picas wide, grouped together regardless of the cuts, which are arranged for appearance values. The result is a splendidly unified text that may well set a style.

*Book Binding and Book Production* (June 1943).
The Museum of Modern Art Archives, NY: Public Information Scrapbook, 60.

# Buildings

## Early buildings

### Rio de Janeiro

p.26    Rio de Janeiro: View from the Copacabana Palace Hotel
p.28    José Maria Jacinto Rebelo: Itamarati Palace, Rio de Janeiro (1851–4)
p.30    Julio Frederico Koeller and Philippe Garçon Rivière: Gloria Church (1842)
        House, Rio de Janeiro (early nineteenth century)
        Ribeiro House, Largo do Boticario, Rio de Janeiro (eighteenth century)
p.32    São Bento, Rio de Janeiro (1652)
        Church of Santo Antonio, Rio de Janeiro
p.34    Fazenda Colubandé, São Gonçalo, near Niteroi RJ (early nineteenth century)
p.36    Fazenda Vassouras, RJ (mid nineteenth century)
p.38    Fazenda Garcia, Petrópolis RJ (gardens by Roberto Burle Marx)

### Rio Grande do Sul

p.40    João Batista Primoli: Church of São Miguel (c.1760)
p.42    Lucio Costa: Museum of the Church of São Miguel (1937–8)

### Minas Gerais

p.44    Congonhas do Campo
p.46    Church, Nosso Senhor do Bom Jesus de Matosinhos, Congonhas do Campo
p.48    Ouro Preto
p.50    Antonio Francisco Lisboa (O Aleijadinho): Nossa Senhora do Carmo, Ouro Preto (1766)
        Chapel of São José, Mariana
p.52    Chapel of São José, Ouro Preto
        São Francisco de Assis, Ouro Preto (1772–94)
p.54    João Domingos Veiga: Chafariz dos Contos, Ouro Preto (1745)
        José Pereira Arouca: Rosario dos Pretos, Ouro Preto (1785)
p.56    Santa Ifigenia, Ouro Preto (1785)

### Espírito Santo

p.56    Penha Convent

### Bahia

p.58    Fort Santa Maria, Salvador (1696)
p.59    Port Montserrat, Salvador (1586)
p.60    Salvador

p.62    Church and Monastery of São Francisco de Assis, Salvador (1710)
        Church of the Third Order of São Francisco de Assis, Salvador
        (1703)
p.64    Church of São Francisco de Assis, Salvador (1710)
p.65    Parish Church of Pilar, Salvador (late eighteenth century)
p.66    Church and Convent, Paraguassú (eighteenth century)


**Paraíba**

p.66    Colonial Church, Guia


**Pernambuco**

p.68    Recife
p.70    Manuel Jaquera Jacomé and Nazzoni: Church of São Pedro dos
        Clérigos, Recife (1729)
        Jaqueira Chapel, Recife (c.1794)
        Church, São Francisco, Olinda (eighteenth century)
p.72    Moraes House, Recife (c.1850)
p.73    Sugar Mill (nineteenth century)
p.74    Church of São Bento, Olinda (third quarter, eighteenth century)
        Mud-walled, palm-thatched fishermen's huts on the Pernambu-
        can coast
        House, Olinda (late seventeenth century)
        Church of São Francisco de Assis, Olinda


**Pará**

p.76    Church of Santo Alexandre Belém (early eighteenth century)
p.78    College of Nazareth, Belém (1789)
        Teatro da Paz

**Modern buildings**

**Reinforced concrete construction**

p.104   National Portland Cement Company, Niterói RJ (1936)
        Saturnini Nunes de Brito: Ministry of Finance, Recife (1942)

**Office buildings, apartments, hotels**

p.106   Lucio Costa: Ministry of Education and Health (1936–45)
p.112   Marcelo and Milton Roberto: Brazilian Press Association (1936–8)
p.116   Apartments, Avenida Augusto Severo, Rio de Janeiro
        Marcelo and Milton Roberto: Institute of Industrial Insurance, Rio
        de Janeiro (1941)
p.118   Gregori Warchavchik: Apartments, Alameda Barão de Limeira,
        São Paulo (1940)
        Henrique Mindlin: Apartments, Paulo (1940)
        Álvaro Vital Brazil: Edifício Esther, São Paulo (1937)

p.122   Apartments, Praia do Flamengo, Rio de Janeiro (1938)
p.124   Apartments, Rua Bolivar, Rio de Janeiro (1940)
p.126   Carlos Frederico Ferreira: Worker's Housing, Realengo RJ (1942)
p.130   Oscar Niemeyer: Hotel, Ouro Preto (1940–2)

## Schools, hospitals, libraries

p.134   Pavalo Camrgo Almeida: Old Peoples' Home, Rio de Janeiro
        Jaques Pilon: Library, São Paulo (1942)
        Santa Terezina Tuberculosis Sanatorium, Salvador (1942)
p.136   Oscar Niemeyer: Obra do Berço Nursery, Rio de Janeiro (1937)
p.140   Álvaro Vital Brazil: Raul Vidal Elementary School, Niterói (1942)
p.142   Carlos Henrique Oliveira Porto: Industrial School, Rio de Janeiro
p.144   Alexander Budddeus: Normal School, Salvador
p.146   Rino Levi: 'Sedes Sapientiæ', São Paulo (1942)
p.148   Marcelo and Milton Roberto: Industrial School, São Paulo (1942)

## Transportation buildings

p.150   Atilio Corrêa Lima: Seaplane Terminal, Santos Dumont Airport,
        Rio de Janeiro (1937–8)
p.154   Marcelo and Milton Roberto: Hangar No. 1, Santos Dumont
        Airport, Rio de Janeiro (1940)
p.156   Atilio Corrêa Lima: Boat Passenger Terminal, Rio de Janeiro
        (1940)

## Miscellaneous

p.158   Luis Nunes: Water Tower, Olinda (1936–7)
p.159   Luis Nunes: Anatomical Laboratory, Recife (1936–7)
p.160   Álvaro Vital Brazil: Instituto Vital Brazil, Niterói, Rio de Janeiro
        (1942)

## Houses

p.162   Oscar Niemeyer: Cavalcanti House, Rio de Janeiro (1940)
p.166   Oscar Niemeyer: Niemeyer House, Rio de Janeiro (1942)
p.168   Oscar Niemeyer: Johnson House, Fortaleza (1942)
p.170   Bernard Rudofsky: João Arnstein House, São Paulo (1941)
p.174   Bernard Rudofsky: Frontini House, São Paulo (1940–1)
p.176   Aldary Henrique Toledo: Sotto Maior House, Secretario RJ (1942)
p.178   Henrique Mindlin: House, São Paulo
        Gregori Warchavchik: House, Rua Bahia, São Paulo (1931)
        José Norberto: Moura House, São Paulo (1940)

## Highways

p.180   Highway Engineering, Belo Horizonte

## Recreation

p.182   Oscar Niemeyer: Casino, Pampulha, Belo Horizonte (1940–2)

p.188   Oscar Niemeyer: Island Restaurant, Pampulha, Belo Horizonte (1940–2)

p.190   Oscar Niemeyer: Yacht Club, Pampulha, Belo Horizonte (1940–2)

p.194   Lucio Costa and Oscar Niemeyer: Brazilian Pavilion, New York World's Fair (1939)

# Appendix: 'Brazil Builds' Panels

## Large Version

Transcribed from 'Brazil Builds' Exhibition Installation List. The Museum of Modern Art, New York

### Older architecture

**Minas Gerais**

| | |
|---|---|
| A–1 | Ouro Preto |
| A–2 | Church, Nossa Senhora do Carmo, Ouro Preto. Corner view |
| A–3 | Church, Nossa Senhora do Carmo, Ouro Preto. Front view |
| A–4 | Congonhas do Campo |
| A–5 | Cathedral, Braga, Portugal |
| A–6 Panel | Church, Nosso Senhor do Bom Jesus de Matosinhos, Congonhas do Campo. Detail |
| A–7 | Church, Nosso Senhor do Bom Jesus de Matosinhos, Congonhas do Campo |
| A–8 | Congonhas do Campo |
| A–9 | Church, Nosso Senhor do Bom Jesus de Matosinhos, Congonhas do Campo |
| A–10 Panel | Church, São Francisco de Assis, Ouro Preto |
| A–11 | Church, São Francisco de Assis, Ouro Preto |
| A–12 | Old Fazenda near Belo Horizonte |
| A–13 | Town Hall of Mariana |
| A–14 | Chafariz dos Contos, Ouro Preto |
| A–15 | Old House at Ouro Preto |
| A–16 | Chapel of São José, Ouro Preto. From Below |
| A–17 | Chapel of São José, Ouro Preto |
| A–18 | Church, Santa Ifigenia, Ouro Preto |

## Bahia

A–19        Salvador
A–20        Fishing Boat, Salvador
A–21        Warehouse, Salvador
A–22        Parish Church of Pilar, Salvador
A–23        Church, São Francisco de Assis, Salvador
A–24 Panel  Church, São Francisco de Assis, Salvador. Plans and details
A–25        Monastery, São Francisco de Assis, Salvador
A–26        Port Montserrat, Salvador
A–27        Fort Santa Maria, Salvador

## Rio de Janeiro

A–28        Ribeiro House, Largo do Boticario, Rio de Janeiro
A–29a Panel Ribeiro House, Largo do Boticario, Rio de Janeiro
A–29b Panel Fazenda Garcia near Petrópolis. Garden plans and photos
A–30a       Fazenda Colubandé, São Gonçalo, near Niterói
A–30b Panel Fazenda Colubandé, São Gonçalo, near Niterói
A–31        Church and Monastery, São Bento, Rio de Janeiro. Refectory
A–32        Church and Monastery, São Bento, Rio de Janeiro. Interior
A–33        Church and Monastery, São Bento, Rio de Janeiro. Sacristy
A–34        Itamarati Palace, Rio de Janeiro
A–35        Gloria Church, Rio de Janeiro
A–36        Rio de Janeiro. View of harbour

## Pernambuco

A–37 Panel  Recife. Sugar Mill, Teatro Santa Isabel, Street
A–38        Recife
A–39 Panel  Church, São Pedro dos Clérigos, Recife. Details
A–40        Recife
A–41        Church, São Francisco, Olinda
A–42        Mud-walled, palm-thatched fishermen's huts on the Pernambucan coast
A–43        Church, São Bento, Olinda
A–44        Church, São Francisco, Olinda
A–45        Old Street, Recife
A–46        Early House, Olinda

## Pará

A–47        Church, Nossa Senhora do Carmo, Belém
A–48        Church, Santo Alexandre Belém
A–49        Church, Nossa Senhora do Carmo, Belém
A–50        Church, Santo Alexandre Belém
A–51        Palácio Azul, Belém
A–52        College of Nazareth, Belém
A–53        College of Nazareth, Belém

The 'Brazil Builds' Exhibition. The Museum of Modern Art, New York, 13 January–28 February 1943.
Installation Panels Redrawn from The Museum of Modern Art Archives, NY: Records of the Department of Circulating Exhibitions, album 'Brazil Builds'.
Drawing by Zilah Quezado Deckker.

**Modern architecture**

### Ministry of Education and Health and the Brazilian Press Association

| | |
|---|---|
| B–1a Panel | Ministry of Education and Health, Rio de Janeiro. Label and plans |
| B–1b Panel | Ministry of Education and Health |
| B–2 | Ministry of Education and Health |
| B–3 | Ministry of Education and Health |
| B–4 Panel | Ministry of Education and Health. Detail of mural |
| B–5 | Ministry of Education and Health. Water tower |
| B–6 | Ministry of Education and Health. Entrance |
| B–7 | Ministry of Education and Health. Auditorium |
| B–8 | Ministry of Education and Health. South façade |
| B–9 | Ministry of Education and Health. Sketch |
| B–10 | Ministry of Education and Health. Mural |
| B–11 Model | Ministry of Education and Health |
| B–12 | Brazilian Press Association, Rio de Janeiro |
| B–13 | Brazilian Press Association |
| B–14 Panel | Brazilian Press Association. Plans and detail |
| B–15 | Brazilian Press Association. Roof |

### Transportation buildings

| | |
|---|---|
| B–16 Panel | Seaplane Station, Santos Dumont Airport, Rio de Janeiro. Plans and detail |
| B–17 | Seaplane Station. Garden view |
| B–18 | Seaplane Station. Staircase |
| B–19 | Seaplane Station. Entrance |
| B–20 | Seaplane Station. Waterfront |
| B–21 | Seaplane Station |
| B–22 Panel | Hangar No. 1, Santos Dumont Airport, Rio de Janeiro. Plans and details |
| B–23 | Hangar No. 1. Façade |
| B–24 | Hangar No. 1. Roof trusses |
| B–25 Panel | Boat Pasenger Station, Rio de Janeiro |
| B–26 | Boat Pasenger Station |
| B–27 | Boat Pasenger Station. Garden |

### Schools

| | |
|---|---|
| B–28 | Normal School, Salvador. Swimming pool |
| B–29 | Normal School. Façade |
| B–30 | Normal School. Kindergarten |
| B–31 Panel | Normal School. Details |
| B–32 | Raul Vidal Elementary School, Niterói. Plans |
| B–33 | Raul Vidal Elementary School |
| B–34 | Raul Vidal Elementary School. Side view |
| B–35 | Raul Vidal Elementary School. Colonnade |
| B–36 | Industrial School, Rio de Janeiro |
| B–37 | Industrial School, Rio de Janeiro |
| B–38 Panel | Industrial School, São Paulo |
| B–39 Panel | 'Sedes Sapientiæ', São Paulo |
| B–40 | 'Sedes Sapientiæ' |

### Brise-soleils

| | |
|---|---|
| B–41 | Brazilian Press Association. *Brise-soleils* |
| B–42 | Brazilian Press Association. *Brise-soleils* |
| B–43 | Wooden *brise-soleils* |
| B–44 | Old Peoples' Home, Rio de Janeiro |
| B–45 Panel | Old Peoples' Home. *Brise-soleils* |
| B–46 | Old Peoples' Home. Street façade |
| B–47 | Instituto Vital Brazil, Niterói. Fixed glass louvres |
| B–48 | Old Peoples' Home. *Brise-soleils* |

### Concrete

| | |
|---|---|
| B–49a | National Portland Cement Company, Niterói |
| B–49b | National Portland Cement Company |
| B–50 | National Portland Cement Company |
| B–51 | Casas Pernambcanas, São Paulo |
| B–52 Panel | Building materials. Labels and photos |
| B–53 | Instituto Vital Brazil |
| B–54 | Instituto Vital Brazil |
| B–55 | Instituto Vital Brazil. Plans and details |
| B–56 | Instituto Vital Brazil. Façade |
| B–57 | Anatomical Laboratory, Recife. Cambogé |
| B–58 | Water Tower at Olinda |
| B–59 | Water Tower at Olinda |

### Hospital

| | |
|---|---|
| B–60 | Santa Terezina Tuberculosis Sanatorium, Salvador |

### Hotel

| | |
|---|---|
| B–61 | Hotel, Ouro Preto |
| B–62 Panel | Hotel, Ouro Preto |
| B–63 | Hotel, Ouro Preto |

### Apartments

| | |
|---|---|
| B–64 Panel | Edifício Esther, São Paulo. Plans and details |
| B–65 | Edifício Esther |
| B–66 | Apartments, Rio de Janeiro |
| B–67 | Apartments, Praia do Flamengo, Rio de Janeiro |
| B–68 | Apartments, Rua Bolivar, Rio de Janeiro |
| B–69 | Apartments, Rio de Janeiro |
| B–70 | Apartments, Avenida Augusto Severo, Rio de Janeiro |
| B–71 | Workers' Housing, Realengo RJ |
| B–72 | Apartments, Alameda Barão de Limeira, São Paulo |

### Houses

| | |
|---|---|
| B–73 Panel | Niemeyer House, Rio de Janeiro. Plans and details |
| B–74 Panel | Cavalcanti House, Rio de Janeiro. Plans and details |
| B–75 | Cavalcanti House. Entrance |
| B–76 | Cavalcanti House. Walled side |
| B–77 | Cavalcanti House. Terrace |

| B–78 | Frontini House, São Paulo |
| B–79a | Frontini House. Inner court |
| B–79b | Frontini House. Exterior |
| B–80 | Frontini House. Plans and views |
| B–81 | Frontini House. Plans and views |
| B–82 | Sotto Maior House, Rio de Janeiro. Elevation |
| B–83 | Sotto Maior. Elevation |
| B–84 Panel | Johnson House, Fortaleza. Plan |
| B–85 Panel | Vital Brazil House, Rio de Janeiro. Plans and photos |
| B–86 | Vital Brazil House. Interior |
| B–87 | João Arnstein House |
| B–88 | João Arnstein House, São Paulo. Label |
| B–89 | Arnstein House. Details |
| B–90 | Arnstein House. Views |
| B–91 | Arnstein House. Terrace |
| B–92 | Arnstein House. Terrace |
| B–93 | Arnstein House. Arbour |

## Recreation

| B–94 | Brazilian Pavilion, New York World's Fair. Entrance |
| B–95 | Brazilian Pavilion. Terrace |
| B–96 Model | Brazilian Pavilion |
| B–97 | Brazilian Pavilion |
| B–98 | Casino, Pampulha, Belo Horizonte. Staircase |
| B–99 | Casino. View from entrance |
| B–100 | Casino. View from water |
| B–101 | Casino. Entrance |
| B–102 Panel | Casino. Plans and interiors |
| B–103 Panel | Casino. Entrance |
| B–104 Panel | Island Restaurant, Pampulha. Plans and views |
| B–105 Panel | Yacht Club. Plans and views |
| B–106 Panel | Yacht Club. Photos and elevation |
| B–107 | Yacht Club. Entrance ramp |

## Day nursery

| B–108 | Day Nursery, Rio de Janeiro |
| B–109 Panel | Day Nursery. Plans |
| B–110 Panel | Day Nursery. Photos |
| B–111 | Day Nursery. Exterior |
| B–112 | Day Nursery. Louvres |

## Civil engineering

| B–113 | Highway, Belo Horizonte |

## Louvre models

| M–1 | Ministry of Education and Health |
| M–2 | Brazilian Press Association |
| M–3 | Yacht Club |

The Museum of Modern Art Archives, NY: Records of the Department of Circulating Exhibitions, II.1/41 (5).
(see Figures 9.3–9.10)

# Small Version

Panel 1      Brazil Builds (title and credits)
Panel 2      The Country
Panel 3      The Architecture
Panel 4      Salvador, Bahia
Photo 5      Third Order of São Francisco, Salvador, 1703
Photo 6      São Francisco de Assis, Salvador, 1710
Photo 7      São Francisco de Assis. Interior
Photo 8      São Francisco de Assis. Monastery cloister
Photo 9      Parish Church of Pilar, Salvador
Photo 10     Forte de Santa Maria, Salvador
Panel 11     Ouro Preto
Photo 12     Nossa Senhora do Carmo, Ouro Preto
Photo 13     Nossa Senhora do Rosário dos Pretos, Ouro Preto
Photo 14     São Francisco de Assis, Ouro Preto
Panel 15     Antonio Francisco Lisboa
Photo 16     Nosso Senhor do Bom Jesus de Matosinhos, Congonhas do
             Campo
Panel 17     Rio de Janeiro
Photo 18     São Bento, Rio de Janeiro
Photo 19     São Bento, Rio de Janeiro
Photo 20     São Bento, Rio de Janeiro
Photo 21     Itamarati Palace, Rio de Janeiro
Photo 22     House in Rio de Janeiro, early nineteenth century
Panel 23     Houses and Fazendas
Photo 24     Fazenda Colubandé, São Gonçalo
Photo 25     Fazenda Garcia near Petrópolis
Panel 26     Eclecticism
Panel 27     Brazil Builds Today
Panel 28     It is less than 15 years...
Panel 29     Brazilian architects found
Panel 30     But the new architecture is Brazilian
Panel 31     Sun control
Panel 32     Reinforced concrete, etc.
Photo 33     Ministry of Education and Health, Rio de Janeiro. Seen from
             the north-west
Photo 34     Ministry of Education and Health, Rio de Janeiro. Seen from
             the north-east
Photo 35     Ministry of Education and Health, Rio de Janeiro. Seen from
             the south-west
Panel 36     Government building
Photo 37     Brazilian Press Association, Rio de Janeiro
Photo 38     Brazilian Press Association, Rio de Janeiro. Louvres
Panel 39     Office building
Photo 40     Seaplane Station, Santos Dumont Airport, Rio de Janeiro.
             Entrance
Photo 41     Seaplane Station. Side façade from bay
Photo 42     Seaplane Station. Canopy

Photo 43    Seaplane Station. Pier
Panel 44    Santos Dumont Airport, Rio de Janeiro
Photo 45    Álvaro Vital Brazil House, Rio de Janeiro
Photo 46    Álvaro Vital Brazil House. Interior
Photo 47    Álvaro Vital Brazil House. Living room
Panel 48    Álvaro Vital Brazil House and Cavalcanti House
Photo 49    Cavalcanti House, Rio de Janeiro
Photo 50    Cavalcanti House
Photo 51    Cavalcanti House
Photo 52    Frontini House, São Paulo. Living room façade
Photo 53    Frontini House. Interior court
Photo 54    Frontini House. Children's pool
Photo 55    Frontini House. Exterior
Panel 56    Frontini House and Arnstein House
Photo 57    João Arnstein House, São Paulo. Living room from court
Photo 58    Arnstein House. Living terrace
Photo 59    Arnstein House. Courtyard
Photo 60    Arnstein House
Photo 61    Apartments, Praia do Flamengo, Rio de Janeiro
Photo 62    Apartments, Rio de Janeiro
Panel 63    Apartments
Photo 64    Workers' Housing, Realengo RJ
Panel 65    Housing
Photo 66    Day Nursery, Rio de Janeiro
Photo 67    Day Nursery
Panel 68    Day Nursery and School
Photo 69    Raul Vidal Elementary School, Niterói
Photo 70    Raul Vidal Elementary School. Exterior
Photo 71    Raul Vidal Elementary School. Loggia
Photo 72    Normal School, Salvador
Photo 73    Normal School
Photo 74    Normal School
Panel 75    Normal School
Photo 76    Island Restaurant, Pampulha, Belo Horizonte
Panel 77    Island Restaurant and Yacht Club
Photo 78    Yacht Club, Pampulha, Belo Horizonte
Photo 79    Yacht Club
Photo 80    Casino, Pampulha, Belo Horizonte
Photo 81    Casino
Photo 82    Casino
Photo 83    Casino
Photo 84    Casino
Panel 85    Casino

The Museum of Modern Art Archives, NY: Records of the Department of Circulating Exhibitions, II.1/41(5).

# Appendix: 'Brazil Builds' Itineraries

## Large Version

| | | |
|---|---|---|
| 1943 | Mar 13–Apr 4 | Boston Museum of Fine Arts, Boston, Massachusetts |
| | Apr 14–May 5 | Vassar College, Poughkeepsie, New York |
| | May 15–Jun 5 | Carnegie Institute, Pittsburgh, Pennsylvania |
| | Jul 15–Aug 15 | Palacio de Bellas Artes, Mexico City, Mexico |
| | Sep 23–Oct 14 | Philadelphia Museum of Art, Philadelphia, Pennsylvania |
| | Oct 24–Nov 14 | Rochester Memorial Art Gallery, Rochester, New York |
| | Nov 26–Dec 20 | Addison Gallery of American Art*, Andover, Massachusetts |
| 1944 | Jan 3–24 | City Art Museum of St. Louis, St. Louis, Missouri |
| | Feb 6–27 | Toledo Museum of Art, Toledo, Ohio |
| | Mar 20–Apr 10 | The T. Eaton Co. Ltd, Toronto, Canada |
| | May 1–22 | University Gallery, University of Minnesota, Minneapolis, Minnesota |
| | May 30–Jun 22 | William Rockhill Nelson Gallery of Art, Kansas City, Missouri |
| | Jul 14–Aug 4 | Taylor Museum, Colorado Springs, Colorado |
| | Sep 22–Oct 15 | California Palace of the Legion of Honor, San Francisco, California |
| 1945 | Jan 10–Feb 4 | Seattle Art Museum, Seattle, Washington |
| | Mar 19–Apr 9 | Cleveland Museum of Art, Cleveland, Ohio |
| 1948 | Jun 9 | Sold to School of Architecture, University of Manitoba, Winnipeg, Canada for $200 |

$75.00 for 3 weeks – $25.00 for models
Packed in 12 boxes weighing 2900 lbs.
(* indicates that the gallery also rented the slide show)

The Museum of Modern Art Archives, NY: Records of the Department of Circulating Exhibitions, II.1/41(5).

# Small Version

| 1944 | Feb 8–28 | Yale University School of Fine Arts, New Haven, Connecticut |
| | Mar 6–27 | College of Art and Design, Ann Arbor, Michigan |
| | Apr 5–26 | Wellesley College, Wellesley, Massachusetts |
| | May 1–26 | Harvard University, Cambridge, Massachusetts |
| | Jul 19–Aug 9 | Dartmouth College, Hanover, New Hampshire |
| | Sep 27–Oct 18 | College of William and Mary, Williamsburg, Virginia |
| | Nov 1–22 | University of North Carolina*, Chapel Hill, North Carolina |
| | Dec 5–21 | Skidmore College, Saratoga Springs, New York |
| 1945 | Jan 18–29 | Philbrook Art Center, Tulsa, Oklahoma |
| | Mar 9–Apr 4 | University of Florida, Gainesville, Florida |
| | Sep 15–Oct 3 | Virginia Museum of Fine Arts*, Richmond, Virginia |
| | Oct 15–Nov 3 | University of New Hampshire, Durham, New Hampshire |
| | Nov 18–Dec 9 | Columbus Gallery of Fine Arts, Columbus, Ohio |
| | Dec 22–Jan 13 | Albright Art Gallery (Albright-Knox), Buffalo, New York |
| 1946 | Mar 1–22 | Worcester Art Museum, Worcester, Massachusetts |
| | Apr 5–26 | Michael Brothers Inc., Athens, Georgia |
| | May 10–31 | Cornell University, Willard Straight Hall, Ithaca, New York |
| 1948 | Jan 12 | Sold to A.A.U.W. Washington Branch for $200 |

$40.00 for 3 weeks
Packed in 2 boxes weighing 360 lbs.
(* indicates that the gallery also rented the slide show)

The Museum of Modern Art Archives, NY: Records of the Department of Circulating Exhibitions, II.1/41(5).

# Slide Show

| 1943 | Nov 26–Dec 20 | Addison Gallery of American Art, Andover, Massachusetts* |
|------|---------------|----------------------------------------------------------|
| 1944 | January | Kappa Kappa Gamma, State College, Pennsylvania |
| | Mar 1–8 | National Gallery of Art, Inter-American Section, Washington, D.C. |
| | Oct 1–8 | University of Manitoba, Winnipeg, Canada |
| | Nov 1–8 | Person Hall Gallery, University of North Carolina, Chapel Hill, North Carolina |
| | Mar 19–26 | State Teachers College, Paterson, New Jersey |
| | Jun 1–8 | Dupont Co., New York |
| | Jul 11–18 | San Francisco Museum of Art, San Francisco, California* |
| | Aug 27–Sep 3 | J.P. Riddle Co., Coral Gables. Florida |
| | Sep 13–20 | Virginia Museum of Fine Arts, Richmond, Virginia |
| 1946 | Dec 3–10 | A & M College of Texas, College Station, Texas |
| 1947 | Nov 30–Dec 7 | Rensselaer Polytechnic Institute, Troy, New York |
| 1952 | Feb 4–18 | University of Manitoba, Winnipeg, Canada |

$10.00 for 1 week

The Museum of Modern Art Archives, NY: Records of the Department of Circulating Exhibitions, II.1/41(5).

## Brazil Version

| | | |
|---|---|---|
| 1943 | Nov 23–Dec 30 | Ministry of Education and Health, Rio de Janeiro |
| 1944 | Feb 18–29 | Edifício Mariana, Attendance: 3,006, Belo Horizonte |
| | Mar 16–Apr 10 | Galeria Prestes Maia, Attendance: 66,388, São Paulo |
| | Apr 29–May 7 | Associação de Engeheiros de Santos, Santos, SP |
| 1945 | Feb 21– | Teatro Municipal, Campinas, SP, Curitiba, PR Florianópolis, SC Porto Alegre, RS |
| | Oct 24– | Jundiaí, SP |
| 1946 | Jul 14–24 | Franca, SP |

Packed in 6 boxes weighing 1375 lbs.

The Museum of Modern Art Archives, NY: Records of the Department of Circulating Exhibitions, II.1/41(5).

# Bibliography

## General Works

Agache, Alfred: *Cidade do Rio de Janeiro: Remodelação, Extensão e Embelezzamento 1926–1936* (Paris: Prefeitura do Rio de Janeiro 1930; French edn *La Remodelation d'une Capitale* Paris 1932)

*Album do Pavilhão do Brasil Feira Mundial de Nova York* (1939)

Amaral, Aracy: *Artes Plásticas na Semana de 22* Coleção Debates 22 (São Paulo: Perspectiva 1970)

Amaral, Aracy: *Blaise Cendrars no Brasil e os Modernistas* (São Paulo: Martins 1970)

*Andrade, Mario de: Cartas de Trabalho* (Brasília: SPHAN Pró-Memória 1981)

Applebaum, Stanley: *The New York World's Fair 1939/1940: in 155 photographs by Richard Wurts and Others* (New York: Dover 1977)

*Arquitetura na Bienal de São Paulo* (São Paulo: Edições Americanas de Arte e Arquitetura 1952)

Artigas, Vilanova: *Caminhos da Arquitetura* (São Paulo: Fundação Vilanova Artigas/Pini 1986)

Banham, Reyner: *Guide to Modern Architecture* (London: Architectural Press 1962)

Banham, Reyner: *The New Brutalism, Ethic or Aesthetic?* (London: Architectural Press 1966)

Banham, Reyner: 'Neo Liberty' *Architectural Review* (April 1959) pp.231–5

Bardi, Pietro Maria: *Lembrança de Le Corbusier: Atenas, Itália, Brasil* (São Paulo: Nobel 1984)

Bardi, Pietro Maria: *The Tropical Gardens of Roberto Burle Marx* (Rio de Janeiro and Amsterdam: Colibris 1964)

Brazil, Álvaro Vital: *Álvaro Vital Brazil: 50 Anos de Arquitetura* (São Paulo: Nobel 1986)

Capanema, Gustavo: 'Testemunho sobre o Edifício do Ministério da Educação e Cultura: 12 December 1965' *Módulo* (May 1985) pp.28–32

Castedo, Leopoldo: *The Baroque Prevalence in Brazilian Art* (New York: Charles Frank 1964)

Cendrars, Blaise: *Brésil des hommes sont venus* (Monaco: Documents d'Art 1952)

Cendrars, Blaise: 'Feuilles de route' *Du monde entier au coeur du monde* (Paris: Denoël 1957)

Cohen, Jean-Louis: 'Le Corbusier and the Mystique of the USSR' *Oppositions* 23 (1981) pp.85–121

Costa, Lucio: *Lucio Costa: registro de uma vivência* (São Paulo: Empresa das Artes 1995)

Curtis, William: *Modern Architecture Since 1900* (Oxford: Phaidon 1982; 2nd edn 1987)

'The Decade 1929–1939: Modern Architecture Symposium 1964' *Journal of the Society of Architectural Historians* (March 1965)

Dorfles, Gillo: *Barocco nell'architettura moderna* (Milan: Editrice Politecnica Tamburini 1951)

Evenson, Norma: *Two Brazilian Capitals* (New Haven: Yale University Press 1973)

Ferraz, Geraldo: *Warchavchik e a Introdução da Nova Arquitetura no Brasil: 1925–1940* Preface by P.M. Bardi (São Paulo: Museu de Arte de São Paulo 1965)

Frampton, Kenneth: *Modern Architecture: a critical history* (London: Thames and Hudson 1980; 2nd edn 1985)

Franck, Klaus: *The Works of Affonso Eduardo Reidy* (Stuttgart: Gerd Hatje; New York: Praeger 1960) Introduction by Siegfried Giedion

Gellman, Irwin F.: *Good Neighbor Diplomacy: United States Policies in Latin America 1933–1945* (Baltimore: John Hopkins University Press 1979)

Giedion, Siegfried (ed.): *A Decade of New Architecture* (Zurich: Girsberger 1951)

Giedion, Siegfried (ed.): *Space Time and Architecture: the growth of a new tradition* (Cambridge MA: Harvard University Press 1941; 5th edn 1967)

Goodwin, Philip L.: *Brazil Builds: architecture new and old 1652–1942* (New York: Museum of Modern Art January 1943; 2nd edn September 1943; 3rd edn November 1944; 4th edn May 1946)

Goodyear, A. Conger: *The Museum of Modern Art: The First Ten Years* (New York: Museum of Modern Art 1943)

Green, David: *The Containment of Latin America: A History of the Myths and Realities of the Good Neighbor Policy* (Chicago: Quadrangle 1971)

Hitchcock, Henry-Russell: *Architecture: Nineteenth and Twentieth Centuries* (Harmondsworth: Penguin Books 1958; repr. 1971)

Hitchcock, Henry-Russell and Philip Johnson: *International Style: Architecture since 1922* (New York: W.W. Norton 1932; repr. 1966)

Hitchcock, Henry-Russell: *Latin American Architecture since 1945* (New York: Museum of Modern Art 1955)

Hobsbawm, Eric: *The Age of Extremes: The Short Twentieth Century* (London: Abacus 1995; 1st publ. 1994) p.135

Homem, Maria Cecília Naclério: *O prédio Martinelli: a ascensão do imigrante e a verticalicão de São Paulo* (São Paulo: Projeto 1984)

*Inter-American Affairs* 5 vols (New York: Columbia University Press 1941–5)

Kutz, Myer: *Rockefeller Power* (New York: Simon and Schuster 1974)

Kidder-Smith, G.E.: *Italy Builds* Introduction by Ernesto Rogers (London: Architectural Press; New York: Reinhold; Milan: Comunità 1955)

Kidder-Smith, G.E.: *Sweden Builds* (New York and Stockholm: Albert Bonnier 1950; 2nd edn New York: Reinhold; London: Architectural Press 1957)

Kidder-Smith, G.E.: *Switzerland Builds* Introduction by Siegfried Giedion (London: Architectural Press, New York and Stockholm: Albert Bonnier 1950)

Kirstein, Lincoln: *The Latin American Collection of the Museum of Modern Art* (New York: Museum of Modern Art 1943)

Kubitschek, Juscelino: 'De Pampulha a Brasília: Os Caminhos da Providência' *Módulo* (December 1975) pp.14–18

*Le Corbusier: Architect of the Century* (London: Arts Council 1987)

*Le Corbusier Archive* 13 and 28 (New York: Garland; Paris: Fondation Le Corbusier 1983)

Le Corbusier: *Précisions sur un état présent de l'architecture et de l'urbanisme* (Paris: Editions Crè 1930; repr. Paris: Vincent Fréal 1960)

Le Corbusier: *La Ville Radieuse* (Boulogne-sur-Seine: Editions de L'Architecture d'Aujourd'hui 1935; repr. Paris: Vincent Fréal 1964; English edn *The Radiant City* London: Faber & Faber 1957)

*Le Corbusier Sketchbooks* 4 vols (London: Thames and Hudson; Paris: Fondation Le Corbusier 1981)

Le Corbusier: *Urbanisme* (Paris: Editions Crè 1925; repr. Paris: Vincent Fréal 1960; *The City of Tomorrow* London: Rodker 1929)

Le Corbusier: *Vers une Architecture* (Paris: Vincent Fréal 1923; *Towards a New Architecture* London: Rodker 1927)

Le Corbusier and P. Jeanneret: *Œuvre Complète* 8 vols (Zurich: Editions d'Architecture Artemis 1984)

Levi, Rino: *Rino Levi* (Milan: Edizione de Comunità 1974)

Lévi-Strauss, Claude: *Tristes Tropiques* (Paris: Plon 1955; London: Picador 1989)

Levine, Robert M.: *The Vargas Regime: The Critical Years 1934–1938* (New York: Columbia University Press 1970)

Lipchitz, Jacques: *My Life in Sculpture* (New York: Viking 1972)

Lynes, Russell: *Good Old Modern: An Intimate Portrait of The Museum of Modern Art* (New York: Atheneum 1973)

McCann, Frank: *The Brazilian–American Alliance 1937–1945* (Princeton: Princeton University Press 1973)

McMurry, Ruth and Muna Lee: *The Cultural Approach Another way in International Relations* (Chapel Hill: 1947)

Mindlin, Henrique: *Brazilian Architecture* Lethaby Lectures, Royal College of Art, London 1961 (Rome: Brazilian Embassy 1961?)

Mindlin, Henrique: *Modern Architecture in Brazil* (Rio de Janeiro and Amsterdam: Colibris; London: Architectural Press; New York: Reinhold; Paris: Vincent Fréal; Munich: Callwey 1956) Preface by Siegfried Giedion

Mock, Elizabeth (ed.): *Built in the USA: 1932–1944* (New York: Museum of Modern Art 1944) Preface by Philip Goodwin

*The Museum of Modern Art: The History and The Collection* (London: Thames and Hudson 1984)

*New York World's Fair: Official Guide Book* (New York 1939)

Newhouse, Victoria: *Wallace K. Harrison, Architect* (New York: Rizzoli 1989)

Niemeyer, Oscar: *As Curvas do Tempo: Memórias* (Rio de Janeiro: Revan 1998)

Oliveira, Lúcia, Mônica Pimenta Velloso Lippi and Angela Maria Castro Gomes: *Estado Novo: Ideologia e Poder* (Rio de Janeiro: Zahar 1982)

Papadaki, Stamo: *Oscar Niemeyer* Masters of World Architecture Series (New York: Braziller 1960)

Papadaki, Stamo: *Oscar Niemeyer: Works in Progress* (New York: Reinhold 1956)

Papadaki, Stamo: *The Works of Oscar Niemeyer* (New York: Reinhold 1950; repr. 1951) Preface by Lucio Costa

Pevsner, Nikolaus: *An Outline of European Architecture* (Harmondsworth: Penguin Books 1943; repr. 1985)

Richards, J.M.: *An Introduction to Modern Architecture* (Harmondsworth: Penguin Books 1940; repr. 1953)

*Rodrigo e seus Tempos* (Rio de Janeiro: SPHAN Pró-Memória 1986) Preface by Lucio Costa

Rodrigues, José Wasth: *Documentário Arquitetônico* (São Paulo: Martins 1944; 4th edn Belo Horizonte: Itatiaia & Universidade de São Paulo 1979)

Santos, Cecília Rodrigues, Margareth Campos da Silva Pereira, Romão Veriano da Silva Pereira and Vasco da Silva (eds): *Le Corbusier e o Brasil* (São Paulo: Tessela/Projeto 1987)

Sartoris, Alberto: *Gli Elementi dell'Architettura Funzionale* (Milan: Hoepli 1932; 2nd edn 1935)

Schwartzman, Simon, Helena Maria Bousquet-Bomeny and Vanda Maria Ribeiro-Costa: *Tempos de Capanema* (Rio de Janeiro: Paz e Terra; São Paulo: Universidade de São Paulo 1984)

Sitwell, Sacheverell: *Southern Baroque Art Revisited* (London: Weidenfeld and Nicolson 1967)

Skidmore, Thomas E. and Peter H. Smith: *Modern Latin America* (New York: Oxford University Press 1984; 2nd edn 1989)

Spade, Rupert: *Oscar Niemeyer* (London: Thames and Hudson 1971)

Stäubli, Willy: *Brasília* (London: Leonard Hill 1966)

Stone, Edward: *The Evolution of an Architect* (New York: Horizon 1962)

*Ten Years of British Architecture: 1945–55* (London: Arts Council 1956) Introduction by John Summerson

Tsiomis, Yannis (ed.): *Le Corbusier Rio de Janeiro 1929–1936* (Centro de Arquitetura e Urbanismo do Rio de Janeiro: Prefeitura da Cidade do Rio de Janeiro 1998)

Wilder, Elizabeth (ed.): *Studies in Latin American Art* (Washington: American Council of Learned Societies 1949) Proceedings of a Conference held in the Museum of Modern Art New York 28–31 May 1945

Wirth, John D.: *The Politics of Brazilian Development 1930–1945* (Stanford: Stanford University Press 1970)

Wright, Frank Lloyd: *An Autobiography* (New York: Longmans Green; London: Faber & Faber 1932; repr. London: Quartet Books 1977)

Zweig, Stefan: *Brazil: Land of the Future* (London: Cassell 1942)

# Foreign Periodicals 1927–64

Brazilian Architecture from 'The Beauties of Brazil' to Brasília.

### Architect and Builder
Cape Town

'Brazil – the playground of modern architecture' (April 1954) pp.52–9


### Architect and Building News

Howard Robertson: 'Building in Strong Sunlight' (16 April 1943) pp.43–6
A. Byden, Percy Johnson-Marshall and H. Modesto: 'Materials in Brazilian
    Architecture and Their Uses' (29 September 1950) pp.361–8
Percy Johnson-Marshall: 'The Contemporary Architecture of Brazil' (9 July
    1953) pp.34–8


### Architects' Journal

'Lessons from Brazil' (31 January 1946) pp.100–2
Sidney Loweth: 'Some New Architecture in Brazil' (31 January 1946)
    pp.105–13
'Exhibition of Architecture in Brazil: London Building Centre' (9 July 1953)
    pp.44–5
Wladimir de Souza: 'Brazil's Architecture: talk at the London Building
    Centre' (30 July 1953) pp.142–3
Cecil Handisyde: 'Brazil' (14 April 1960) pp.572–83


### Architect's Year Book

Henry-Russell Hitchcock: 'The Place of Painting and Sculpture in Relation to
    Modern Architecture' No. 2 (1947) pp.12–23
Affonso Eduardo Reidy: 'Pedregulho Neighbourhood Unit' No. 6 (1955)
    pp.95–108
Gordon Graham: 'Modern Architecture in Brazil: an appreciation' No. 7
    (1956) pp.72–8


### Architectural Design

Sidney Loweth: 'Brazilian Schools' (September 1945) pp.227–31
Peter Craymer: 'Fourth Centenary Exhibition of São Paulo: Oscar Niemeyer,
    Zenon Helio Uchôa Lotufo and Eduardo Kneese de Mello'; 'Offices in
    Rio de Janeiro: M.M.M. Roberto' (March 1955) pp.86–8; p.89
'Students' Hall of Residence, University City, São Paulo: Rino Levi' (Decem-
    ber 1955) p.387
'Two Hospitals in Brazil, Cancer Hospital and Children Hospital: Rino Levi'
    (January 1956) pp.9–12
'House in Rio de Janeiro: Sergio Bernardes' (July 1956) p.236
'Maison du Brésil, Cité Universitaire, Paris' (July 1959) pp.283–4

### Architectural Forum

'Office Building for Ministry of Education and Health, Rio de Janeiro' (February 1943) pp.37–44

'Brazil Builds' (April 1943) pp.12, 122

'IRB Building, Rio de Janeiro: Marcelo and Milton Roberto' (August 1944) pp.66–76

'Steel for Brazil' (May 1945) pp.16, 20

Donald Newton: 'Letter from Brazil' (February 1946) pp.58, 62

Special Issue: Brazil (November 1947) pp.65–112

'Niemeyer's Church' (March 1950) p.48

'Arched Industrial Building: M.M.M. Roberto' (November 1950) pp.136–7

Walter McQuade: 'Brasília's Beginning' (April 1959) pp.97–103

'Corbu's Brazil in Paris: "Maison du Brésil" ' (November 1959) p.169

Douglas Haskell: 'Brasília: a new type of national city' (November 1960) pp.126–33


### Architectural Record

'ABI: From New Techniques Spring New Forms' (December 1940) pp.74–9

'Cantilever Hangar, Santos Dumont Airport, Rio de Janeiro: Marcelo Roberto' (December 1942) pp.41–4

'Architecture of Brazil' (January 1943) pp.34–56

'Prize winning apartments in Brazil: Gregori Warchavchik' (October 1944) pp.88–9

'Instituto Central do Cancer, São Paulo: Rino Levi and Roberto Cerqueira Cesar' (February 1950) pp.108–11

'Office Building for São Paulo: Rino Levi and Roberto Cerqueira Cesar' (January 1952) pp.154–8

'Instituto Central do Cancer, São Paulo: Rino Levi and Roberto Cerqueira Cesar' (February 1954) pp.202–5

'Roberto Burle Marx: Art and the Landscape' (October 1954) pp.145–51

'Residences: Rino Levi' (April 1955)

Carleton Sprague-Smith: 'Architecture of Brazil' (April 1956) pp.187–94

'South American House on a Mountainside, Rio de Janeiro: Affonso Eduardo Reidy' (June 1956) pp.173–5

'Neighbourhood Public Housing Units in Rio de Janeiro: Affonso Eduardo Reidy' (July 1958) pp.166–70

'Brasília: A New City Rises' (January 1959) pp.14–15


### Architectural Review

Special Issue: The New York World's Fair 1939 (April 1939)

'Shops: Bernard Rudofsky' (May 1940) pp.167–8

John Summerson: 'The Brazilian Contribution' (May 1943) p.135

Special Issue: Brazil. J. Sousa-Leão: 'The Background' pp.58–64; Sachaverell Sitwell: 'The Brazilian Style' pp.65–8; 'Modern Buildings' pp.69–77; G.E. Kidder-Smith: 'The Architects and the Modern Scene' pp.78–84 (March 1944)

'Day Nursery in Rio: Oscar Niemeyer' (April 1944) pp.106–7

'Social Centre, Pampulha: Oscar Niemeyer'; 'Cavalcanti House and Niemeyer House: Oscar Niemeyer' (May 1944) pp.118–24; 130–4

'House at São Paulo: Bernard Rudofsky' (June 1944) pp.157–62

'House at São Paulo: Bernard Rudofsky' (November 1944) pp.135–8

Joaquim Cardoso: 'Rebirth of the Azulejo' (December 1946) pp.178–82

'Rio de Janeiro Airport: Marcelo and Milton Roberto' (March 1947) pp.83–9

Claude Vincent: 'The Modern Garden in Brazil' (May 1947) pp.165–72

Claude Vincent: 'The Background and the Sculpture' (May 1948) pp.203–9

'In Search of a New Monumentality: a symposium by Gregor Paulsson, Henry-Russell Hitchcock, William Holford, Siegfried Giedion, Walter Gropius, Lucio Costa, Alfred Roth' (September 1948) pp.117–28

'Il Juventude' (October 1948) p.197

'Jockey Club Brazileiro' (December 1948) pp.295–8

'Cinema and Hotel in São Paulo: Rino Levi (December 1949) pp.350–3

P.J. Marshall: 'South America Scrapbook: Rio de Janeiro. São Paulo' (February 1950) pp.123–6

'Wall Surfaces in Brazil' (April 1950) pp.221–30

'Flats at Rio de Janeiro: Lucio Costa' (August 1950) pp.88–94

Alf Byden: 'Report on Brazil', 'From the Drawing Boards of Affonso Eduardo Reidy and Oscar Niemeyer' (October 1950) pp.221–32

'New Neighbourhood at Pedregulho: Affonso Eduardo Reidy' (October 1950) pp.249–58

'Three Houses in Brazil' (November 1950) pp.303–6

'Factory at Rio de Janeiro: M.M.M. Roberto' (January 1951) pp.25–8

'Three Buildings by Rino Levi in São Paulo' (December 1951) pp.368–75

'Pedregulho Neighbourhood: gymnasium and primary school: Affonso Eduardo Reidy' (July 1952) pp.16–19

'Companhia Nacional de Seguros: Rino Levi' (August 1952) p.129

'Museum of Art in São Paulo: Lina Bo Bardi' (September 1952) pp.160–3

'Brazilian Preview' (July 1953) pp.10–15

'Three Houses by Sergio Bernardes' (March 1954) pp.162–7

'Museum of Modern Art in Rio de Janeiro: Affonso Eduardo Reidy' (May 1954) pp.336–40

'Report on Brazil: Peter Craymer, Walter Gropius, Hiroshi Ohye, Max Bill, Ernesto Rogers' (October 1954) pp.234–50

'Flats in Rio de Janeiro: Jorge Machado Moreira' (September 1956) pp.168–71

William Holford: 'Brasília, a New Capital City for Brazil' (December 1957) pp.395–402

J.M. Richards: 'Brasília' (February 1959) pp.94–104

'Hospital at São Paulo: Rino Levi' (August 1959) pp.109–12

'House at São Paulo: Rino Levi' (November 1960) pp.338–40

### Architecture d'Aujourd'hui

'Cinéma UFA-Palace a São Paulo: Rino Levi' (September 1938) pp.62–4

'Maison de week-end près de São Paulo: Rino Levi'; 'Immeuble a São Paulo: Rino Levi' (February 1939) pp.26; 53

'Immeuble a Usage de Bureaux a Rio de Janeiro: Angelo Bruhns' (June 1939) p.22

'Immeuble a Rio de Janeiro: A. Vital Brasil et A. Marinho' (August 1939) p.25

Pierre Guegen: 'Chapelle a Pampulha: Oscar Niemeyer, Peintures de Portinari' No. 9 (December 1946) pp.54–6

André Bloch: 'Amérique Latine' No. 10 (March 1947)

'Reception des architectes Brésilien a Paris par L'Architecture d'Aujourd'hui' No. 12 (July 1947)

Spécial: 'Architecture au Brésil' No. 13–14 (September 1947)

'Habitations Collective au Brésil' No. 16 (January 1948) pp.22–39

'Habitations Individuelles au Brésil' No. 18–19 (July 1948) pp.72–82

'Concours du Jockey Clube Brésilien'; 'Immeuble Commercial a São Paulo: Lucjan Korngold' No. 21 (December 1948) pp.64–5; 73–82

'Ecole d'Art Dramatique au Brésil: A. Rocha Miranda et J. de Souza Reis'; 'Theatre a Rio de Janeiro: Oscar Niemeyer'; 'Cinéma-Hotel a São Paulo: Rino Levi' No. 23 (May 1949) pp.15; 27; 49–51

'Ecole à Pedregulho: Affonso Eduardo Reidy' No. 25 (August 1949) p.48

'Usine Sotreq a Rio de Janeiro: M.M.M. Roberto'; Rino Levi: 'L'architecture est un art et une science: Conference'; 'Hôtel à Bahia: Paulo Antunes Ribeiro et Diógenes Rebouças' No. 27 (December 1949) pp.26–30; 50–1; 88–90

'Immeuble d'Appartements à São Paulo: Rino Levi et Roberto Cerqueira Cesar' No. 31 (September 1950) pp.16–17

'Urbanism au Brésil: Unité d'Habitation au Pedregulho, projet d'Urbanisation de la Butte Santo Antonio, Affonso Eduardo Reidy' No. 33 (December 1950) pp.56–70

'Groupe Scolaire, Unité d'Habitation Saint André, São Paulo: Carlos F. Ferreira', 'Ecole Professionnelle, Rio de Janeiro: M.M.M. Roberto' No. 34 (February 1951) pp.74–7

'La Première Biennale de São Paulo' No. 38 (December 1951) pp.v–vii

Spécial Brésil No. 42–3 (August 1952)

'Immeuble Antonio Ceppas, Rio de Janeiro: Jorge Machado Moreira' No. 45 (November 1952) pp.36–7

'Maison pour un critique d'art, São Paulo: Lina Bo Bardi'; 'Maison, São Paulo: Oswaldo A. Bratke'; 'Résidence, Rio de Janeiro: Paulo Antunes Ribeiro' No. 49 (October 1953) pp.38–41; 50–1; 62–3

Mario Pedrosa: 'L'Architecture Moderne au Brésil: Conference' No. 50–1 (December 1953) pp.xxi–xxiii

'Maison Rio de Janeiro: Oscar Niemeyer' pp.2–3; Maison São Paulo: Rino Levi' pp.4–5; 'Résidence Rio de Janeiro: Sergio Brenardes' p.6; 'Unité d'habitation de Pedregulho: Affonso Reidy' p.25; 'Ensemble Résidentiel Belo Horizonte: Oscar Niemeyer' pp.26–7; 'Hôtel Bahia: Ribeiro et Rebouças' p.32; 'Jardins de L'Aéroport de Rio: Roberto Burle-Marx' p.33; Banque a Salvador: Paulo Antunes Ribeiro' pp.42–3; 'Hôpital A.C. Camargo: Rino Levi' pp.82–3; 'Musée d'Art Moderne: Affonso Reidy' pp.100–1; 'Deuxième Biennale d'Architecture de São Paulo' pp.102–3 No. 52 (January 1954)

'Cité Universitaire de Rio de Janeiro: Jorge Machado Moreira'; 'Centre Résidentiel Universitaire a São Paulo: Rino Levi' No. 53 (March 1954) pp.72–7; p.84

'Poste de Contrôle des Courses Motonautiques: Marcos Konder Netto' No. 55 (July 1954) p.84

'Quelquer examples d'équipement le séjour: Brésil, Oscar Niemeyer' No. 56 (September 1954) p.43

' "Habitations Individuelles: Rino Levi"; Hôpital Sul-América a Rio de Janeiro: Oscar Niemeyer et Hélio Uchôa' No. 62 (November 1955) pp.24–9; 77–80

'Construction en Pays Chaud: Brésil' No. 67–8 (November 1956) pp.152–67

Rino Levi: 'Problèmes de Circulation et de Stationnement au Brésil' No. 70 (February 1957) pp.80–2

' "L'Art Sacre et la Critique Architecturale": Chapelle de Saint-François, Pampulha: Oscar Niemeyer' No. 71 (April 1957) p.v

'Construction Scolaires: Eneas Silva' No. 72 (June 1957) pp.96–101

'Aperçu sur la Jeune Architecture Brésilienne' No. 73 (August 1957) pp.70–1

'Unité Résidencialle de Gávea a Rio de Janeiro: Affonso Eduardo Reidy', 'Immeuble à São Paulo, Rino Levi et Roberto Cerqueira Cesar' No. 74 (October 1957) pp.93–5

'Interbau – Exposition Internationale de la Construction Berlin, June–April 1957: Oscar Niemeyer' No. 75 (December 1957) p.9

'Centres Sportifs à São Paulo: Icaro de Castro Mello' No. 76 (February 1958) pp.12–13, 26–7, 38, 62–3

'Le Siége du Parlement de la nouvelle capitale du Brésil' No. 76 (February 1958) pp.78–9

'Pavillon du Brésil, Exposition Internationale de Bruxelles 1958: Sergio Bernardes et jardin de Roberto Burle Marx' No. 78 (June 1958) p.32

'Brasília Nouvelle Capitale du Brésil' No. 80 (October 1958) pp.48–71

'Inauguration de la Maison du Brésil à la Cité Universitaire de Paris' No. 84 (June 1959) p.xi

'Hôpital Albert Einstein à São Paulo: Rino Levi et Roberto Cerqueira Cesar' No. 84 (June 1959) pp.60–2

'Coupole Géodesique en aluminium, São Paulo: David Libeskind' No. 85 (August 1959) pp.92–3

'Congrès International des Critiques d'Art a Brasília' No. 86 (October 1959) pp.vi–vii

'Habitations Individuelles: David Libeskind' No. 86 (October 1959) pp.24–6

'Brésil Actualités' No. 90 (June 1960) pp.1–69

'Brasília' No. 101 (April 1962) pp.22–37.

### Architettura

'Visita alla Fiera Mondiale di Nuova York' (July 1939) pp.395–407

P. Carbonara: 'Tre Edificio in São Paulo del Brasile: Rino Levi' (May 1938) pp.275–86

'Progetto per l'Università del Brasile a Rio de Janeiro: Marcello Piacentini e Vittorio Morpurgo' (September 1938) pp.521–50

### Architettura Chronache e Storia

Mario Salvatori: 'Ingegneria versus architettura: Chiesa a Belo Horizonte: Oscar Niemeyer' No. 8 (June 1956) p.139

Lina Bo Bardi: 'Lettera dal Brasile' No. 9 (July 1956) pp.182–7

'Recente Opera de Oscar Niemeyer' No. 12 (October 1956) pp.426–7

'Centro Governativo in Brasile' No. 22 (August 1957) p.254

'Palazzo del Governatore a Brasile: Oscar Niemeyer' No. 45 (July 1959) p.189

'Il Formalismo di Oscar Niemeyer', 'Inchiesta su Brasília' No. 51 (January 1960) pp.579, 608–19

'Museo d'Arte Moderna: Affonso Eduardo Reidy' No. 73 (November 1961) p.480

'Sede della Banca Sud-America: Rino Levi, Roberto Cerqueira Cesar, Carvalho Franco'; 'Yacht Club a Belo Horizonte: Oscar Niemeyer' (October 1962) pp.394–5; 396

### Arquitectura
Habana

'Arquitectura Contemporanea Brasileña' (November 1954) pp.474–84

### Arquitectura
Mexico

'Una Exposición de Le Corbusier en Brasil' (March 1952) pp.115–16

'Cinco Casas del Brasil: Sergio Bernardes' (March 1957) pp.11–26

'Casa en São Paulo: Eduardo Corona'; 'Conjunto Urbano Pedregulho en Rio de Janeiro: Affonso Eduardo Reidy'; Geraldo Ferraz: 'Roberto Burle Marx y sus Jardines' (June 1957) pp.90–2; 98–106; 107–12

'Fabrica en São Paulo: Eduardo Corona' (December 1957) pp.243–4

Número dedicado al Brasil (December 1958)

### Art Bulletin

Robert C. Smith: 'The Colonial Architecture of Minas Gerais' (June 1939) pp.110–59

Henry-Russell Hitchcock: 'Brazil Builds' (December 1943) pp.383–5

Robert C. Smith: 'Recent Publications in the Fine Arts of Brazil and Portugal' (July 1944) pp.124–8

### Art et Decoration
Librairie Centrale des Beaux Arts

'Maison sous le soleil: Rino Levi' (1949) pp.16–18

### Art News

Robert C. Smith: 'Brazil Builds on Tradition and Today' (February 1943) pp.14–19, 33

### Arts & Architecture
California

Philip Goodwin: 'Brazil Builds for the New World' (February 1943) pp.20–3

'House in Brazil: Jacobo Mauricio Ruchti' (September 1944) p.29
'House and Studio in Brazil: Oswaldo Bratke' (October 1948) pp.32–3
Lucio Costa: 'The architect and the Contemporary Society' (October 1954)
    pp.14–15, 34–8
'House in Brazil: Sergio Bernardes' (July 1956) pp.18–19
'Brasília a New Capital City' (April 1959) pp.15–21


### *Atlantic Monthly*
Boston

Lucio Costa: 'Testimony of a Carioca Architect' (February 1956) pp.43–5


### *Aujourd'hui Art et Architecture*

'Habitation Individuelle au Brésil' (January–February 1955) pp.33–5
'Musée d'Art à São Paulo: Lina Bo Bardi et G.C. Palanti', 'Musée d'Art
    Moderna à Rio de Janeiro: Affonso Eduardo Reidy' (March–April
    1955) pp.62–5
'Œuvre de l'Architecte A.E. Reidy' (November 1955) pp.48–55
'Musée d'Art Moderne, Caracas, Venezuela: Oscar Niemeyer' (March
    1956) pp.48–9
'Exposition Internationale du Bâtiment 1957: Oscar Niemeyer' (April 1957)
    pp.62–3
'La Nouvelle Capitale du Brésil: Oscar Niemeyer' (June 1957) pp.56–61
'Le Musée d'Art Moderne de Rio de Janeiro: Affonso Eduardo Reidy' (May
    1959) pp.20–2
Pierre Guegen: 'Jardin au Brésil' (May 1959) pp.94–9
Gérald Gassiot-Talabot: 'Affonso Eduardo Reidy' (July 1964) pp.48–52


### *Bauingenieur*

'Einige Eisenbetonbauten in Brasilien' No. 9/10 (1938)


### *Baukunst und Werkform*

'Des Brasilianische Pavillion' (December 1959)
'Das Wohngebiet Pedregulho, Das Wohngebiet Gávea: Affonso Eduardo
    Reidy' (January 1962) pp.17–24


### *Builder*

'*The Times* Brazil Number: Review' (8 July 1927) p.43
Basil Marriot: 'Contemporary Brazilian Architecture: Exhibition at the
    London Building Centre' (July 1953) pp.88–9


### *Building*

'The Architecture of Brazil: Exhibition at the London Building Centre' (July
    1953) pp.270–1


### *Burlington Magazine*

J. Sousa-Leão: 'Portuguese Tiles in Brazilian Architecture' (April 1944)
    pp.83–7

**Cahiers d'Art**

Gregori Warchavchik: 'L'Architecture d'Aujourd'hui dans l'Amérique du
Sud' (February 1931) pp.105–9

**Carnegie Magazine**

'Brazil's Leadership' (May 1943) pp.51–3

**Casabella**

Bernard Rudofsky: 'Cantieri di Rio de Janeiro' No.136 (April 1939)
pp.12–17
'Cronaca della Esposizione Universale di New York' No.141 (September
1939) pp.22–40
'Un negozio di orologi a São Paulo: Bernard Rudofsky' No.143 (November
1939) pp.20–2
Anna Maria Cotta and Attilio Marcolli: 'Considerazioni su Brasilia' No.218
(1958) pp.33–9
'La Maison du Brésil nella Città Universitaire di Parigi: architetto Le Corbusier, d'accordo con Lucio Costa' No.248 (February 1961) pp.4–14

**Chantiers**

Pierre-Louis Flouquet: 'L'Architecture Moderne au Brésil' (October 1947)
pp.132–40

**Civil and Structural Engineers Review**

'Office Blocks, Hotels and Flats in Brazil' (January 1954) pp.25–9

**College Art Journal**

Walter Curt Behrendt: 'Brazil Builds' (March 1945) p.174

**Comunità**

Giulio C. Argan: 'Architettura Moderna in Brasile' (1954) pp.48–52

**Concrete Quarterly**

'Brazil: notes on a tour organized by the Cement and Concrete Association' (April–June 1960) pp.2–17
'Hospital Albert Einstein: Rino Levi' (April 1960) pp.18–24

**Le Constructeur de Béton Armé**

'Le Pont Rio de Peixe au Brésil' (February 1932)

**Domus**

'Architettura Moderna al Brasile: Gregori Warchavchik' No.64 (April 1933)
p.177
Carlo Pagani: 'Due ville in Brasile: Dell'architetto Alvaro Vidal Brasil e
dell'architetto Rino Levi' No.222 (June 1947) pp.2–9

L.C. Olivieri: 'Brasile – da Le Corbusier architetto allo "Stile Le Corbusier"' No. 229 (January 1948) pp. 1–4

L.C. Olivieri: 'Villa Arnstein e Villa Frontini: Bernard Rudofsky' No. 234 (January 1949) pp. 1–9

'Il quartiere Pedregulho a Rio de Janeiro: Affonso E. Reidy' No. 254 (January 1951) pp. 2–4

Carlo Santi: 'Oscar Niemeyer' No. 255 (February 1951) pp. 15–18

'Casa a São Paulo: Rino Levi' No. 258 (May 1951) pp. 6–7

'Teatro a São Paulo: Rino Levi' No. 259 (June 1951) pp. 6–9

'Un Edificio e una villa: Rino Levi' No. 264–5 (December 1951) pp. 40–3

'Stile de Niemeyer' No. 278 (January 1953) pp. 8–9

'Burle Marx o dei giardini brasiliani', 'La "casa de vidro": Lina Bo Bardi' No. 279 (February 1953) pp. 14–18; pp. 19–26

Gio Ponti: 'Una grande esposizione semplice, ideata da Niemeyer'; 'Graticci Brasiliani' (April 1953) p. 1; 6–7

'Museo sulla sponda dell'oceano: Lina Bo Bardi' No. 286 (September 1953) p. 15

'Antologia di Rino Levi' No. 287 (October 1953) pp. 5–8

'I giardini per la esposizione di São Paulo' No. 290 (January 1954) p. 2

'Il patio-pergola: Rino Levi' No. 292 (March 1954) pp. 16–19

'La casa di Oscar Niemeyer' No. 302 (January 1955) pp. 10–14

' "L'isola universitaria" di Rio, un'impresa brasiliana: Jorge Machado Moreira' No. 310 (September 1955) pp. 1–2

'A Caracas, il Museo d'Arte Moderna di Oscar Niemeyer' No. 317 (April 1956) pp. 2–8

'A Brasília: Oscar Niemeyer' No. 331 (June 1957) pp. 1–2

'A Berlino gli edifici dell'Hansaviertel: Oscar Niemeyer' No. 333 (August 1957) p. 5

Gillo Dorfles: 'Il Congresso di Brasília' No. 361 (December 1959) pp. 29, 74


### Engineering News-Record

Rolf Schjodt: 'Long Rigid-Frame Bridge Erected by Cantilever Method' (6 August 1931) pp. 208–9

Arthur J. Boarse: 'Latin America Building is Challenging' (19 October 1944) pp. 121–8

Arthur J. Boarse: 'South American Building Codes' (19 April 1945) pp. 68–77

Arthur J. Boarse: 'Brazilian Concrete Building Design Compared with United States Practice' (28 June 1945) pp. 80–8


### House and Garden

New York

'Brazilian Modern Reorients Old Tradition' (March 1943) pp. 30–1


### Interior

'Architecture in the United States of Brazil' (February 1943) pp. 24–5

'Outdoor Living Rooms' (May 1943) pp. 19–23, 56

### Journal of the Royal Architectural Institute of Canada

Pegeen Synge: 'Modern Architecture in Brazil' (October 1943) pp.167–71
Philip Goodwin: 'New Architecture at Belo Horizonte' (October 1943) pp.172–5

### Journal of the Royal Institute of British Architects

'Brazil Builds' (May 1943) pp.155–8
Robert R. Prentice: 'Conditions of Practice in Brazil' (July 1947) pp.433–4
'Conversation in Brasile: Robert Harbison and George Balcombe' (November 1961) pp.490–4

### Kunst ins Volk

'Moderne Brasilianische Bauten: Rino Levi' (September–October 1950) pp.415–19

### Magazines of Art

F.A. Gutheim: 'Buildings at the Fair' (May 1939) pp.286–9, 316
Philip Goodwin: 'New Architecture at Belo Horizonte, Brazil' (March 1943) pp.90–3
'Brazil – Workshop of Sculpture' (November 1945) pp.266–7

### La Maison

'Interview de l'Architecte Brésilien Rino Levi' (November 1949) pp.334–9

### Metron

'Uno stadio nazionale in Brasile: Oscar Niemeyer' No. 2 (1945) pp.24–7
'Appartamento: Lucio Costa' No. 29 (1948) p.9
'Sistemazione di un Museo in Brasile: Lina Bo Bardi' No. 30 (1948) pp.34–5
'Cinema e Hotel: Rino Levi' No. 37 (1950) pp.47–9
'Cinema e Hotel: Rino Levi' No. 38 (1950) pp.7–12
'Edificio d'abitazione a São Paulo del Brasile: Vilanova Artigas' No. 48 (1953) pp.34–8
Natalio David Firszt: 'L'Irrazionale nell'architettura di Oscar Niemeyer: Fabrica Duchen' No. 52 (1954) pp.10–15

### Official Architecture and Planning

'Official Architecture in Brazil: Exhibition at the London Building Centre' (August 1953) pp.388–9

### Oeil

Françoise Choay: 'Le Pavillon du Brésil que Le Corbusier vient d'achever à la Citè Universitaire de Paris' (September 1959) pp.54–9

### Pencil Points

'Brazilian Architecture: Living and Building Below the Equator' (January 1943) pp.54–61
Bernard Rudofsky: 'On Architecture and Architects' (April 1943) pp.62–4
Bernard Rudofsky: 'Notes on Patios', 'Three Patio Houses: Bernard Rudofsky' (June 1943) pp.44–8
'Brazilian Concrete Building Design Compared with United States Practice: review' (April 1945) pp.105–6
Richard Neutra: 'Sun Control Devices' (October 1946) pp.88–91
'Chapel of St. Francis Pampulha, Brazil: Oscar Niemeyer' (December 1946) pp.52–5

### Plan

H.W. Maxwell: 'Building in Brazil' (March 1946) pp.4–10

### Polytechnisch Tijoschrift

Prague
'Brazilian architecture, examples of modern work: I' (2 April 1946) pp.16–22
'Brazilian architecture, examples of modern work: II' (13 April 1946) pp.15–19

### Progressive Architecture
[Old *Pencil Points*]

'Recent Brazilian Work' (April 1947) pp.47–64
'Maternity Hospital, São Paulo: Rino Levi and Roberto Cerqueira Cesar' (December 1949) pp.48–54
'Apartment House, São Paulo: Rino Levi and Roberto Cerqueira Cesar' (August 1952) pp.63–7
'Geodetic and Plastic Expressions Abroad: Pier Luigi Nervi, Oscar Niemeyer' (June 1953) pp.111–16
'Dormitories and Student Club: Rino Levi' (November 1953) pp.15–16
'Neighbourhood Group, Rio de Janeiro: Affonso Eduardo Reidy' (August 1955) pp.104–9
'Report from Brazil' (December 1956) pp.77–9
'Bridgehead to "Brasília"' (April 1957) pp.136–8
Sibyl Moholy-Nagy: 'Brasília: Majestic Concept or Autocratic Monument?' (October 1959) pp.88–9
Ray C. Smith: 'In Latin America: After Corbu, What's Happening?' (September 1966) pp.140–61

### Schweizerrische Bauzeitung

F. Stussi: 'Eindrücke aus Brasilien' (7 May 1955) pp.269–77

### South African Architectural Record

Harrie Biermann: 'Observation on Fenestration in Brazil' (July 1950) pp.150–62

### *Stile*

Carlo Perogalli: 'San Francesco in Brasile: Oscar Niemeyer' (October 1946) pp.14–15

### *Studio*

Bryan Holme: 'New York Commentary: 'Brazil Builds' (July 1943) pp.28–9
Paulo T. Boavista: 'Modern Architecture' (October 1943) pp.121–9

### *Technique des Travaux*

'Le Théâtre João Caetano' (February 1931)
Claude Vincent: 'L'Architecture Brésilienne, vue a travers l'Exposition du Musée de l'Art Moderne de Rio de Janeiro' (May–June 1953) pp.130–40

### *Techniques et Architecture*

'Réglage de l'Ensoleillement' (July–August 1943) pp.207–9
'Brésil' (July–August 1944) pp.350–69
'Soleil et Architecture' (September–October 1944) pp.151–2

### *Travel*

Elizabeth B. Mock: 'Building for Tomorrow' (June 1943) pp.26–32

### *Werk*

'Ministerium für Erziehung und Gesundheit in Rio de Janeiro' (January 1948) pp.1–5
Special Issue: Siegfried Giedion: 'Moderne Architektur und Kunst in Brasilien'; Lucio Costa: 'Imprévu et impotance de la contribution des architectes brésiliens au développement actuel de l'architecture contemporaine' (August 1953)
'Museu de Arte Moderna, Rio de Janeiro: Affonso Eduardo Reidy' (September 1955) pp.277–9
Creed Küenzle: 'Brasília, eine Haupstadt in Bau' (1959) pp.259–62

### *Zodiac*

'Rapporto Brasile' (May 1960) pp.56–139

# Brazilian Periodicals 1924–45

A selection of contemporary sources.

### *Acrópole*
São Paulo (1938–71)

'Edifício Esther: Álvaro Vital Brazil e Adhemar Marinho' (May 1938) pp.54–66

'Faculdade de Filosofia do Instituto "Sedes Sapientiæ": Rino Levi' (August 1943) pp.65–73

'A Exposição "Brazil Builds"' (March 1944)

'"Brazil Builds" e os Edifícios Públicos Paulistas' (May 1944) p.23

'A Exposição "Brazil Builds" em Jundiaí' (December 1945) pp.209–10


### *Architectura no Brasil* [sic]
Rio de Janeiro (1921–6)

José Mariano Filho: 'Os Dez Mandamentos do Estilo Neo-Colonial aos Jovens Architectos' (September 1924) p.161

'Salão de Architectura de 1925' (November 1925) pp.25–33

'Projecto de Residência: Lucio Costa e F. Valentim' (February–March 1926) pp.16–23

'Concurso de Anteprojetos para o Pavilhão do Brasil na Exposição de Philadelphia' (April–May 1926) pp.86–7


### *Arquitetura e Urbanismo*
Rio de Janeiro (1936–42)

'Goiânia, nova capital: Atilio Corrêa Lima' (March–April 1937) pp.60–3

'O Palácio da Imprensa: Marcelo e Milton Roberto' (March–April 1937) pp.64–72

'Aeroporto Santos Dumont, Estação de Hidro-aviões: Ata do Julgamento do Concurso' (March–April 1937) pp.99–100

'Edital do Concurso de Ante-projeto para a Estação Central do Aeroporto Santos Dumont' (March–April 1937) pp.102–3

'Concurso de Ante-projetos para a Estação Central do Aeroporto Santos Dumont' (March–April 1937) pp.211–12

'Ligação do Aeroporto Santos Dumont com a Cidade' (July–August 1937) pp.213–14

'Aeroporto Santos Dumont: Termo de Julgamento do Concurso de Ante-projetos, Ante-projetos classificados' (November–December 1937) pp.295–313

'Paris – 1937' (November–December 1937) pp.333–4

'Exposição Mundial de Nova York: concurso de ante-projetos para o pavilhão brasileiro' (January–February 1938) pp.50–2

'Feira Mundial de Nova York: Termo de Julgamento do Concurso de Ante-projetos para o Pavilhão Brasileiro' (March–April 1938) pp.98–9

'Residência Daudt de Oliveira: Lucio Costa e F. Valentim' (September–October 1938) pp.238–41

'Estação de Hidro-aviões do Aeroporto Santos Dumont: Atilio Corrêa Lima' (November–December 1938) pp.286–95

'O Pavilhão Brasileiro na Feira Mundial de Nova York: Lucio Costa e Oscar Niemeyer' (May–June 1939) pp.471–9

'O Brasil na Feira Mundial de Nova York' (May–June 1939) p.530

'Projeto de Residência para o escritor Oswald de Andrade: Oscar Niemeyer' (May–June 1939) pp.502–3

'O Edifício do Ministério da Educação e Saúde: Lucio Costa, Oscar Niemeyer, Affonso Reidy, Jorge Moreira, Carlos Leão e Ernani Vasconcellos' (July–August 1939) pp.543–50

'O Pavilhão do Brasil na Exposição da California' (July–August 1939) pp.557–9

'O Edifício da ABI: Marcelo e Milton Roberto' (September–December 1940) pp.261–78

### Concreto
Rio de Janeiro (1931–?)

'Emilio Baumgart' (October 1943) pp.107–8
'Emilio Baumgart' (Special Issue, June 1945) pp.173–293

### Revista da Diretoria de Engenharia da Prefeitura do Distrito Federal (PDF)
Rio de Janeiro (1932–59)

'Ante-projeto de um edifício destinado a conter dependências de Serviços Municipais: Affonso Eduardo Reidy' (July 1932) pp.2–5

'Apartamentos Econômicos Gambôa: Warchavchik e Lucio Costa' (July 1932) p.6

'Estudo para o Palácio da Prefeitura do Distrito Federal: Affonso Eduardo Reidy' (July 1934) pp.3–13

'Clube Esportivo: Anteprojeto Oscar Niemeyer Filho' (January 1935) pp.236–40

'Concurso de Anteprojetos para o Ministério da Educação e Saúde Pública' (September 1935) pp.510–19

'Diretoria do Serviço Technico do Café: Anteprojeto Carlos Leão' (September 1935) pp.520–7

Lucio Costa: 'Razões da Nova Arquitetura' (January 1936) pp.3–9

Le Corbusier: 'Le Préfet Passos, 12 August 1936' (September 1936) p.243

'Ante-projeto para a ABI: Jorge Machado Moreira e Ernani M. de Vasconcellos' (September 1936) pp.261–70

'Ante-projeto para a ABI: Oscar Niemeyer Filho, Fernando Saturnino de Brito e Cassio Veiga de Sá' (November 1936) pp.334–41

Lucio Costa: 'Uma Questão de Oportunidade' (May 1937) pp.120–39

'Universidade do Brasil: Ante-projecto Lucio Costa, Affonso Reidy, Oscar Niemeyer Filho, F.F. Saldanha, José de Souza Reis, Jorge M. Moreira, Angelo Bruhns, Eng. Paulo Fragoso' (May 1937) pp.120–35

'Obra do Berço: Oscar Niemeyer Filho' (May 1937) pp.140–1

'Projeto do Ministério da Educação e Saúde: Le Corbusier e Pierre Jeanneret' (July 1937) pp.182–3

'Cidade Universitária do Rio de Janeiro: Le Corbusier e Pierre Jeanneret' (July 1937) pp.184–6

'Instituto Nacional de Puericultura: Estudo Oscar Niemeyer Filho, Olavo Rdig de Campos, José de Souza Reis' (July 1937) pp.180–91

'Colégio Pedro II: Ante-projeto Carlos Leão' (July 1937) pp.200–1

'Maternidade: Ante-projeto Oscar Niemeyer Filho' (September 1937) pp.272–3

'Projeto para Sede da 8ª Divisão de Viação': Affonso Eduardo Reidy' (September 1937) pp.274–5

Le Corbusier: 'O Problema das Favelas Parisienses' (September 1937) pp.284–6

'Aeroporto Santos Dumont: Estação Central, Ante-projeto Herminio de Andrade e Silva e Edwaldo M. de Vasconcellos' (September 1937) pp.271–83

'O Edifício Central do Aeroporto Santos Dumont: Marcelo e Milton Roberto' (July 1938) pp.414–20

'Urbanização da Esplanada do Castelo: Affonso Eduardo Reidy' (September 1938) pp.604–7

'Hotel de Ouro Preto: Oscar Niemeyer Filho' (March 1942) pp.82–7

'As Obras da Pampulha em Belo Horizonte: Oscar Niemeyer Filho' (April 1943) pp.112–24

'Instituto Superior de Filosofia, Ciências e Letras "Sedes Sapientiæ", São Paulo: Rino Levi' (September 1942) pp.274–82

'Projeto de um Conjunto de Edifícios para o Centro Comercial de São Paulo: Rino Levi' (January 1943) pp.35–44


**Revista Polytechnica**
São Paulo (Escola Polytechnica) (1904–?)

'Predio de Habitação do Tipo Semi-Intensivo: Rino Levi' (March–June 1935)
'Um Predio de Apartamentos: Rino Levi' (July–October 1935)
'Cine Ufa – Palácio: Rino Levi' (January–April 1937)
'Casa de Campo junto de Santo Amaro: Rino Levi' (May–August 1937)


**Revista do Serviço Público**
Rio de Janeiro

'O Palácio do Ministério da Educação' (November 1945) pp.75–98

## Archives

Serviço do Patrimônio Histórico e Artístico Nacional, Rio de Janeiro:
PCMESP–SPHAN: Processo de Construção do Ministério da Educação e Saúde Pública – Serviço do Patrimônio Histórico e Artístico Nacional
PRPPC–SPHAN: Projeto de Recuperação e Preservação do Palácio da Cultura – Serviço do Patrimônio Histórico e Artístico Nacional
Centro de Pesquisa e Documentação em História Contemporânea do Brasil, Fundação Getúlio Vargas, Rio de Janeiro:
CE: CPC–CPDOC/FGV: Colunas da Educação: Construção do Palácio Capanema, Centro de Pesquisa e Documentação em História Contemporânea do Brasil/Fundação Getúlio Vargas
Fondation Le Corbusier, Paris (FLC)
The Museum of Modern Art, New York:
MoMA Archives, NY: AHB [AAA]: The Museum of Modern Art Archives, NY: Alfred H. Barr, Jr. Papers [Archives of American Art]
MoMA Archives, NY: CE: The Museum of Modern Art Archives, NY: Records of the Department of Circulating Exhibitions
MoMA Archives, NY: PI: The Museum of Modern Art Archives, NY: Public Information Scrapbook
MoMA Department of Registration: The Museum of Modern Art Department of Registration

## Interviews

Lucio Costa, December 1988 and August 1993
Oscar Niemeyer, August 1993
Roberto Cerqueira Cesar, October 1988
Pietro Maria Bardi, October 1988
Augusto Guimarães Filho, November 1988

## Correspondence

G.E. Kidder-Smith 1988–90
Elizabeth Mock 1990

# Index

Entries in **bold type** denote figures.

Aalto, Alvar 93, 165, 167
Academia Imperial de Belas Artes, Rio de Janeiro 9
Ackerman, Carl 99
*Acrópole* 192, 194
Adams, William Howard
  *Roberto Burle Marx: The Unnatural art of the Garden* 171 n26
Agache, Alfred
  Rio de Janeiro: plan 19, 26, **26**, 35, 40, 47, 66, 178, **179**,
    **Plate 1**
Algiers
  Hôtel de Ville 32
  Maison de l'Agriculture 32
  Maison Locative 20, 32, 40, 66
  Quartier de la Marine, Algiers: project 174
Amaral, Tarsila do 2
Andrade, Carlos Drummond de 20, 27
Andrade, Mario de 9, 20, 189, 192
Andrade, Oswaldo de 9
Andrade, Rodrigo Mello Franco de 15, 20, 27
*Ante-Projeto* 194
Antonio, Celso 36, 38
  'Mulher Reclinada', Brazilian Pavilion, New York World's Fair 1939
    60
  'Mulher Reclinada', Ministry of Education and Health, Rio de
    Janeiro 46
Aranha, Oswaldo 101
*Architect and Building News* 176
*Architect's Journal* 166
*Architectural Forum* 61, 115, 153, 154
*Architectural Record* 61, 111, 153, 156
*Architectural Review* 61, 145, 159, **160**, 164, 165, 166, 170
*Architecture d'Aujourd'hui* 160, **161**, 164
*Arquitetura Contemporânea* 194
*Arquitetura e Engenharia* 194
*Arquitetura e Urbanismo* 56, 178
*Art Bulletin* 159
*Art News* 157
Artigas, João Batista Vilanova 170, 200–1
  Faculdade de Arquitetura e Urbanismo, São Paulo 170, 201, **Plate
    23**
Asplund, Gunnar 93, 169

Baker, Josephine 18
Banham, Reyner
  *Guide to Modern Architecture* 93 n3
  *The New Brutalism* 170, 201
Bardi, Lina Bo 201–2
  Museu de Arte de São Paulo 170, 202, **Plate 21**
  SESC-Pompéia Cultural Centre, São Paulo **201**, 202
Bardi, Pietro Maria 180–1, 182, 202
Barr, Alfred 89–90, 91, 104, 106, 114, 116, 121–2, 124, 127, 131,
  134
Barragan, Luis 169
Bauer, Catherine 150
Baumgart, Emilio Henrique 13, **14**, 44
Belém 116, 128, 137, 138
Belo Horizonte 76, 116, 120, 139, 142
  Banco da Lavoura 199, **199**
  Pampulha 15, 64, 76–8, 129, 139, 140, 141, 193, 195, 196, 202,
    204
    Casa de Baile 76–8, **77**, **Plate 11**
    Casino 76–8, **78**, **79**, 151, 157, **Plate 10**
    Church of São Francisco 76–8, 160, 166, **Plate 12**, **Plate 13**
    Kubitschek House 77
    Yacht Club 76–8, **79**, 128
Bienais de São Paulo 165, 167, 183, 193, **193**, 197, 198, 199, 200
Bill, Max 165
Bliss, Lillie 89
*Brasil Constroi* 194
Brasília 76, 166, 170, 183, 186, 197, 198, 202–3, 204, 208
  Cathedral 204
  Companhia de Urbanização da Nova Capital (NOVACAP) 202
  Congresso Nacional **Plate 24**
  Esplanada do Ministérios 202
  Ministério da Justiça 204
  Ministério do Exército:gardens 198, **Plate 28**
  Panteão da Pátria 204, **Plate 27**
  Praça dos Três Poderes 202, **Plate 25**
  *superquadras* 198, 202, **Plate 26**
Brazil
  *brasilidade* 20, 25, 56
  Declaration of War 1942 97–9
  Estado Novo 21, 25, 47, 56, 119, 202

Brazil (*cont.*)
  relations with the United States 95–101
  military government 1964 168, 202–3, 208
  Revolução de 30 2, 14–15, 20–1, 25, 27, 47, 202, 204, 208
Brazil Builds
  'Brazil Builds' exhibition 1, 2, 7, 49, 89, 93, 100, 101, 105, 111–24,
    127–34, **127**, **128**, **129**, **130**, **131**, **132**, **133**, 170, 172, 173,
    177, 188–93, 200, 207–8
    in the popular press 147–51, **147**, **152**, **153**, **154**, **155**, 170
    in the professional press 152–61, **156**, **160**, **161**, 164, 165,
      170, 192–4
  *Brazil Builds* 1, 2, 7, **43**, **44**, 49, 61–2, **62**, 64, 67, **68**, 69, **69**, 71,
    **71**, **72**, **73**, 75, **75**, 76, **76**, 77–8, **77**, **78**, **79**, 80, 81, **81**, 83, **83**,
    95, 116, **117**, **118**, **119**, **120**, **121**, **122**, 123, 124, 135–43, **136**,
    177, 178, 196, 199, 204, 207–8, **Plate 16**
    in the popular press 151–2, 191–3
    in the professional press 153, 155, 158, 160, 176, 194–195
Brazilian Style 20, 48, 54, 64, 68, 79, 159, 160, 165, 167–70, 174,
  193, 196–7, 199, 200–4, 208,
  national character 7, 20, 56, 60–1, 140–1, 148, 168, 207
  reactions against 195, 200–1, 203, 204
  regional identity 142, 160, 167–70, 172, 188, 207
Brecheret, Victor 10
Brito, Fernando Saturnino de 140
Brito Filho, Francisco Saturnino Rodrigues de 32, 50 n17
Bruhns, Angelo 50 n19, 55
Burle Marx, Roberto 15, 140, 169, 194, 198
  Brazilian Press Association, Rio de Janeiro: garden 67, 140
  Copacabana, Rio de Janeiro: pavement 198
  Fazenda Garcia, Petrópolis: garden 140
  Ministério do Exército, Brasília: garden 198, **Plate 28**
  Ministry of Education and Health, Rio de Janeiro: garden 46, 140,
    198
  Pampulha, Belo Horizonte: landscaping 76, 140
  Parque da Cidade, Brasília 198
  Parque Glória-Flamengo, Rio de Janeiro 198, **Plate 17**
  *superquadras*, Brasília: landscaping 198, **Plate 26**
  Schwartz House, Rio de Janeiro: garden 16, 198
  Sitio Santo Antônio da Bica 198

*California Arts & Architecture* 155, **156**
Campos, Francisco 15
Camus, Marcel 53 n85
Capanema, Gustavo 7, 20, 26–9, 32–6, 39, 44–9, 76, 116, 118, 133,
  135, 139, 188–9, **191**, 204
Cardoso, Joaquim 20
Carson, Alice M. 113, 124, 127
Carvalho Franco, Roberto 199
Carvalho, Alberto Monteiro de **19**, 32–4
*Casabella* 61, 111
Castedo, Leopoldo
  *The Baroque Prevalence in Brazilian Art* 168
Cavalcanti, Emiliano Di 10, **10**
Cendrars, Blaise 18
Cerqueira Cesar, Roberto 199
Chicago
  860 Lakeshore Drive 176
  comparison to São Paulo 64
  Illinois Institute of Technology 175–6, **175**
Clark, Stephen C. 104

Claudius-Petit, Eugène 182
*Concreto* 13
Congrès Internationaux d'Architecture Moderne (CIAM) 13, 167, 180
Corrêa Lima, Atilio 15, 69, 116
  Boat Passenger Station, Rio de Janeiro 64, 69, **71**, 128, 157
  Goiânia: plan 68
  Seaplane Terminal, Rio de Janeiro 67–70, **70**, **72**, **73**, 117, 128,
    141, 196, **Plate 8**
Costa, Lucio 10–11, 15–18, **16**, 33, 34, 65, 111, 112, 116–17, 140,
  164, 170, 177–8, 181–2, 186, 195, 196–7, 200, 203
  Argentine Embassy, Rio de Janeiro 11
  at SPHAN 20, 75, 117, 196
  as theoretician of Modernism 20, 32, 127
  Brasília: plan 202
  Brazilian Pavilion, New York World's Fair 1939 54
    collaboration with Niemeyer 56–62, **58**, **59**, **60**, **61**, 111
    competition entry 56
  Brazilian Pavilion, Philadelphia Exposition 11
  Cidade Universitária, Rio de Janeiro: project 29, 47–9, **49**
  Director of Escola Nacional de Belas Artes, Rio de Janeiro 15–16,
    29, 66, 75, 79
  Fontes House, Rio de Janeiro **11**
  Gamboa Housing, Rio de Janeiro 16
  Maison du Brésil, Cité Universitaire, Paris 183–4, **185**
  Ministry of Education and Health, Rio de Janeiro 29–35, 39, 47, 60
    *see also* Rio de Janeiro: Ministry of Education and Health
  Museum of the Church of São Miguel 20, 75, **75**
  Parque Guinle, Rio de Janeiro 197, **197**, 199, 200, 202
  'Razões da Nova Arquitetura' 17–18
  'Salão de 31' 15
  Schwartz House, Rio de Janeiro 16, **16**
Courter, Elodie 112, 124
Craymer, Peter 165
Cunha, Euclides da
  *Os Sertões* 7
Curtis, William
  *Modern Architecture since 1900* 169

Disney, Walt 101
*Domus* 160
Drexler, Arthur 107, 169, 171 n25

Eames, Charles 106
Eames, Ray 155, **156**
Entenza, John 155
Ervi, Aarne 165
Escola Nacional de Belas Artes, Rio de Janeiro 7, **8**, 9, 10, 15, 19, 29,
  65, 66, 68, 75, 79, 194, 198

Fairbanks, Douglas, Jr. 101
Fantl, Ernestine 92
Ferraz, Geraldo 194
Fertin, Mario
  Ministry of Education and Health, Rio de Janeiro: competition entry
    **28**
Frampton, Kenneth
  *Modern Architecture: a Critical History* 169–70
Franck, Klaus
  *The Works of Affonso Eduardo Reidy* 164
Franklin, Benjamin 99

Freire, Gilberto 20
French Mission of 1816 138, 167–8
Fry, Maxwell 165

Galvão, Raphael
  Ministry of Education and Health, Rio de Janeiro: competition entry
    **28**
Giedion, Siegfried 165, 167
  *A Decade of New Architecture* 167, 172
  *Modern Architecture in Brazil*, preface 167
  *The Works of Affonso Eduardo Reidy*, preface 164, 167
  *Space, Time and Architecture* 142, 167
Giorgi, Bruno
  'Juventude', Ministry of Education and Health, Rio de Janeiro **45**, 46
Goodwin, Philip 83, 111, **113**, 115
  as architect 114–15
      Food Building, New York World's Fair 1939 115
      Museum of Modern Art, New York 115
  *Brazil Builds see* Brazil Builds
  Chairman of the Architectural Committee, Museum of Modern Art,
    New York 92, 95, 104, 113, 114, 115
  trip to Brazil 1942 7, 89, 114, 116–21, 192
Goulart, João 202–3
Gouthier, Hugo 183
Grandjean de Montigny, August Henri Victor 9, 167–8
Gropius, Walter 16, 17, 83, 93, 165
  Bauhaus, Dessau 83
Guarnieri, Camargo 105
Guevara, Ernesto 'Ché' 203
Guilbert, Jacques 62 n3

*Habitat* 194
d'Harnoncourt, René 107
Harrison, Wallace K. 57, 104, 113, 124
  Albany Mall 175
  Metropolitan Opera House, New York 175
  Radio City Music Hall, New York 150
  Rockefeller Center, New York 150, 172
  Trylon and Perisphere, New York World's Fair 1939 57, **57**
  United Nations Headquarters, New York 172–5, **173**
Henrich, Janet 112
Hitchcock, Henry-Russell 54, 91–3, 159
  *Architecture: Nineteenth and Twentieth Centuries* 167–8
  *Latin American Architecture since 1945* 74, 165, 194, 196, 197,
    200
  *The International Style: Architecture since 1922* 91, 136, 142, 207
Holanda, Sérgio Buarque de 20
Holford, William 166

Instituto de Arquitetos do Brasil (IAB) 27, 55, 67, 123, 189, 193
International Exhibitions 54–5
  New York 1939 54–63, 111, 115, 173
  Paris 1937 55
  Philadelphia 1926 11, 54–5
  Saint Louis 1904 54
  San Francisco 1939 55

Jefferson, Thomas 99
Johnson, Philip 90, 91, 92, 107
  *The International Style: Architecture since 1922* 91, 136, 142, 207

Johnson-Marshall, Percy 165
Jordy, William 175
*Journal of the Royal Institute of British Architects* 158–9

Kablin, Mina 11, 13
Kahn, Louis
  Capitol, Dacca 169
Kidder-Smith, George Everard 112, 113, 114, 116, 121, 192
  as photographer 112, 116, 121–2, 123, 124, 136, 149, 152–3,
    158, 160
  *Brazil Builds* 116, 136, 160
      *see also* Brazil Builds
  *Italy Builds* 116
  *Sweden Builds* 116
  *Switzerland Builds* 116
  'The Architects and the Modern Scene' 159
  trip to Brazil 1942 116–21
Kirstein, Lincoln 106, 116, 117
Kubitschek, Juscelino 76, 77, 183, 193, 202–3

LaGuardia, Fiorello 97
Lambert, Jacques 99
Le Corbusier 16, 17, 18, **19**, 82, 165, 174
  Armée du Salut, Paris 115, 178, 185
  Capitol, Chandigarh 169, 174
  Centrosoyuz Building, Moscow 18, 20, 29–30, 33, 36, 37, 178,
    185
  Cité Universitaire, Rio de Janeiro: project 36, 47, **48**
  Errazuris House, Chile: project 20, 77, 186
  French Embassy, Brasília: project 183
  influence of Rio de Janeiro 5, 18–19, 184–5
  *La Charte d'Athènes* 202
  *La Ville Radieuse* 20, 32
  League of Nations, Geneva: project 20, 35, 47, 71
  Lotissement, Barcelona 20, 41
  Maison de la Culture, Firminy 182
  Maison de Week-end, Paris 177
  Maison du Brésil, Cité Universitaire, Paris 183–4, **185**
  Maison Locative, Algiers 20, 32, 40, 67
  Ministry of Education and Health, Rio de Janeiro: participation 7,
    20, 25, 32–8, 47, 177–82
  *Œuvre Complète 1910–29* 30
  *Œuvre Complète 1929–34* 20, 30
  *Œuvre Complète 1934–38* 38, 47, 75, 111, 177, **179**, 182
  *Œuvre Complète 1938–46* 178, **179**, **180**, 185
  Palace of the Soviets, Moscow 36
  Pavillon des Temps Nouveau, Paris 177
  Pavillon Suisse, Paris 115, 178, 184, 185
  *Précisions* 5, 19, 20
  Quartier de la Marine, Algiers: project 174
  Rio de Janeiro: plan 19, 36, **Plate 2, Plate 3**
  Swiss Embassy, Brasília: project 183
  trip to Brazil 1929 18–20, **19**, 137, 184–5, **Plate 2, Plate 3**
  trip to Brazil 1936 32–8, 47, 184–5
  trip to Brazil 1962 186
  trip to New York 1935 93
  *Une Maison Un Palais* 32
  United Nations Building, New York: participation 173–4
  Unité d'Habitation, Marseilles 173–4, 178, 184, 186
  *Urbanisme* 32

Le Corbusier (*cont.*)
   villa, La Tremblade 177
   Villa Savoye, Poissy 18
   Ville Contemporaine 18, 19
Leão, Carlos 15, 16, **16**, 17, 19, 74, 199
   Ministry of Education and Health, Rio de Janeiro
      collaboration with Costa 29, 32, 33, 34, 47,
         *see also* Rio de Janeiro: Ministry of Education and Health
Léger, Fernand 18
Lehmbruck, Wilhelm
   *Kneeling Woman* 155, **156**
Levi, Rino 11, 78, 82, 83, 164, 199
   Sedes Sapientiæ, São Paulo 64, 82–3, **83**, **84**, 157, **Plate 9**
   *see also* Rino Levi Associados
Lévi-Strauss, Claude 99, 126 n48
   *Tristes Tropiques* 23, 51 n42, 84 n1
*Life* 148
Lipchitz, Jacques 104
   'Prometheus', Ministry of Education and Health, Rio de Janeiro 46,
      47, 118, 130
London
   Churchill Gardens Housing 176, **177**
   Economist Building 169
   Royal Festival Hall 176
   State House 176, **177**
Los Angeles
   comparison to Rio de Janeiro 117
   County General Hospital 32

Mafaldi, Anita 10
*Magazine of Arts* 60
Mallet-Stevens, Rob 13
Mariano, José 7, 9, 15, 188
   Solar do Monjobe, Rio de Janeiro 9
Marinho, Adhemar 79
Markelius, Sven 165
Martins, Carlos 116, 147
Martins, Maria 147
Matarazzo Sobrinho, Francisco 193
Matthew, Robert 165
   Royal Festival Hall, London 176
McAndrew, John 92, 113
McCray, Porter 107
McKenna, Rosalie 166
McKnight Kauffer, Edgard 135, **136**, **Plate 16**
Memória, Archimedes 29
   Ministry of Education and Health, Rio de Janeiro: competition entry
      **28**, 29
Mendelsohn, Eric 93
Mies van der Rohe, Ludwig 16, 17, 83, 93, 165, 175
   860 Lakeshore Drive, Chicago 176
   Farnsworth House, Plano, Illinois 176
   Illinois Institute of Technology, Chicago 175–6, **175**
   Seagram Building, New York 176
Milhaud, Darius 193
Mindlin, Henrique 195
   *Modern Architecture in Brazil* 165, 182, **184**, 195, **195**, 196, 200
Mock, Elizabeth 92, 112, 113, **113**, 124, 172
   *Brazil Builds* 135, 148
      *see also* Brazil Builds

*Built in USA: since 1932* 124, 186 n3
*Modern Gardens and the Landscape* 169
*Módulo* 165, 194
Moholy-Nagy, Sybil 166
Monbeig, Pierre 99
Monteiro, General Góes 98
Morais, Vinícius de 20, 53 n85
Morales de los Rios, Adolfo 50 n11
   Escola Nacional de Belas Artes, Rio de Janeiro 7, **8**, 25
Moreira, Jorge Machado 15, 198, 200
   Cidade Univeritária, Ilha do Fundão, Rio de Janeiro 198–9
      Faculdade de Arquitetura e Urbanismo 198–9, **199**
      Instituto de Puericultura 198
      Politécnica 198
Moreira and Vasconcellos
   Brazilian Press Association, competition entry 65, **65**, 67
   Ministry of Education and Health, Rio de Janeiro
      collaboration with Costa 29, 33, 47
      competition entry 29–30, **30**
      *see also* Rio de Janeiro: Ministry of Education and Health
Moses, Herbert 64, 65, 66
Moya, Antonio Garcia 21 n5
Museum of Modern Art, New York 89–93, 103–7
   exhibitions
      'A New House by Frank Lloyd Wright: Fallingwater' 93
      'Airways to Peace' 104
      'America Can't Have Housing?' 92
      'American Sources of Modern Art' 104
      'Americans 1942: Eighteen Artists from Nine States' 104
      'Americans 1943: Realists and Magic Realists' 104, 132
      'Architecture and Furniture by Alvar and Aito Aalto' 93
      'Architecture of Japan' 107
      'Architecture without Architects' 169
      'Arts in Therapy' 131
      'Bauhaus 1919–1928' 93
      'Brazil Builds' *see* Brazil Builds
      'Britain at War' 104
      'Built in USA: since 1932' 93
      'Built in USA: Post-War Architecture' 107
      'Camouflage for Civilian Defense' 104
      'Cândido Portinari of Brazil' 105, **106**
      'Cuban Paintings Today' 105
      'Development by Louis I. Kahn of the design for the Second
         Capital of Pakistan at Dacca' 169
      'Early Modern Architecture: Chicago 1870–1910' 92
      'Faces and Places in Brazil: Photographs by Genevieve Naylor'
         105, 127
      'Festival of Brazilian Music' 105
      'Fifteen Latin American Painters' 105
      'Fourteen Americans' 104
      'German Art of the Twentieth Century' 107
      'Graphic Arts from Mexico and Argentine' 105
      'Indian Art of the United States' 104
      'Industrial Design Competition for 21 American Republics' 106
      'La Pintura Contemporanea Norteamericana' 106
      'Latin America Colonial Art' 105
      'Latin America Contemporary Art' 105
      'Latin America Pre-Colombia Art' 105
      'Latin American Architecture Since 1945' 107, 165
      'Louis Sullivan 1856–1924' 92

'Machine Art' 92
'Mies Van der Rohe' 93
'Modern Architecture in California' 93, 136
'Modern Architecture in England' 93
'Modern Architecture: International Exhibition' 89, 91–2, **91**, 114, 207
'Modern Cuban Painters' 105
'Modern Exposition Architecture' 93
'Modern Gardens and the Landscape' 169
'Modern Mexican Paintings' 105
'Modern Painters of Brazil' 105
'Murals by Cândido Portinari' 105
'Norman Bel Geddes' War Manoeuvre Models' 104
'Objects 1900 and Today' 92
'Organic Design in Home Furnishings' 106
'Paintings from Latin America in the Museum Collection' 106
'Paintings from Ten American Republics' 105
'Prints from Europe and Japan' 107
'Recent Works by Le Corbusier' 93, 136
'Rivera, Orozco, Siqueiros' 105
'Road to Victory' 104
'Stockholm Builds' 93, 112, 116, 134
'T.V.A. Architecture and Design' 93
'The Americas Co-operate' 106
'The Architecture of Eric Mendelsohn 1914–1940' 93
'The Architecture of Henry Hobson Richardson and His Time' 92
'The Latin American Collection of the Museum of Modern Art' 106
'The Lesson of War Housing' 104
'The Modern Movement in Italy' 107
'The Philadelphia Savings Fund Society Building by Howe and Lescaze' 92
'The Popular Art of Mexico' 105
'The Skyscraper USA' 107
'The Wooden House in America' 104
'Twenty Centuries of Mexican Art' 104
'Three Mexican Artists' 104
'United Hemisphere Posters' 106, **106**
'Useful Objects in Wartime' 104
'Walker Evans: Photographs of Nineteenth Century Houses' 92
'Watercolours and Drawings by Six Cuban Painters' 105
policy to Latin America 104
policy to Modern architecture 91–3, 111, 169, 207–8
policy to United States government 103, 104, 111, 208
publications 136
    *Architecture without Architects* 169
    *Brazil Builds* see Brazil Builds
    *Built in USA: since 1932* 124, 186 n3
    *Complexity and Contradiction in Architecture* 169
    *Latin American Architecture since 1945* see Hitchcock, Henry-Russell
    *Modern Architecture: International Exhibition* 91, **91**
    *Roberto Burle Marx: The Unnatural art of the Garden* 171 n25
    *What is Modern Architecture?* 124
Mussolini, Benito 7

Naylor, Genevieve 105, 127
Neo-Colonial movement 7, 9, 10, 11, **11**, 15, 17, 55, 188
Neutra, Richard 93
    visit to Brazil 1945 200

New York
    Lever House 176, **176**
    Metropolitan Opera House 175
    Museum of Modern Art, New York 115
    Radio City Music Hall 115, 150
    Rockefeller Center 150, 172
    Seagram Building 176
    United Nations Headquarters 172–5, **173**
    World's Fair 1939 57, **57**, **Plate 14**
        Brazilian Pavilion 54, 56–62, **58**, **59**, **60**, **62**, 111–12, 131
        Food Building 115
        Theme Centre 57
        Trylon and Perisphere 57
Niemeyer, Oscar 15, 47, 75–6, 111, 112, 116, 117, 118, 123, 133, 164, 165, 178, 186, 194, 196, 200
    apartment buildings in the *superquadras*, Brasília 202, **Plate 26**
    Banco Boavista, Rio de Janeiro 196
    Brazilian Pavilion, New York World's Fair 1939
        collaboration with Costa 56–62, **58**, **59**, **60**, **62**, 111, 193
        competition entry 56
    Brazilian Press Association, Rio de Janeiro: competition entry 65, **65**
    Cathedral, Brasília 204
    Congresso Nacional, Brasília 202, **Plate 24**
    Hotel, Ouro Preto 75
    Ibirapuera Exhibition Buildings, São Paulo 196, **Plate 18**
    Memorial da America Latina, São Paulo 204, **204**
    Ministério da Justiça, Brasília 204
    Ministry of Education and Health, Rio de Janeiro 29, 33, 47, 157, 182, **183**
        see also Rio de Janeiro: Ministry of Education and Health
    Niemeyer House, Gávea, Rio de Janeiro 196, **Plate 19**
    Obra do Berço, Rio de Janeiro 75, **76**, 130
    Pampulha, Belo Horizonte 64, 76–8, **76**, 139, 141, 193, 195, 196, 204
        Casa de Baile 76–8, **77**, **Plate 11**
        Casino 76–8, **78**, **79**, 151, 157, **Plate 10**
        Church of São Francisco 76–8, 160, 166, **Plate 12**, **Plate 13**
        Kubitschek House 77
        Yacht Club 76–8, **79**, 128
    Panteão da Pátria, Brasília 204, **Plate 27**
    Parti Communiste Français, Paris 203, **203**
    United Nations Building, New York: participation 172–5, **174**
Niterói
    Instituto Vital Brazil **81**, 82
    Raul Vidal Elementary School 81–2, 128
Noyes, Eliot 104
Nunes, Luiz 15
    Anatomical Laboratory, Recife 140
    Water Tower, Olinda 140, 149

Ocampo, Vitoria 18
Ohye, Hiroshi 165
Olinda
    Water Tower 140, 149
Orozco, José Clemente 105
Ouro Preto 20, 75, 120, **121**
    Hotel 75

Pani, Mario 165
Papadaki, Stamo 196
    *The Works of Oscar Niemeyer* 164, 174, **174**, 182, **183**

Paris
  Armée du Salut 115, 178, 185
  Brazilian Pavilion, Exhibition 1937 55
  comparison to Rio de Janeiro 117
  Maison de Week-end 177
  Maison du Brésil, Cité Universitaire 183–4, **185**
  Parti Communiste Français 203, **203**
  Pavillon des Temps Nouveau 177
  Pavillon Suisse 115, 178, 184, 185
  UNESCO Building 164
Passos, Francisco de Oliveira
  Teatro Municipal, Rio de Janeiro 7, **8**, 25
Passos, Pereira 7, 33, 36
Pedro II, Emperor of Brazil 99
*Pencil Points* 153–4
Pevsner, Nicholas
  *An Outline of European Architecture* 168, 184
  *Pioneers of the Modern Movement* 142
Piacentini, Marcello 7, 11, 27, 29, 32, 47, 82, 201
Picasso, Pablo
  'Guernica' 155, **156**
Picchia, Paulo Menotti Del 9, 189–91
Pinheiro, Gerson
  Ministry of Education and Health, Rio de Janeiro: competition entry **28**
Ponti, Gio 201
Portinari, Cândido **16** 105, **106**, 116–7, 118, 165, 193, 194
  Brazilian Pavilion, New York World's Fair 1939: paintings 60
  Church of São Francisco, Pampulha: *azulejos* and murals 77, **Plate 12**, **Plate 13**
  Ministry of Education and Health, Rio de Janeiro: *azulejos* and murals **45**, 46–7, **Plate 6**
Portinho, Carmen 17
Powell and Moya
  Churchill Gardens Housing, London 176, **177**
Prado, Paulo 9, 18
Prestes, Luís Carlos 202
*Progressive Architecture* 166
Przyrembel, Georg 21 n5

Rebelo, Jose Maria Jacinto 159, 168
Recife 116, 120, **122**
  Anatomical Laboratory 140
Reidy, Affonso Eduardo 15, 17, 29, 33, 164, 200
  Albergue da Boa Vontade, Rio de Janeiro 140
  Gávea Residential Neighbourhood, Rio de Janeiro 198
  Ministry of Education and Health, Rio de Janeiro
    collaboration with Costa 29, 33, 47
    competition entry 29–30, **30**
  Museu de Arte Moderna, Rio de Janeiro 182, 198, **Plate 22**
  Pedregulho Residential Neighbourhood, Rio de Janeiro 197–8
*Revista da Directoria de Engenharia da Prefeitura do Distrito Federal (PDF)* 17, 27, 29
*Revista de Arquitetura* 30
Richards, James M. 166
  *An Introduction to Modern Architecture* 168
Richardson, Henry Hobson 92
Rino Levi Associados 199
  Banco Sul Americano, São Paulo 199
  Brasília: plan 202
  Instituto Central do Câncer, São Paulo 199

Rio de Janeiro 5, 116, 117, 200, **Plate 17**
  A Noite building 13, **14**, 16
  Albergue da Boa Vontade 140
  Avenida Rio Branco 7, **8**, 25, 54, 67, 138, 142
  Banco Boavista 196
  Biblioteca Nacional 7, **8**, 25
  Boat Passenger Station 64, 69, **71**, 128, 157
  Brazilian Press Association 64–7, **65**, **68**, **69**
  Cidade Universitária, Ilha do Fundão 198
  Cidade Universitária: project 15, 27, 47–9, **49**
  comparison to Los Angeles 117
  comparison to Paris 7, 26, 117
  Copacabana Palace Hotel 116
  Escola Nacional de Belas Artes 7, **8**, 25
  Fontes House **11**
  Gamboa Housing 16
  Gávea Residential Neighbourhood 198
  Hangar Nº1 70–1, **73**
  Hotel Gloria 19, 34
  Industrial School 122
  Ministry of Education and Health 7, 15, 20, 25–53, 54, 56, 59, 64, 65, 67, 75, 83, 123, 196, 197, 198, 199, 202, 207
    competition 27–30, **28**, **30**
    first Costa project 29–32, **31**
    final Costa project 39–47, **39**, **40**, **41**, **42**, **43**, **44**, **45**, **46**, **178**, **Plate 4**, **Plate 5**, **Plate 6**
    in 'Brazil Builds' 112, 117–8, 128, 130, **131**, 133, **133**, 134, 147–8
    in *Brazil Builds* **43**, **44**, 49, 139, 140–1
    in the popular press 147, **147**, 148, 150–1, **152**, **153**, **154**, 186–8, **189**, **190**, **191**
    in the professional press 111, 154–5, **156**, 157, 160, **161**, 166–7, 168, 169, 170, 194, 195, 196
    influence 172–6
    Le Corbusier 177–8, 182, 186, **179**, **180**, **181**, **184**
      project for Castelo 36–8, **37**, **38**
      project for Santa Luzia 35–6, **35**, 38
  Ministry of Finance 25, 141, 188
  Monroe Palace 54
  Museu de Arte Moderna 198, **Plate 22**
  Niemeyer House 196, **Plate 19**
  Obra do Berço 75, **76**, 130
  Parque Glória-Flamengo 198, **Plate 17**
  Parque Guinle 197, **197**, 199, 200, 202
  Pedregulho Residential Neighbourhood 197–8
  Santos Dumont Airport 64, 67–8, 71–4, **70**, **75**, **Plate 7**
  São Bento Monastery 138
  Schwartz House 16, **16**
  Seaplane Station 69–70, **70**, **72**, **73**, 117, 128, 141, 196, **Plate 8**
  Solar do Monjobe 9
  Teatro Municipal 7, **8**, 25
Rivera, Diego 91, 104, 105
Roberto, M. M. 140, 164, 199
  Brazilian Press Association, Rio de Janeiro 64–7, **65**, **68**, **69**
  Hangar Nº1, Rio de Janeiro 70–1, **73**, 153
  Parque Guinle, Rio de Janeiro 199
  Santos Dumont Airport, Rio de Janeiro, 67–8, 71–4, **70**, **74**, **Plate 7**
Roberto, M. M. M. 199
  Brasília: plan 202

Roberto, Marcelo 65–6, 116, 199
Roberto, Mauricio 199
Roberto, Milton 15, 66, 199
Robertson, Howard 176, 186 n2
Rockefeller Brothers Foundation 107
Rockefeller, Abby Aldrich 89, 90, 105
Rockefeller, Blanchette 103
Rockefeller, John Davison III 103
Rockefeller, John Davison Jr. 89, 91
Rockefeller, Nelson 90, 100–1, 103–4, 105, 113, 115, 123, 124, 135, 172–3
Rodrigues, José Wasth
    *Documentário Arquitetônico* 9
Rogers, Ernesto 165
Roosevelt, Franklin Delano 2, 96, 97, 98, 100, 101, 103, 104
Rubinstein, Artur 193
Rudofsky, Bernard 78, 106, 111, 141, 157–8, 169
    *Architecture without Architects* 169
    Arnstein House, São Paulo 78, 130, 131, 169
    Frontini House, São Paulo 78

Saarinen, Eero 106
Saint-Exupéry, Antoine de 18, 137
Sakakura, Junzo 165
Salvador 116, 120, 138
São Paulo 9, 14, 64, 78–9, 99, 116, 133, 140, 200
    Arnstein House 78, 130, 131, 169
    Banco Sul Americano 199
    comparison to Chicago 64
    Edifício Esther 64, 79–81, **80**, 196
    Faculdade de Arquitetura e Urbanismo 170, 201, **Plate 23**
    Frontini House 78
    House, Rua Bahia 140
    House, Rua Itápolis 11–12, **12**
    Ibirapuera Exhibition Buildings 196, **Plate 18**
    Instituto Central do Câncer 199
    Martinelli Building 13
    Memorial da America Latina 204, **204**
    Museu de Arte de São Paulo 170, 202, **Plate 21**
    Public Library 141
    Sedes Sapientiæ 64, 82–4, **83**, **84**, 157, **Plate 9**
    SESC-Pompéia Cultural Centre **201**, 202
Semana de Arte Moderna 1922 9–10, **10**, 11, 13, 15, 18, 189
Serviço do Patrimônio Histórico e Artístico Nacional (SPHAN) 20, 75, 117, 196
Severo, Ricardo 9
Siqueiros, David Alfaro 105
Sitwell, Sacheverell 159
Skidmore, Louis 176
Skidmore, Owings and Merrill
    Lever House, New York 176, **176**
Smith, Robert Chester 105, 112, 122, 138, 157
Smithson, Alison and Peter
    Economist Building, London 169
Souza Aguiar, Eduardo 45–6, 50 n11, 55
Souza Aguiar, Francisco Marcelino de
    Biblioteca Nacional, Rio de Janeiro 7, **8**, 25, 67
    Monroe Palace, Rio de Janeiro 54
Souza Leão, Joaquim de 159
Souza Reis, José de 20

Sprague-Smith, Carleton 133
Stokowski, Leopoldo 101
Stone, Edward Durrell
    Museum of Modern Art, New York 115
Sullivan, Louis 92
Sullivan, Mary Quinn 89
Summerson, John 159
    *Georgian London* 137

*The Times* 7, **8**, 170, 188
Toscanini, Arturo 101
Trehearne and Norman, Preston and Partners
    State House, London 176, **177**

United States
    Division of Cultural Relations 100
    Farm Security Administration 103
    Good Neighbour policy 55, 96–101, 208
    Monroe Doctrine 95–6
    New Deal 2, 96, 103, 208
    Office of Inter-American Affairs (OIAA) 100–1, 104, 106–7, 113, 123–4, 133, 135, 136, 173, 192
    Truman Doctrine 101
    Works Progress Administration 103

Vargas, Getúlio 2, 14–15, 20–1, 25, 27, 29, 32, 33, 34, 47, 54, 55, 64, 97, 135, 139, 202, 203, 208
Vasconcellos, Ernani 15, 199
    *see also* Moreira and Vasconcellos
Vauthier, Louis 159, 168
Venturi, Robert
    *Complexity and Contradiction in Architecture* 169
Villa-Lobos, Heitor 2, 9, 15, 25, 105
Vital Brazil, Álvaro 15, 79, 81–2, 199
    Banco da Lavoura, Belo Horizonte 199, **199**
    Edifício Esther, São Paulo 64, 79–81, **80**, 196
    Instituto Vital Brazil, Niterói 81, **81**
    Raul Vidal Elementary School, Niterói 81–2

Warchavchik, Gregori 11–13, 15, 16–17, **16**, 82, 140, 170
    'Acerca da Arquitetura Moderna' 11
    Gamboa Housing, Rio de Janeiro 16
    House, Rua Bahia, São Paulo 140
    House, Rua Itápolis, São Paulo 11–12, **12**
    Schwartz House, Rio de Janeiro 16, **16**
Welles, Orson 101
*Werk* 160
Wheeler, Monroe 90–1, 104, 112, 135–6
Wiener, Paul Lester 56, 111, 112, 157
Wilder, Elizabeth 150–1
William E. Rudge's Sons 135–6
Wittenborn, George 135–6
Wright, Frank Lloyd 92, 93
    visit to Brazil 1931 15, 65
Wurster, William 169

Zamoiski, August 78
Zé Carioca 25, 101, **Plate 15**
Zweig, Stefan
    *Brazil, Land of the Future* 87, 109